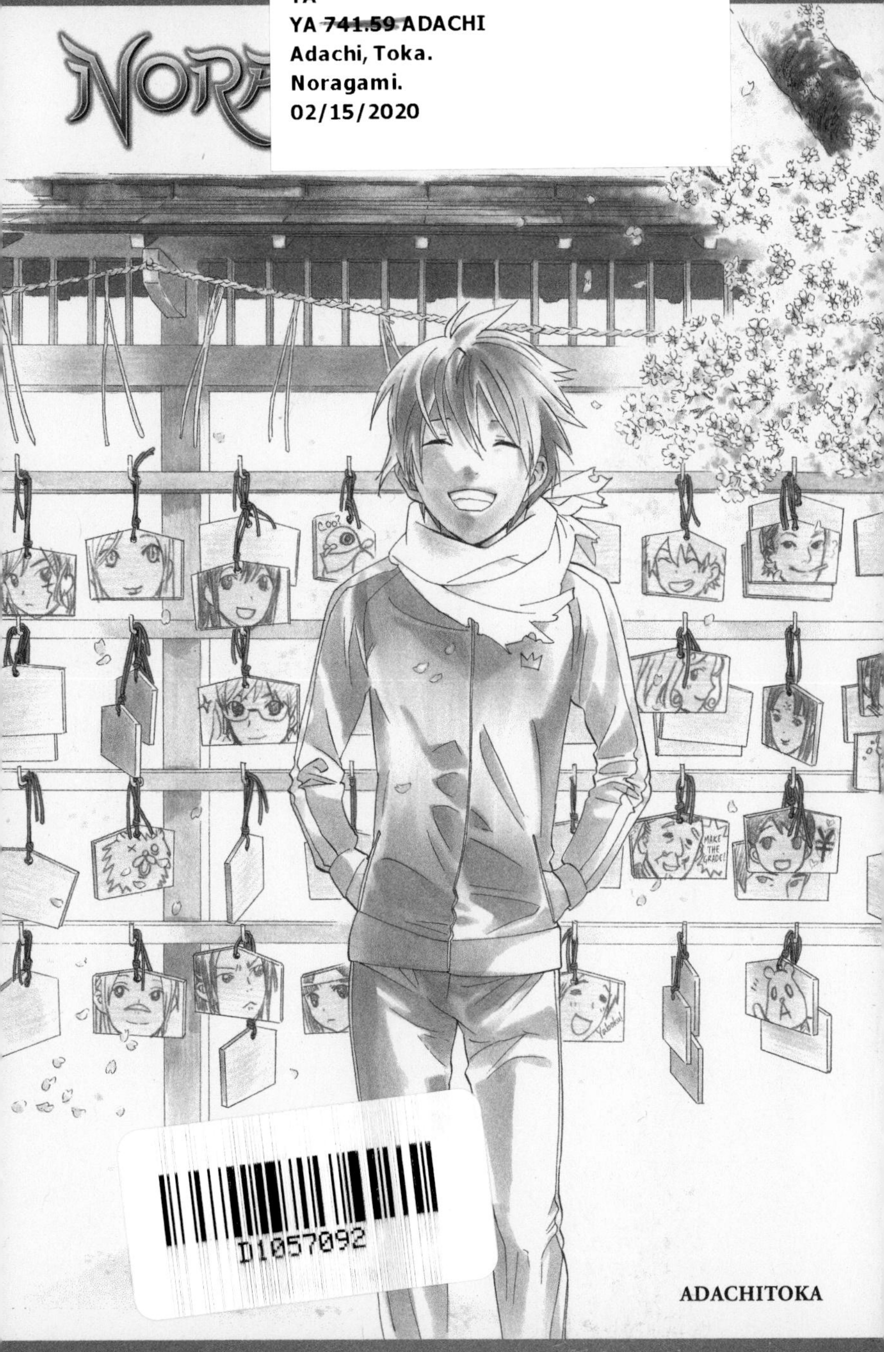
NORA
MAKE THE GRADE!



ADACHITOKA

# characters

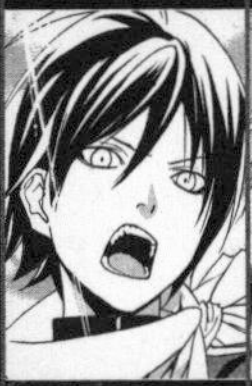

## YATO

A minor deity who always wears a sweatsuit.

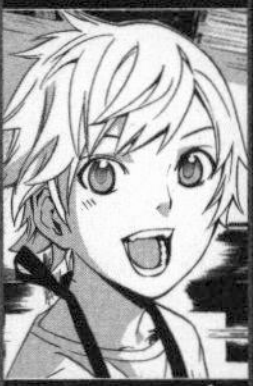

## YUKINÉ

Yato's shinki who turns into swords.

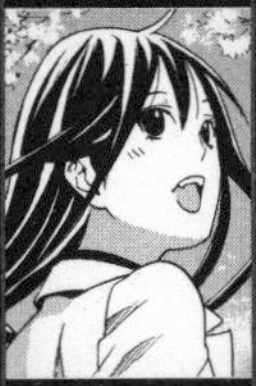

## HIYORI IKI

A high school student who has become half ayakashi.

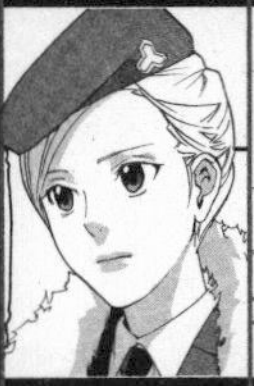

## BISHAMONTEN

A powerful warrior god, one of the Seven Gods of Fortune.

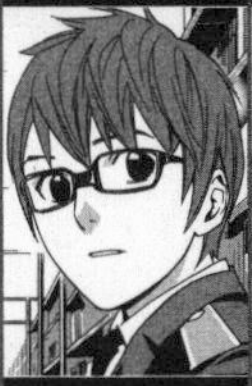

## KAZUMA

A navigational shinki who serves as guide to Bishamon.

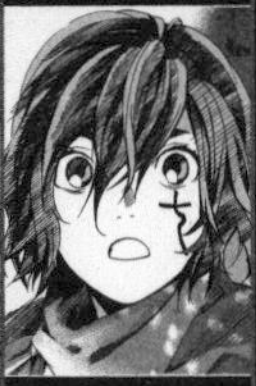

## NANA

A powerful shinki who once rebelled against the Heavens.

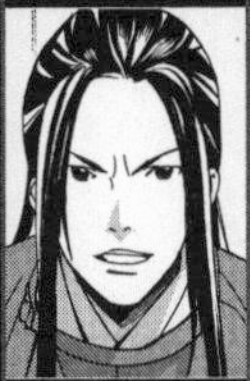

## TAKEMIKAZUCHI

A warrior god who longs for the chaos of war.

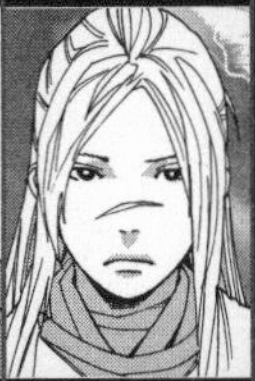

## KIUN

Takemikazuchi's shinki who has earned the title of Thunder Blade.

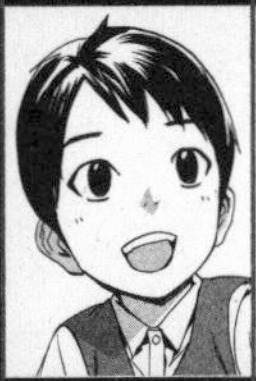

## EBISU

A business-god in the making, one of the Seven Gods of Fortune.

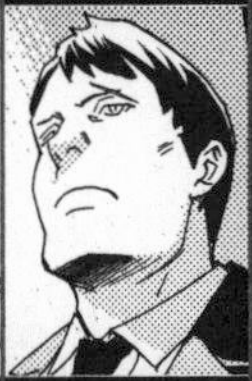

## KUNIMI

A shinki who enhances Ebisu's motor skills.

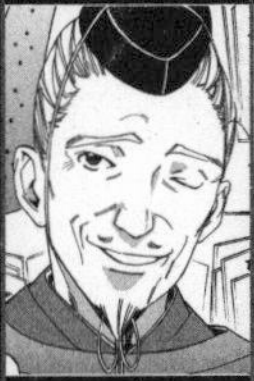

## TENJIN

The god of learning, Sugawara no Michizane.

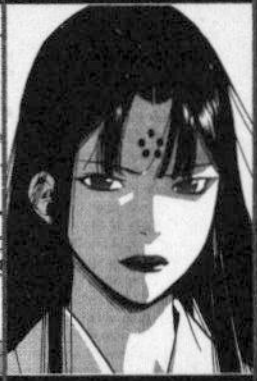

## TSUYU

A spirit of the plum tree, Tenjin's attendant.

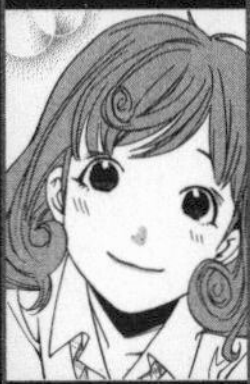

## KOFUKU

A goddess of poverty who calls herself Ebisu after the god of fortune.

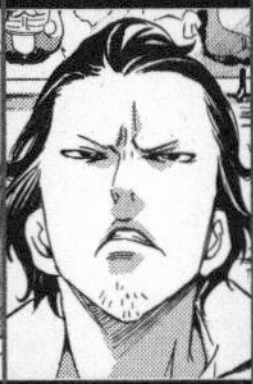

## DAIKOKU

Kofuku's shinki who summons storms.

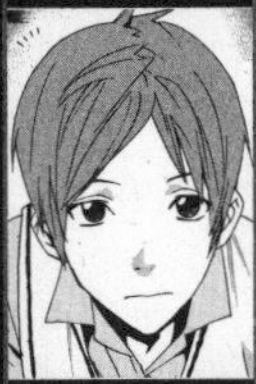

## KÔTO FUJISAKI

Yato's "father."

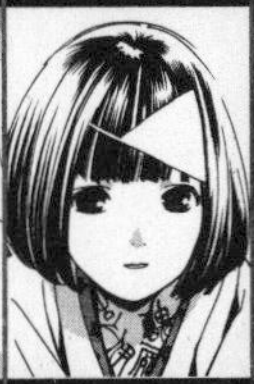

## STRAY

A shinki who serves an unspecified number of deities.

## SHINATSUHIKO

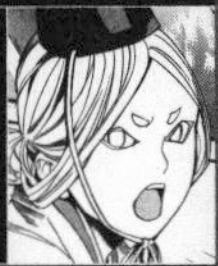

## SAKUYA-BIMÉ

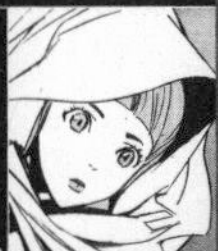

## KAGUTSUCHI

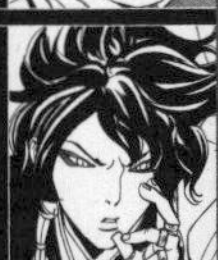

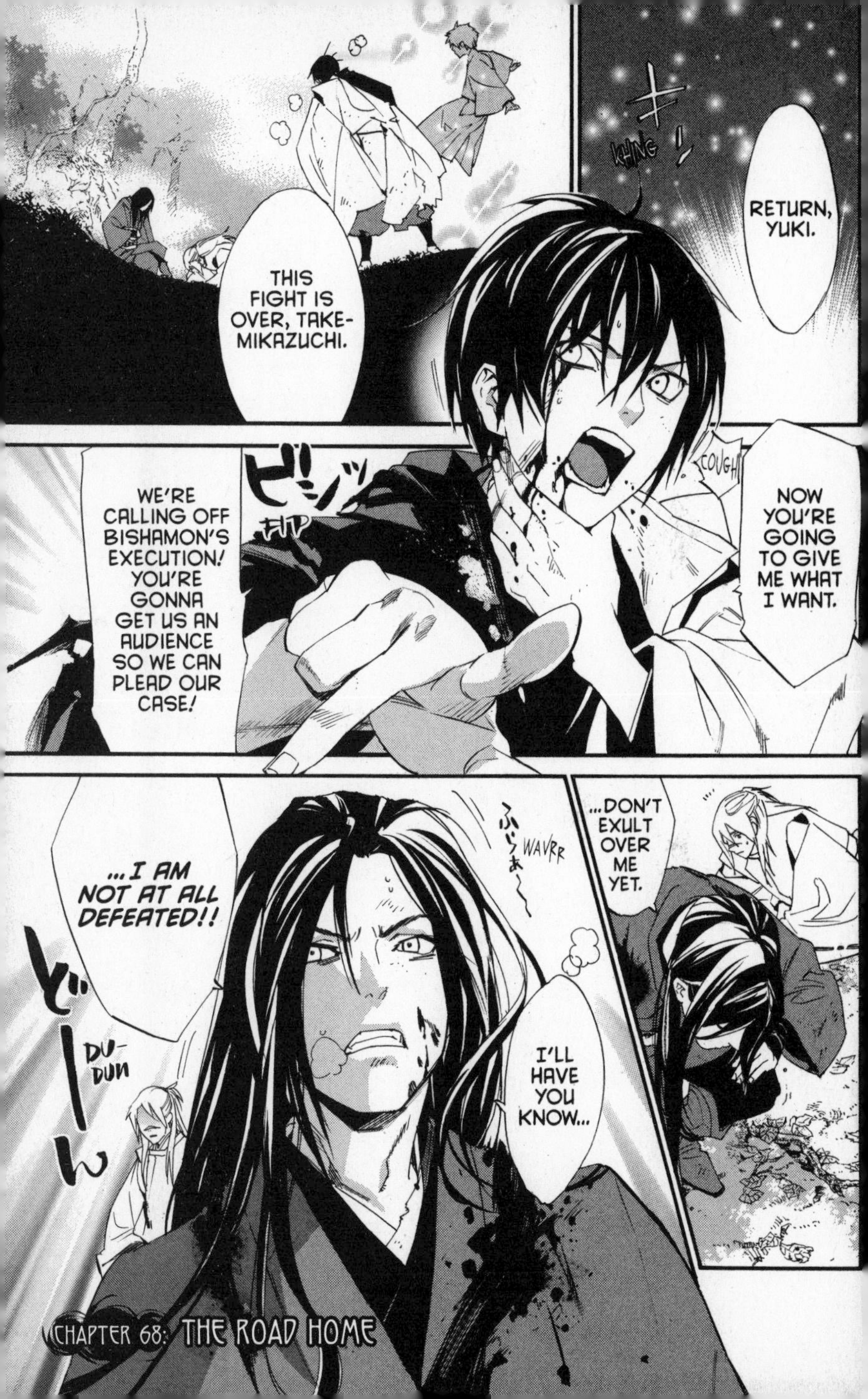
KHING
RETURN, YUKI.
THIS FIGHT IS OVER, TAKE-MIKAZUCHI.
COUGH
NOW YOU'RE GOING TO GIVE ME WHAT I WANT.
FTIP
WE'RE CALLING OFF BISHAMON'S EXECUTION! YOU'RE GONNA GET US AN AUDIENCE SO WE CAN PLEAD OUR CASE!
...DON'T EXULT OVER ME YET.
WAVRR
I'LL HAVE YOU KNOW...
...I AM NOT AT ALL DEFEATED!!
DU-DUN
CHAPTER 68: THE ROAD HOME

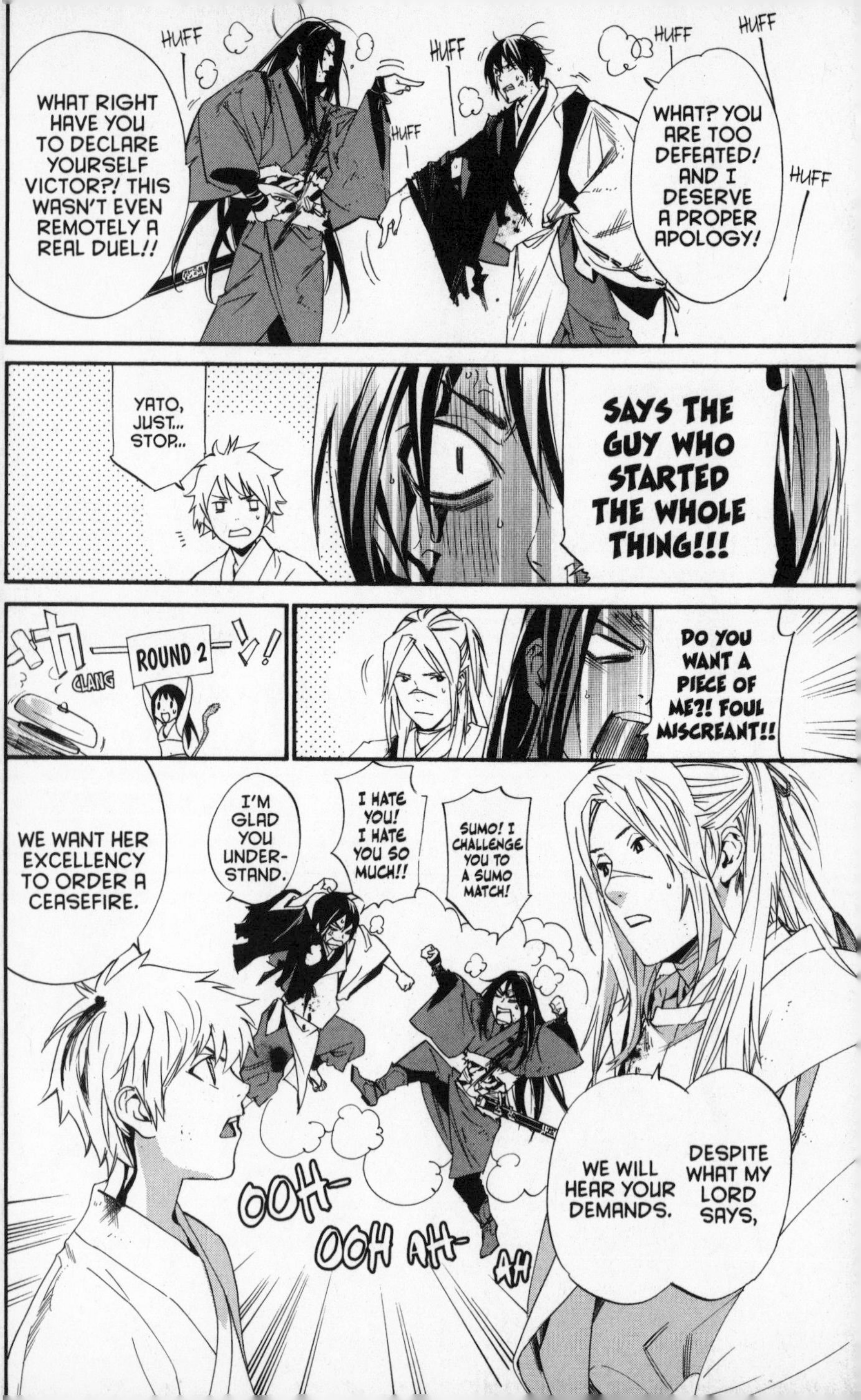
HUFF
HUFF
WHAT? YOU ARE TOO DEFEATED! AND I DESERVE A PROPER APOLOGY!
HUFF
HUFF
HUFF
HUFF
WHAT RIGHT HAVE YOU TO DECLARE YOURSELF VICTOR?! THIS WASN'T EVEN REMOTELY A REAL DUEL!!
SAYS THE GUY WHO STARTED THE WHOLE THING!!!
YATO, JUST... STOP...
DO YOU WANT A PIECE OF ME?! FOUL MISCREANT!!
ROUND 2
CLANG
DESPITE WHAT MY LORD SAYS,
WE WILL HEAR YOUR DEMANDS.
SUMO! I CHALLENGE YOU TO A SUMO MATCH!
I HATE YOU! I HATE YOU SO MUCH!!
I'M GLAD YOU UNDER-STAND.
WE WANT HER EXCELLENCY TO ORDER A CEASEFIRE.
OOH-
OOH AH-
AH

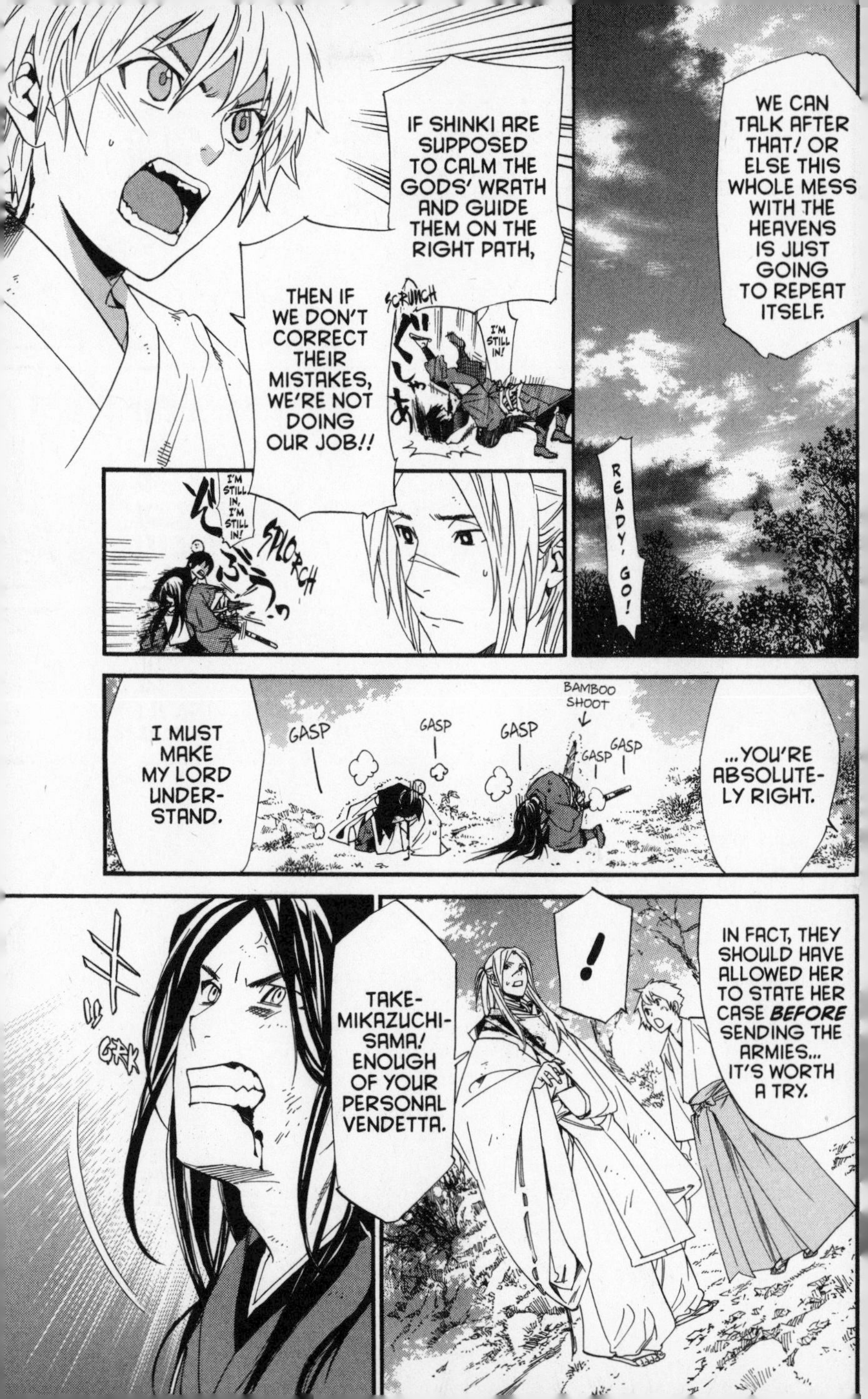
WE CAN TALK AFTER THAT! OR ELSE THIS WHOLE MESS WITH THE HEAVENS IS JUST GOING TO REPEAT ITSELF.
READY, GO!
IF SHINKI ARE SUPPOSED TO CALM THE GODS' WRATH AND GUIDE THEM ON THE RIGHT PATH,
THEN IF WE DON'T CORRECT THEIR MISTAKES, WE'RE NOT DOING OUR JOB!!
SCRUNCH
I'M STILL IN!
I'M STILL IN, I'M STILL IN!
SPLORCH
...YOU'RE ABSOLUTE-LY RIGHT.
GASP
GASP
BAMBOO SHOOT
GASP
GASP
GASP
I MUST MAKE MY LORD UNDER-STAND.
IN FACT, THEY SHOULD HAVE ALLOWED HER TO STATE HER CASE *BEFORE* SENDING THE ARMIES... IT'S WORTH A TRY.
!
TAKE-MIKAZUCHI-SAMA! ENOUGH OF YOUR PERSONAL VENDETTA.
GRK

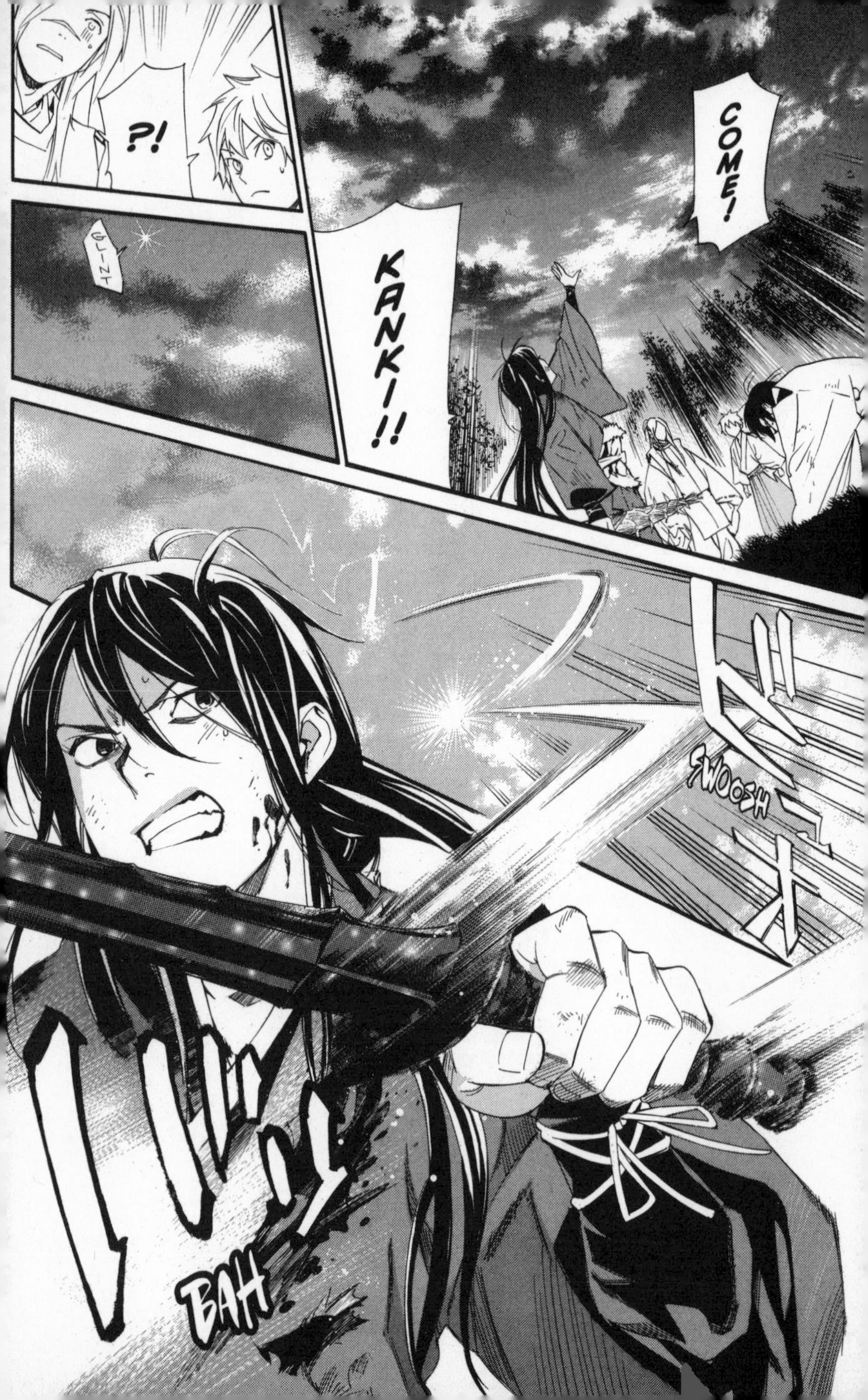
COME!
KANKI!!
?!
GLI-NT
SWOOSH
BAH

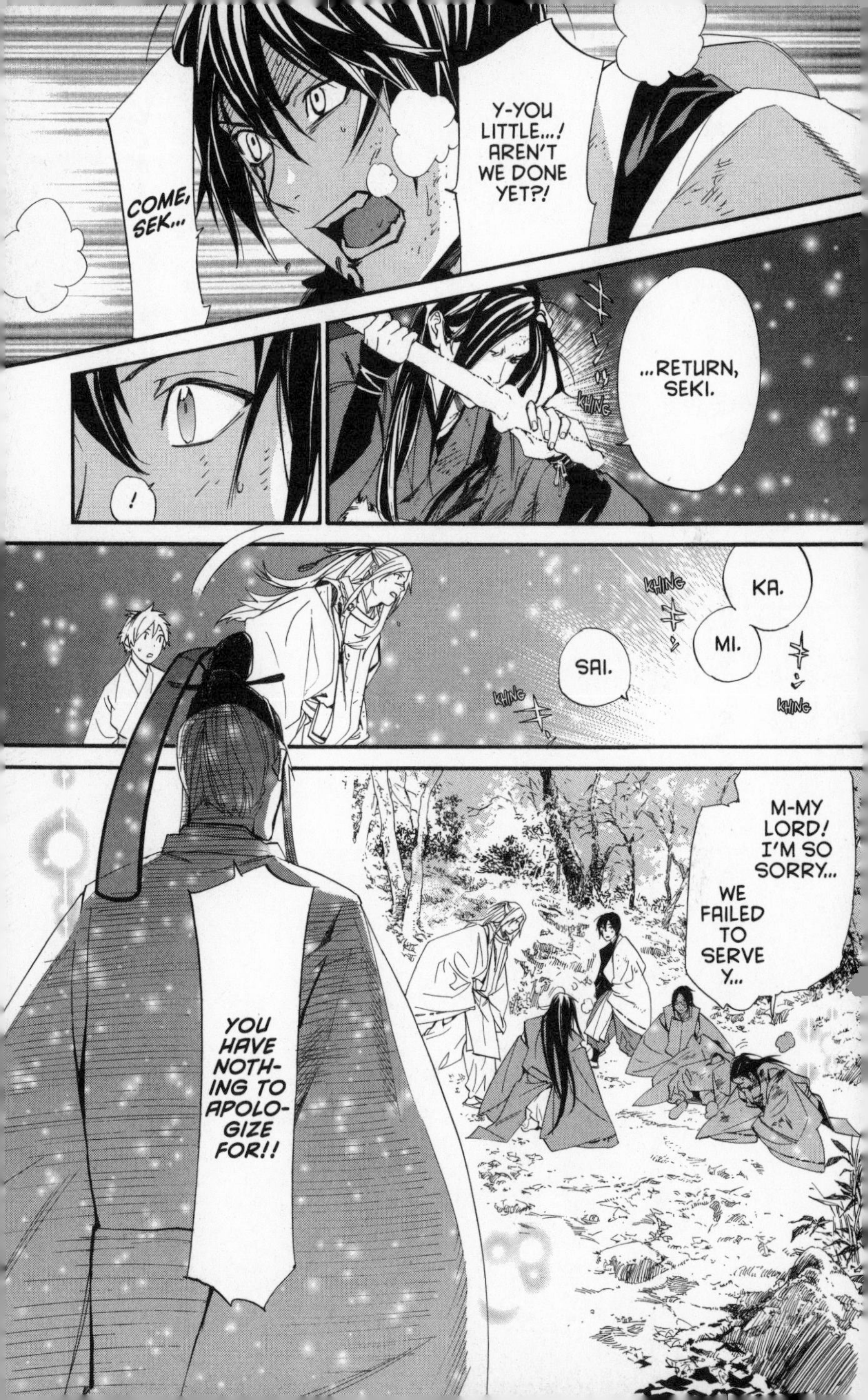
Y-YOU LITTLE...! AREN'T WE DONE YET?!
COME, SEK...
...RETURN, SEKI.
KHING
!
KA.
MI.
SAI.
KHING
KHING
KHING
M-MY LORD! I'M SO SORRY...
WE FAILED TO SERVE Y...
YOU HAVE NOTH-ING TO APOLO-GIZE FOR!!

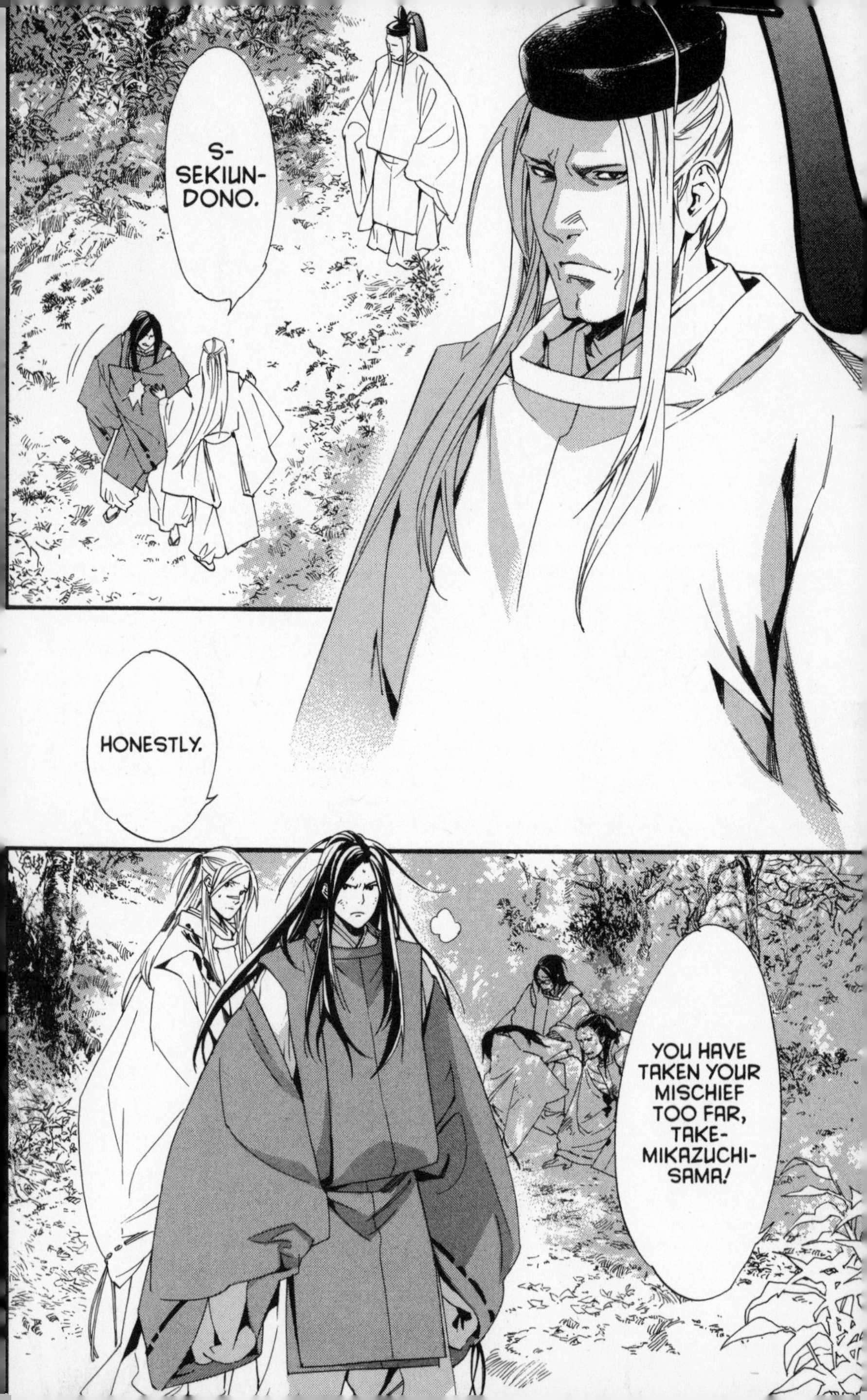
S-SEKIUN-DONO.
HONESTLY.
YOU HAVE TAKEN YOUR MISCHIEF TOO FAR, TAKE-MIKAZUCHI-SAMA!

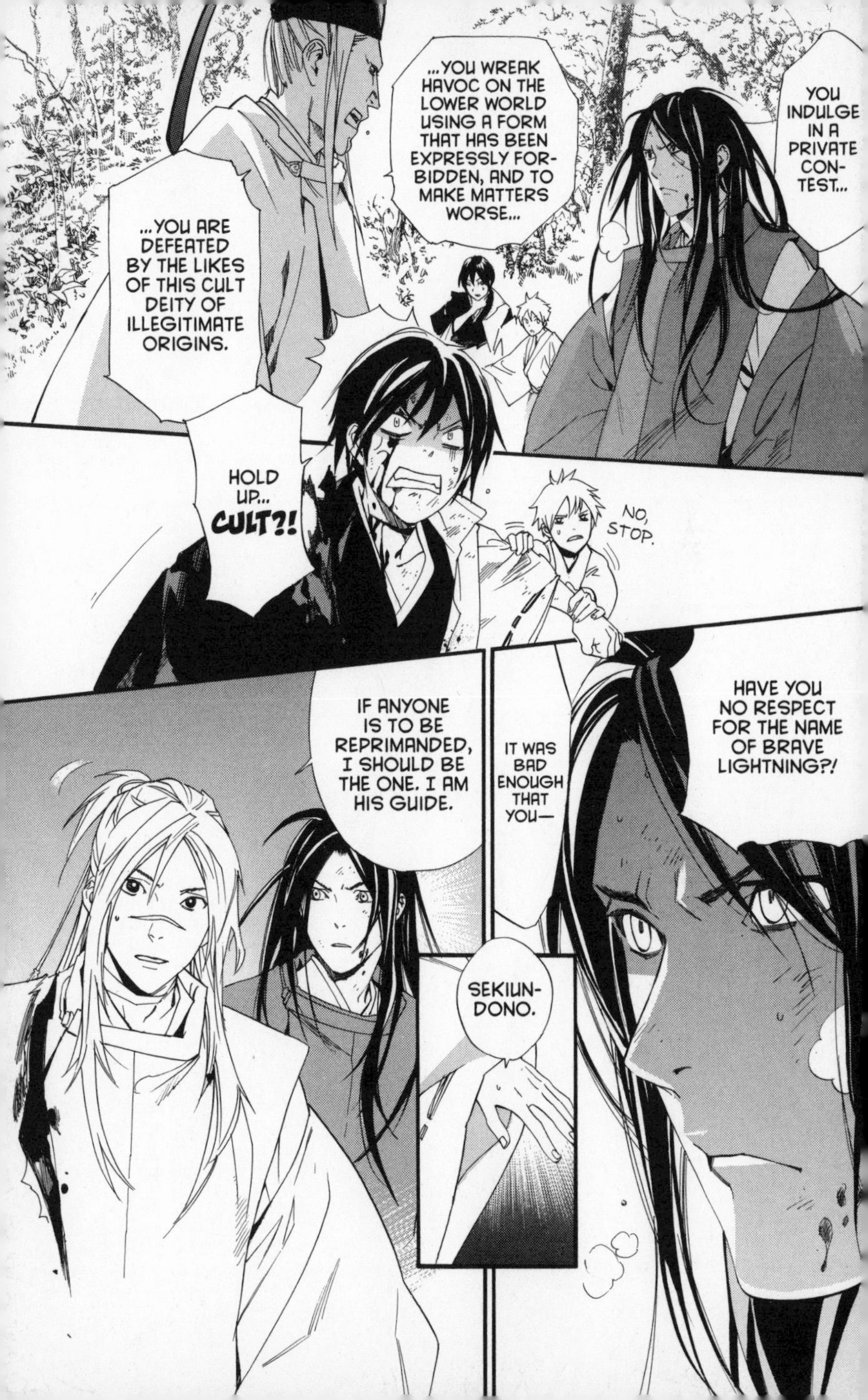
YOU INDULGE IN A PRIVATE CON-TEST...
...YOU WREAK HAVOC ON THE LOWER WORLD USING A FORM THAT HAS BEEN EXPRESSLY FOR-BIDDEN, AND TO MAKE MATTERS WORSE...
...YOU ARE DEFEATED BY THE LIKES OF THIS CULT DEITY OF ILLEGITIMATE ORIGINS.
NO, STOP.
HOLD UP... CULT?!
HAVE YOU NO RESPECT FOR THE NAME OF BRAVE LIGHTNING?!
IT WAS BAD ENOUGH THAT YOU—
IF ANYONE IS TO BE REPRIMANDED, I SHOULD BE THE ONE. I AM HIS GUIDE.
SEKIUN-DONO.

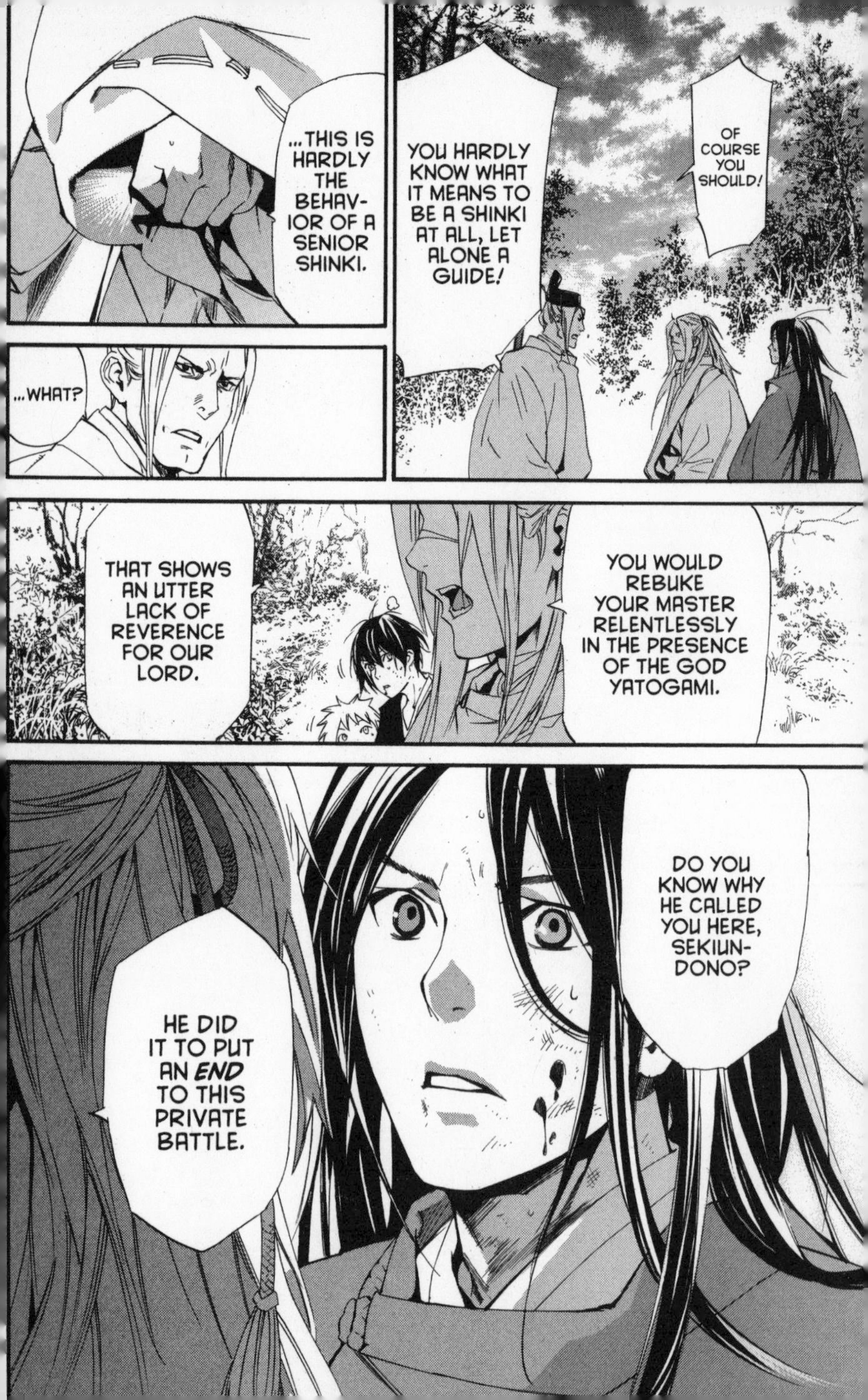
OF COURSE YOU SHOULD!
YOU HARDLY KNOW WHAT IT MEANS TO BE A SHINKI AT ALL, LET ALONE A GUIDE!
...THIS IS HARDLY THE BEHAV-IOR OF A SENIOR SHINKI.
...WHAT?
YOU WOULD REBUKE YOUR MASTER RELENTLESSLY IN THE PRESENCE OF THE GOD YATOGAMI.
THAT SHOWS AN UTTER LACK OF REVERENCE FOR OUR LORD.
DO YOU KNOW WHY HE CALLED YOU HERE, SEKIUN-DONO?
HE DID IT TO PUT AN *END* TO THIS PRIVATE BATTLE.

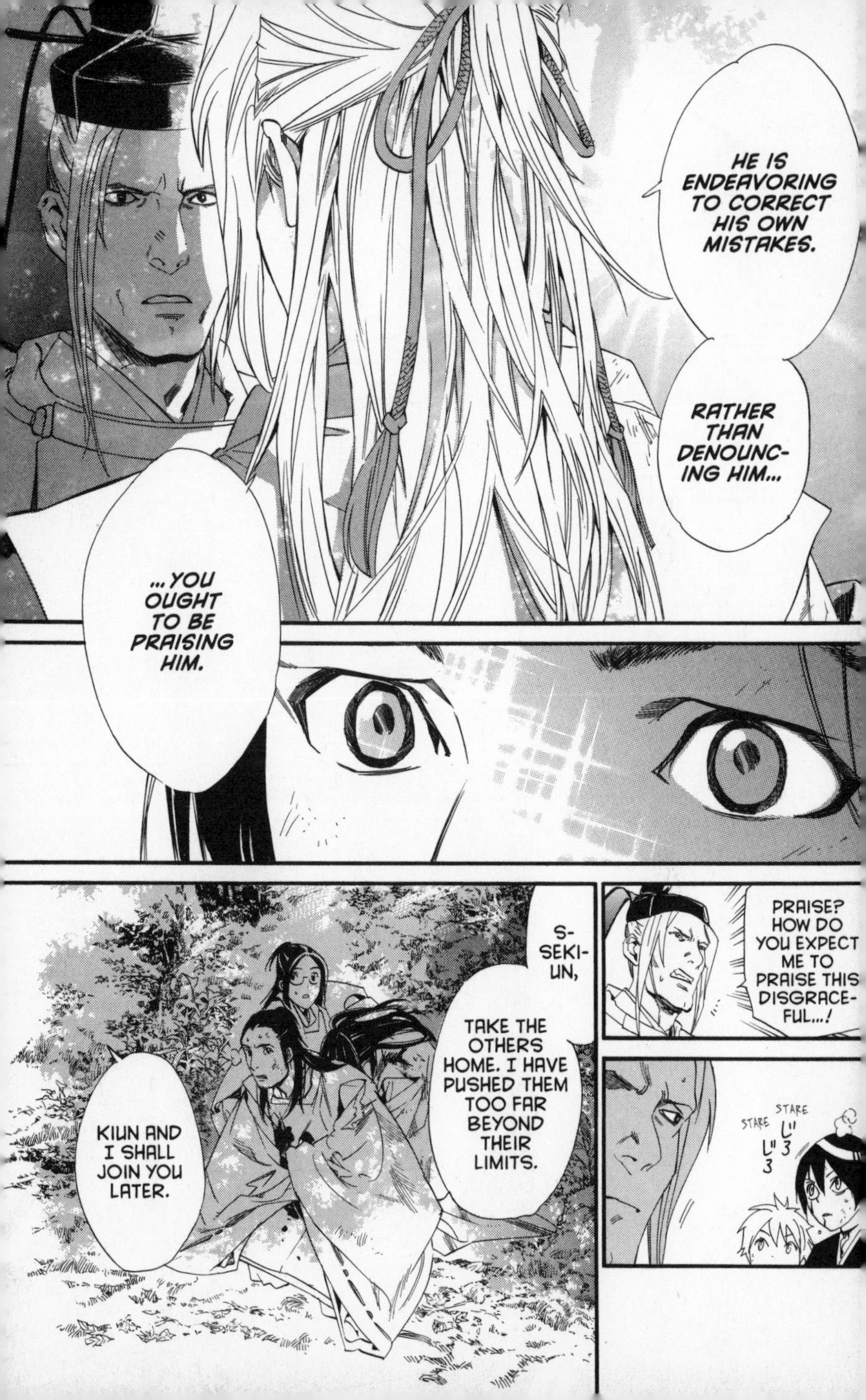
HE IS ENDEAVORING TO CORRECT HIS OWN MISTAKES.
RATHER THAN DENOUNCING HIM...
...YOU OUGHT TO BE PRAISING HIM.
PRAISE? HOW DO YOU EXPECT ME TO PRAISE THIS DISGRACEFUL...!
STARE
STARE
S-SEKI-UN,
TAKE THE OTHERS HOME. I HAVE PUSHED THEM TOO FAR BEYOND THEIR LIMITS.
KIUN AND I SHALL JOIN YOU LATER.

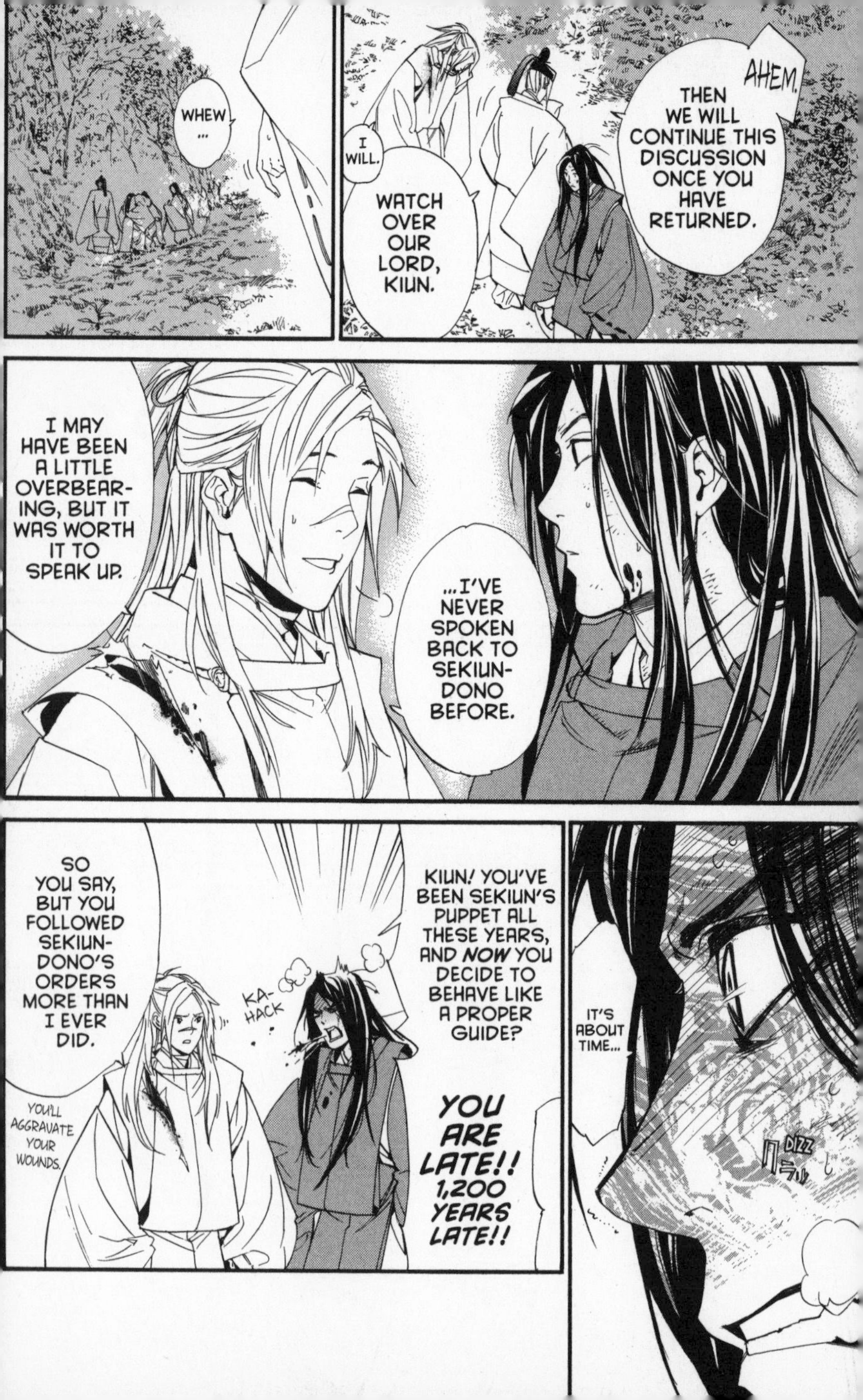
AHEM.
THEN WE WILL CONTINUE THIS DISCUSSION ONCE YOU HAVE RETURNED.
I WILL.
WATCH OVER OUR LORD, KIUN.
WHEW ...
...I'VE NEVER SPOKEN BACK TO SEKIUN-DONO BEFORE.
I MAY HAVE BEEN A LITTLE OVERBEAR-ING, BUT IT WAS WORTH IT TO SPEAK UP.
IT'S ABOUT TIME...
DIZZ
KIUN! YOU'VE BEEN SEKIUN'S PUPPET ALL THESE YEARS, AND NOW YOU DECIDE TO BEHAVE LIKE A PROPER GUIDE?
YOU ARE LATE!! 1,200 YEARS LATE!!
KA-HACK
SO YOU SAY, BUT YOU FOLLOWED SEKIUN-DONO'S ORDERS MORE THAN I EVER DID.
YOU'LL AGGRAVATE YOUR WOUNDS.

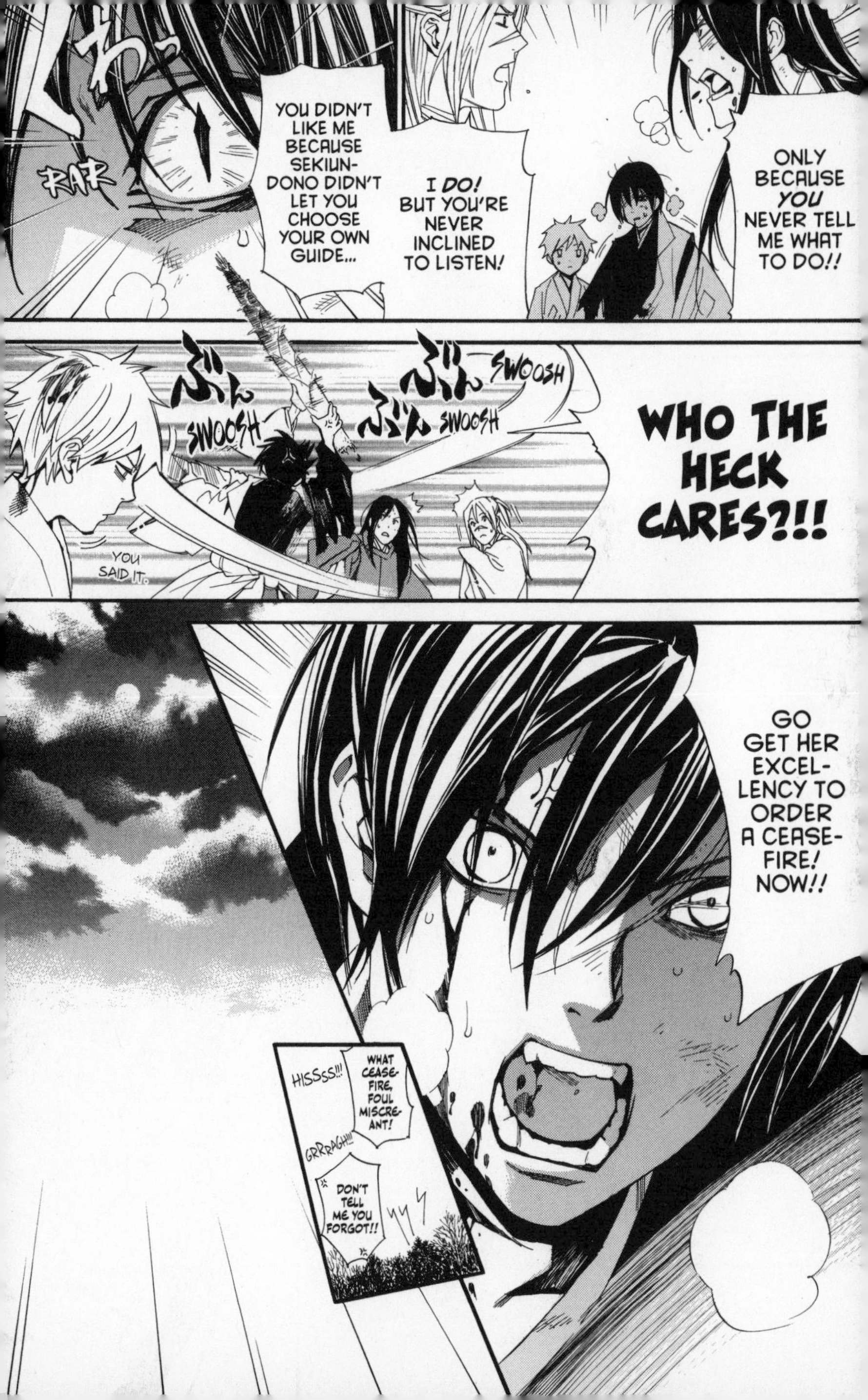
ONLY BECAUSE *YOU* NEVER TELL ME WHAT TO DO!!
I *DO!* BUT YOU'RE NEVER INCLINED TO LISTEN!
YOU DIDN'T LIKE ME BECAUSE SEKIUN-DONO DIDN'T LET YOU CHOOSE YOUR OWN GUIDE...
RAR
WHO THE HECK CARES?!!
SWOOSH
SWOOSH
SWOOSH
YOU SAID IT.
GO GET HER EXCEL-LENCY TO ORDER A CEASE-FIRE! NOW!!
WHAT CEASE-FIRE, FOUL MISCRE-ANT!
HISSSS!!!
GRRRAGH!!!
DON'T TELL ME YOU FORGOT!!

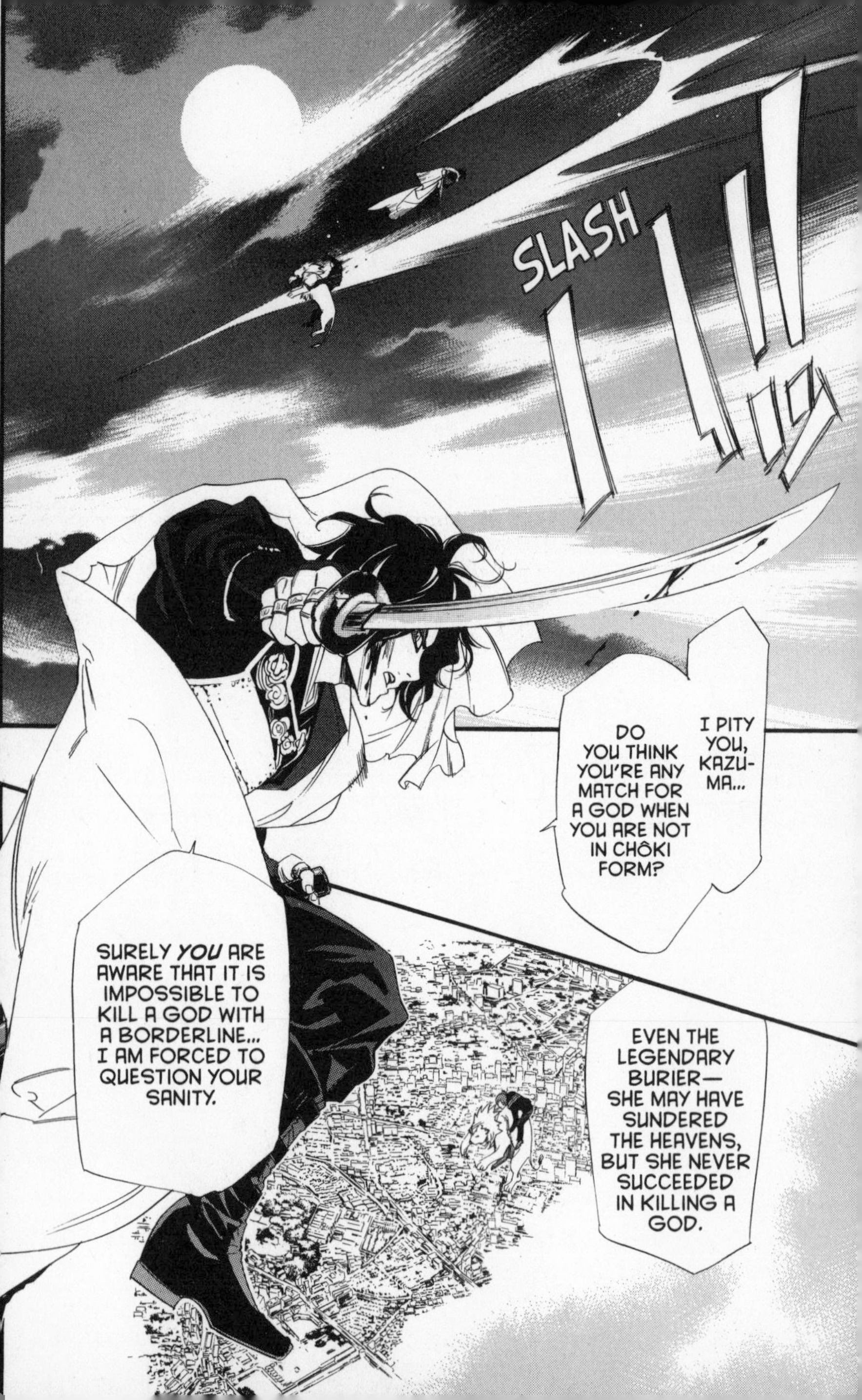
SLASH
I PITY YOU, KAZUMA...
DO YOU THINK YOU'RE ANY MATCH FOR A GOD WHEN YOU ARE NOT IN CHÔKI FORM?
SURELY *YOU* ARE AWARE THAT IT IS IMPOSSIBLE TO KILL A GOD WITH A BORDERLINE... I AM FORCED TO QUESTION YOUR SANITY.
EVEN THE LEGENDARY BURIER—SHE MAY HAVE SUNDERED THE HEAVENS, BUT SHE NEVER SUCCEEDED IN KILLING A GOD.

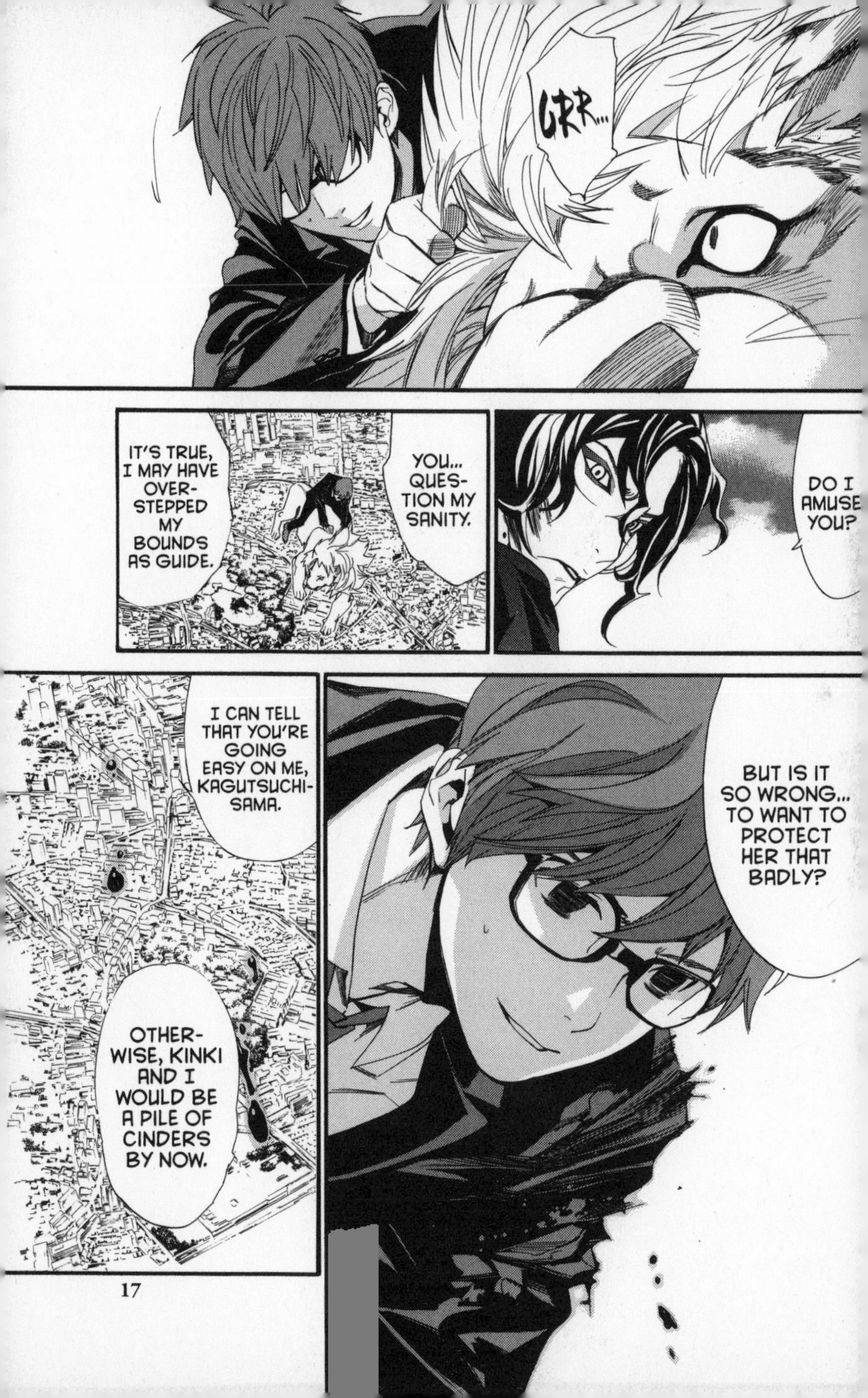
GRR...
DO I AMUSE YOU?
YOU... QUES-TION MY SANITY.
IT'S TRUE, I MAY HAVE OVER-STEPPED MY BOUNDS AS GUIDE.
BUT IS IT SO WRONG... TO WANT TO PROTECT HER THAT BADLY?
I CAN TELL THAT YOU'RE GOING EASY ON ME, KAGUTSUCHI-SAMA.
OTHER-WISE, KINKI AND I WOULD BE A PILE OF CINDERS BY NOW.

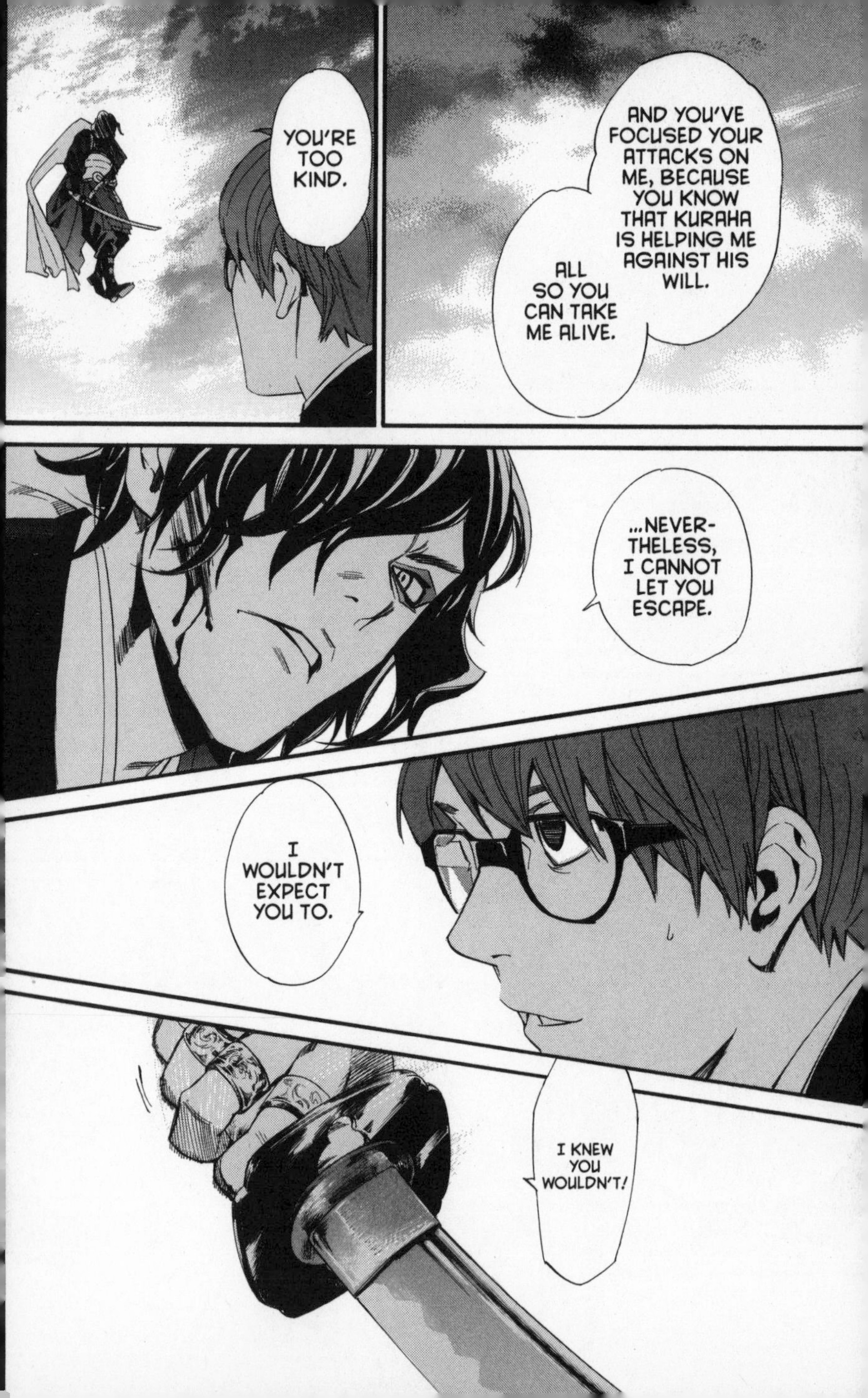
AND YOU'VE FOCUSED YOUR ATTACKS ON ME, BECAUSE YOU KNOW THAT KURAHA IS HELPING ME AGAINST HIS WILL.
ALL SO YOU CAN TAKE ME ALIVE.
YOU'RE TOO KIND.
...NEVER-THELESS, I CANNOT LET YOU ESCAPE.
I WOULDN'T EXPECT YOU TO.
I KNEW YOU WOULDN'T!

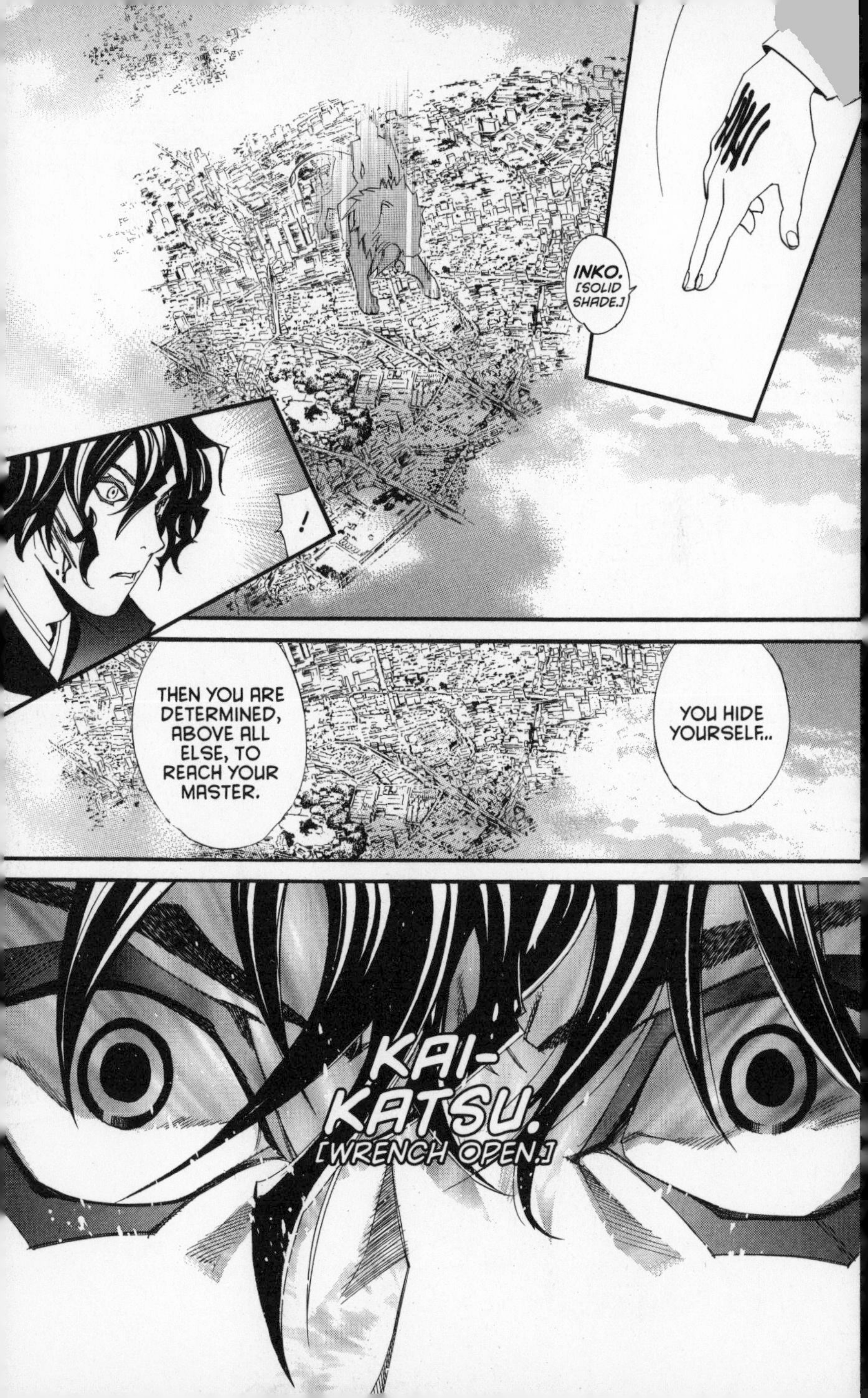
INKO.
[SOLID SHADE.]
!
YOU HIDE YOURSELF...
THEN YOU ARE DETERMINED, ABOVE ALL ELSE, TO REACH YOUR MASTER.
KAI-KATSU.
[WRENCH OPEN.]

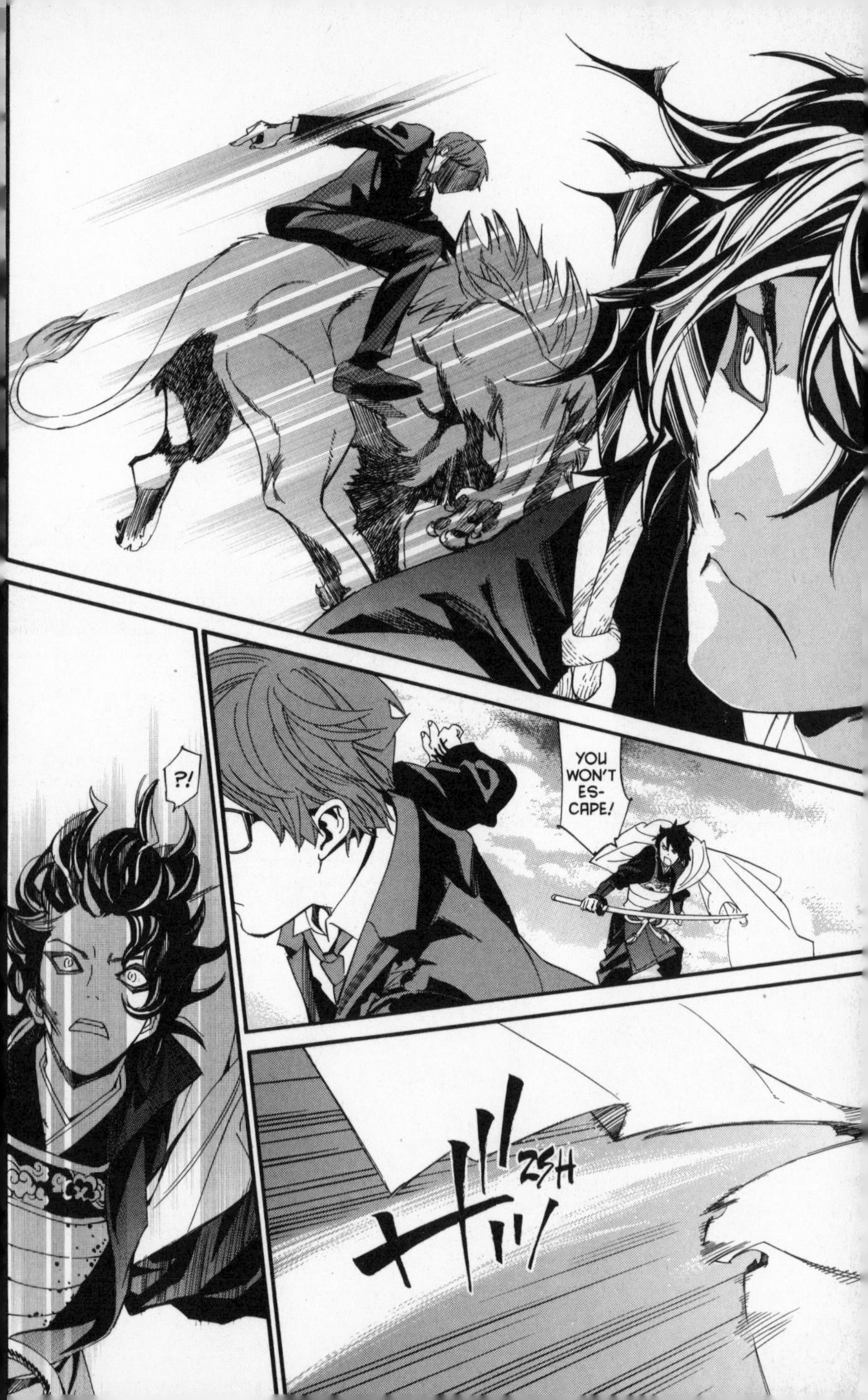
YOU WON'T ES-CAPE!
?!
ZSH

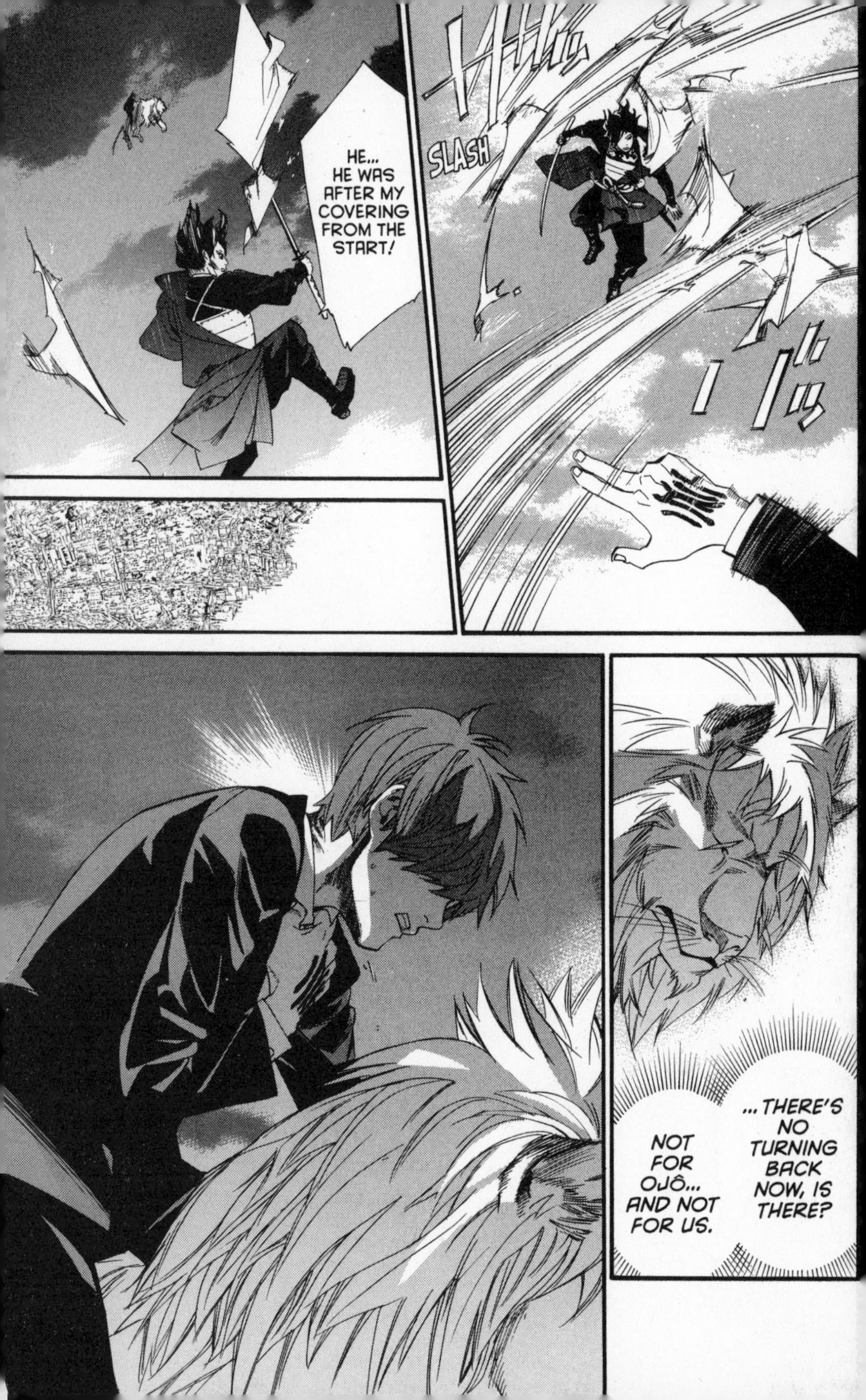
SLASH
HE... HE WAS AFTER MY COVERING FROM THE START!
...THERE'S NO TURNING BACK NOW, IS THERE?
NOT FOR OJÔ... AND NOT FOR US.

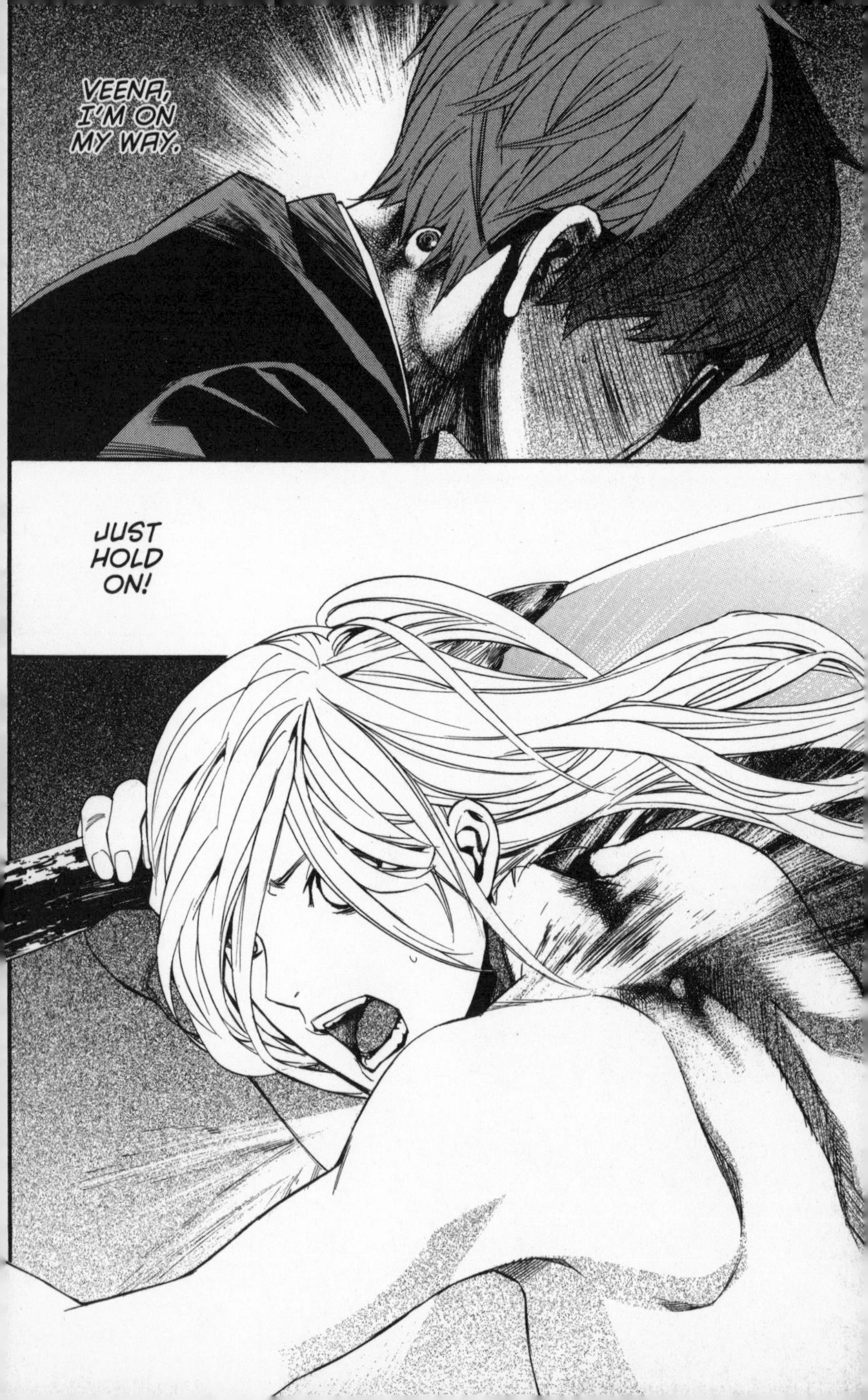
VEENA, I'M ON MY WAY.
JUST HOLD ON!

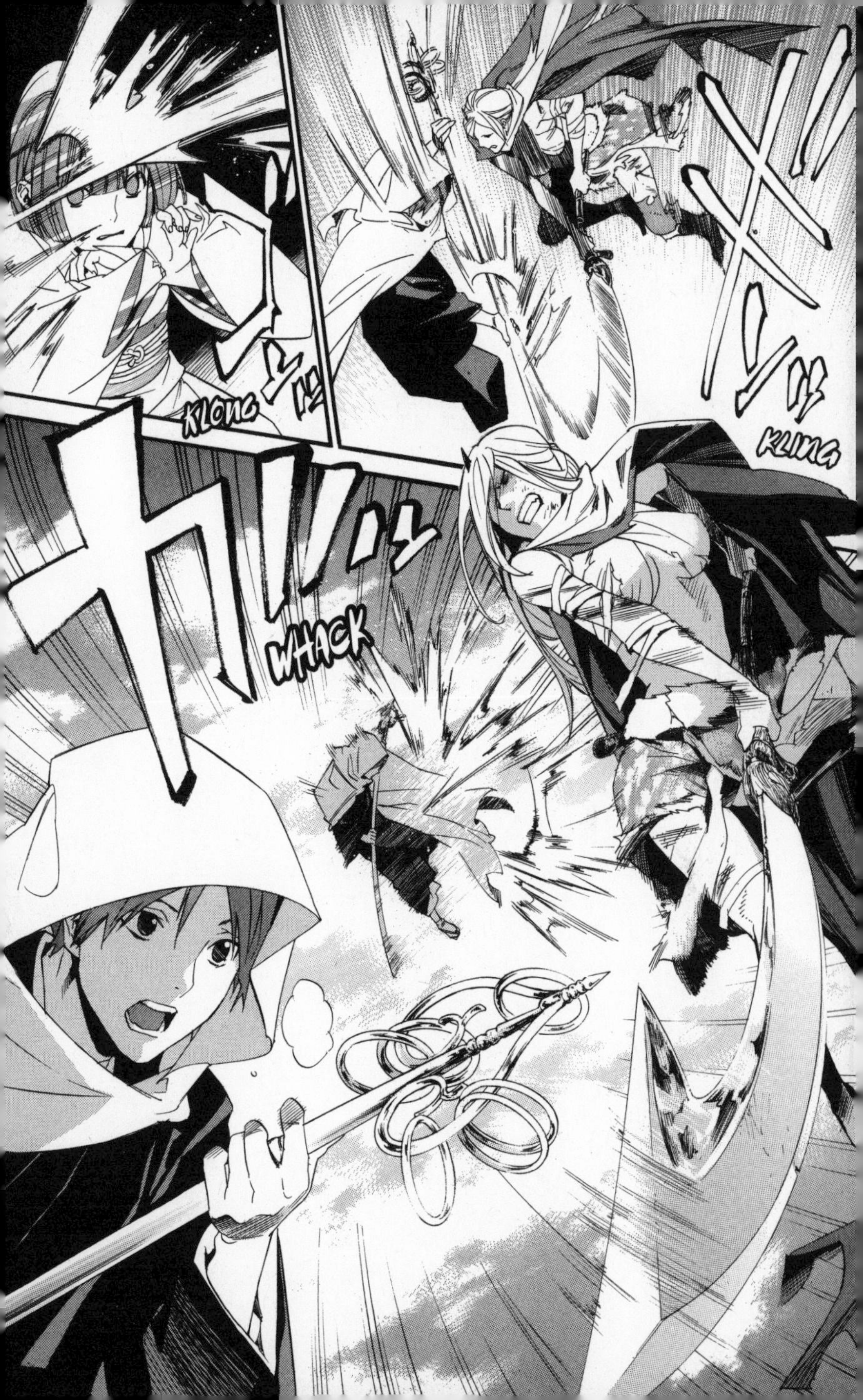
KLING
KLONG
WHACK

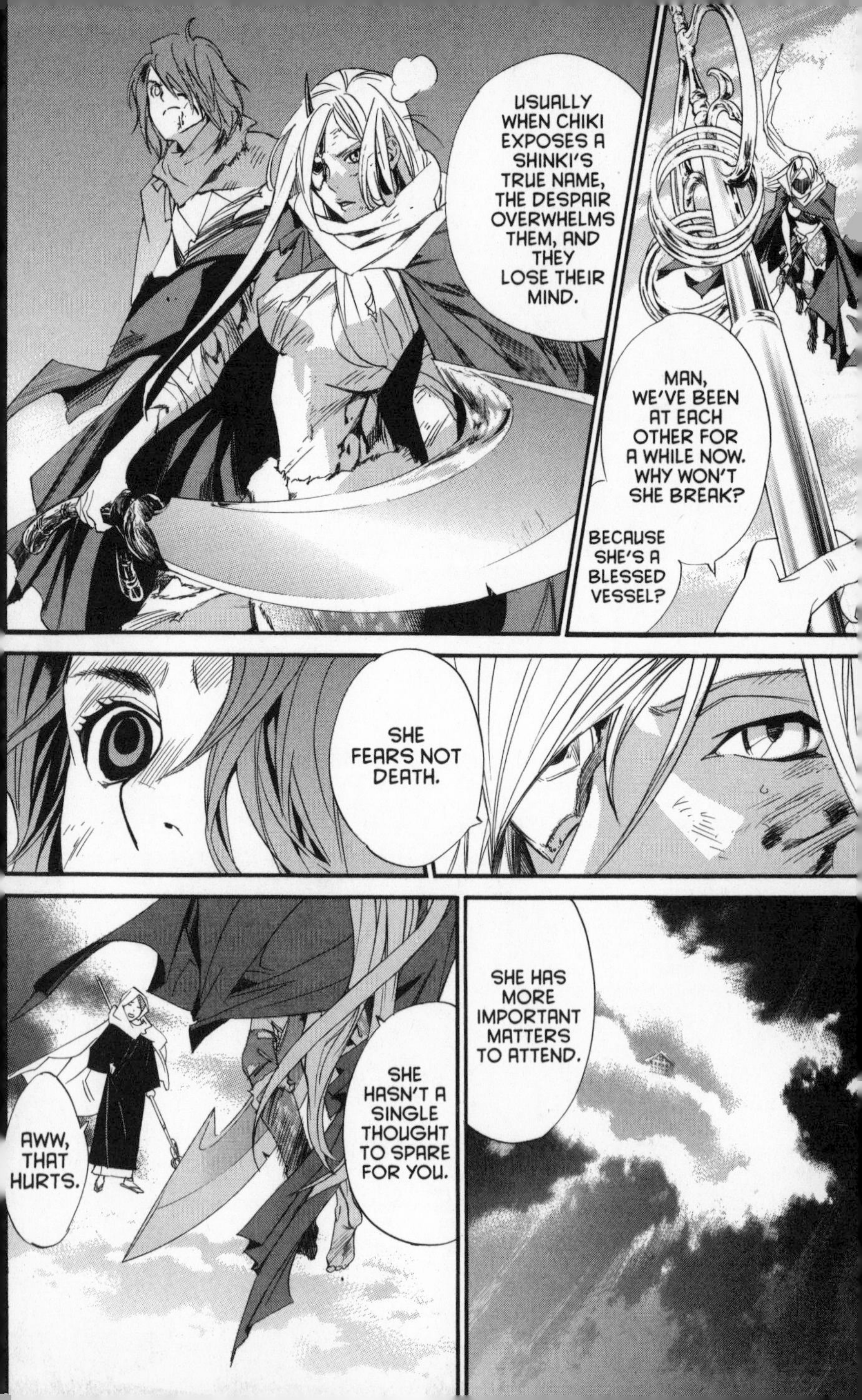
MAN, WE'VE BEEN AT EACH OTHER FOR A WHILE NOW. WHY WON'T SHE BREAK?
BECAUSE SHE'S A BLESSED VESSEL?
USUALLY WHEN CHIKI EXPOSES A SHINKI'S TRUE NAME, THE DESPAIR OVERWHELMS THEM, AND THEY LOSE THEIR MIND.
SHE FEARS NOT DEATH.
SHE HAS MORE IMPORTANT MATTERS TO ATTEND.
SHE HASN'T A SINGLE THOUGHT TO SPARE FOR YOU.
AWW, THAT HURTS.

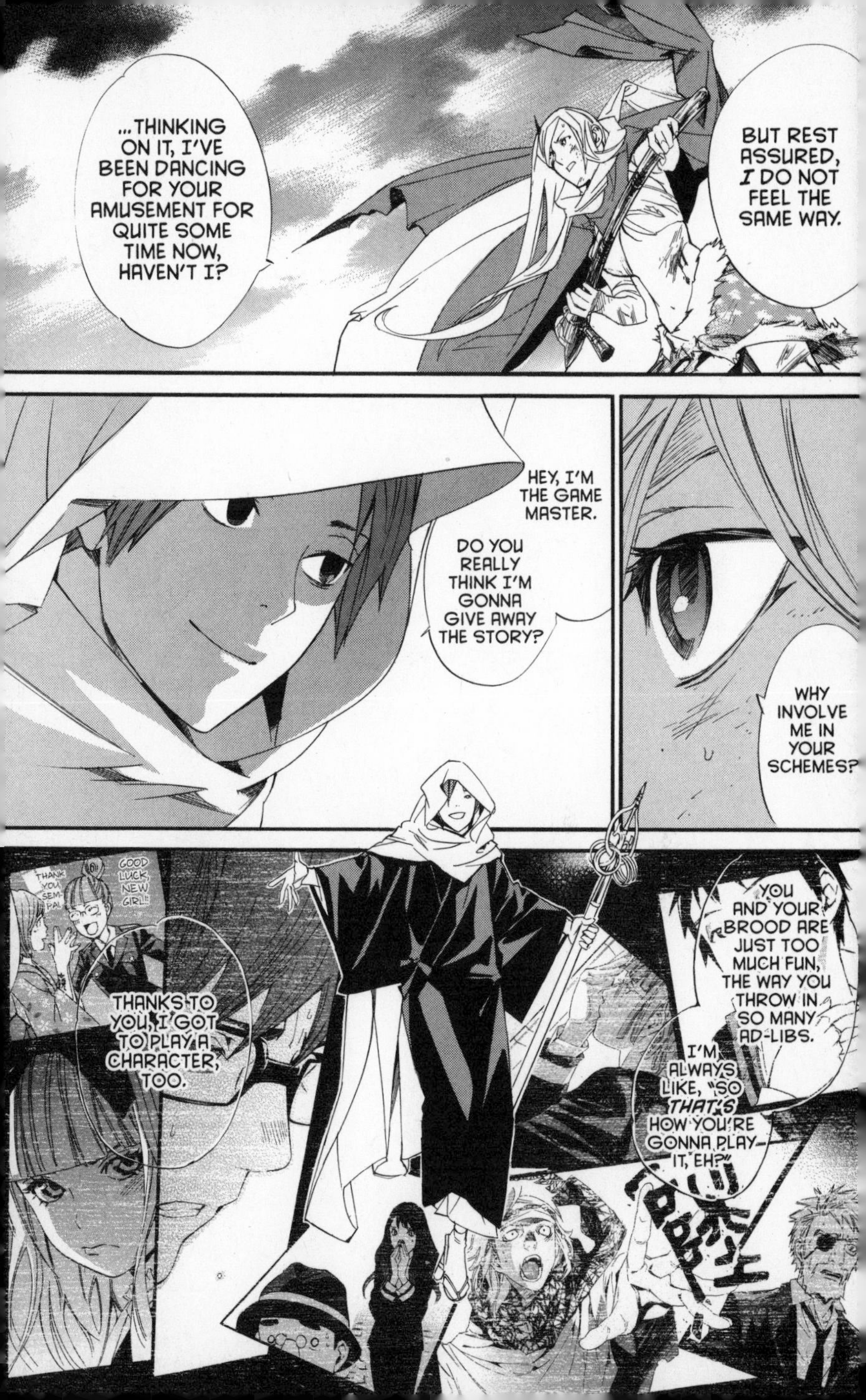
...THINKING ON IT, I'VE BEEN DANCING FOR YOUR AMUSEMENT FOR QUITE SOME TIME NOW, HAVEN'T I?
BUT REST ASSURED, *I* DO NOT FEEL THE SAME WAY.
WHY INVOLVE ME IN YOUR SCHEMES?
HEY, I'M THE GAME MASTER.
DO YOU REALLY THINK I'M GONNA GIVE AWAY THE STORY?
YOU AND YOUR BROOD ARE JUST TOO MUCH FUN, THE WAY YOU THROW IN SO MANY AD-LIBS.
I'M ALWAYS LIKE, "SO *THAT'S* HOW YOU'RE GONNA PLAY IT, EH?"
THANKS TO YOU, I GOT TO PLAY A CHARACTER, TOO.
GOOD LUCK, NEW GIRL!!
THANK YOU, SEM-PAI.

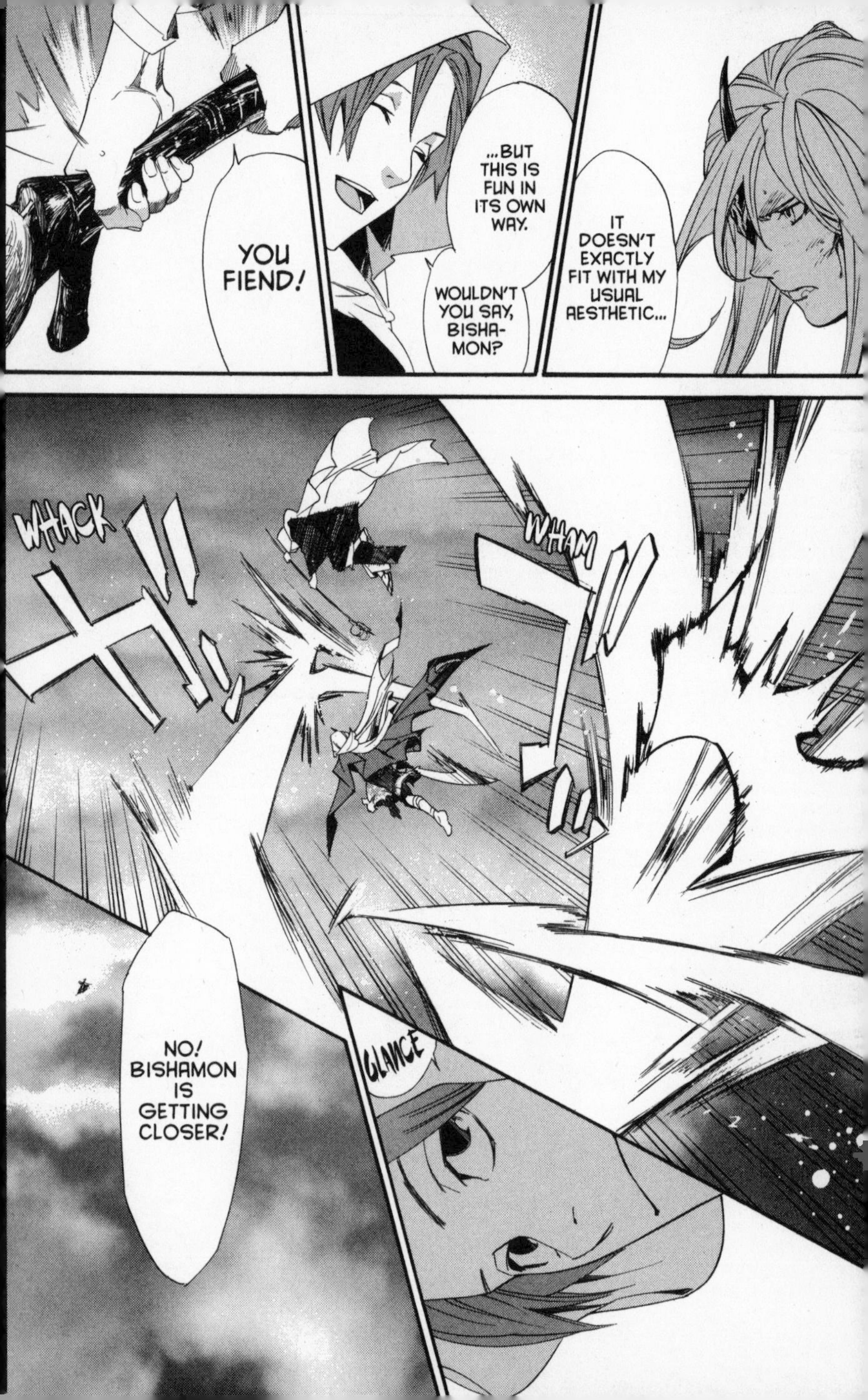
IT DOESN'T EXACTLY FIT WITH MY USUAL AESTHETIC...
...BUT THIS IS FUN IN ITS OWN WAY.
WOULDN'T YOU SAY, BISHAMON?
YOU FIEND!
WHAM
WHACK
GLANCE
NO! BISHAMON IS GETTING CLOSER!

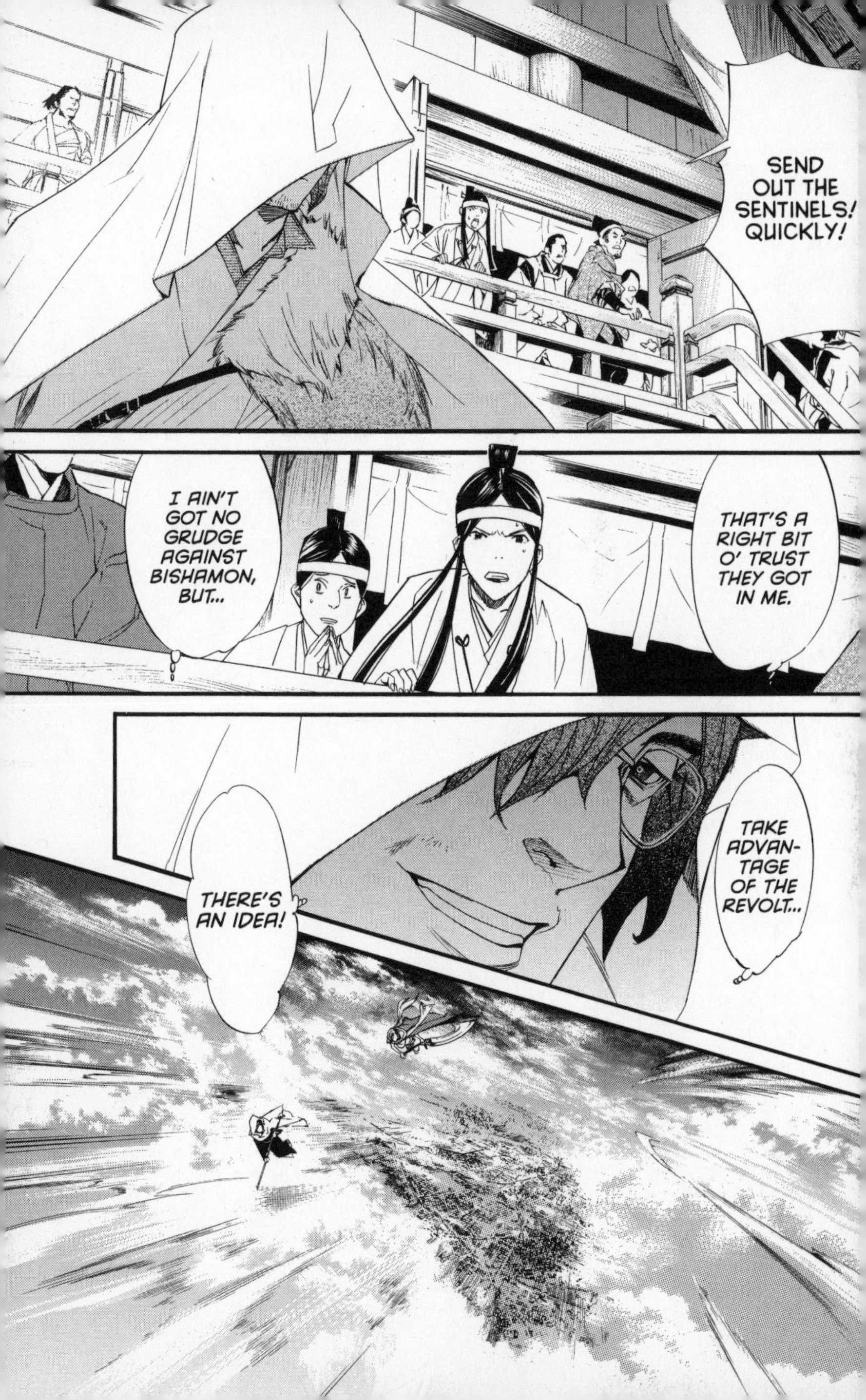
SEND OUT THE SENTINELS! QUICKLY!
THAT'S A RIGHT BIT O' TRUST THEY GOT IN ME.
I AIN'T GOT NO GRUDGE AGAINST BISHAMON, BUT...
TAKE ADVAN-TAGE OF THE REVOLT...
THERE'S AN IDEA!

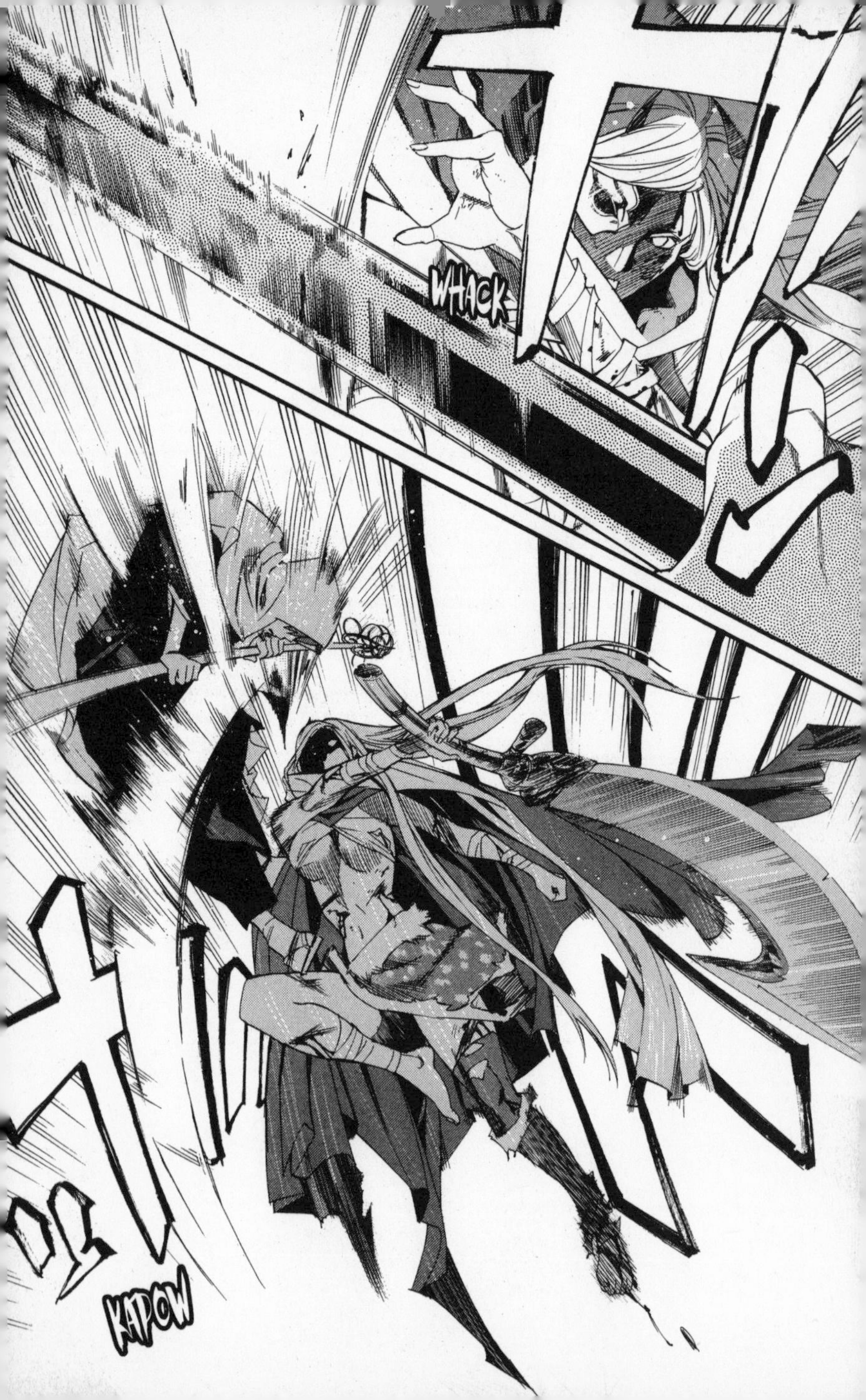
WHACK
KAPOW

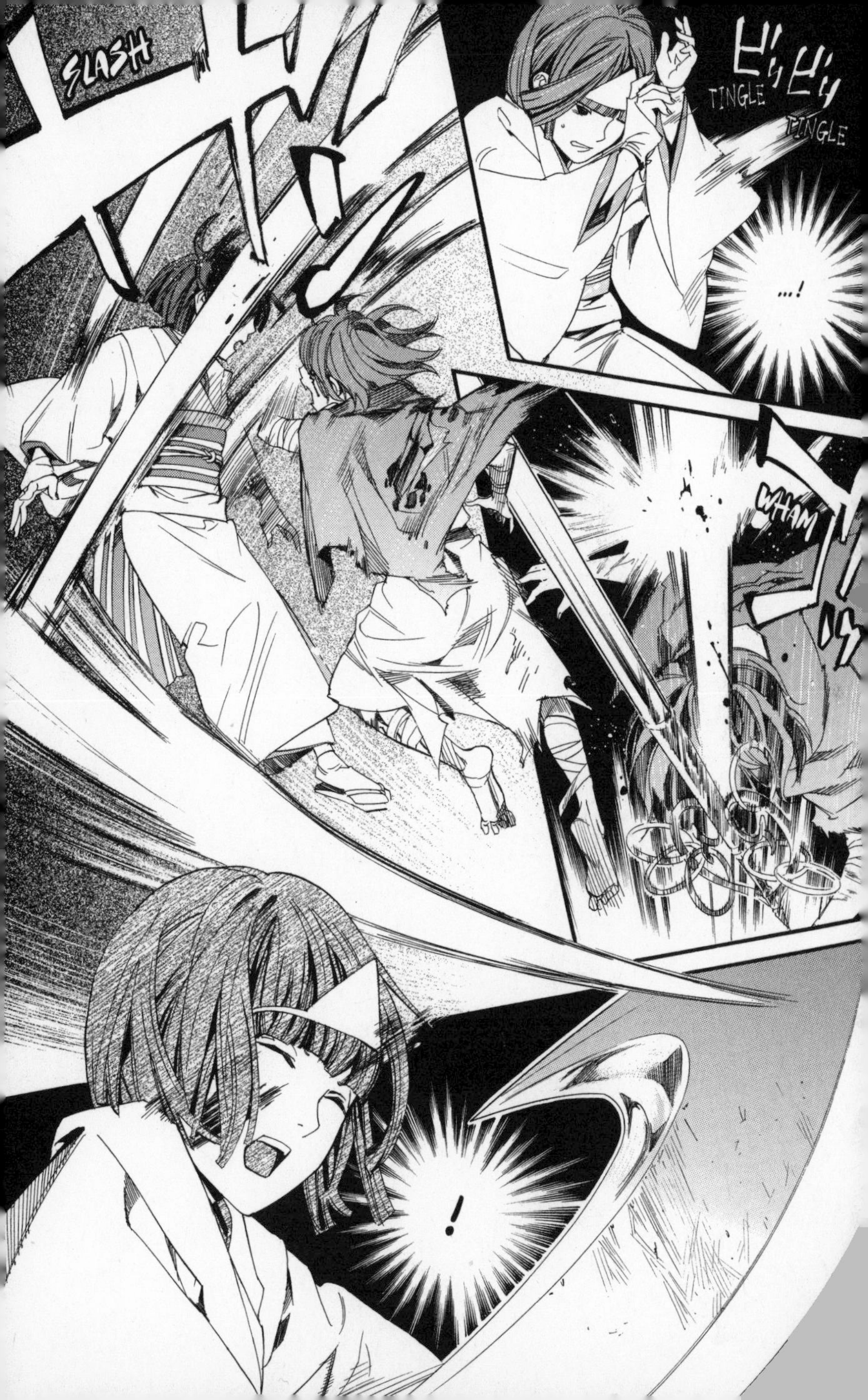
ビリビリ
TINGLE
TINGLE
...!
SLASH
WHAM
!

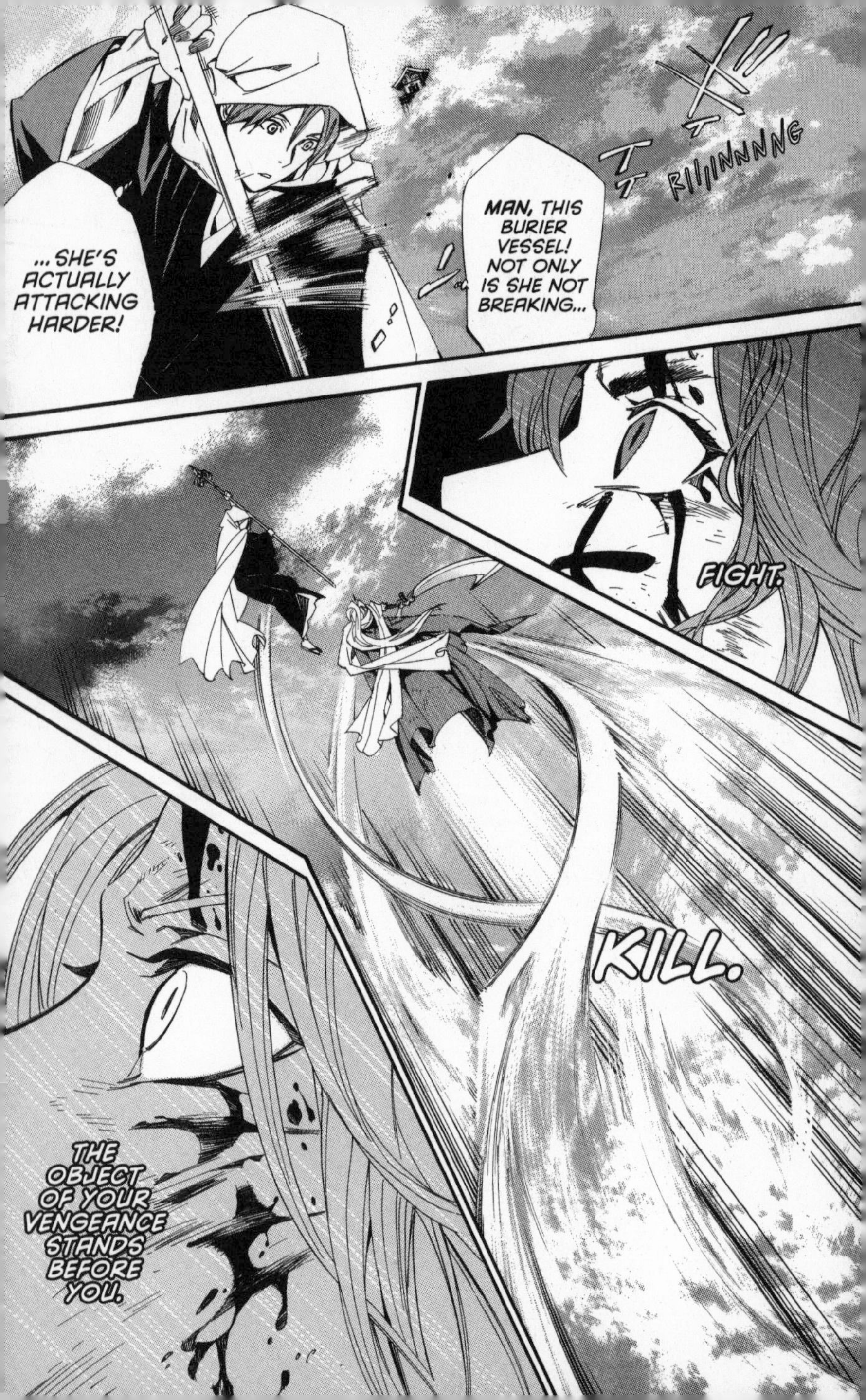
RIIIINNNNG
MAN, THIS BURIER VESSEL! NOT ONLY IS SHE NOT BREAKING...
...SHE'S ACTUALLY ATTACKING HARDER!
FIGHT.
KILL.
THE OBJECT OF YOUR VENGEANCE STANDS BEFORE YOU.

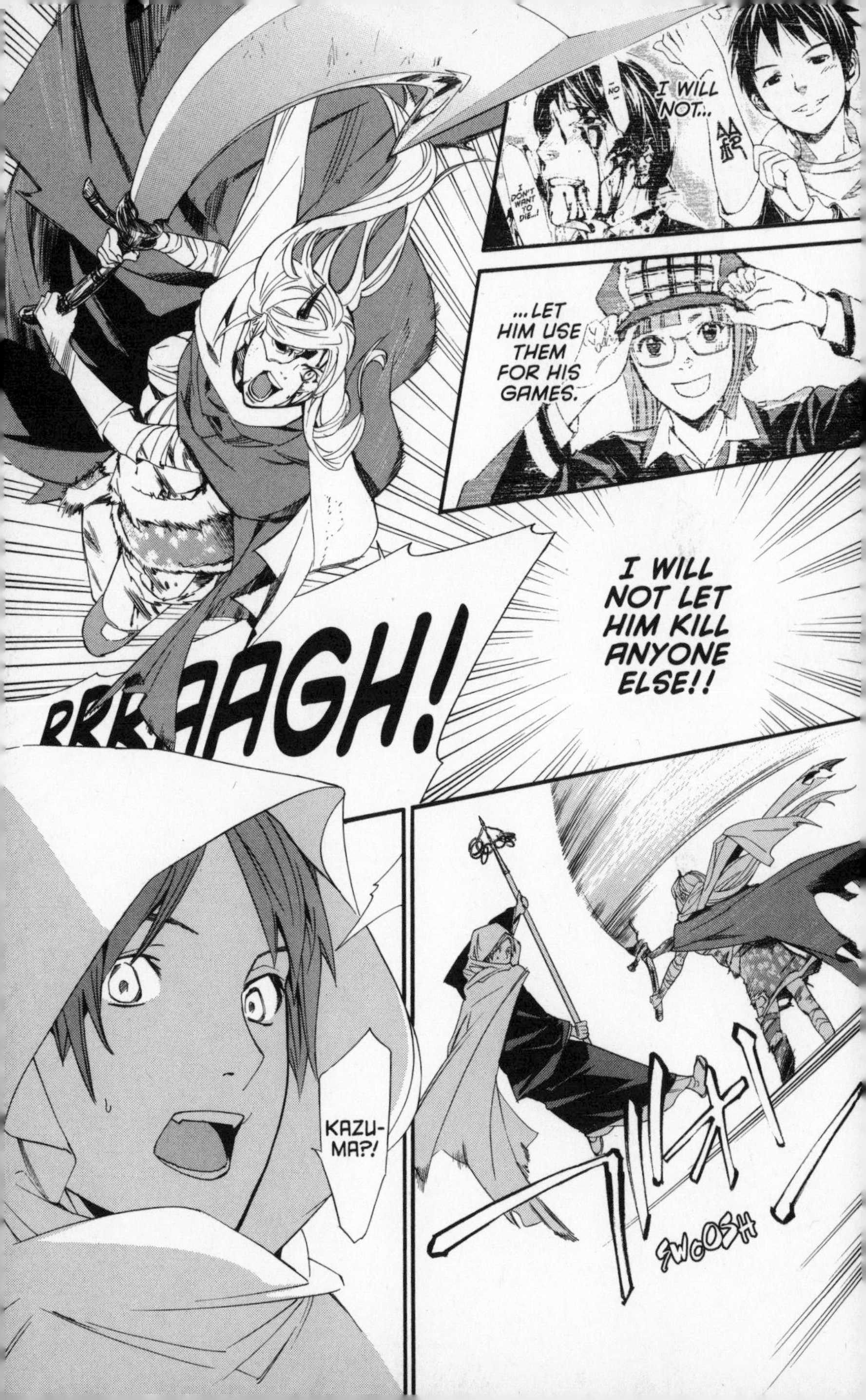
I WILL NOT...
NO
I DON'T WANT TO DIE...!
...LET HIM USE THEM FOR HIS GAMES.
I WILL NOT LET HIM KILL ANYONE ELSE!!
RRRAAGH!
SWOOSH
KAZU-MA?!

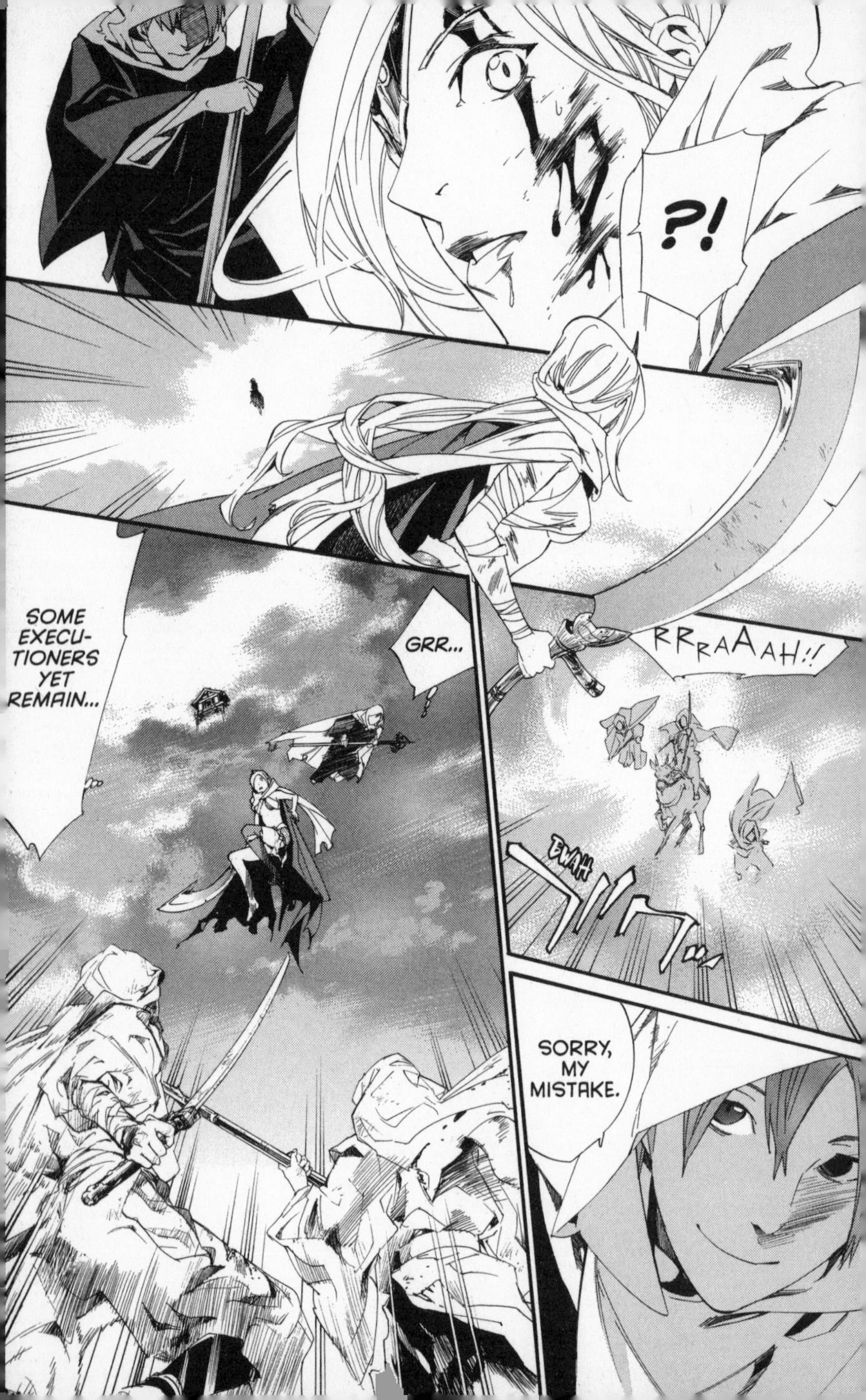
?!
RRRAAAH!!
EWAH
GRR...
SOME EXECUTIONERS YET REMAIN...
SORRY, MY MISTAKE.

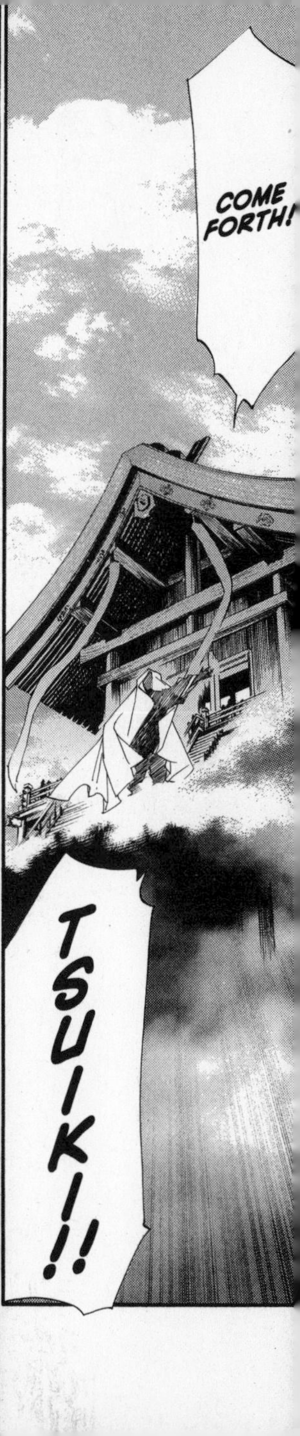
COME FORTH!
TSUKI!!
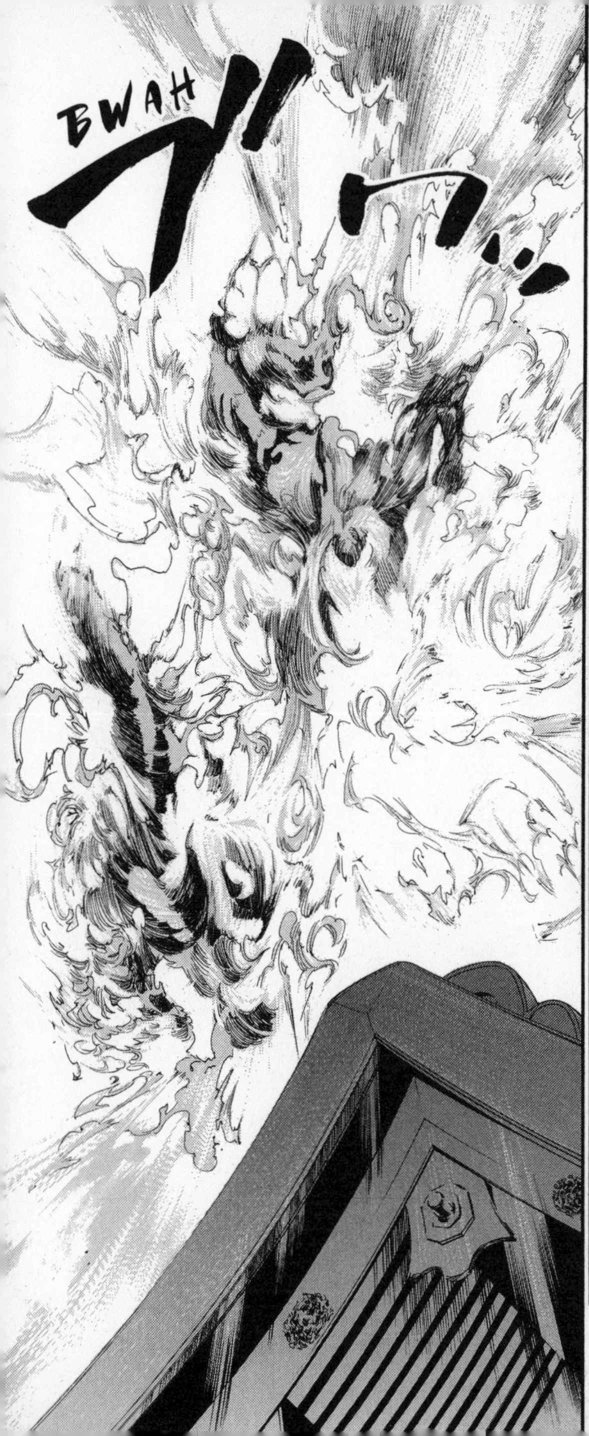
BWAH

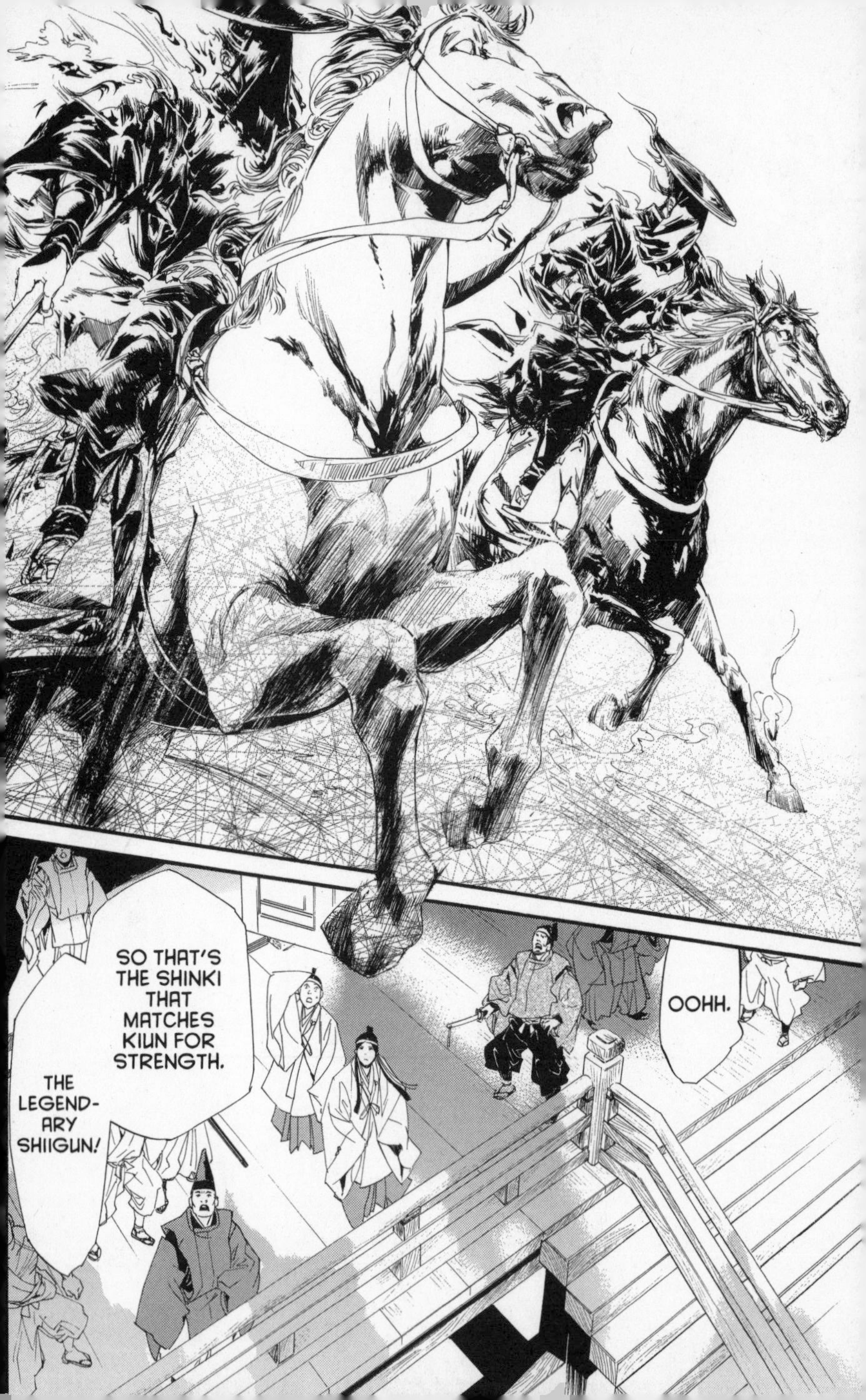
OOHH.
SO THAT'S THE SHINKI THAT MATCHES KIUN FOR STRENGTH.
THE LEGENDARY SHIIGUN!

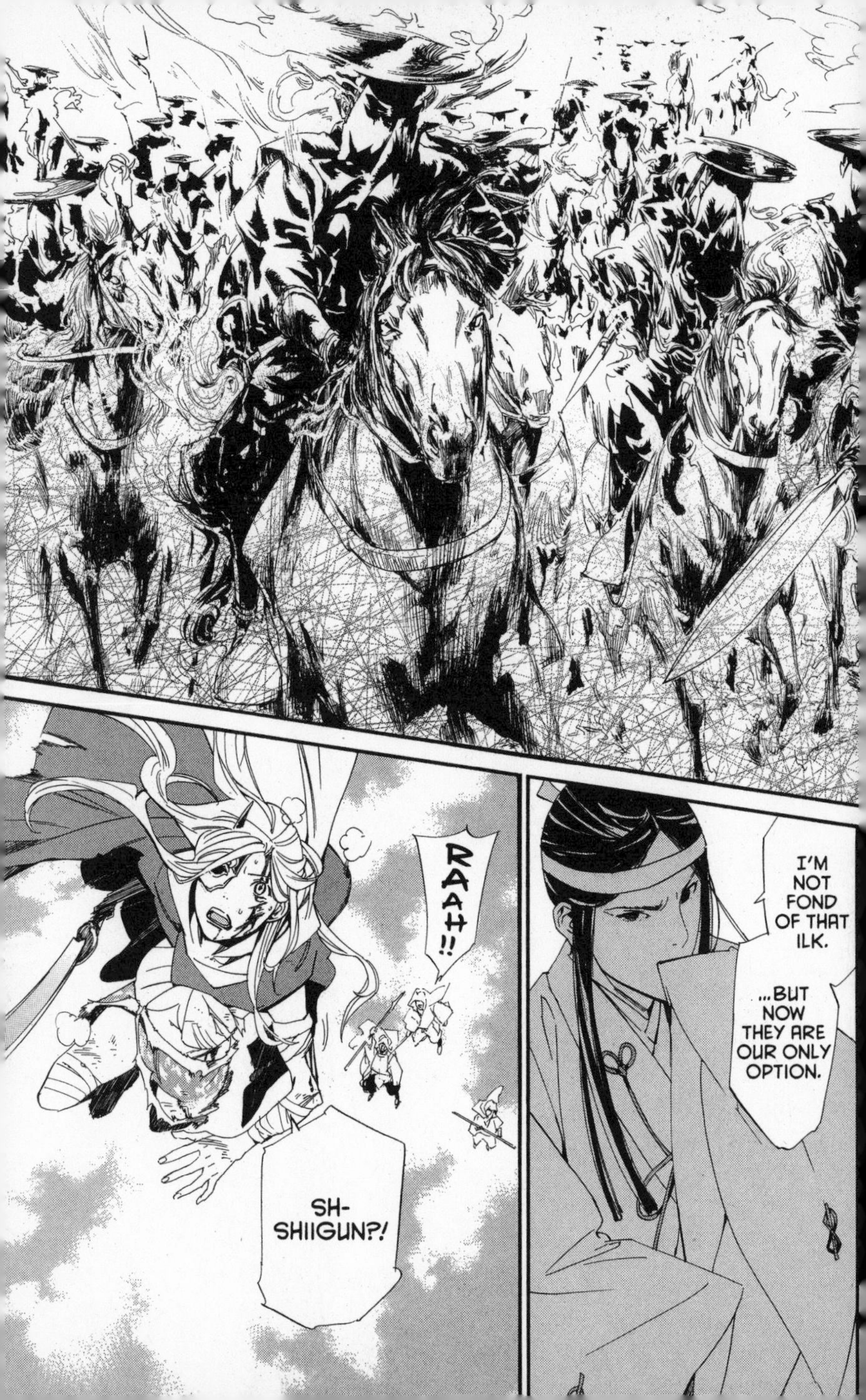
I'M NOT FOND OF THAT ILK.
...BUT NOW THEY ARE OUR ONLY OPTION.
RAAAH!!
SH-SHIIGUN?!

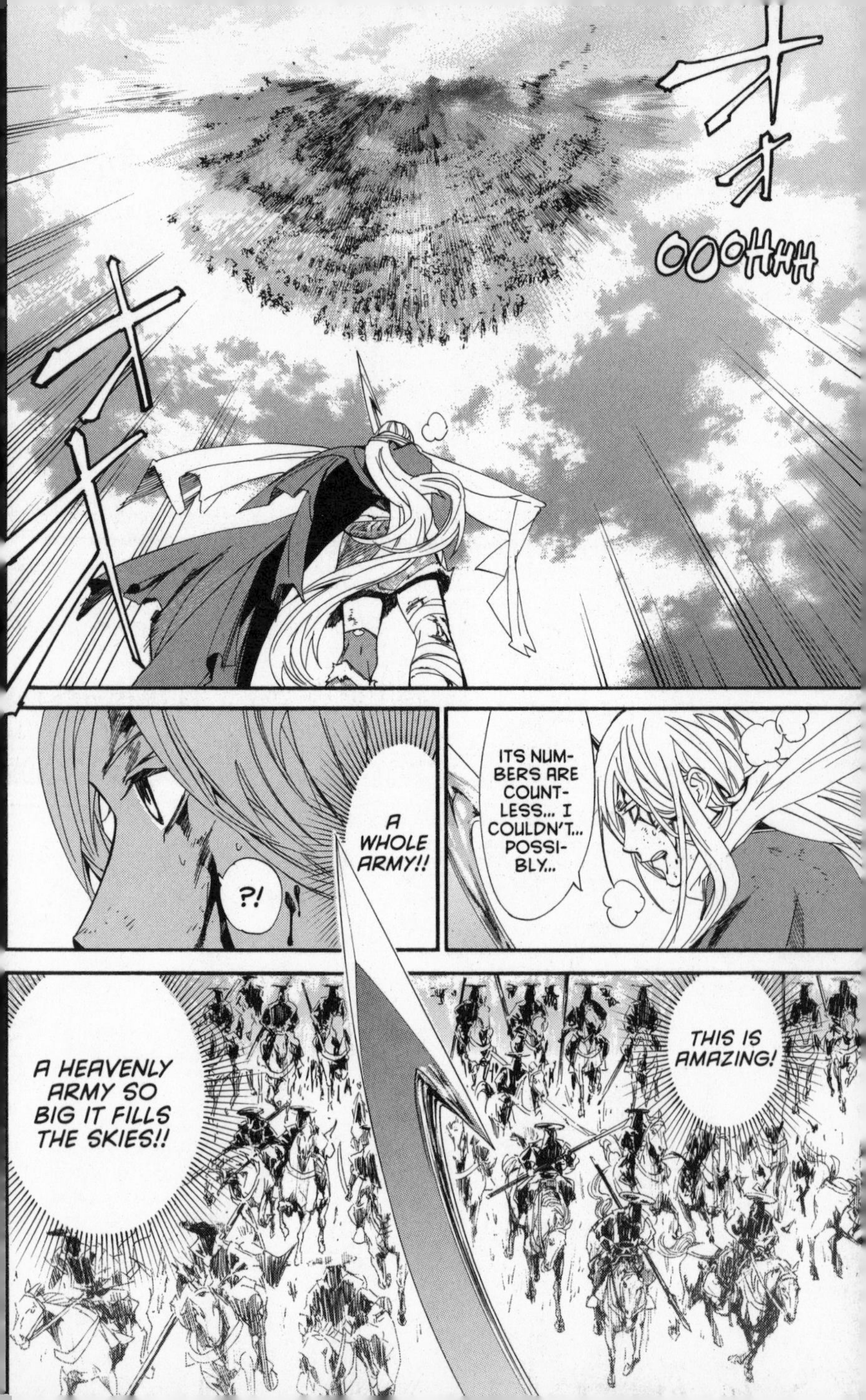

オオ
OOOHHH
オオ
ITS NUMBERS ARE COUNTLESS... I COULDN'T... POSSIBLY...
A WHOLE ARMY!!
?!
THIS IS AMAZING!
A HEAVENLY ARMY SO BIG IT FILLS THE SKIES!!

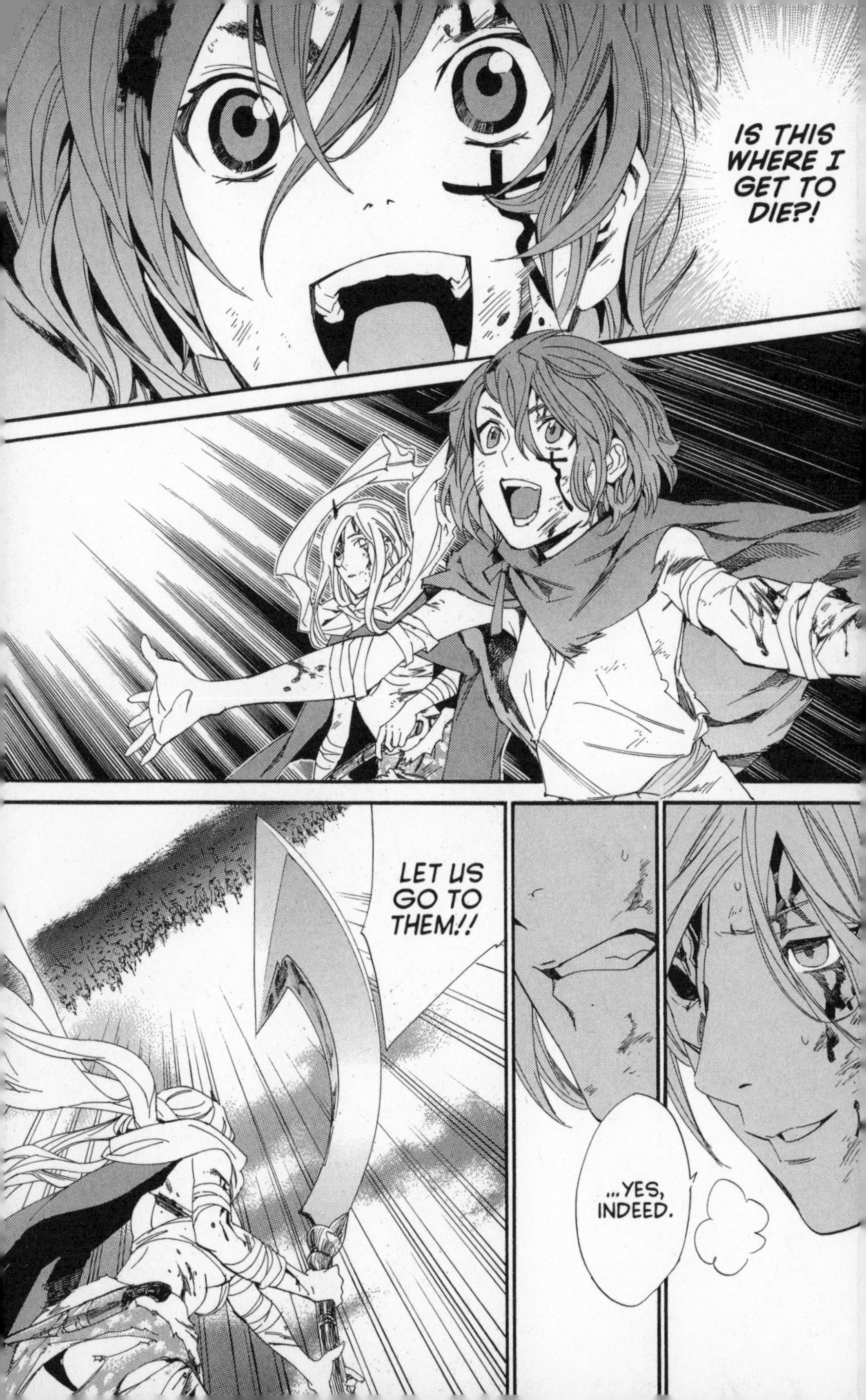
IS THIS WHERE I GET TO DIE?!
...YES, INDEED.
LET US GO TO THEM!!

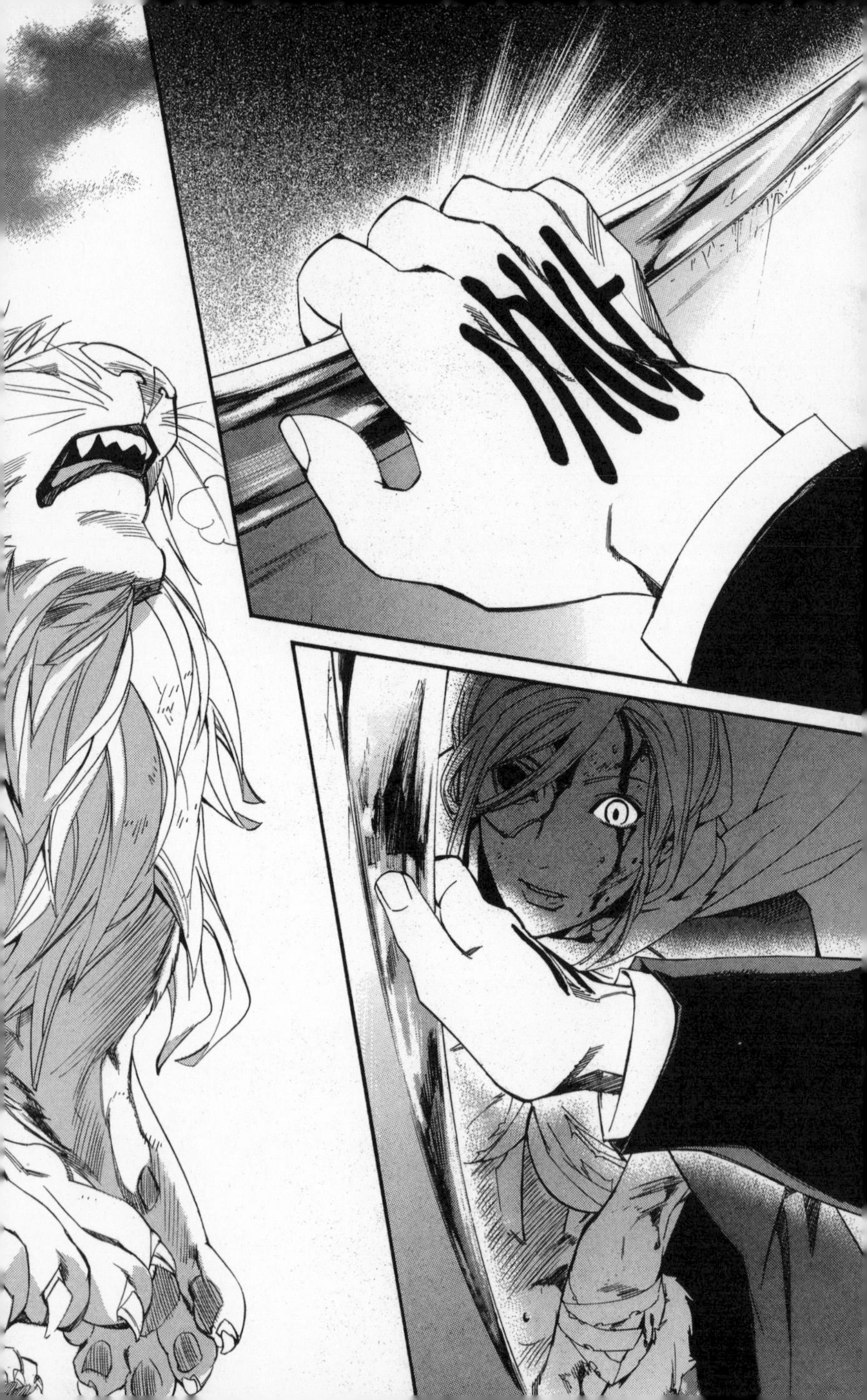

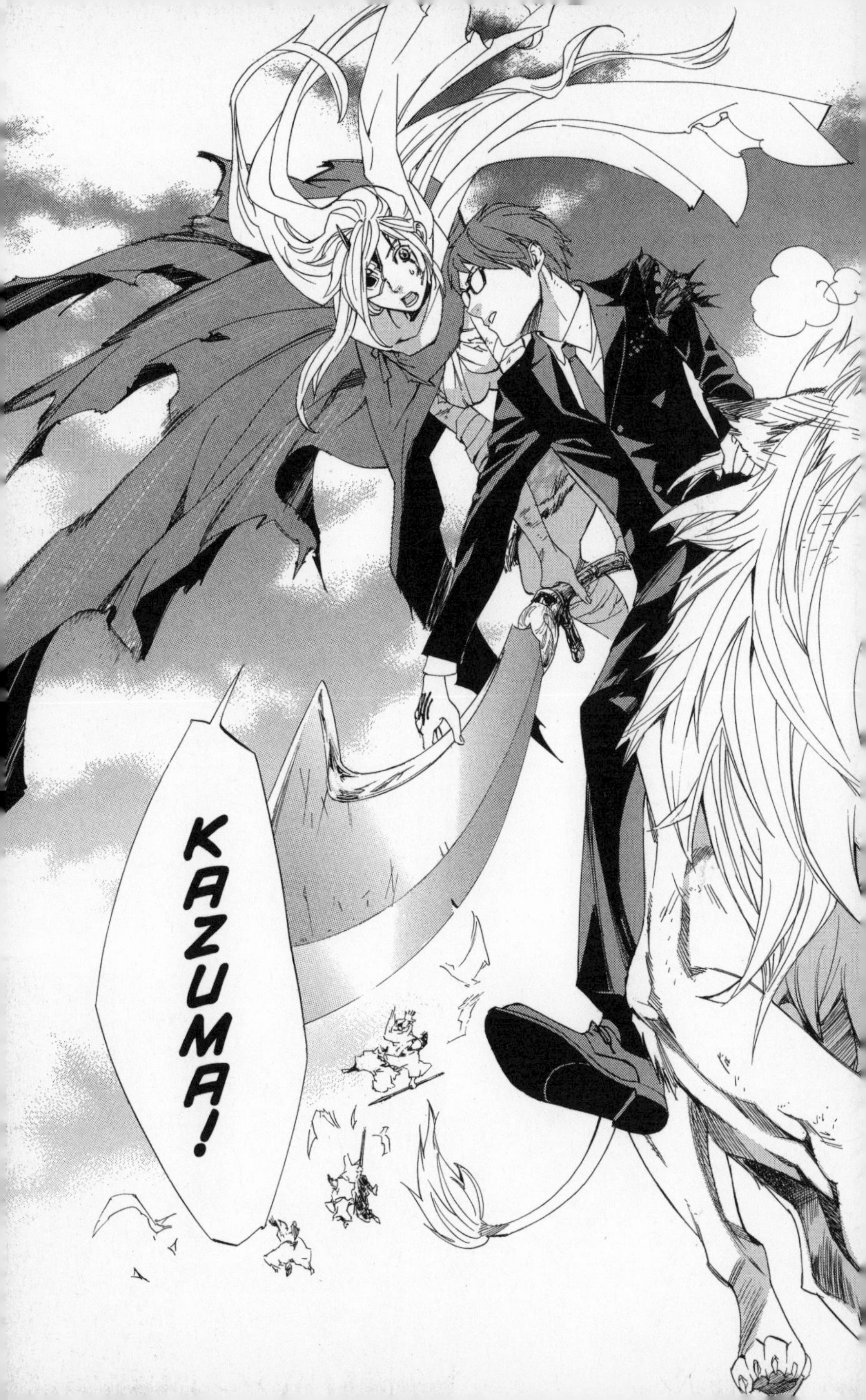
KAZUMA!

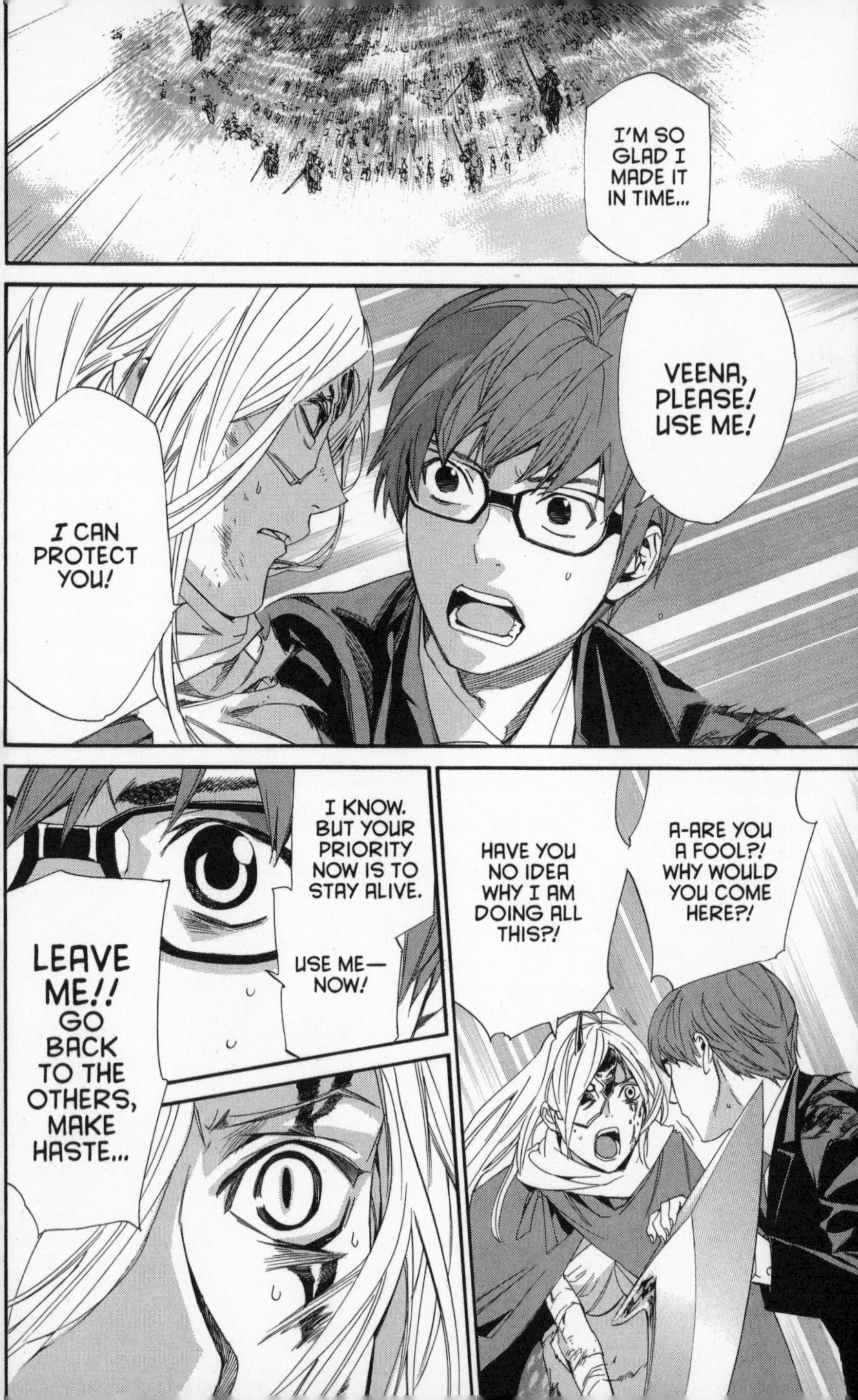
I'M SO GLAD I MADE IT IN TIME...
VEENA, PLEASE! USE ME!
*I* CAN PROTECT YOU!
A-ARE YOU A FOOL?! WHY WOULD YOU COME HERE?!
HAVE YOU NO IDEA WHY I AM DOING ALL THIS?!
I KNOW. BUT YOUR PRIORITY NOW IS TO STAY ALIVE.
USE ME— NOW!
LEAVE ME!! GO BACK TO THE OTHERS, MAKE HASTE...

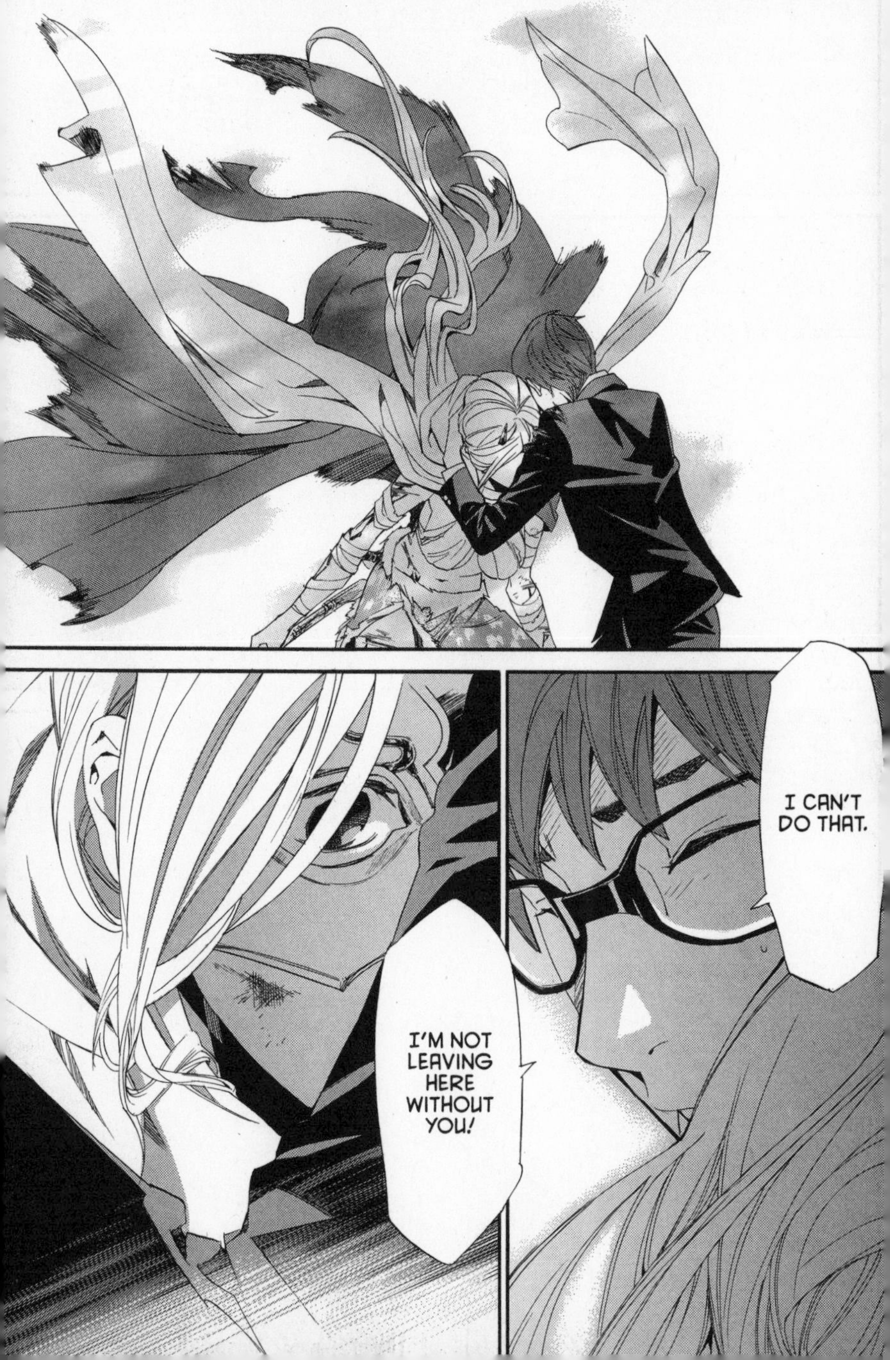
I'M NOT LEAVING HERE WITHOUT YOU!
I CAN'T DO THAT.

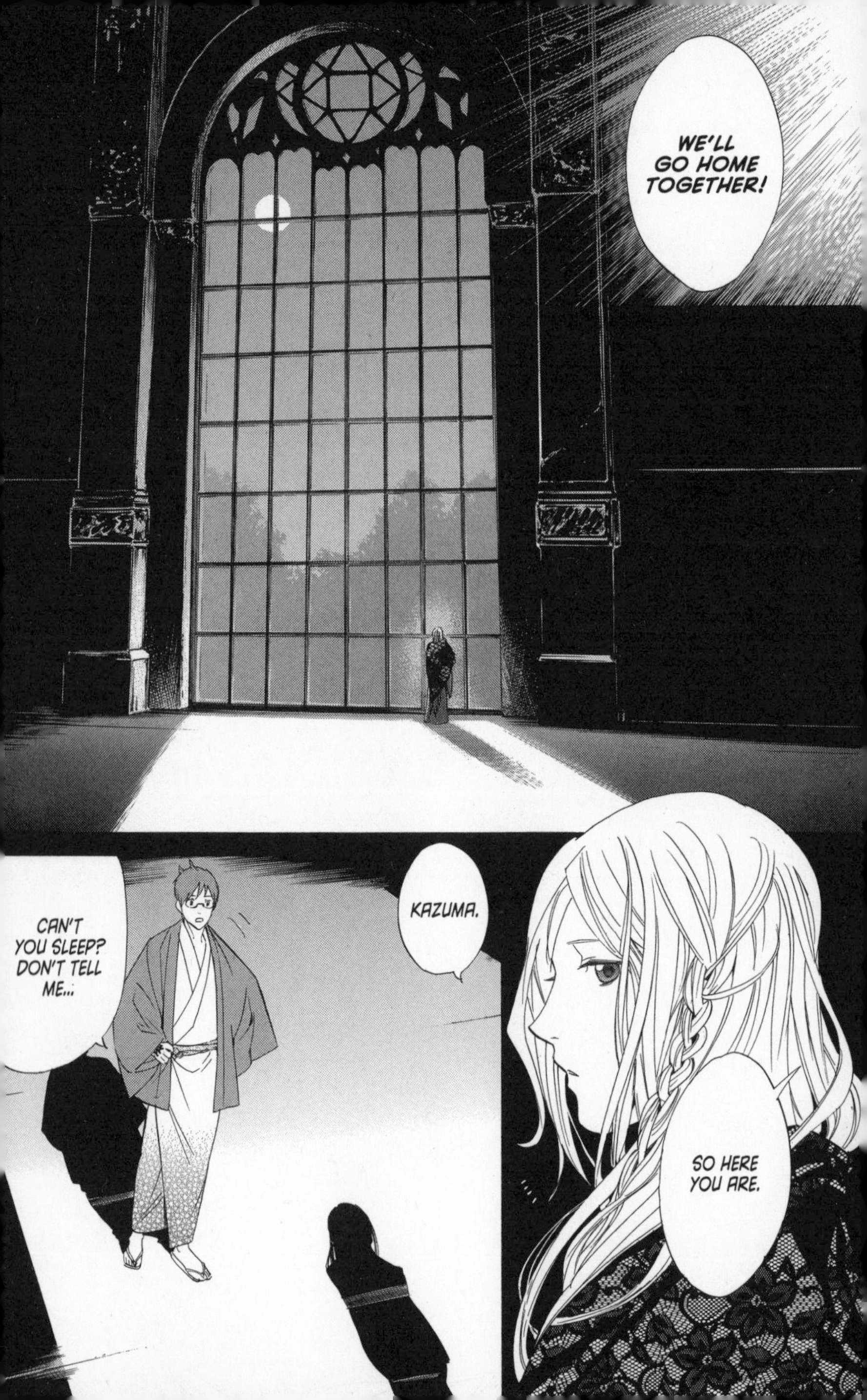
WE'LL GO HOME TOGETHER!
SO HERE YOU ARE.
KAZUMA.
CAN'T YOU SLEEP? DON'T TELL ME...

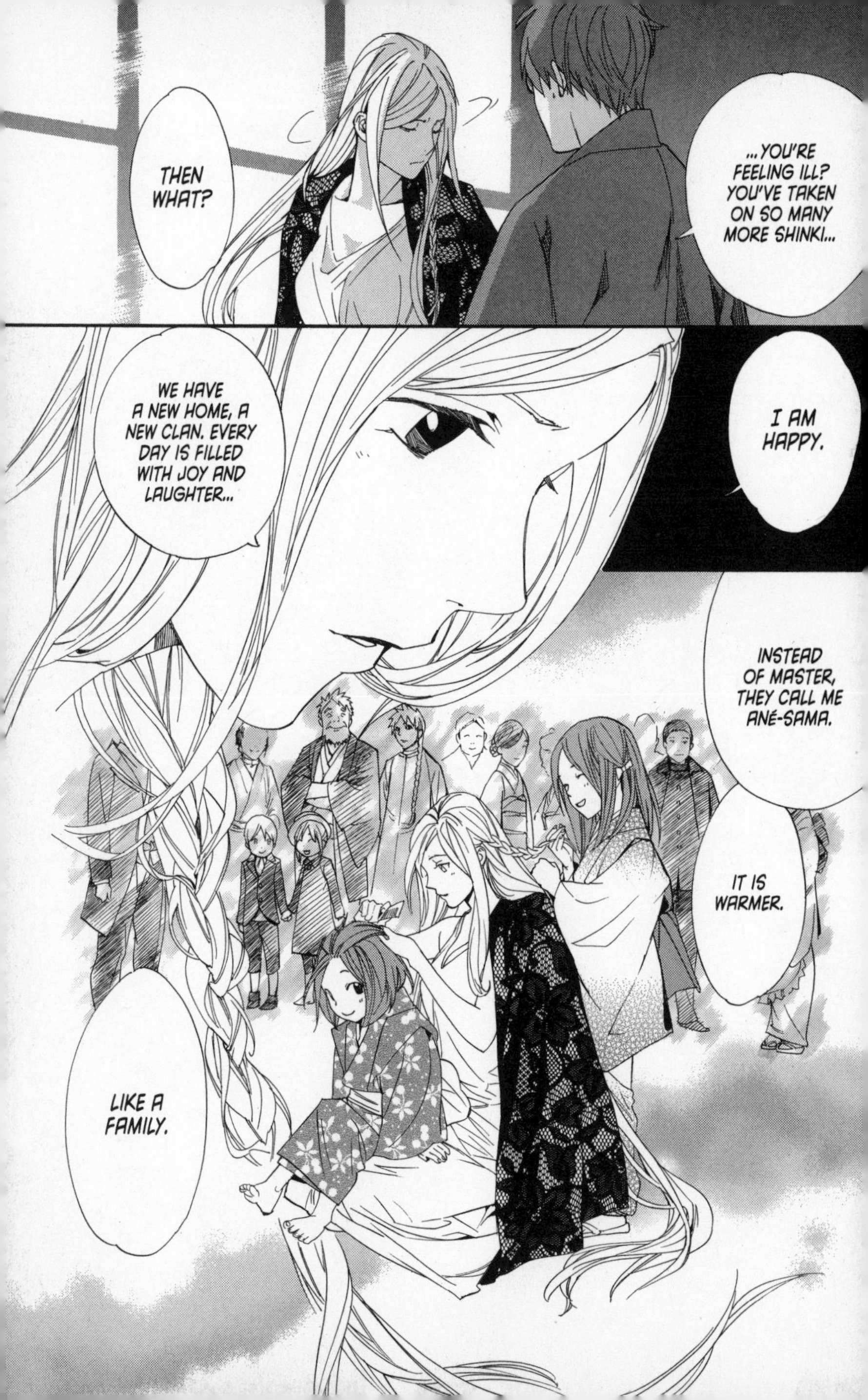
...YOU'RE FEELING ILL? YOU'VE TAKEN ON SO MANY MORE SHINKI...
THEN WHAT?
I AM HAPPY.
WE HAVE A NEW HOME, A NEW CLAN. EVERY DAY IS FILLED WITH JOY AND LAUGHTER...
INSTEAD OF MASTER, THEY CALL ME ANÉ-SAMA.
IT IS WARMER.
LIKE A FAMILY.

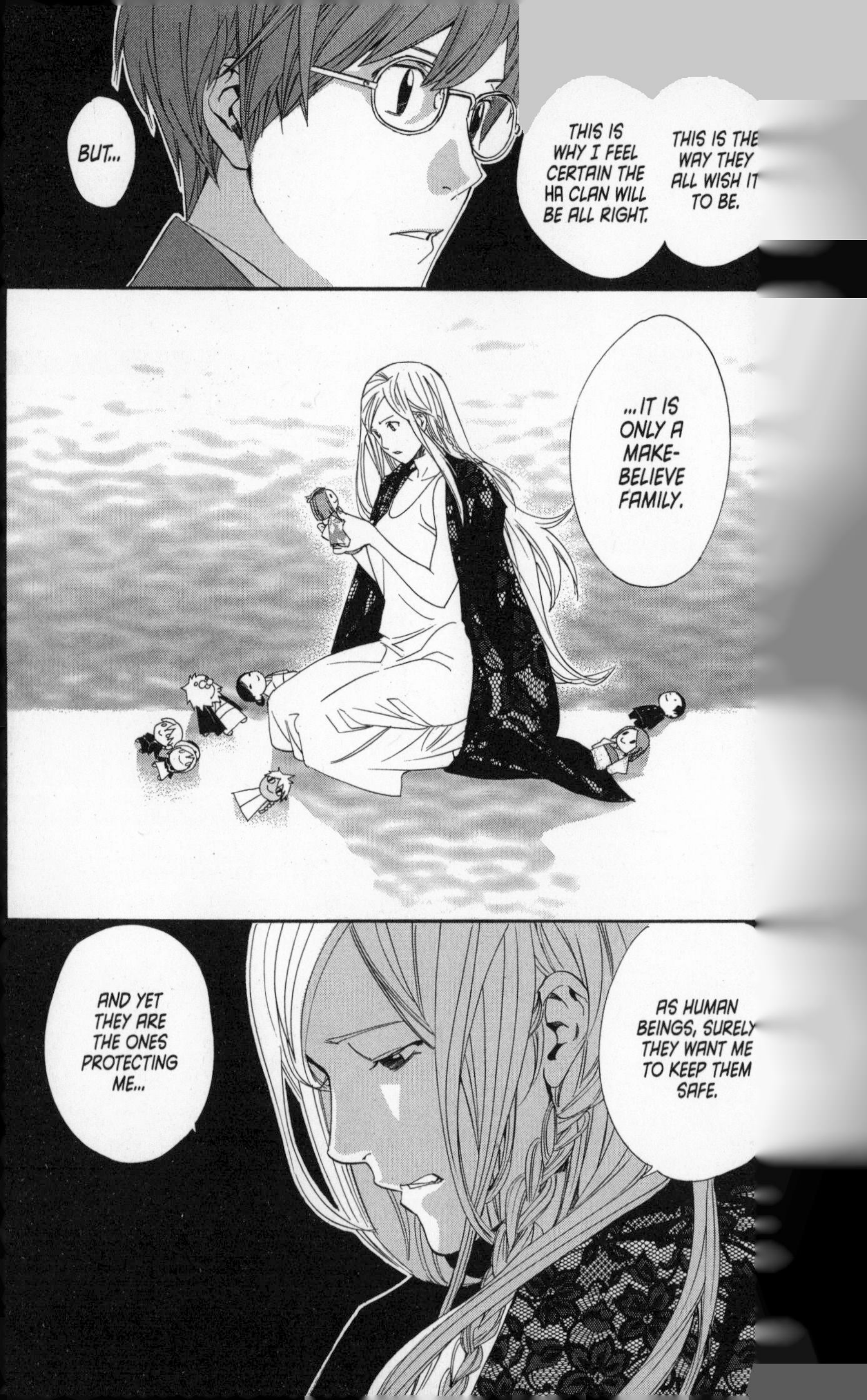
THIS IS THE WAY THEY ALL WISH IT TO BE.
THIS IS WHY I FEEL CERTAIN THE HA CLAN WILL BE ALL RIGHT.
BUT...
...IT IS ONLY A MAKE-BELIEVE FAMILY.
AS HUMAN BEINGS, SURELY THEY WANT ME TO KEEP THEM SAFE.
AND YET THEY ARE THE ONES PROTECTING ME...

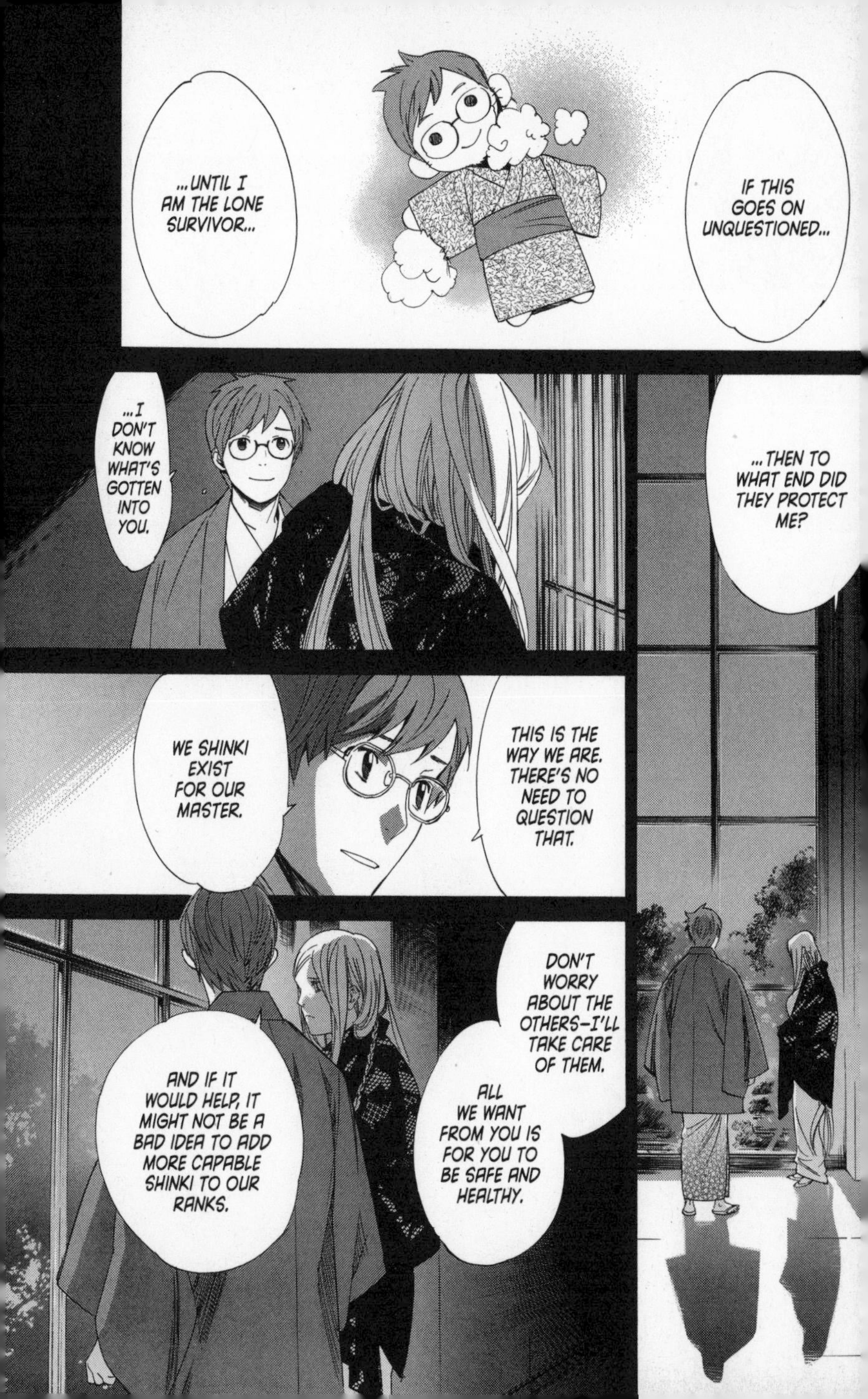
IF THIS GOES ON UNQUESTIONED...
...UNTIL I AM THE LONE SURVIVOR...
...THEN TO WHAT END DID THEY PROTECT ME?
...I DON'T KNOW WHAT'S GOTTEN INTO YOU.
THIS IS THE WAY WE ARE. THERE'S NO NEED TO QUESTION THAT.
WE SHINKI EXIST FOR OUR MASTER.
DON'T WORRY ABOUT THE OTHERS—I'LL TAKE CARE OF THEM.
ALL WE WANT FROM YOU IS FOR YOU TO BE SAFE AND HEALTHY.
AND IF IT WOULD HELP, IT MIGHT NOT BE A BAD IDEA TO ADD MORE CAPABLE SHINKI TO OUR RANKS.

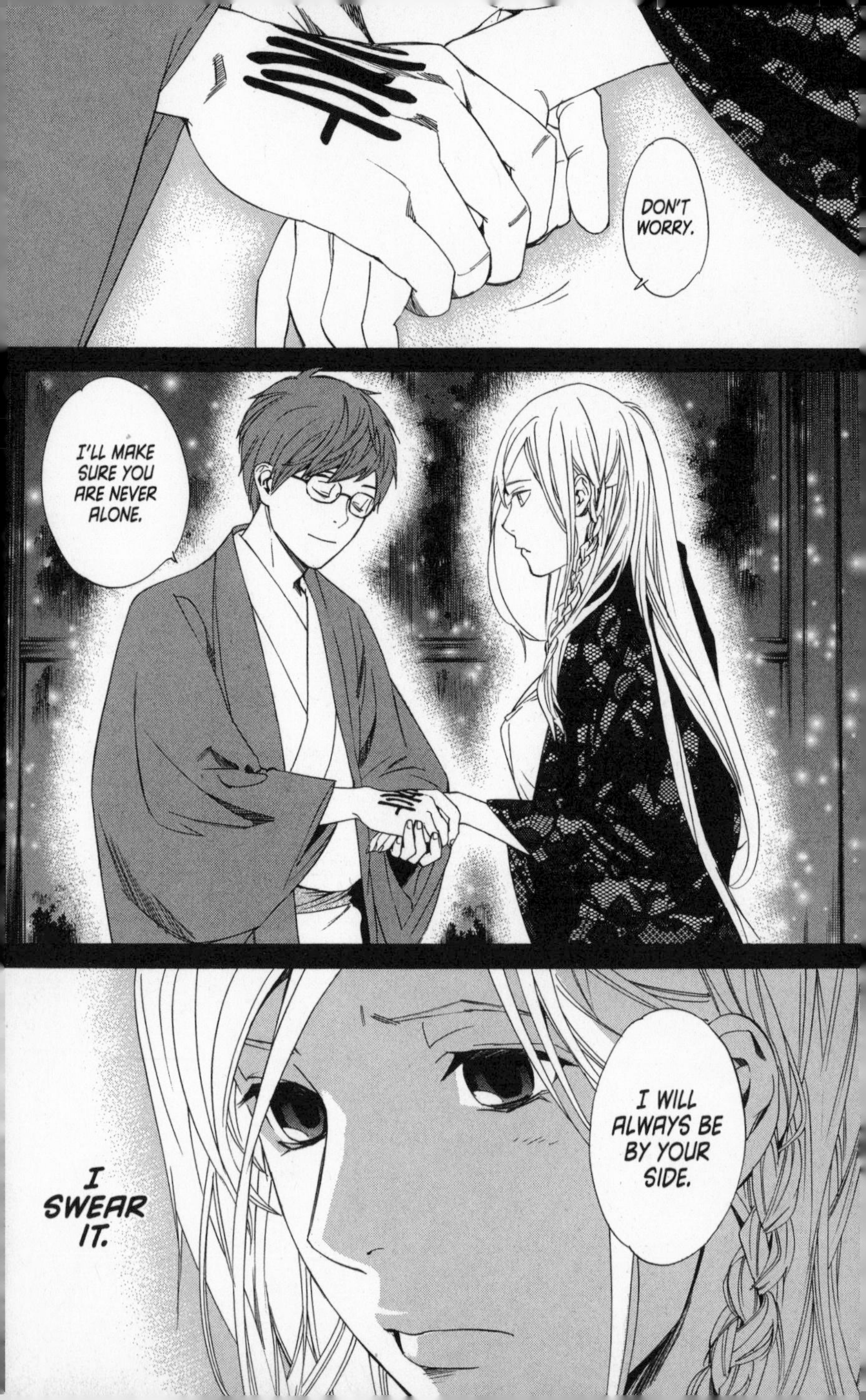
DON'T WORRY.
I'LL MAKE SURE YOU ARE NEVER ALONE.
I WILL ALWAYS BE BY YOUR SIDE.
I SWEAR IT.

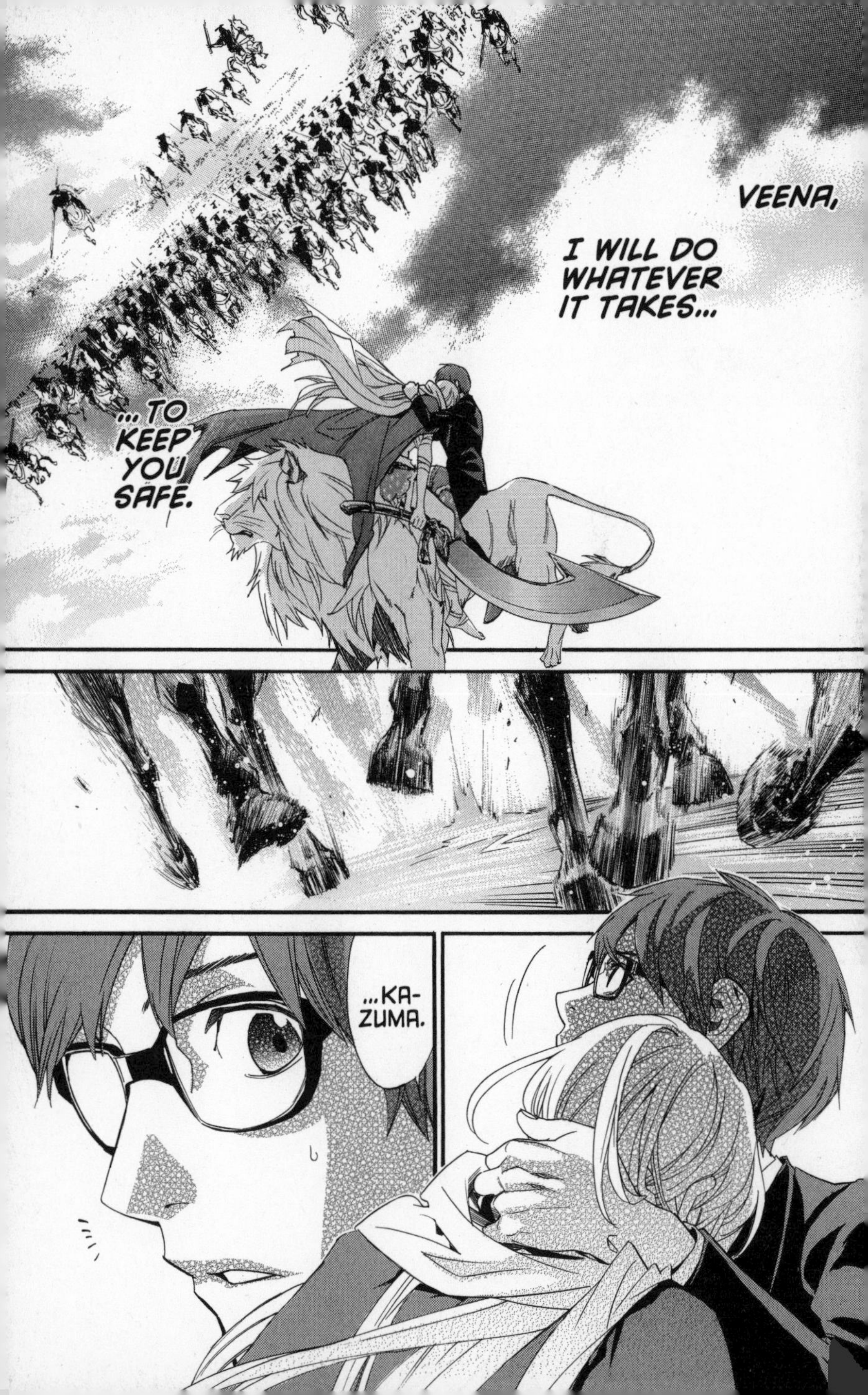
VEENA,
I WILL DO WHATEVER IT TAKES...
...TO KEEP YOU SAFE.
...KA-ZUMA.

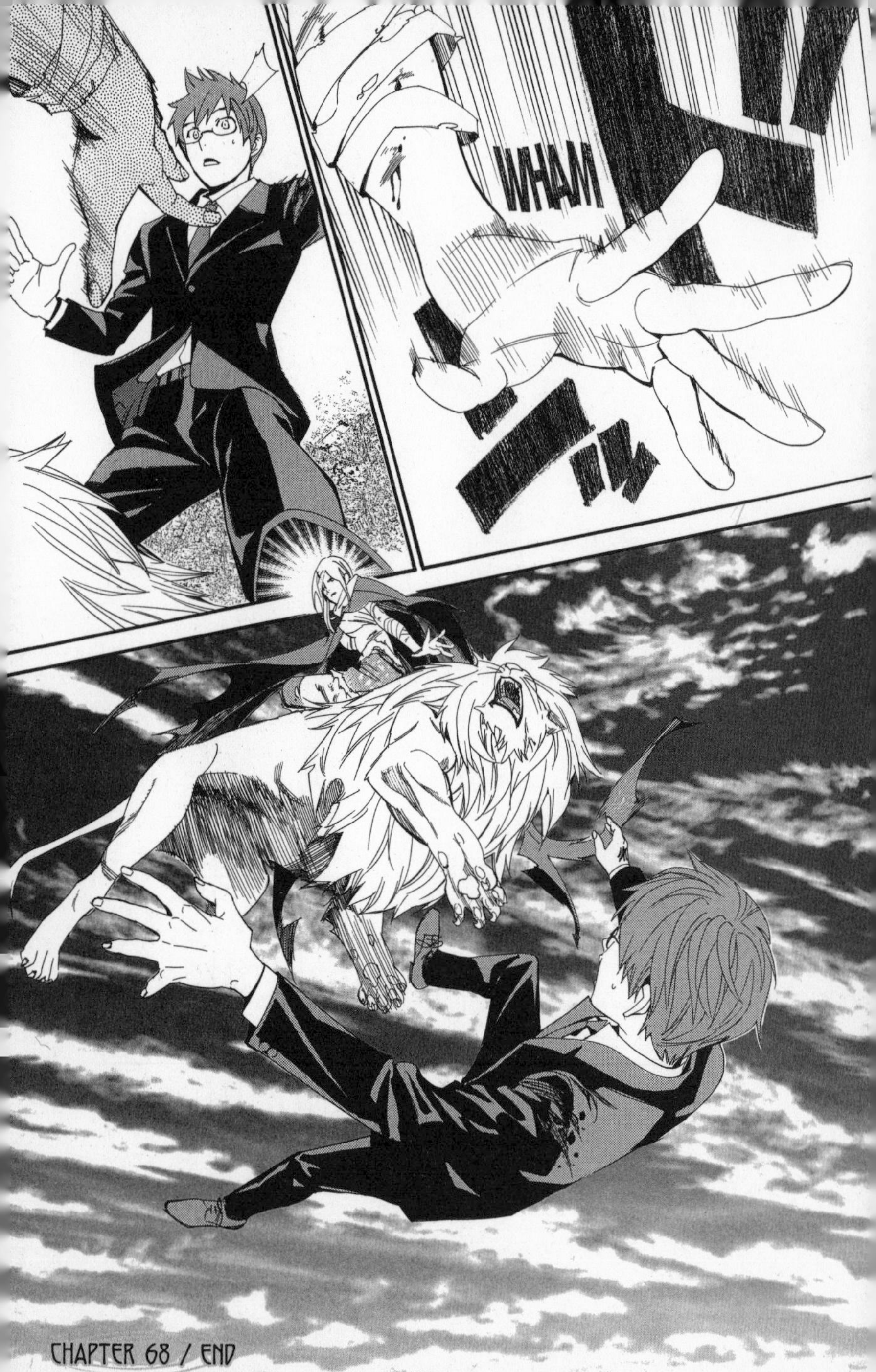
WHAM

CHAPTER 68 / END

封

[illegible]

神

[illegible]

夏

[illegible]

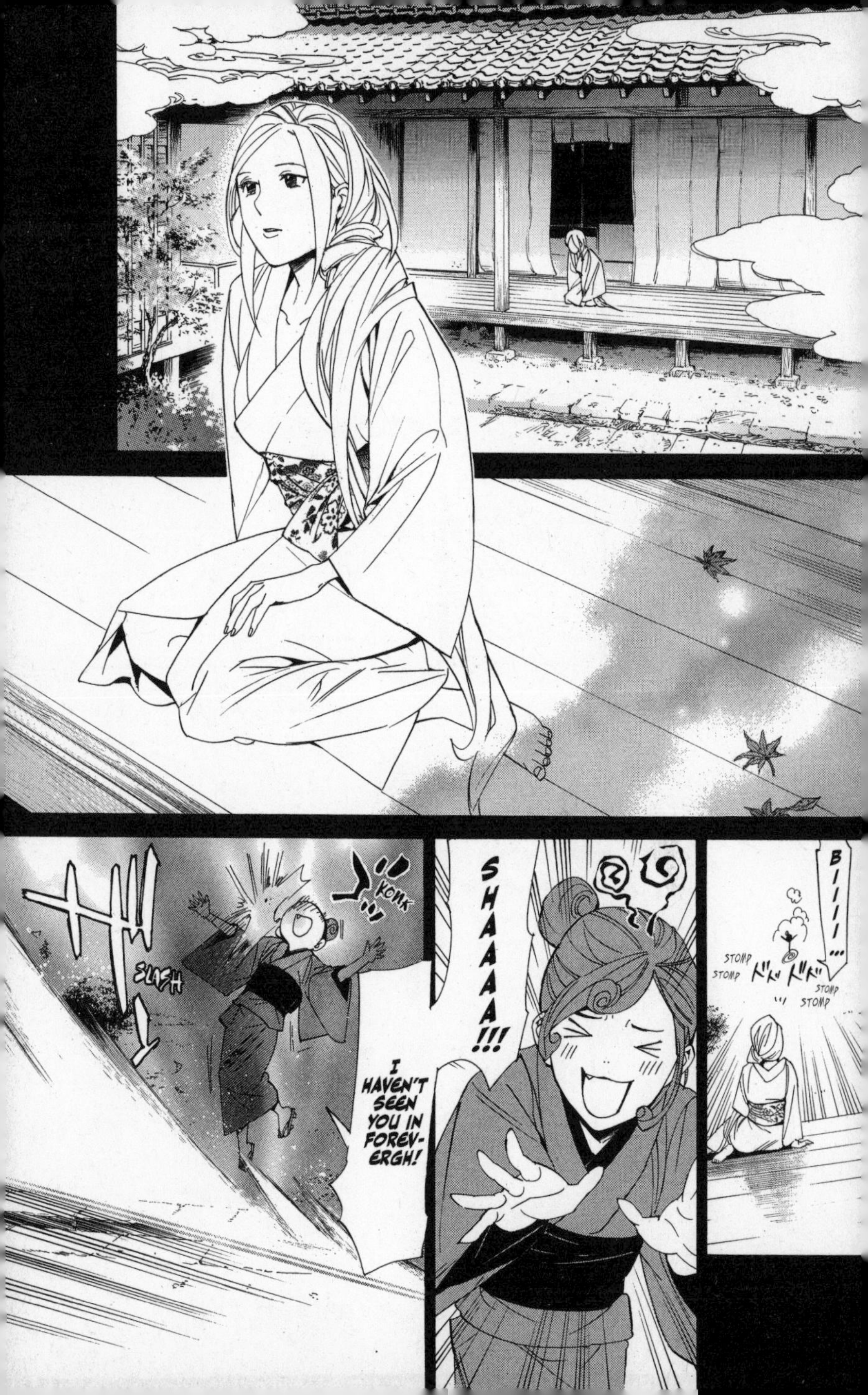

BIIII...
STOMP STOMP
STOMP STOMP
SHAAAAA!!!
I HAVEN'T SEEN YOU IN FOREV-ERGH!
KONK
SLASH

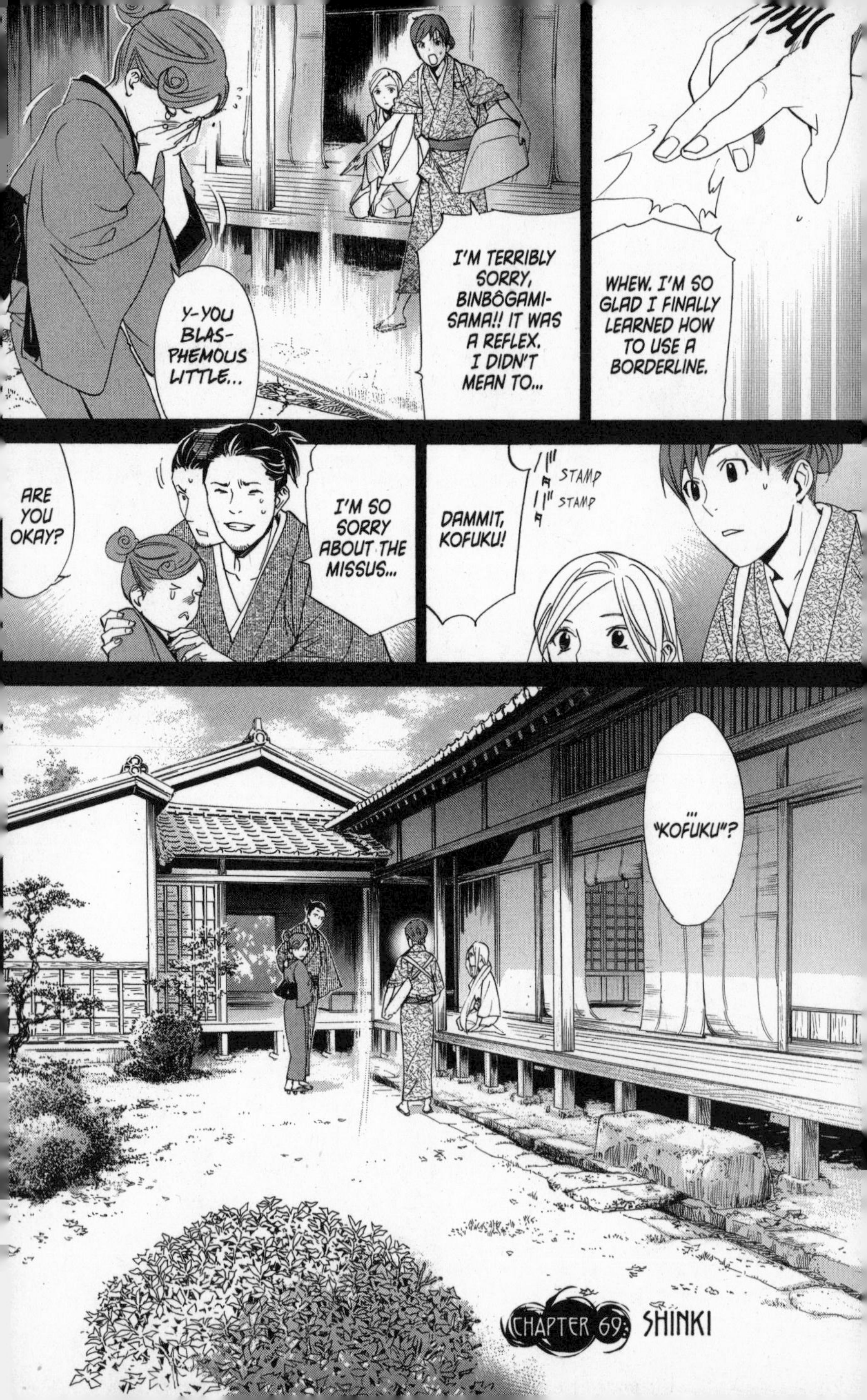
WHEW. I'M SO GLAD I FINALLY LEARNED HOW TO USE A BORDERLINE.
I'M TERRIBLY SORRY, BINBÔGAMI-SAMA!! IT WAS A REFLEX. I DIDN'T MEAN TO...
Y-YOU BLAS-PHEMOUS LITTLE...
STAMP
STAMP
DAMMIT, KOFUKU!
I'M SO SORRY ABOUT THE MISSUS...
ARE YOU OKAY?
... "KOFUKU"?
CHAPTER 69: SHINKI

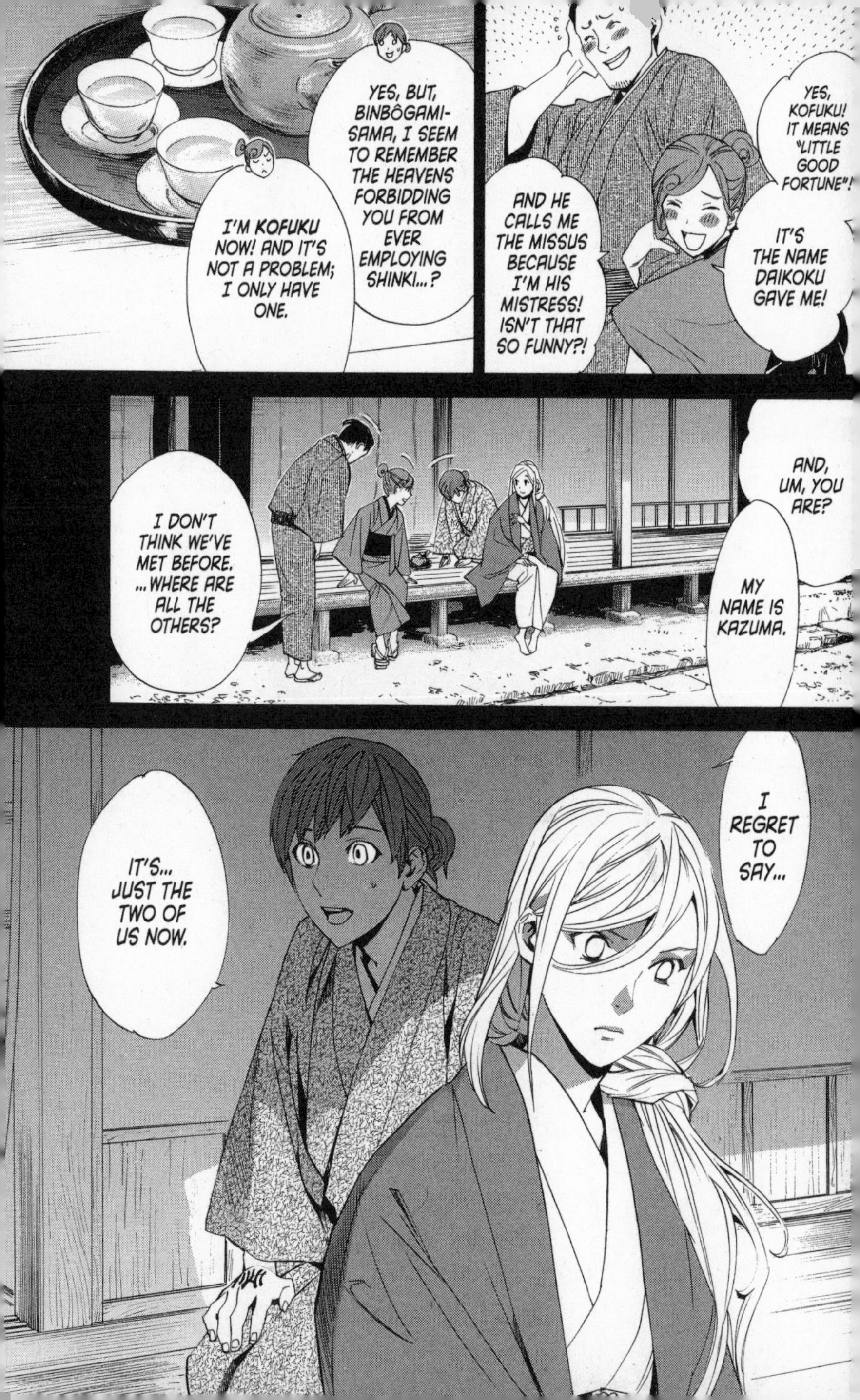
YES, KOFUKU! IT MEANS "LITTLE GOOD FORTUNE"!
IT'S THE NAME DAIKOKU GAVE ME!
AND HE CALLS ME THE MISSUS BECAUSE I'M HIS MISTRESS! ISN'T THAT SO FUNNY?!
YES, BUT, BINBÔGAMI-SAMA, I SEEM TO REMEMBER THE HEAVENS FORBIDDING YOU FROM EVER EMPLOYING SHINKI...?
I'M KOFUKU NOW! AND IT'S NOT A PROBLEM; I ONLY HAVE ONE.
AND, UM, YOU ARE?
MY NAME IS KAZUMA.
I DON'T THINK WE'VE MET BEFORE. ...WHERE ARE ALL THE OTHERS?
I REGRET TO SAY...
IT'S... JUST THE TWO OF US NOW.

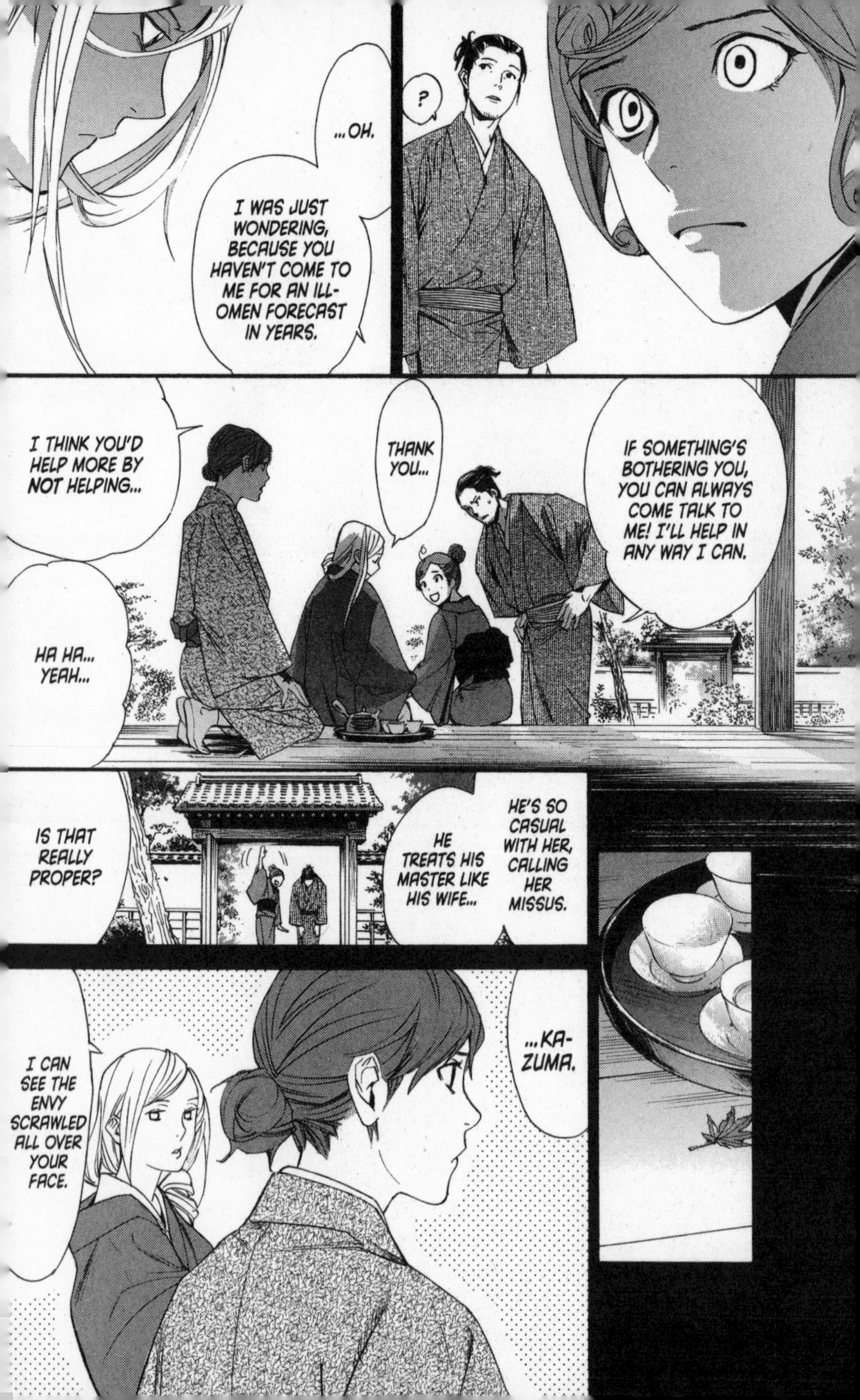
?
...OH.
I WAS JUST WONDERING, BECAUSE YOU HAVEN'T COME TO ME FOR AN ILL-OMEN FORECAST IN YEARS.
IF SOMETHING'S BOTHERING YOU, YOU CAN ALWAYS COME TALK TO ME! I'LL HELP IN ANY WAY I CAN.
THANK YOU...
I THINK YOU'D HELP MORE BY NOT HELPING...
HA HA... YEAH...
HE'S SO CASUAL WITH HER, CALLING HER MISSUS.
HE TREATS HIS MASTER LIKE HIS WIFE...
IS THAT REALLY PROPER?
...KA-ZUMA.
I CAN SEE THE ENVY SCRAWLED ALL OVER YOUR FACE.

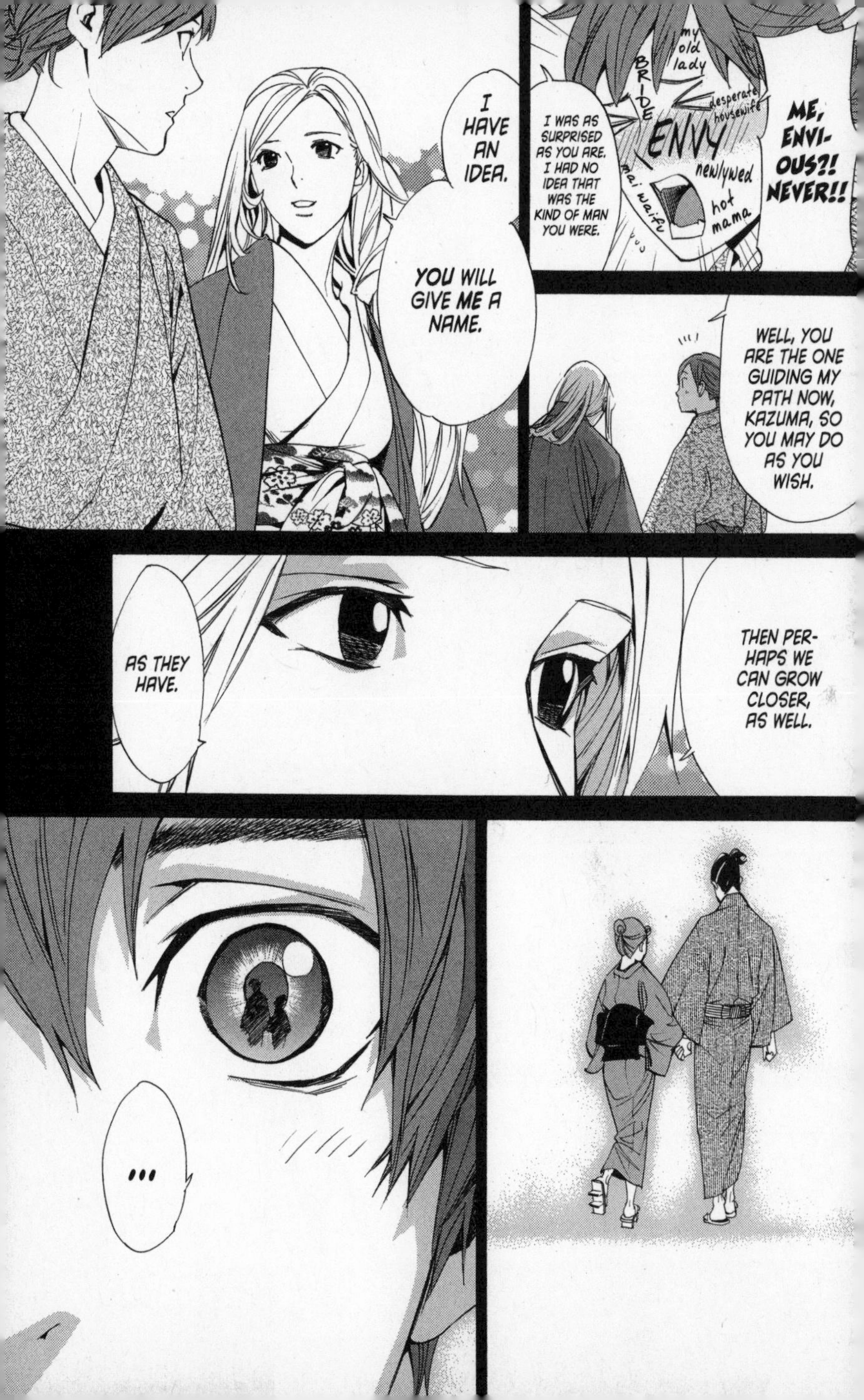
I WAS AS SURPRISED AS YOU ARE. I HAD NO IDEA THAT WAS THE KIND OF MAN YOU WERE.
ME, ENVI-OUS?! NEVER!!
my old lady
BRIDE
desperate housewife
ENVY
newlywed
mai waifu
hot mama
WELL, YOU ARE THE ONE GUIDING MY PATH NOW, KAZUMA, SO YOU MAY DO AS YOU WISH.
I HAVE AN IDEA.
YOU WILL GIVE ME A NAME.
THEN PER-HAPS WE CAN GROW CLOSER, AS WELL.
AS THEY HAVE.
...

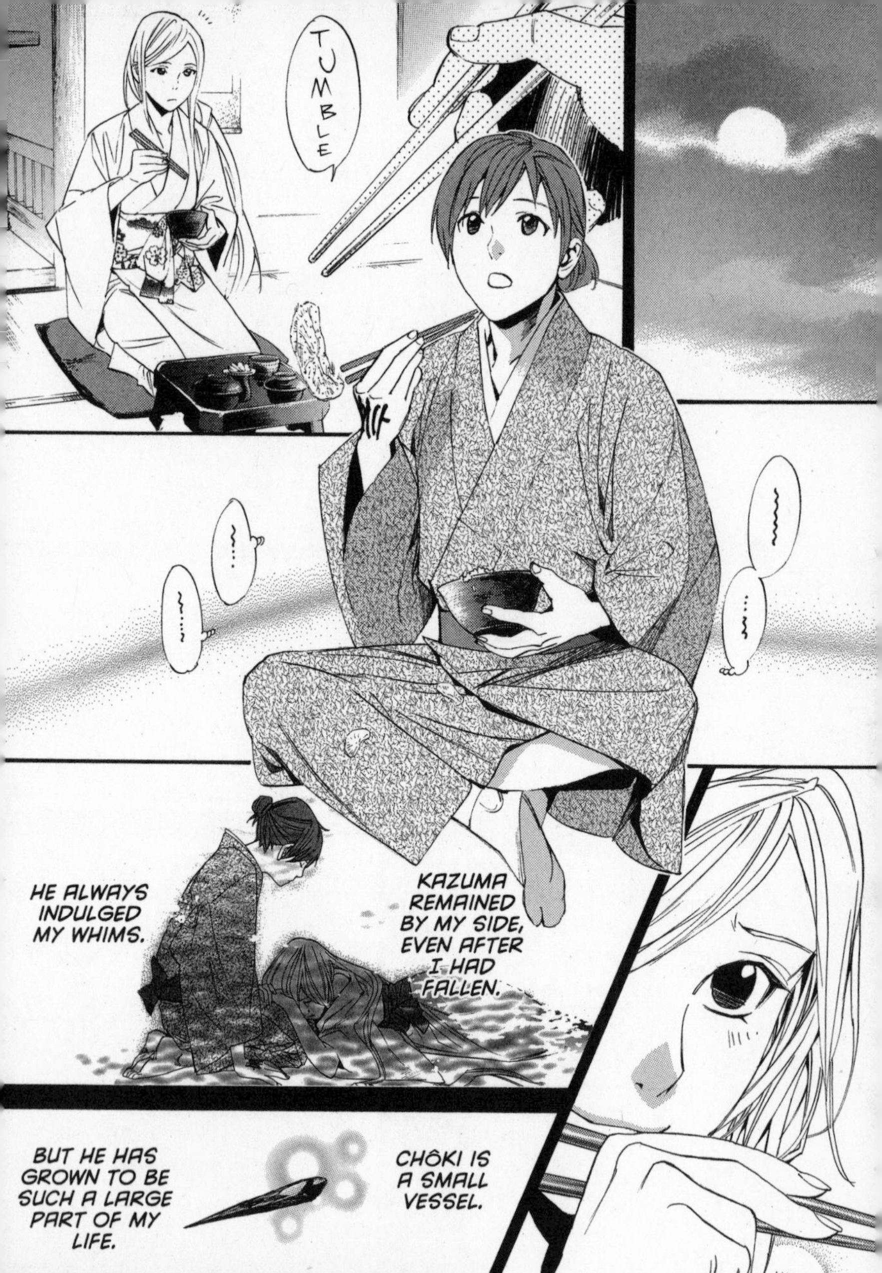
TUMBLE
HEE
KAZUMA REMAINED BY MY SIDE, EVEN AFTER I HAD FALLEN.
HE ALWAYS INDULGED MY WHIMS.
CHÔKI IS A SMALL VESSEL.
BUT HE HAS GROWN TO BE SUCH A LARGE PART OF MY LIFE.

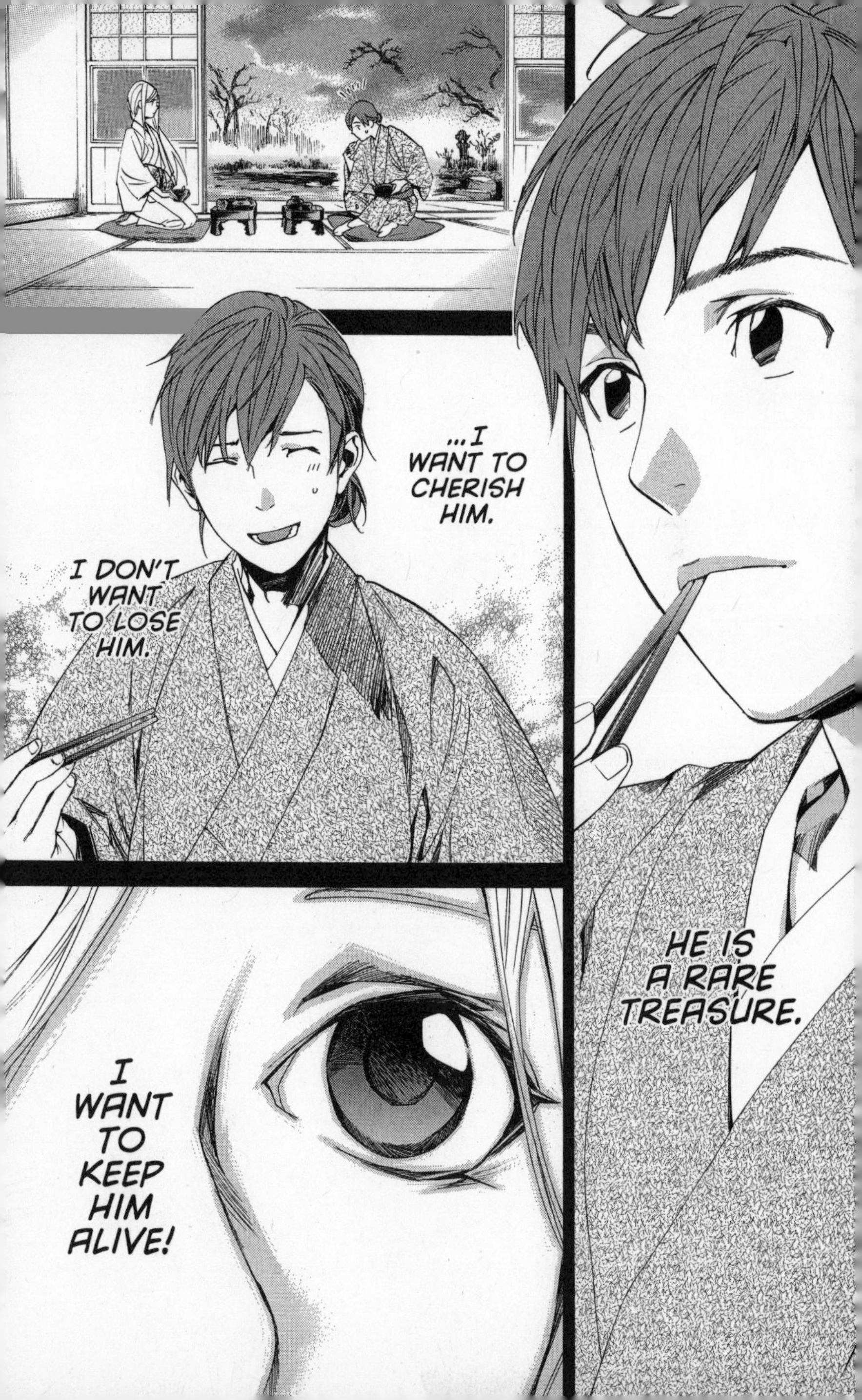
HE IS A RARE TREASURE.
...I WANT TO CHERISH HIM.
I DON'T WANT TO LOSE HIM.
I WANT TO KEEP HIM ALIVE!

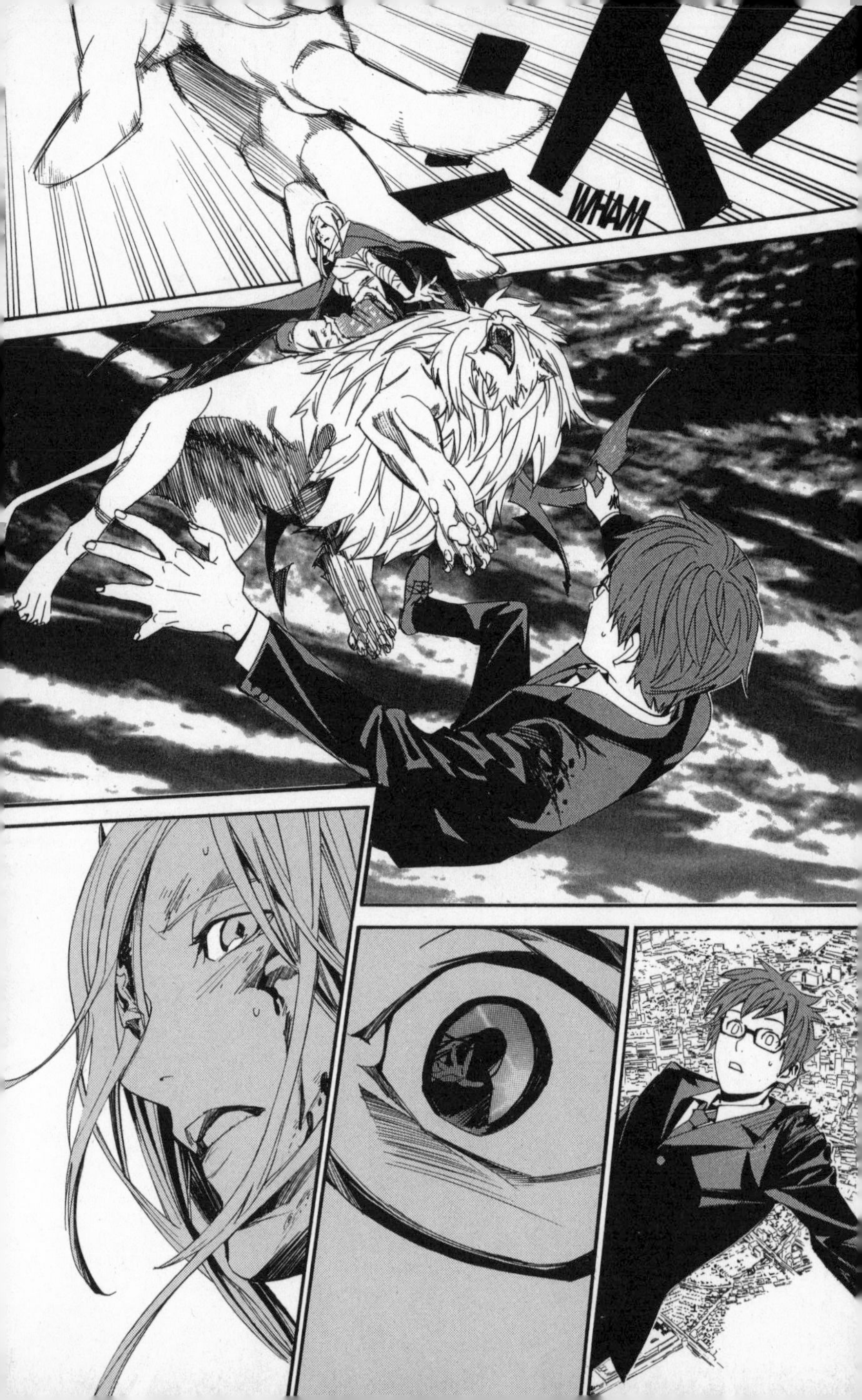
WHAM

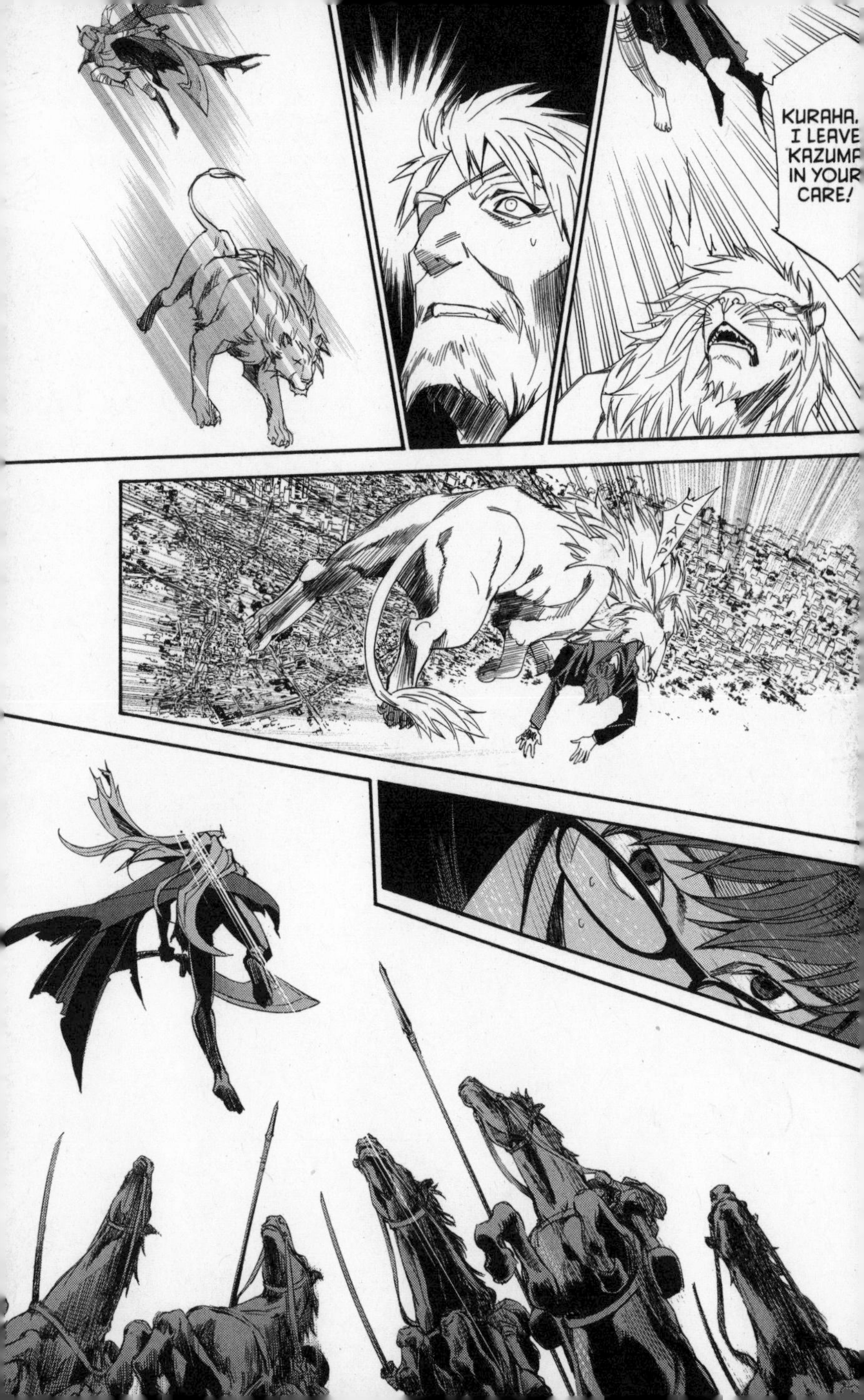
KURAHA, I LEAVE KAZUMA IN YOUR CARE!
CLAMP

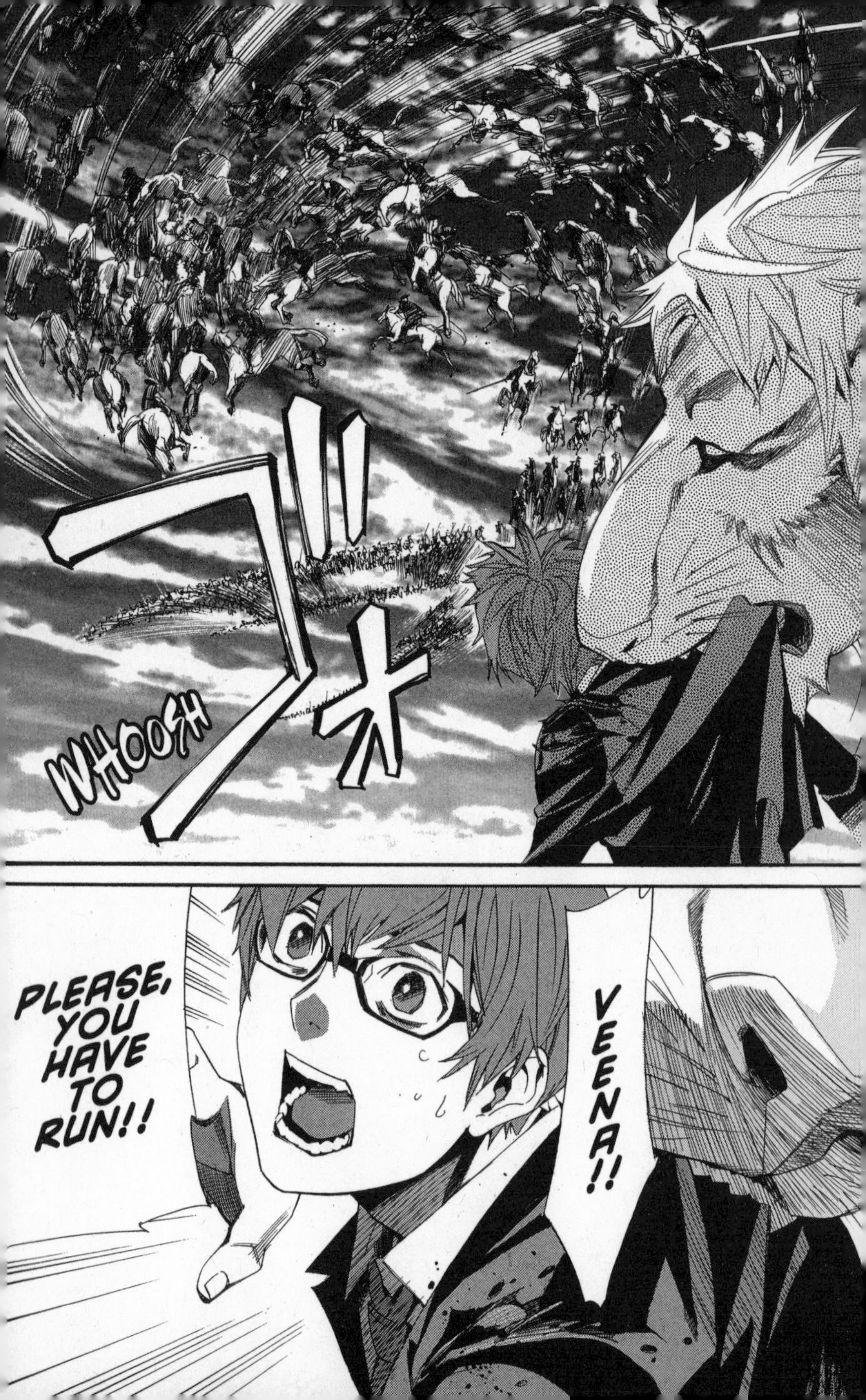
WHOOSH
ブオ
VEENA!!
PLEASE, YOU HAVE TO RUN!!

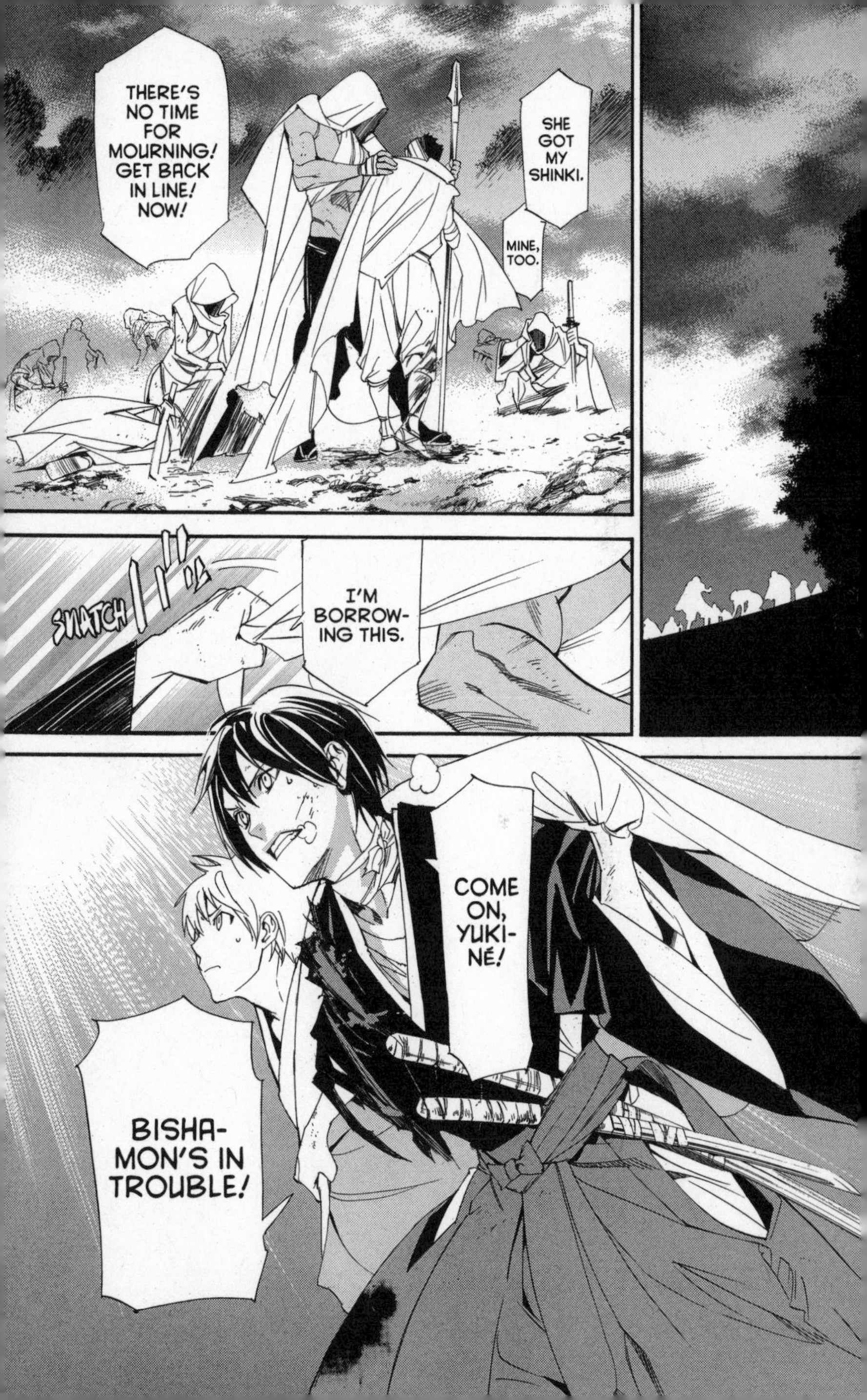
SHE GOT MY SHINKI.
MINE, TOO.
THERE'S NO TIME FOR MOURNING! GET BACK IN LINE! NOW!
I'M BORROWING THIS.
SNATCH
COME ON, YUKINÉ!
BISHAMON'S IN TROUBLE!

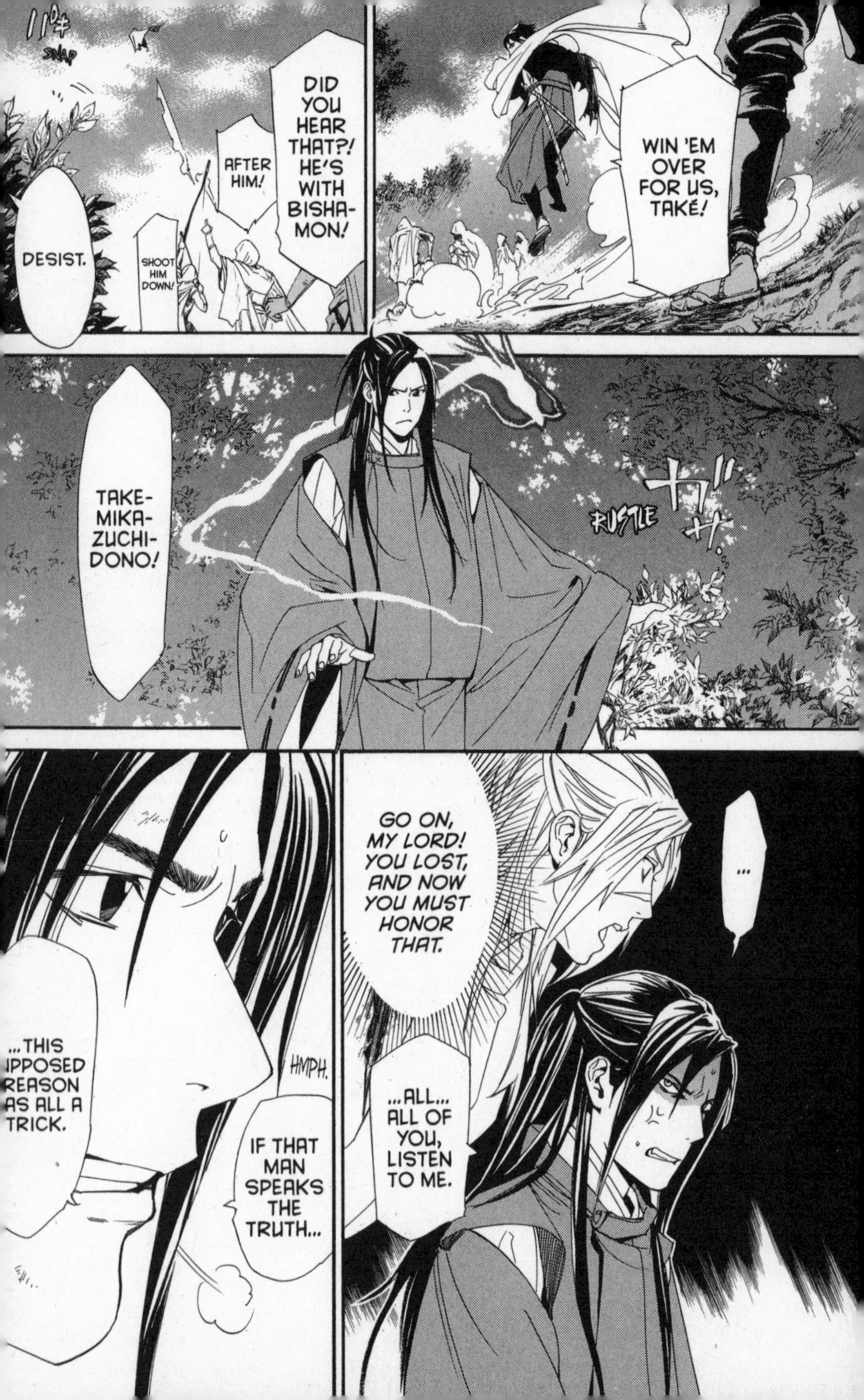
WIN 'EM OVER FOR US, TAKÉ!
SNAP
DID YOU HEAR THAT?! HE'S WITH BISHAMON!
AFTER HIM!
SHOOT HIM DOWN!
DESIST.
TAKEMIKAZUCHI-DONO!
RUSTLE
...
GO ON, MY LORD! YOU LOST, AND NOW YOU MUST HONOR THAT.
...ALL... ALL OF YOU, LISTEN TO ME.
HMPH.
IF THAT MAN SPEAKS THE TRUTH...
...THIS
IPPOSED
REASON
AS ALL A
TRICK.

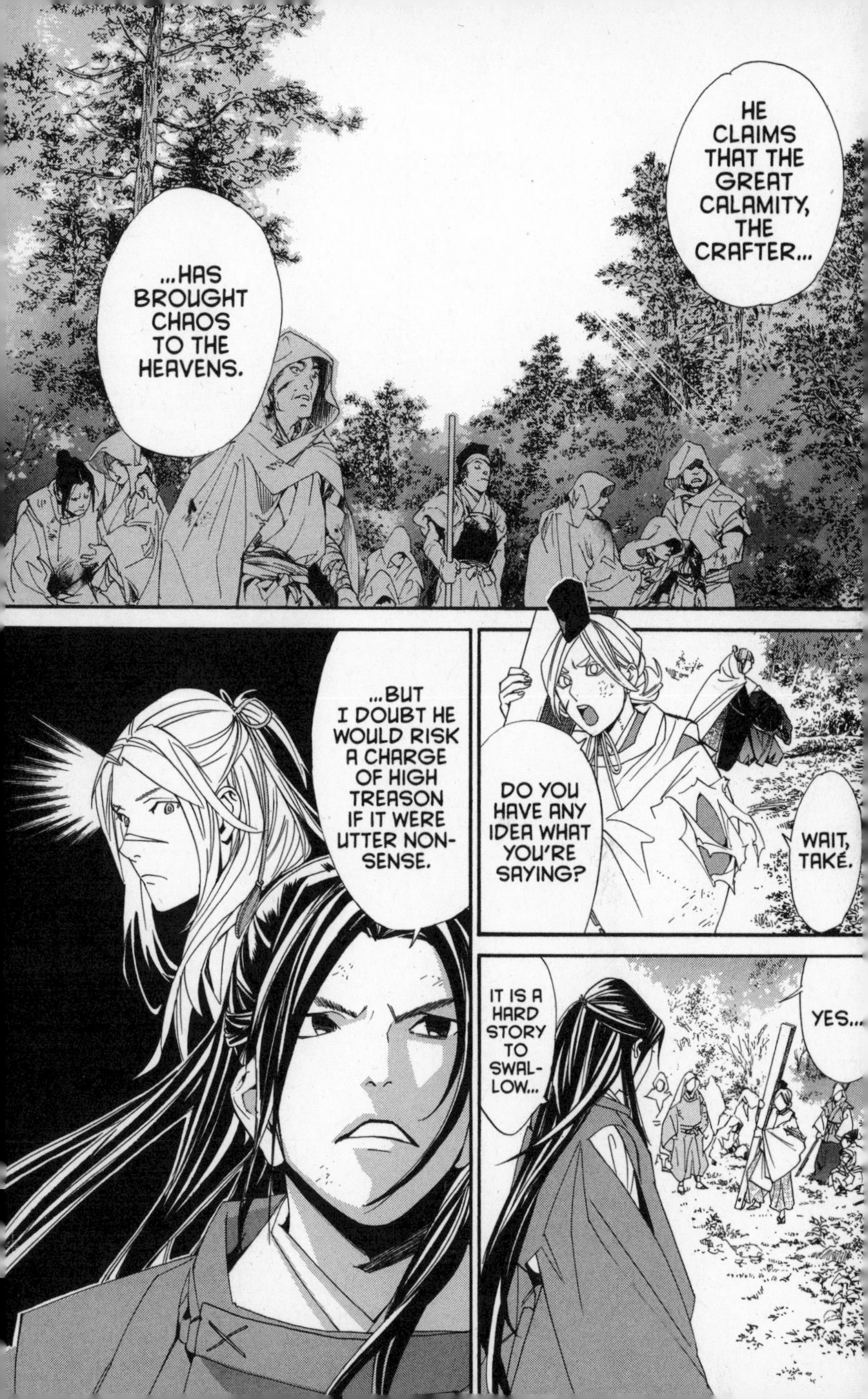
HE CLAIMS THAT THE GREAT CALAMITY, THE CRAFTER...
...HAS BROUGHT CHAOS TO THE HEAVENS.
WAIT, TAKÉ.
DO YOU HAVE ANY IDEA WHAT YOU'RE SAYING?
...BUT I DOUBT HE WOULD RISK A CHARGE OF HIGH TREASON IF IT WERE UTTER NON-SENSE.
YES...
IT IS A HARD STORY TO SWAL-LOW...

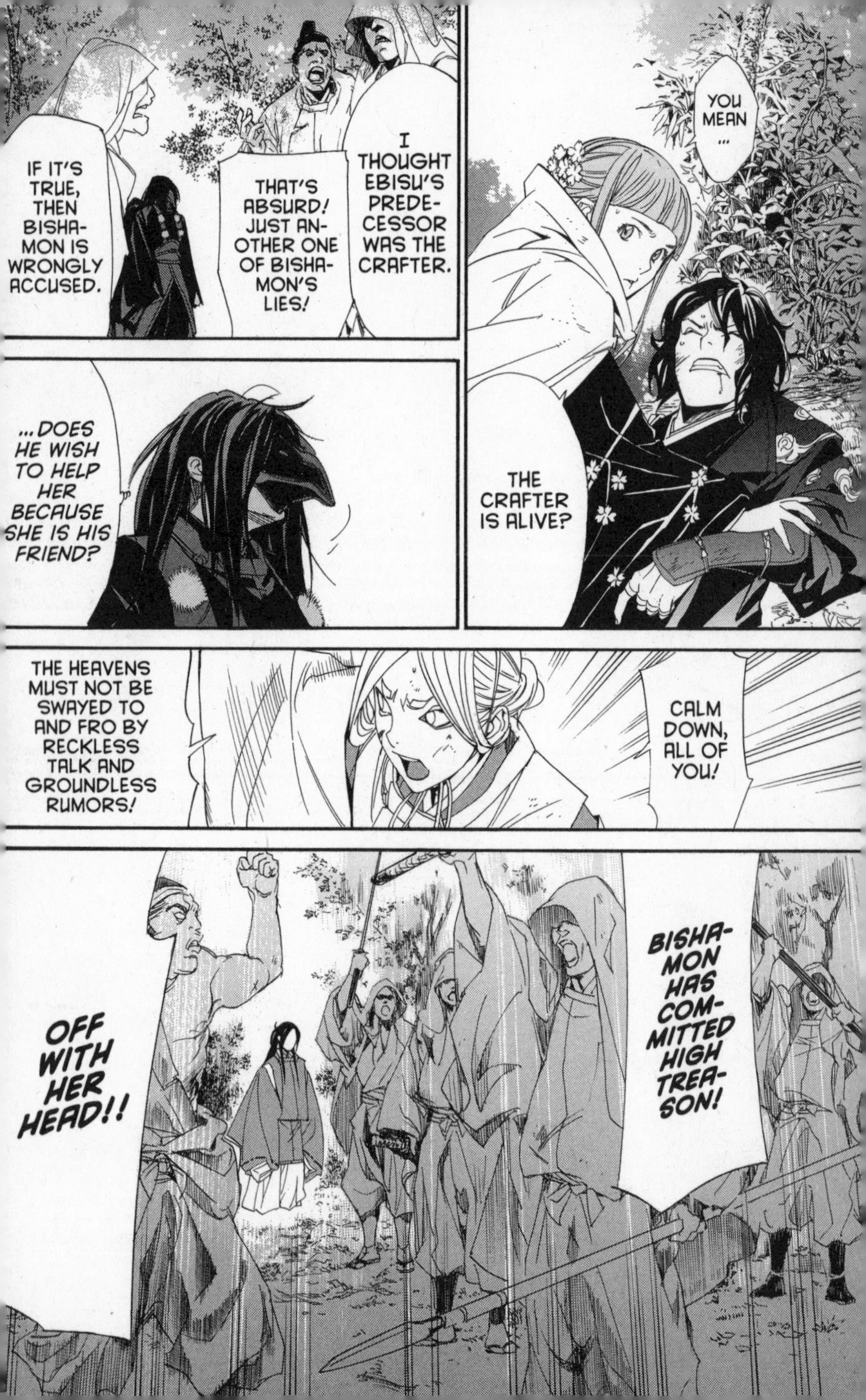
YOU MEAN ...
THE CRAFTER IS ALIVE?
I THOUGHT EBISU'S PREDE-CESSOR WAS THE CRAFTER.
THAT'S ABSURD! JUST AN-OTHER ONE OF BISHA-MON'S LIES!
IF IT'S TRUE, THEN BISHA-MON IS WRONGLY ACCUSED.
...DOES HE WISH TO HELP HER BECAUSE SHE IS HIS FRIEND?
CALM DOWN, ALL OF YOU!
THE HEAVENS MUST NOT BE SWAYED TO AND FRO BY RECKLESS TALK AND GROUNDLESS RUMORS!
BISHA-MON HAS COM-MITTED HIGH TREA-SON!
OFF WITH HER HEAD!!

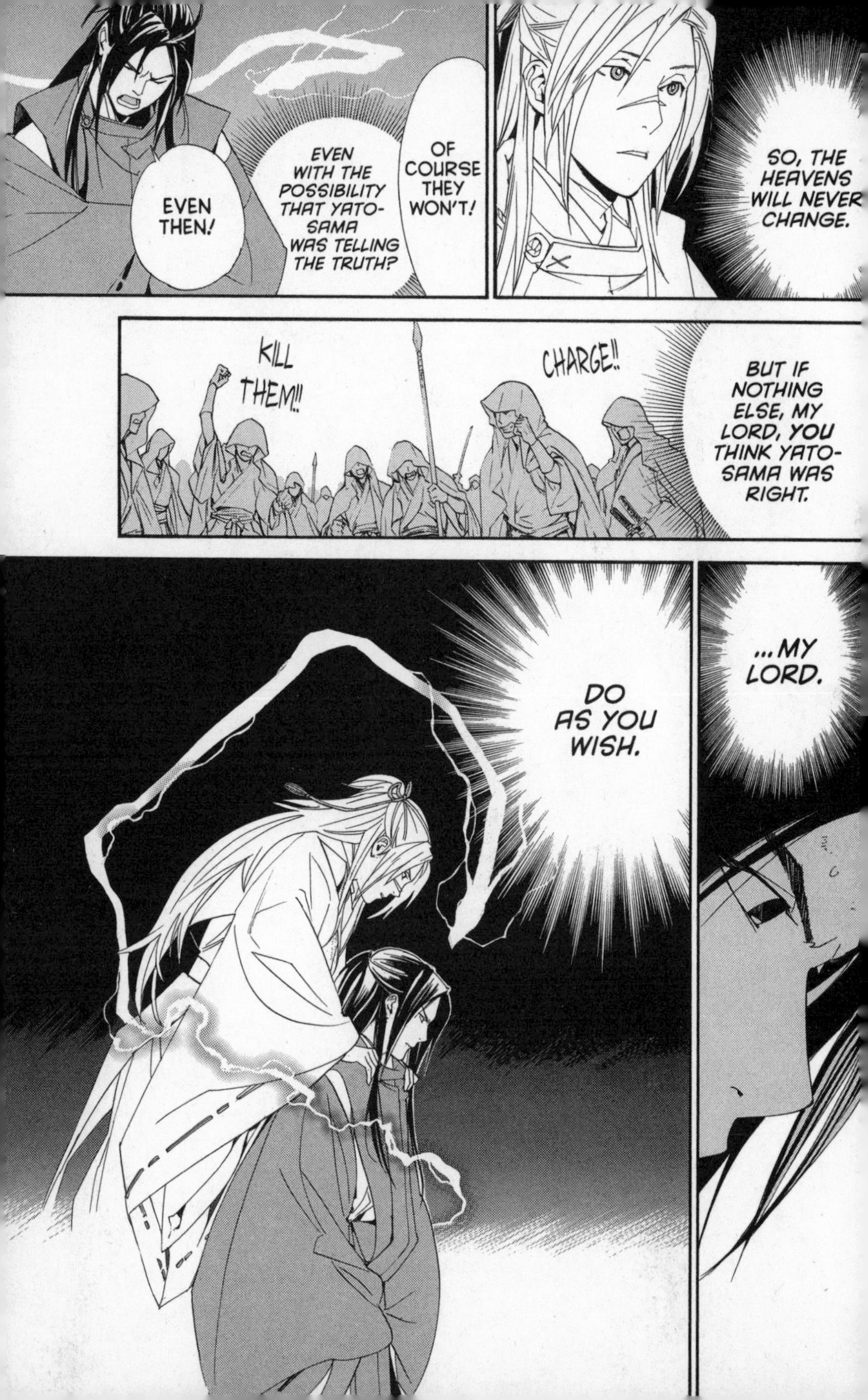
SO, THE HEAVENS WILL NEVER CHANGE.
OF COURSE THEY WON'T!
EVEN WITH THE POSSIBILITY THAT YATO-SAMA WAS TELLING THE TRUTH?
EVEN THEN!
BUT IF NOTHING ELSE, MY LORD, YOU THINK YATO-SAMA WAS RIGHT.
CHARGE!!
KILL THEM!!
...MY LORD.
DO AS YOU WISH.

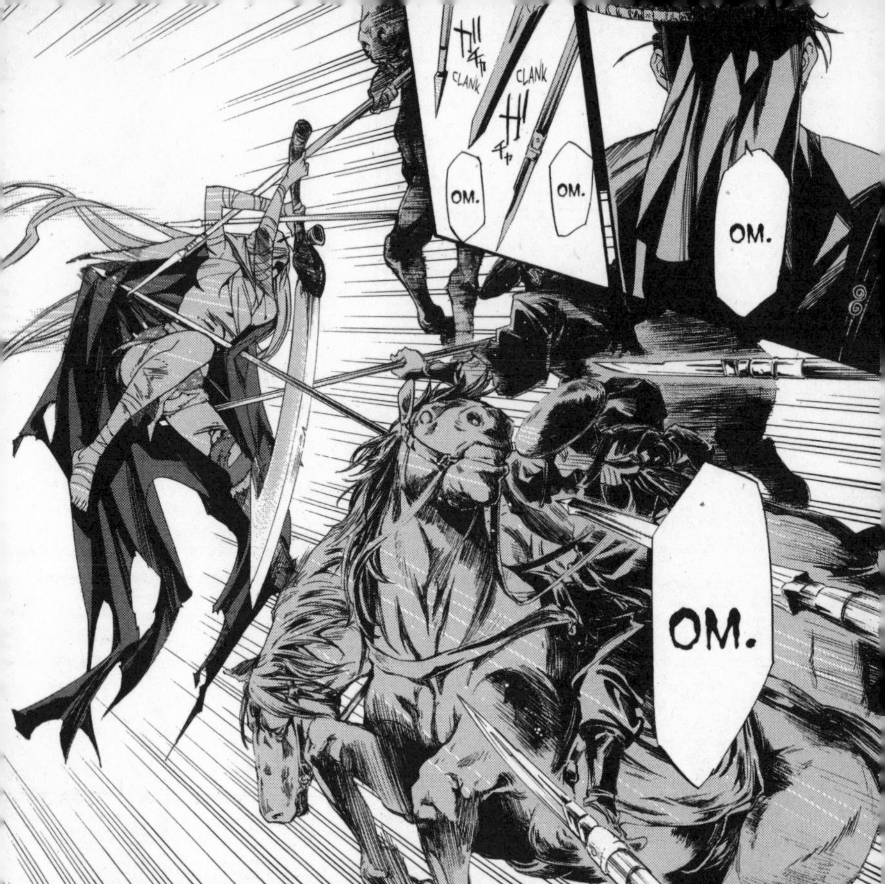
OM.
CLANK
OM.
CLANK
OM.
OM.
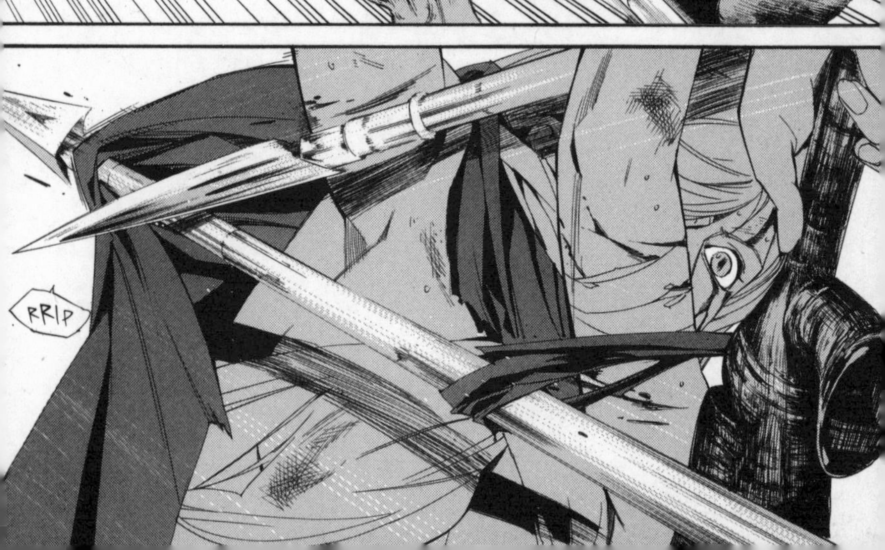
RRIP

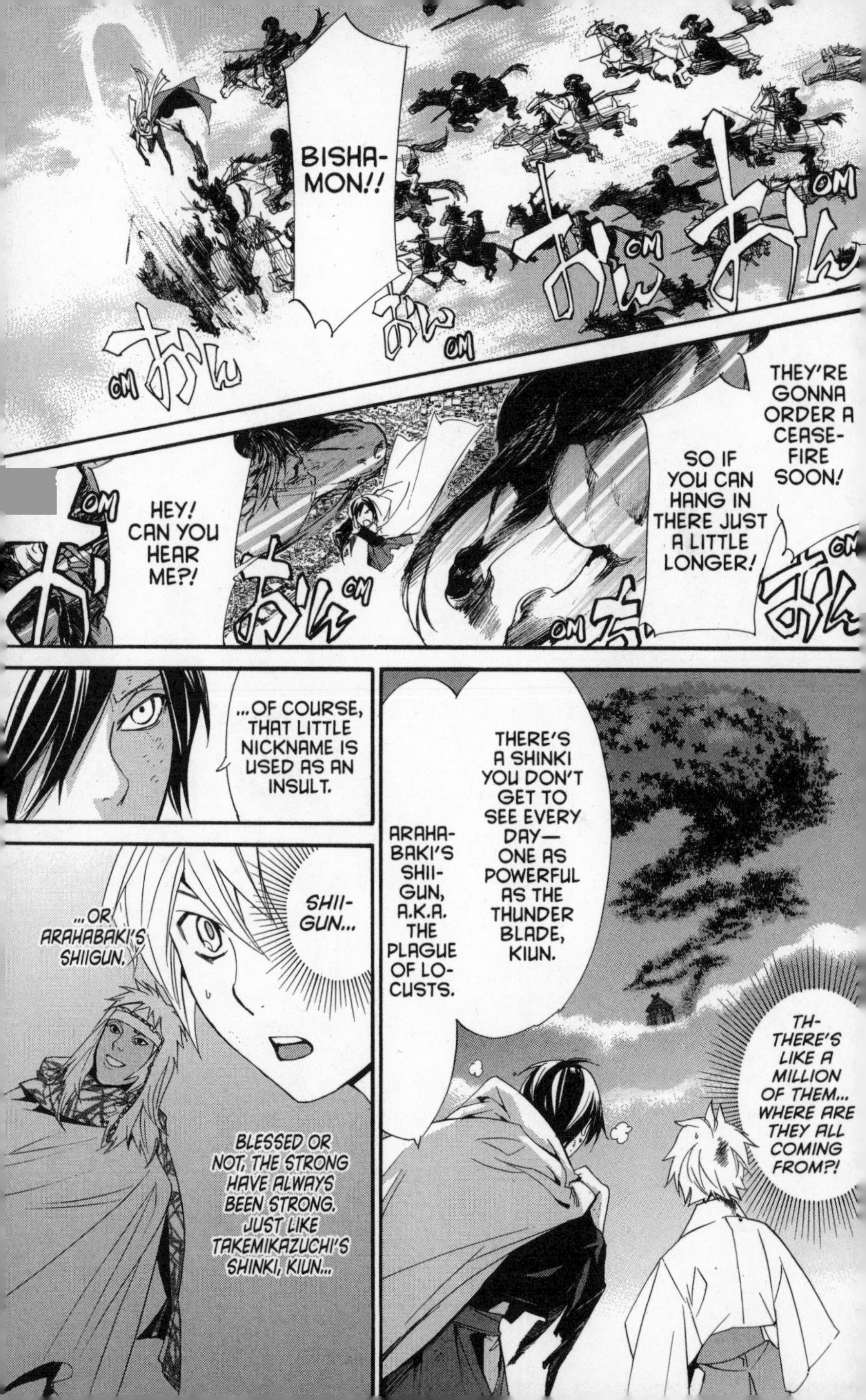
OM
OM
BISHA-MON!!
OM
OM
THEY'RE GONNA ORDER A CEASE-FIRE SOON!
SO IF YOU CAN HANG IN THERE JUST A LITTLE LONGER!
OM
OM
HEY! CAN YOU HEAR ME?!
OM
TH-THERE'S LIKE A MILLION OF THEM... WHERE ARE THEY ALL COMING FROM?!
THERE'S A SHINKI YOU DON'T GET TO SEE EVERY DAY—ONE AS POWERFUL AS THE THUNDER BLADE, KIUN.
ARAHA-BAKI'S SHII-GUN, A.K.A. THE PLAGUE OF LO-CUSTS.
...OF COURSE, THAT LITTLE NICKNAME IS USED AS AN INSULT.
SHII-GUN...
...OR ARAHABAKI'S SHIIGUN.
BLESSED OR NOT, THE STRONG HAVE ALWAYS BEEN STRONG. JUST LIKE TAKEMIKAZUCHI'S SHINKI, KIUN...

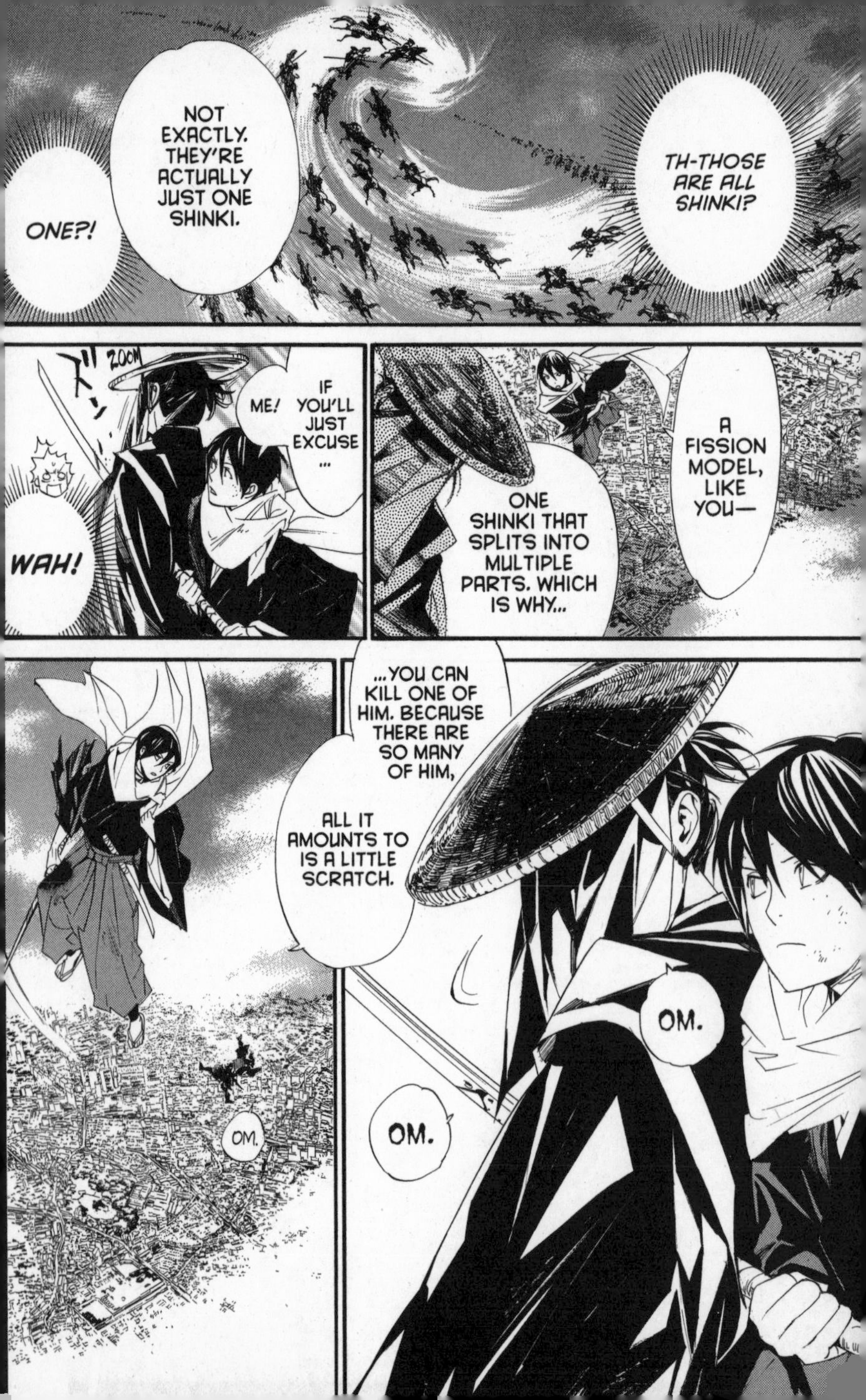
TH-THOSE ARE ALL SHINKI?
NOT EXACTLY. THEY'RE ACTUALLY JUST ONE SHINKI.
ONE?!
A FISSION MODEL, LIKE YOU—
ONE SHINKI THAT SPLITS INTO MULTIPLE PARTS. WHICH IS WHY...
ZOOM
IF YOU'LL JUST EXCUSE ...
ME!
WAH!
...YOU CAN KILL ONE OF HIM. BECAUSE THERE ARE SO MANY OF HIM,
ALL IT AMOUNTS TO IS A LITTLE SCRATCH.
OM.
OM.
OM.

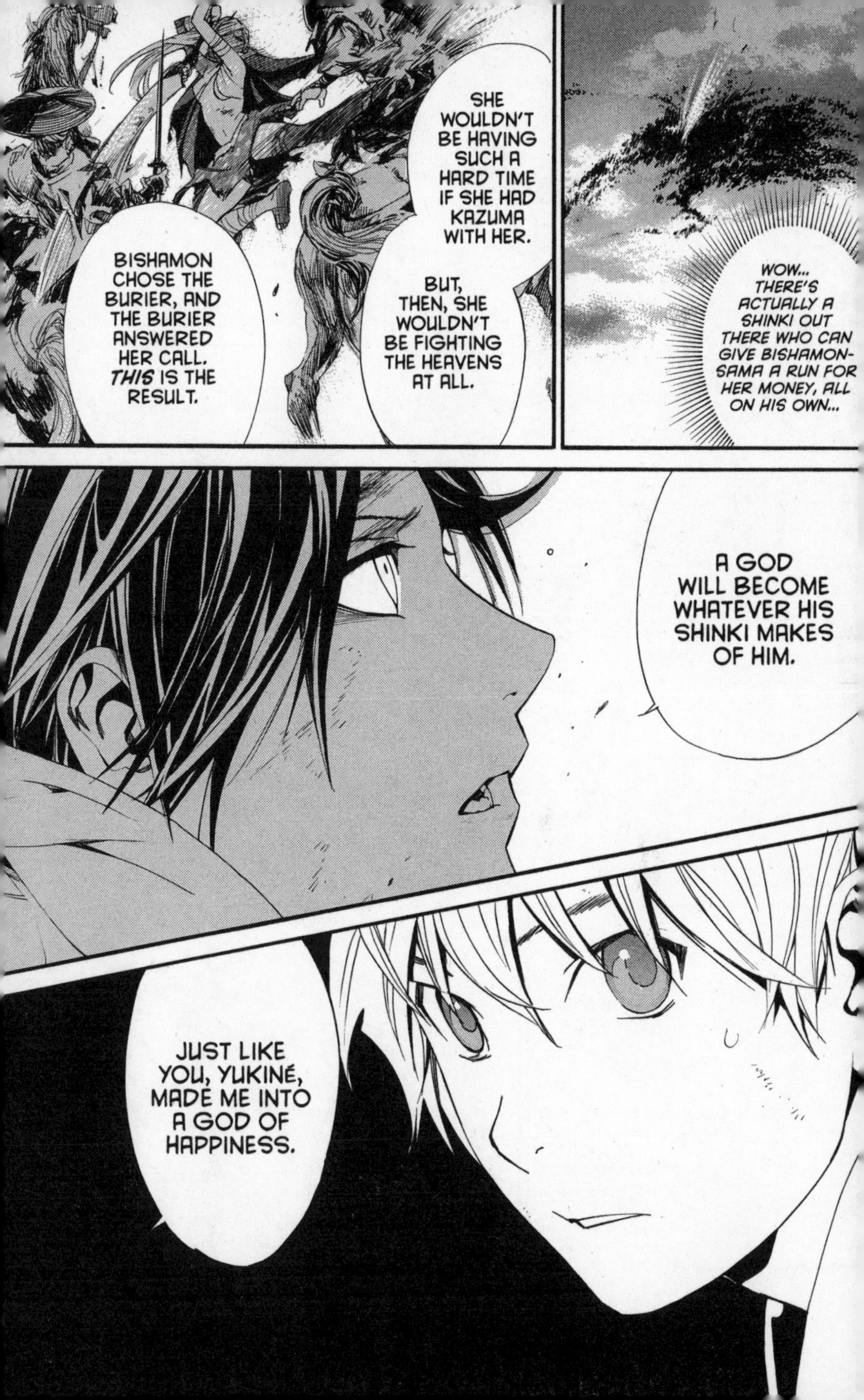
WOW... THERE'S ACTUALLY A SHINKI OUT THERE WHO CAN GIVE BISHAMON-SAMA A RUN FOR HER MONEY, ALL ON HIS OWN...
SHE WOULDN'T BE HAVING SUCH A HARD TIME IF SHE HAD KAZUMA WITH HER.
BUT, THEN, SHE WOULDN'T BE FIGHTING THE HEAVENS AT ALL.
BISHAMON CHOSE THE BURIER, AND THE BURIER ANSWERED HER CALL. *THIS* IS THE RESULT.
A GOD WILL BECOME WHATEVER HIS SHINKI MAKES OF HIM.
JUST LIKE YOU, YUKINÉ, MADE ME INTO A GOD OF HAPPINESS.

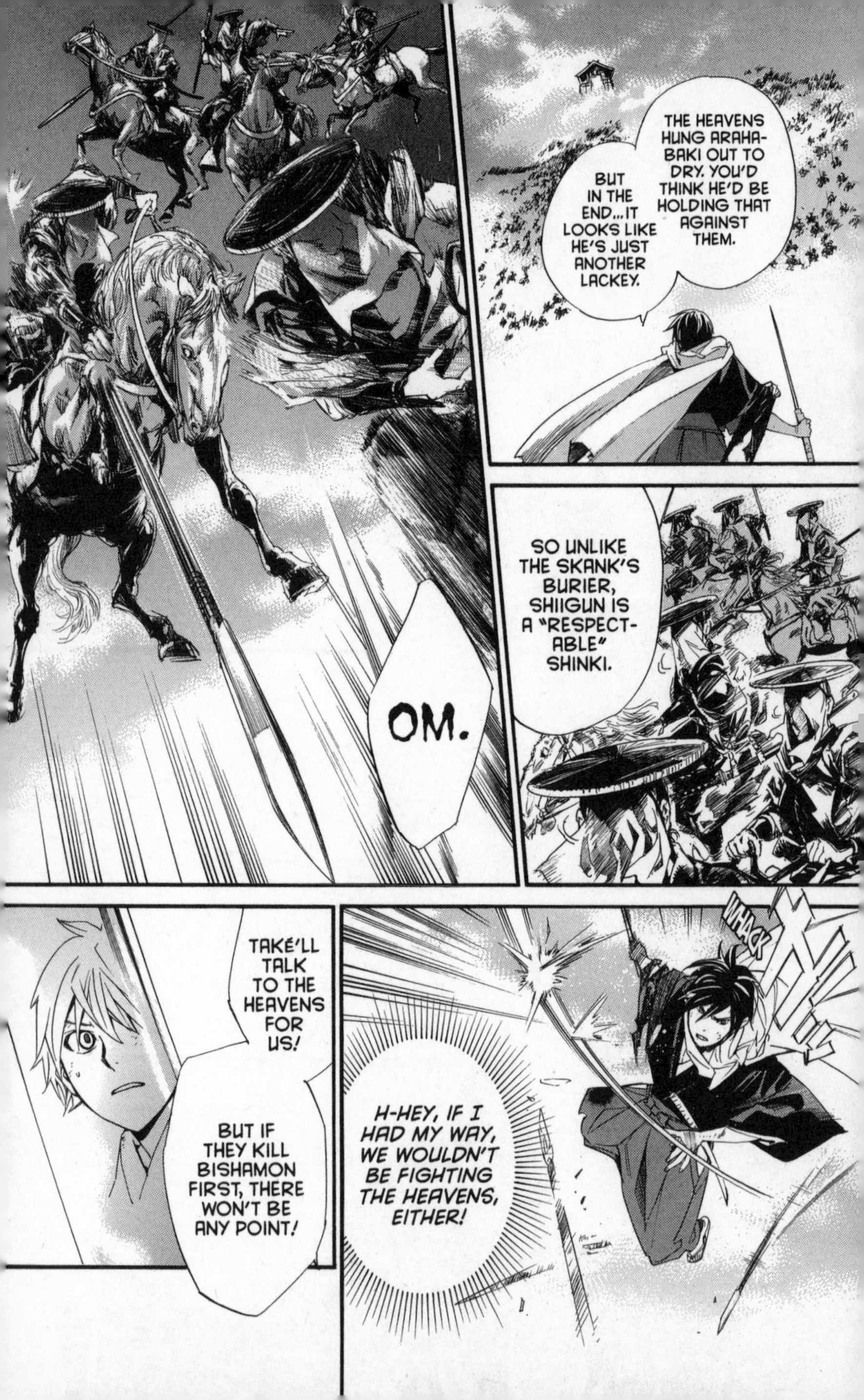
THE HEAVENS HUNG ARAHA-BAKI OUT TO DRY. YOU'D THINK HE'D BE HOLDING THAT AGAINST THEM.
BUT IN THE END...IT LOOKS LIKE HE'S JUST ANOTHER LACKEY.
SO UNLIKE THE SKANK'S BURIER, SHIIGUN IS A "RESPECT-ABLE" SHINKI.
OM.
WHACK
H-HEY, IF I HAD MY WAY, WE WOULDN'T BE FIGHTING THE HEAVENS, EITHER!
TAKÉ'LL TALK TO THE HEAVENS FOR US!
BUT IF THEY KILL BISHAMON FIRST, THERE WON'T BE ANY POINT!

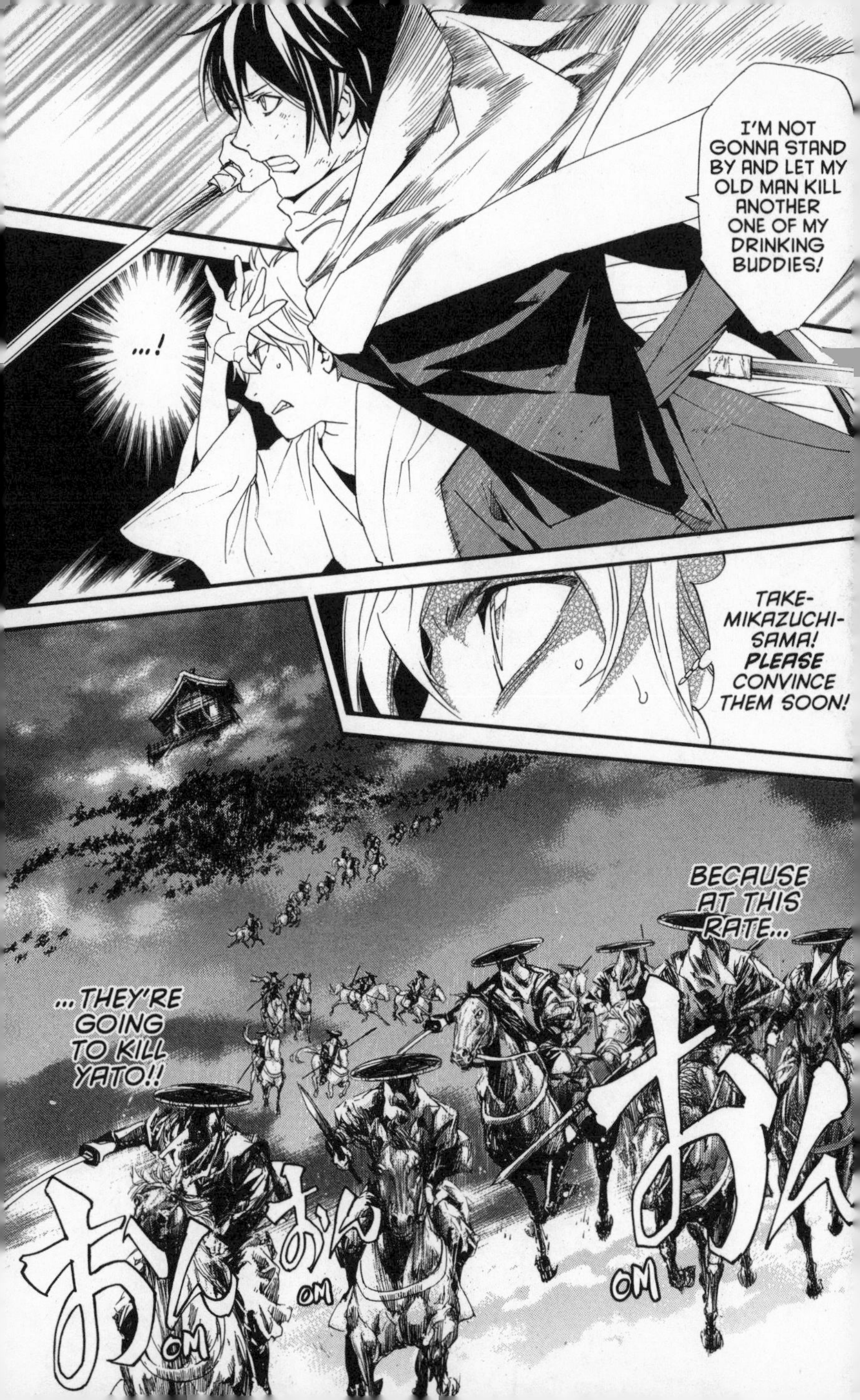
I'M NOT GONNA STAND BY AND LET MY OLD MAN KILL ANOTHER ONE OF MY DRINKING BUDDIES!
...!
TAKE-MIKAZUCHI-SAMA! PLEASE CONVINCE THEM SOON!
BECAUSE AT THIS RATE...
...THEY'RE GOING TO KILL YATO!!
OM
OM
OM

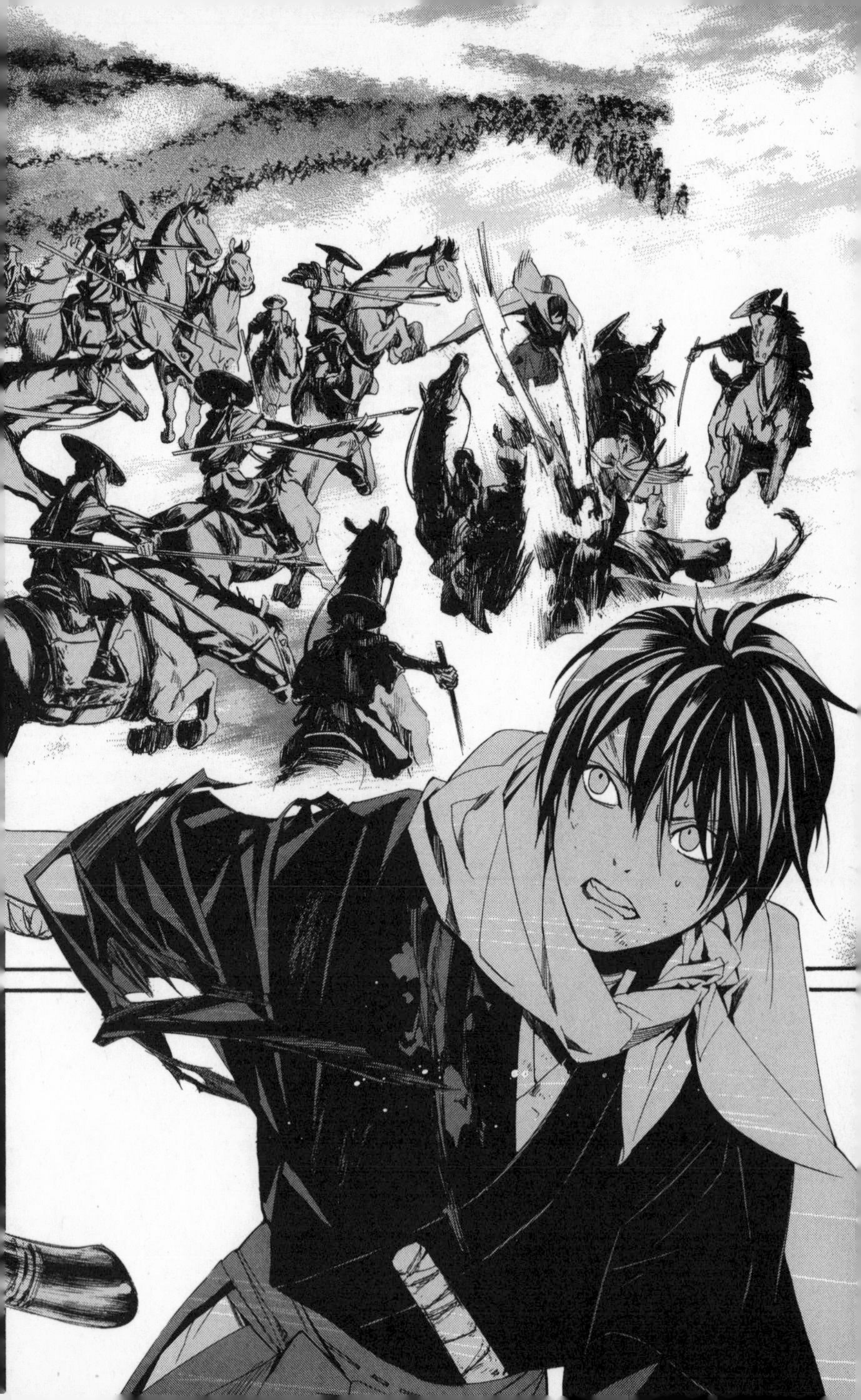

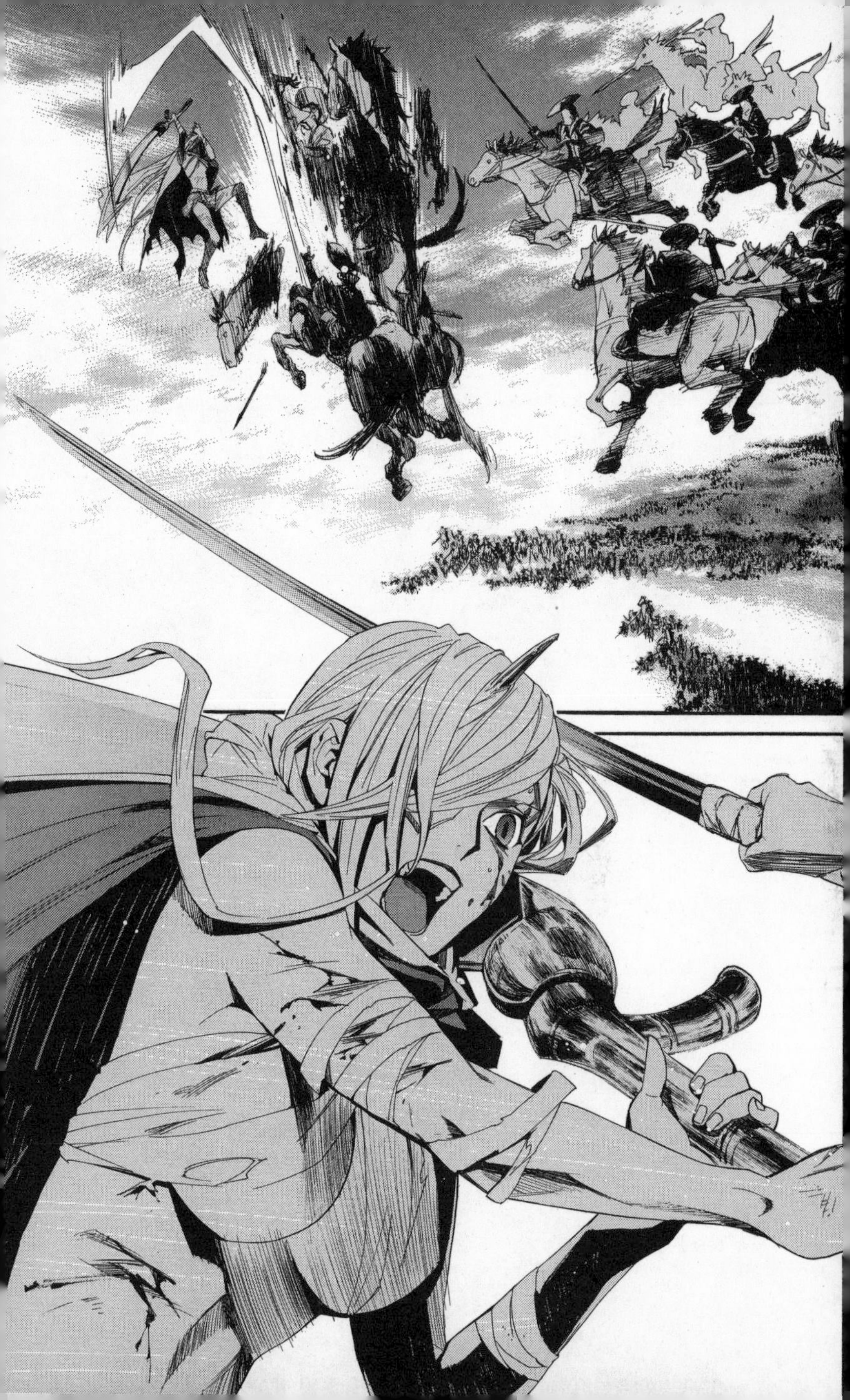

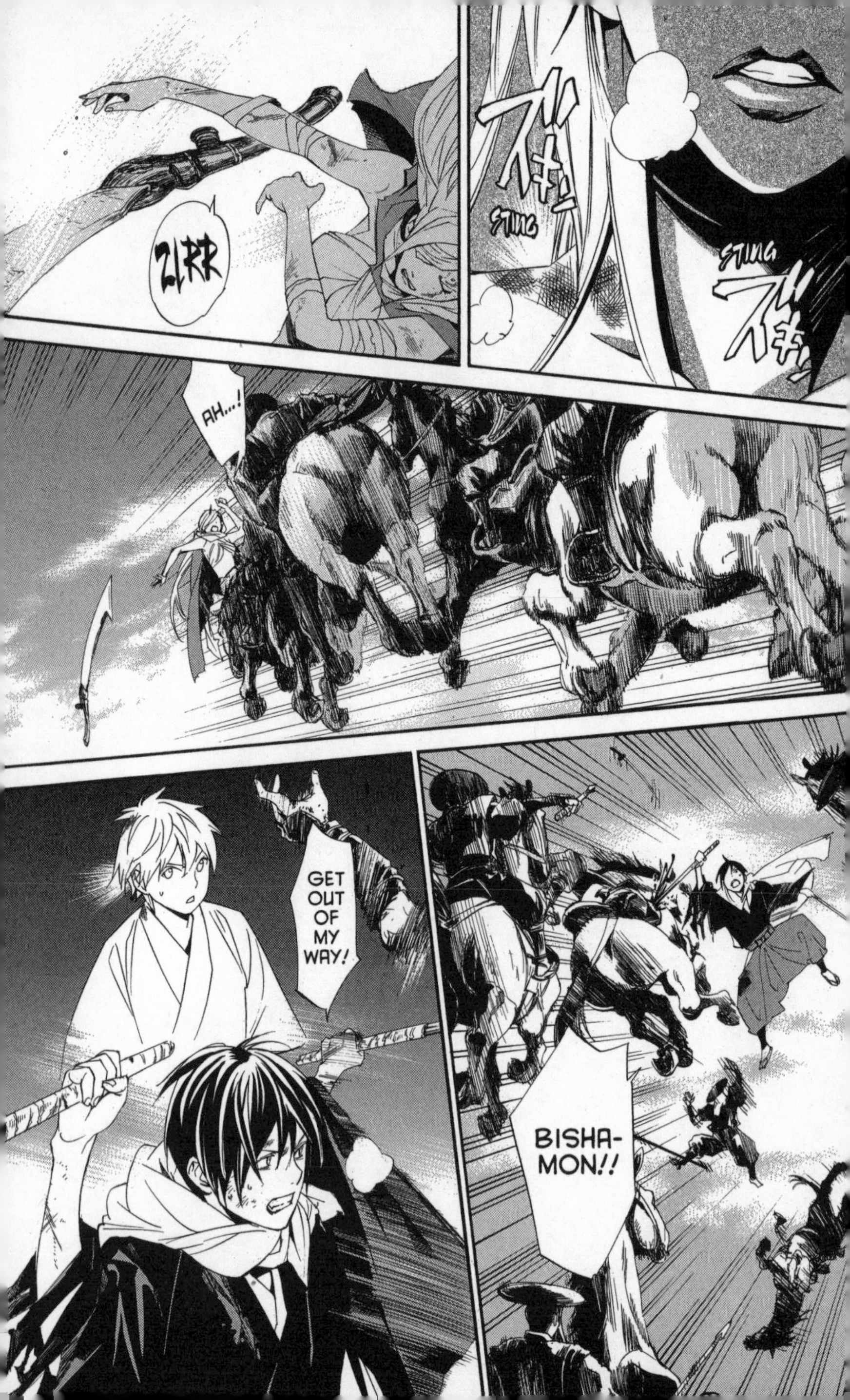
STING
STING
ZIRR
AH...!
BISHA-MON!!
GET OUT OF MY WAY!

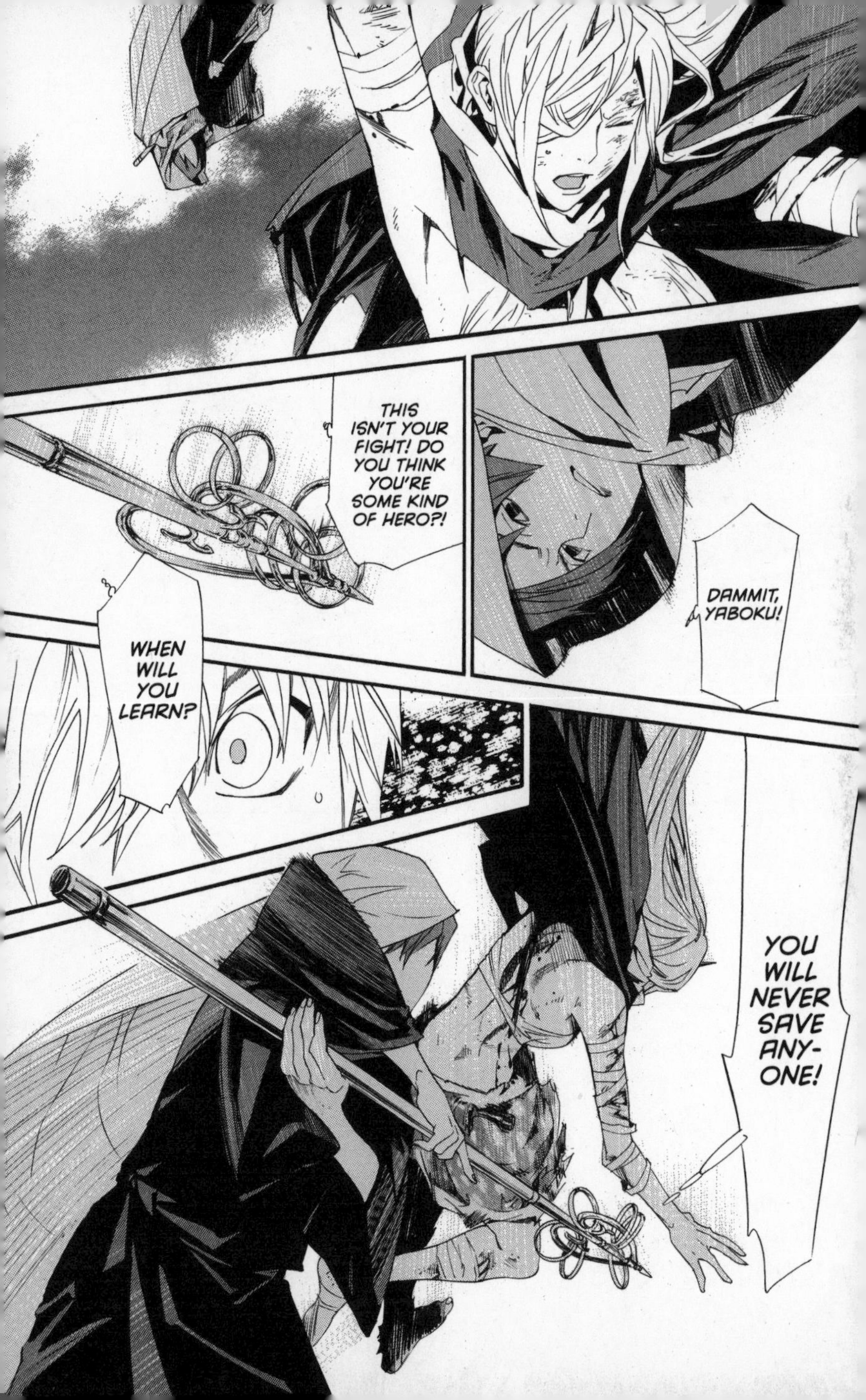
DAMMIT, YABOKU!
THIS ISN'T YOUR FIGHT! DO YOU THINK YOU'RE SOME KIND OF HERO?!
WHEN WILL YOU LEARN?
YOU WILL NEVER SAVE ANY-ONE!

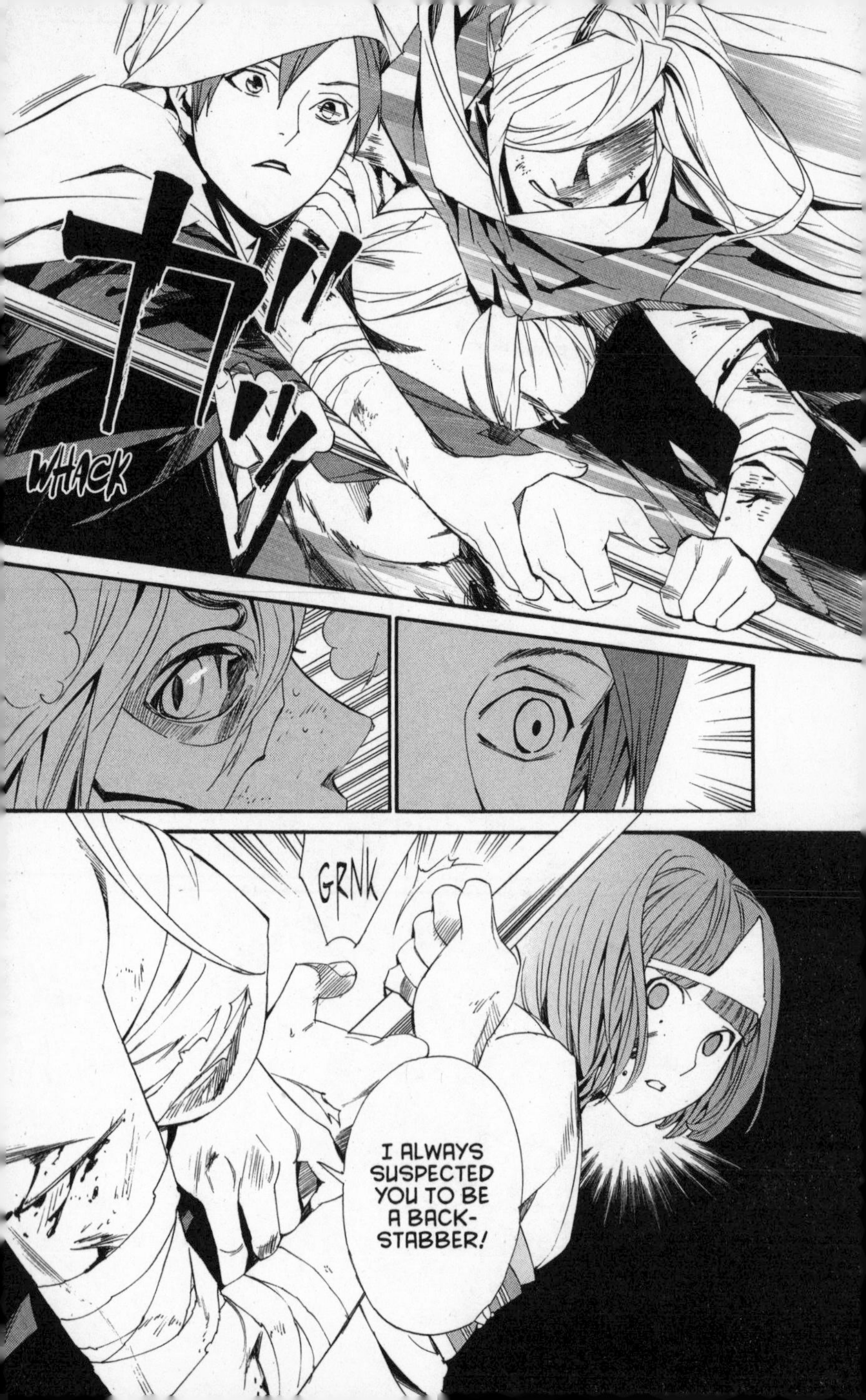
WHACK
GRNK
I ALWAYS SUSPECTED YOU TO BE A BACK-STABBER!

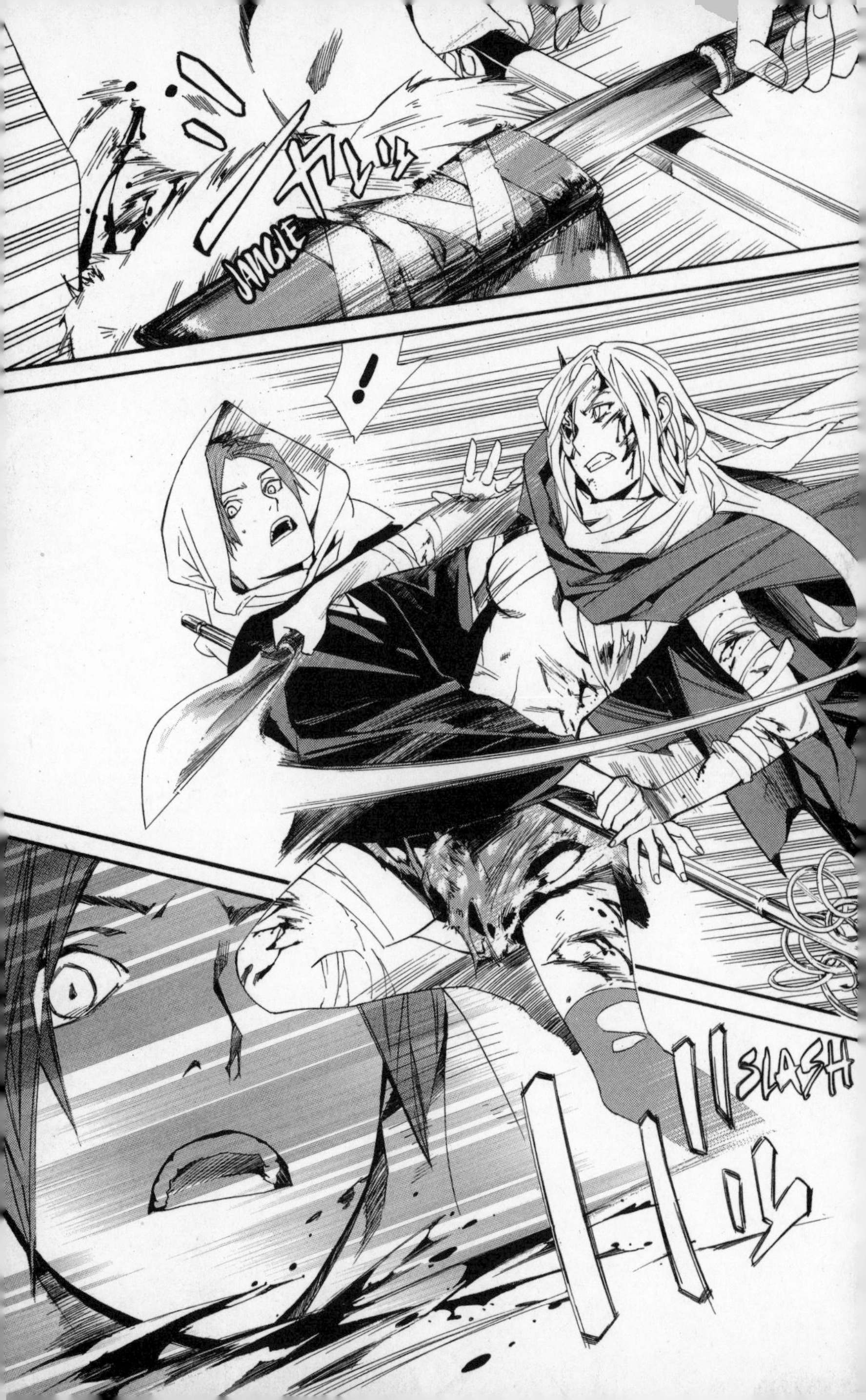
JANGLE
!
SLASH

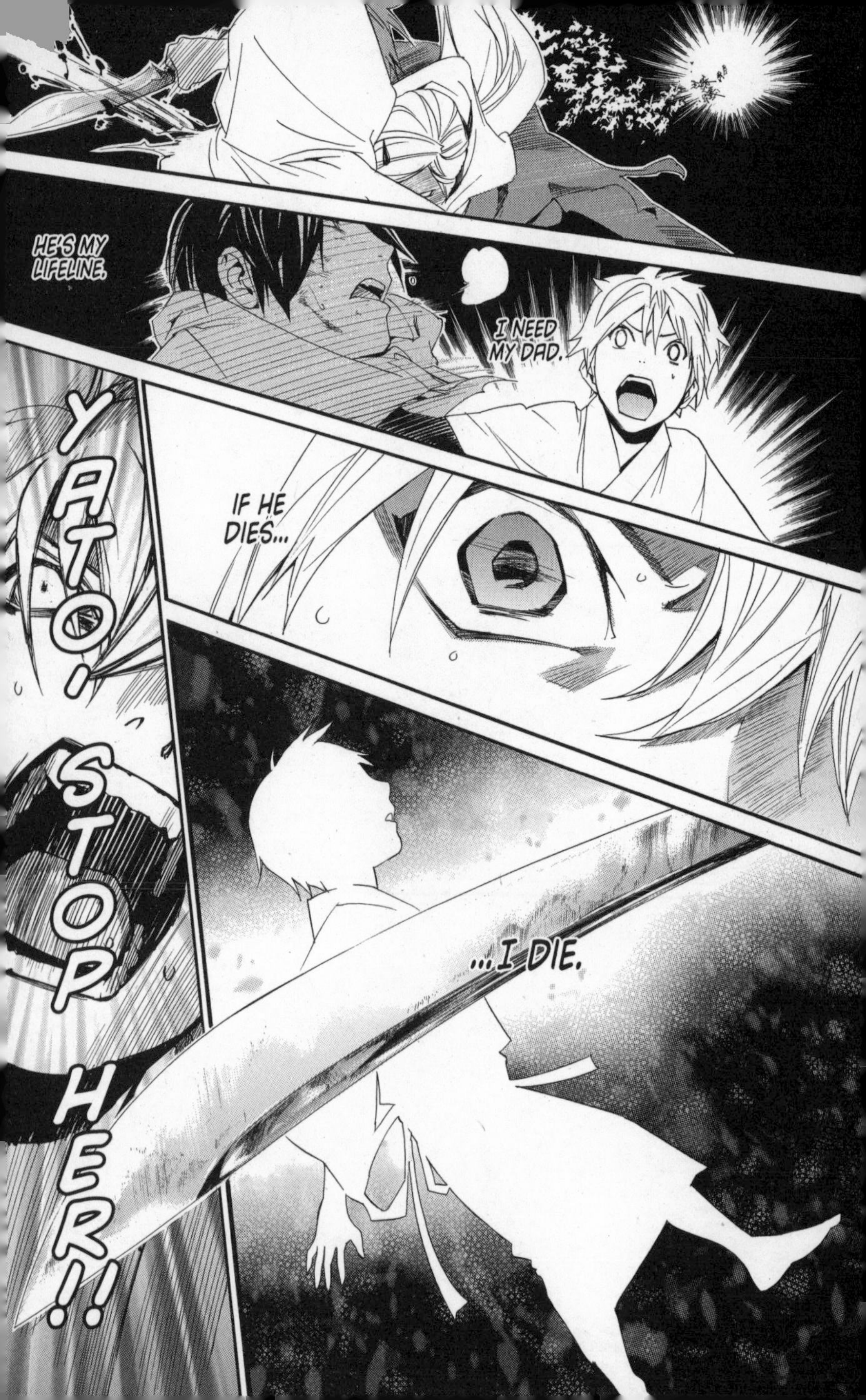
HE'S MY LIFELINE.
I NEED MY DAD.
YATO! STOP HER!!
IF HE DIES...
...I DIE.

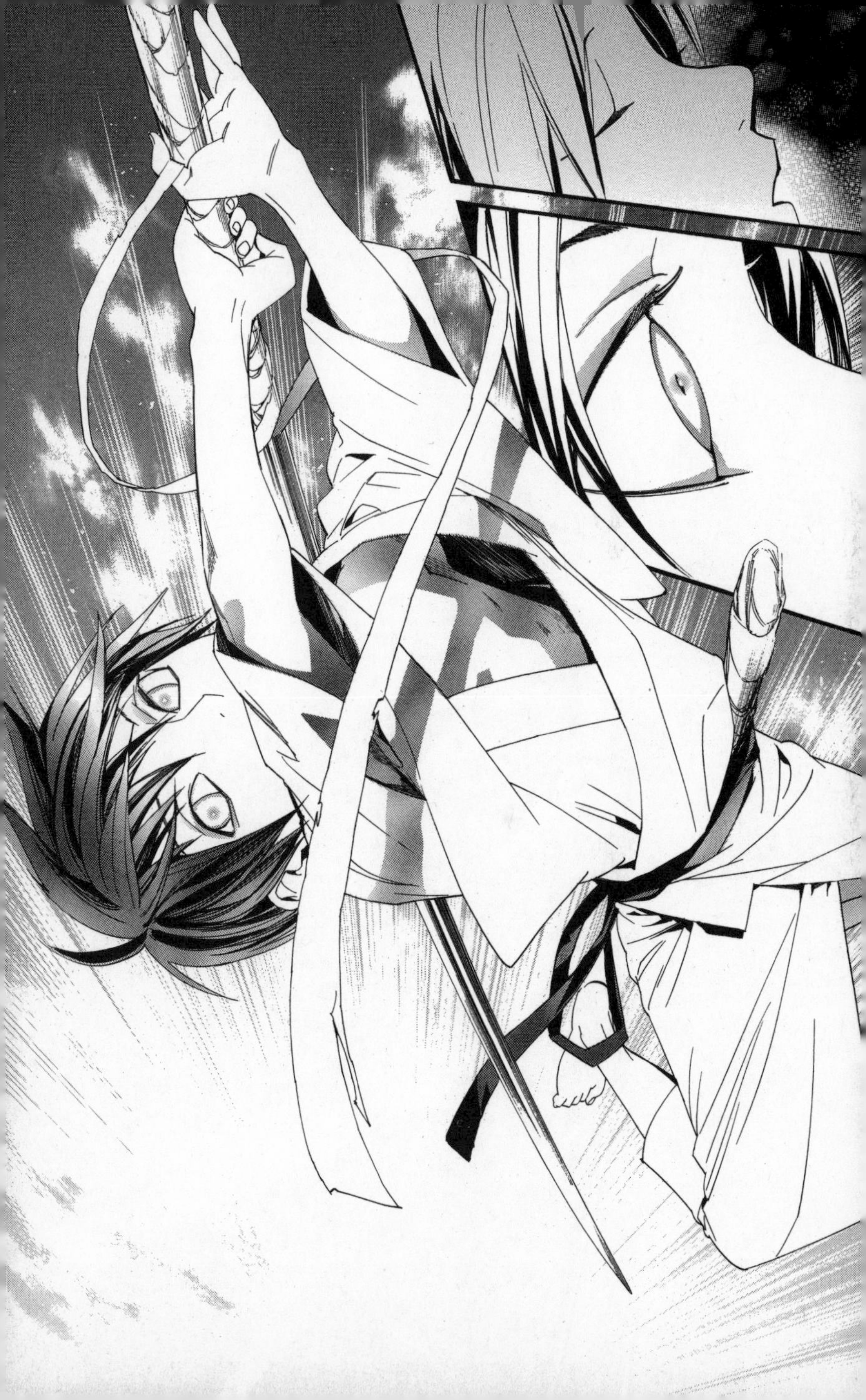

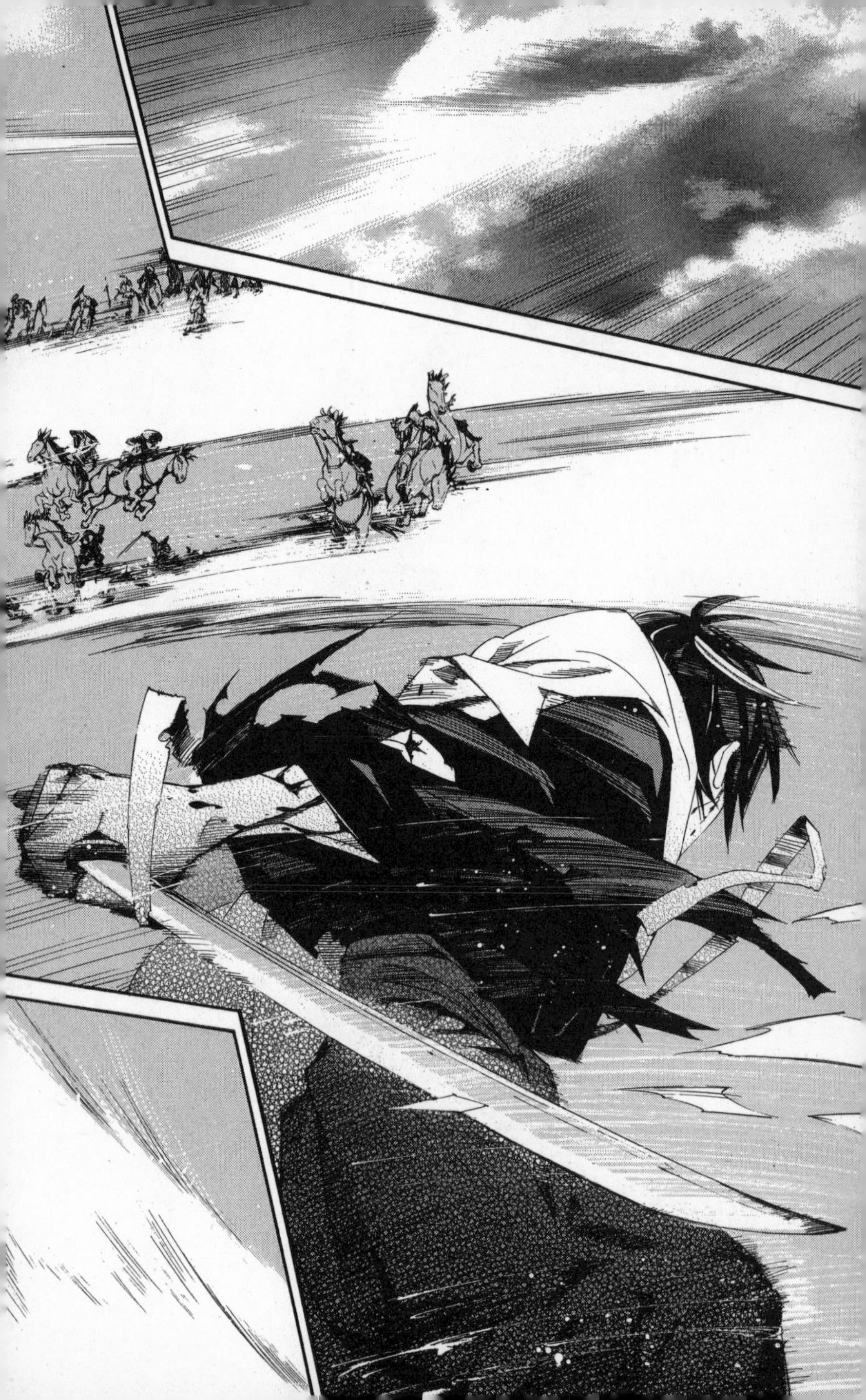

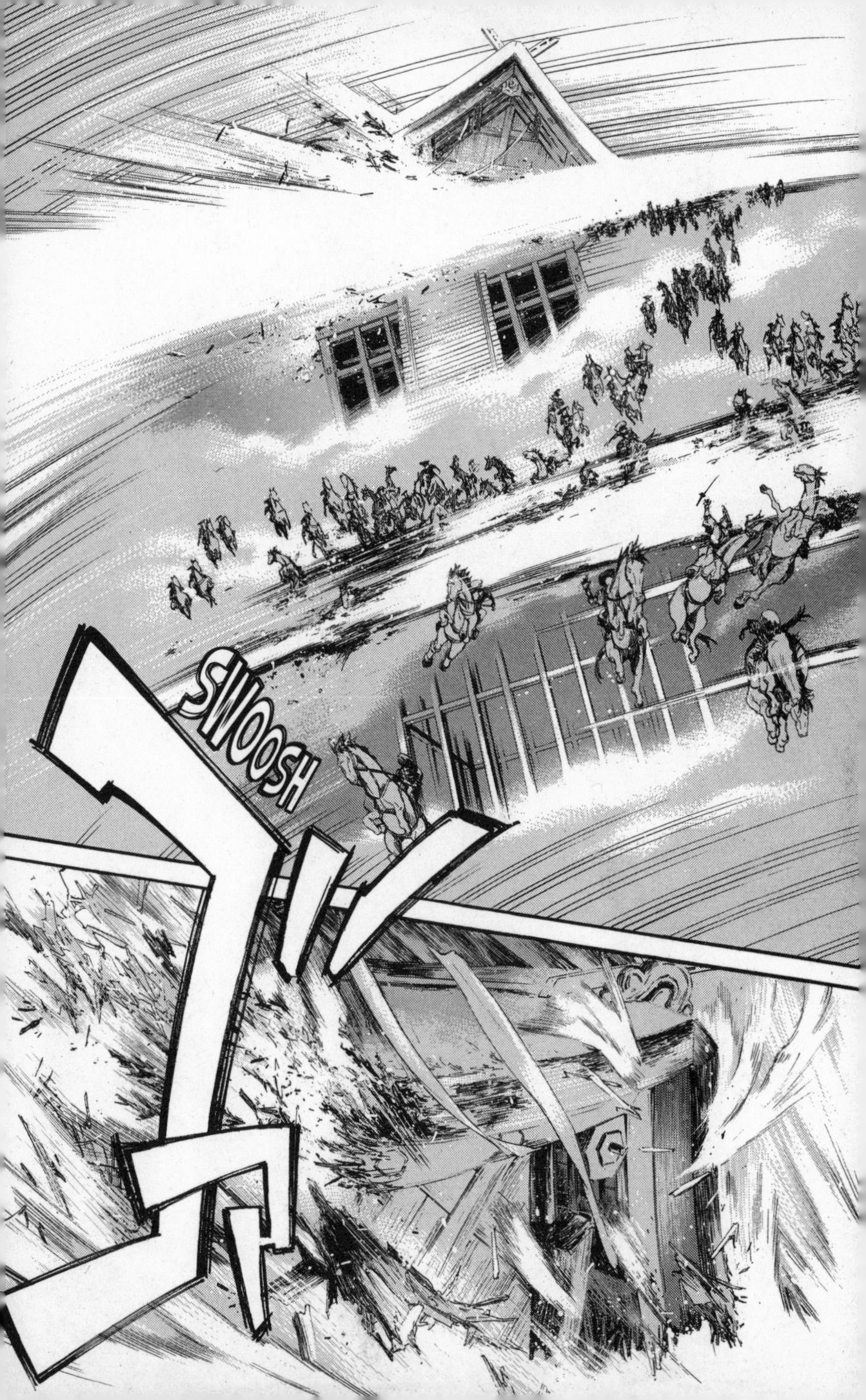
SWOOSH

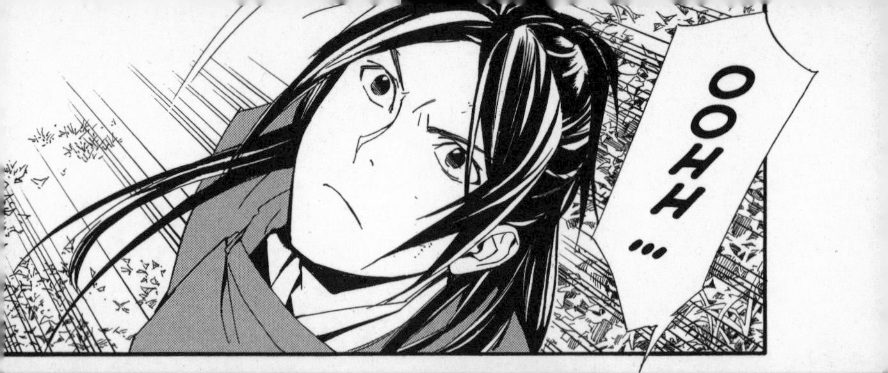
OOHH...
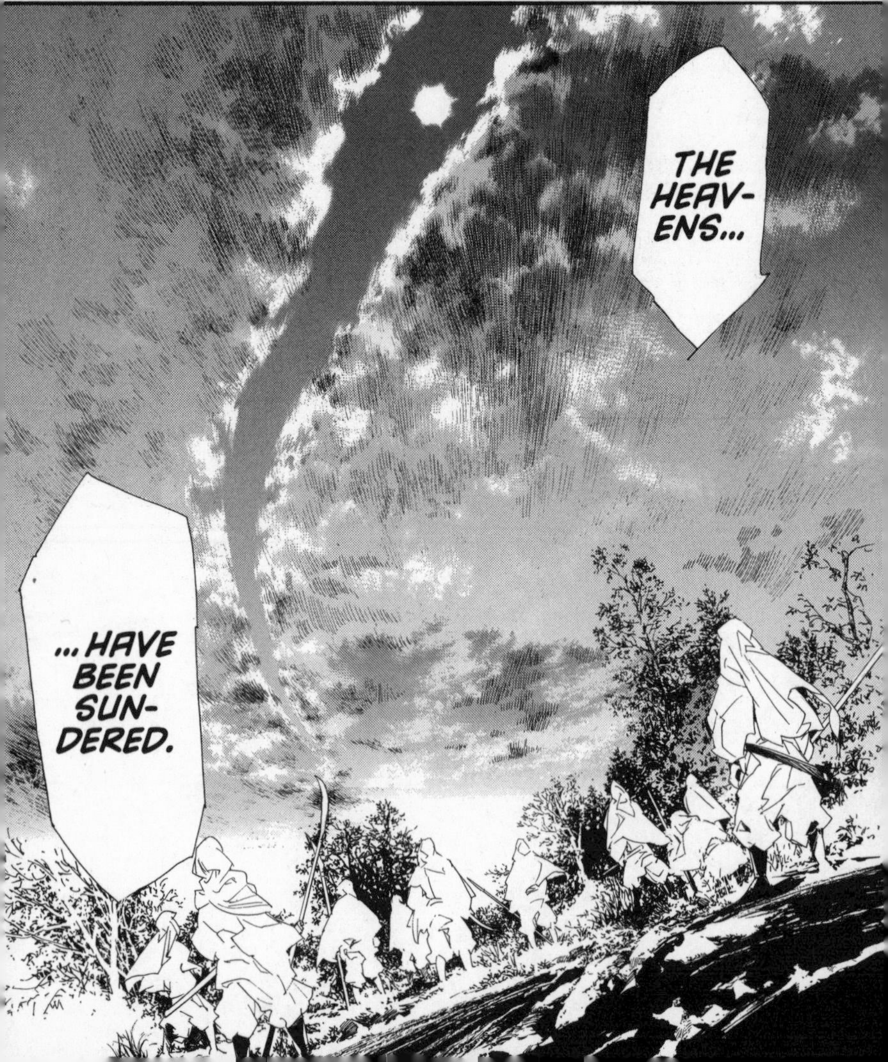
THE HEAVENS...
...HAVE BEEN SUNDERED.

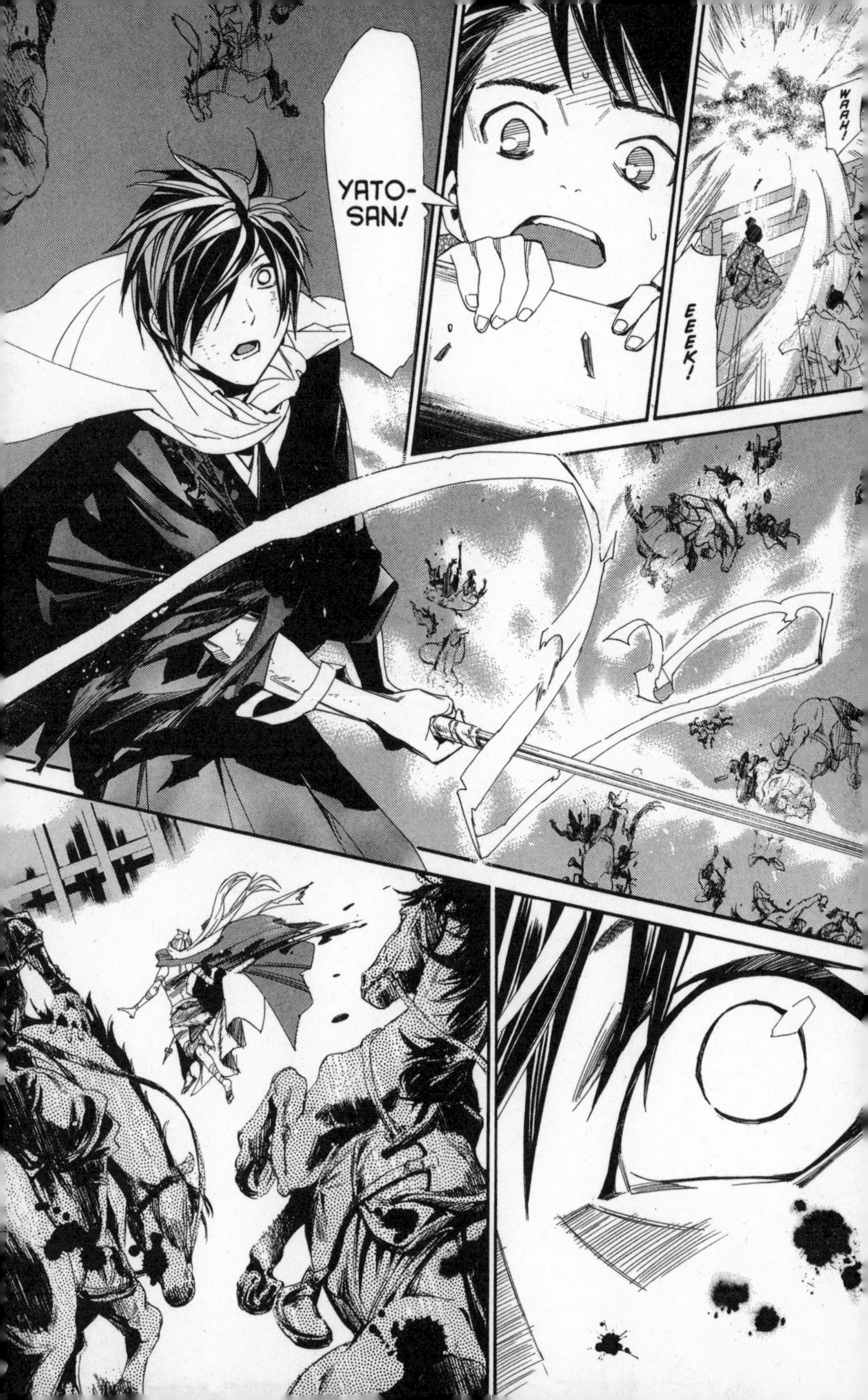
WAAH!
EEEK!
YATO-SAN!

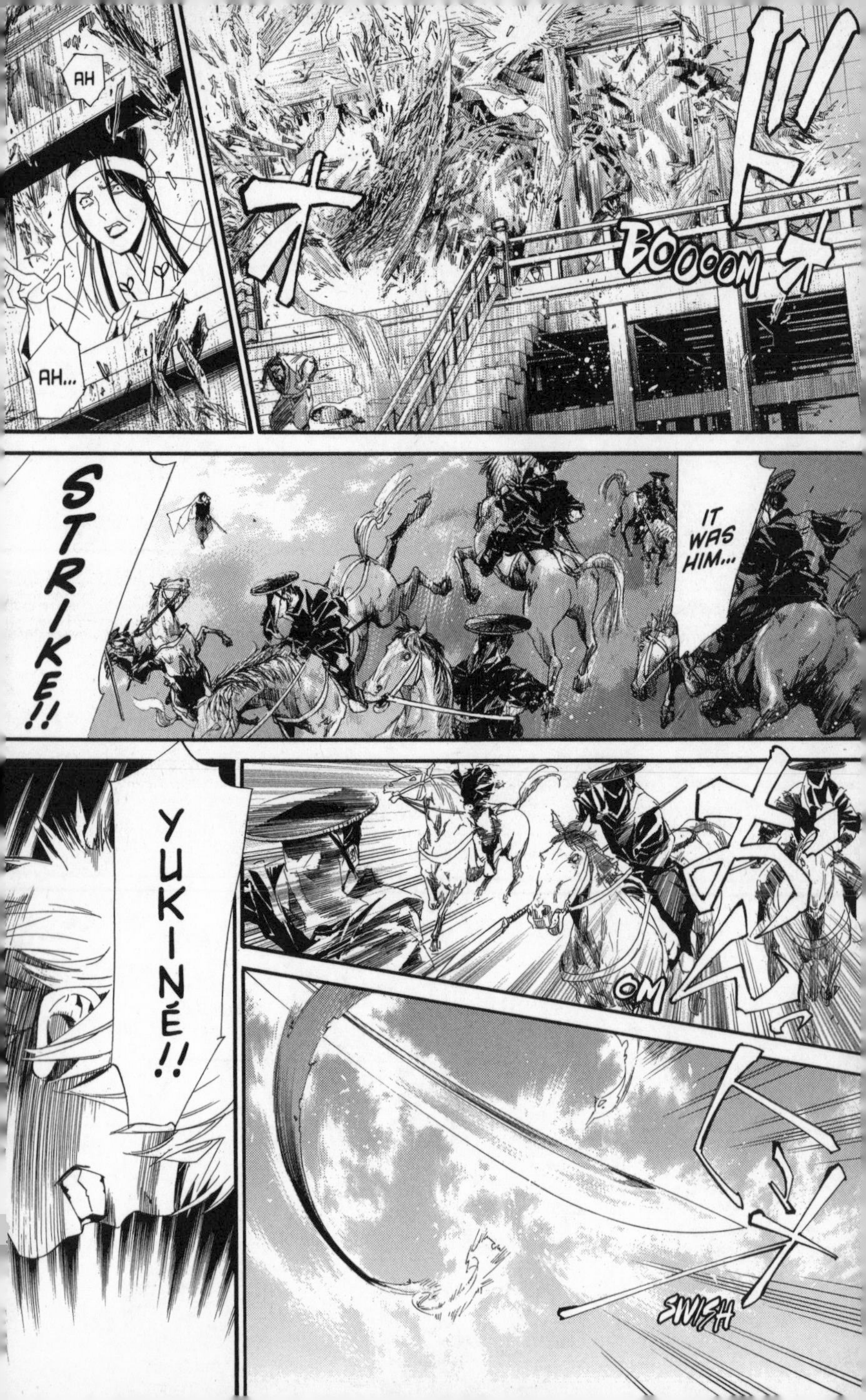
BOOOOM
AH
AH...
IT WAS HIM...
STRIKE!!
OM
SWISH
YUKINÉ!!

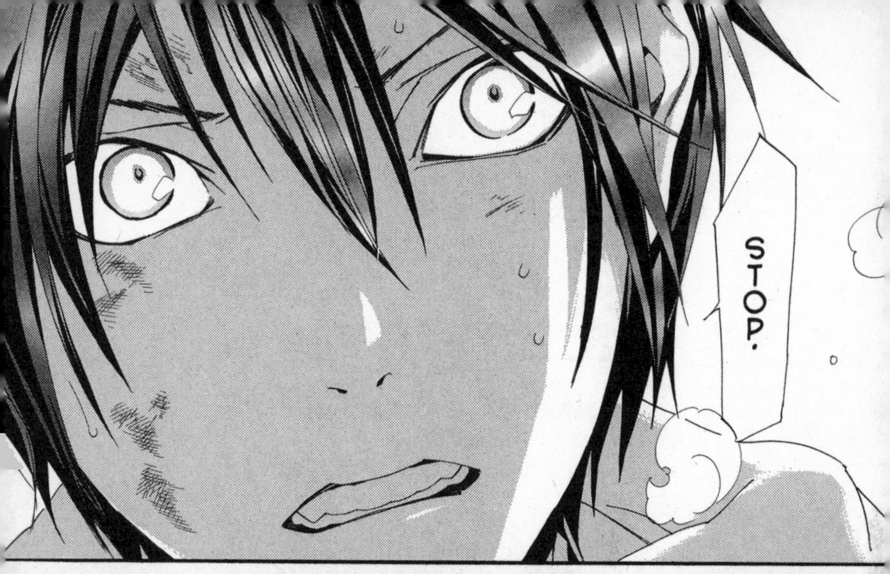
STOP.
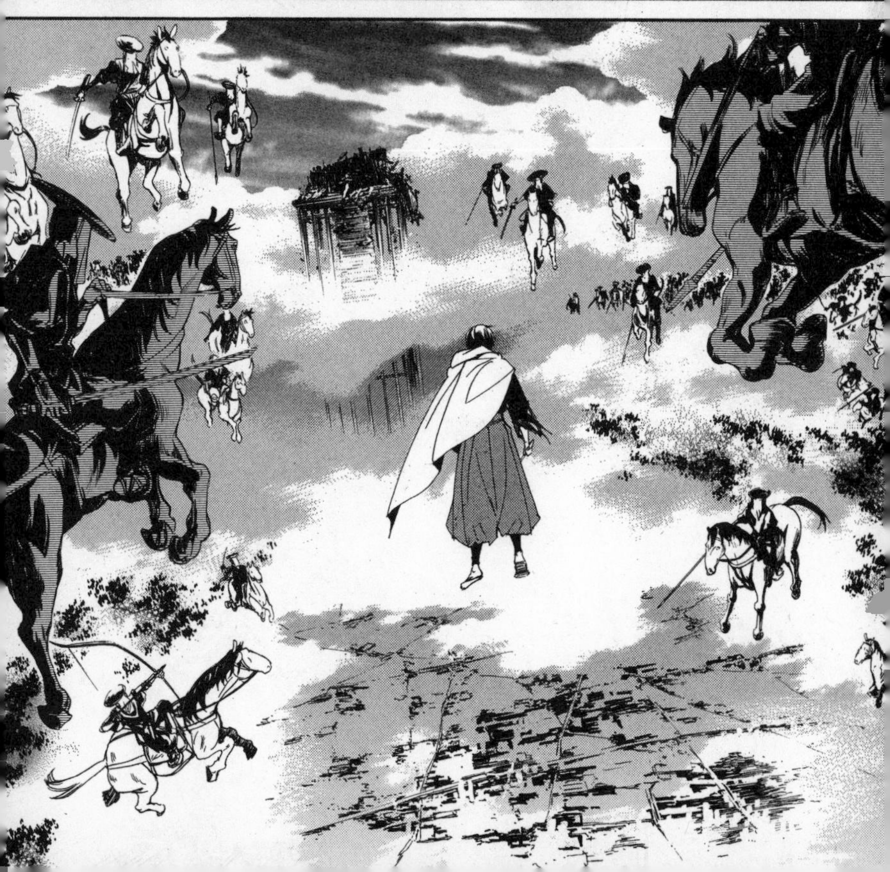

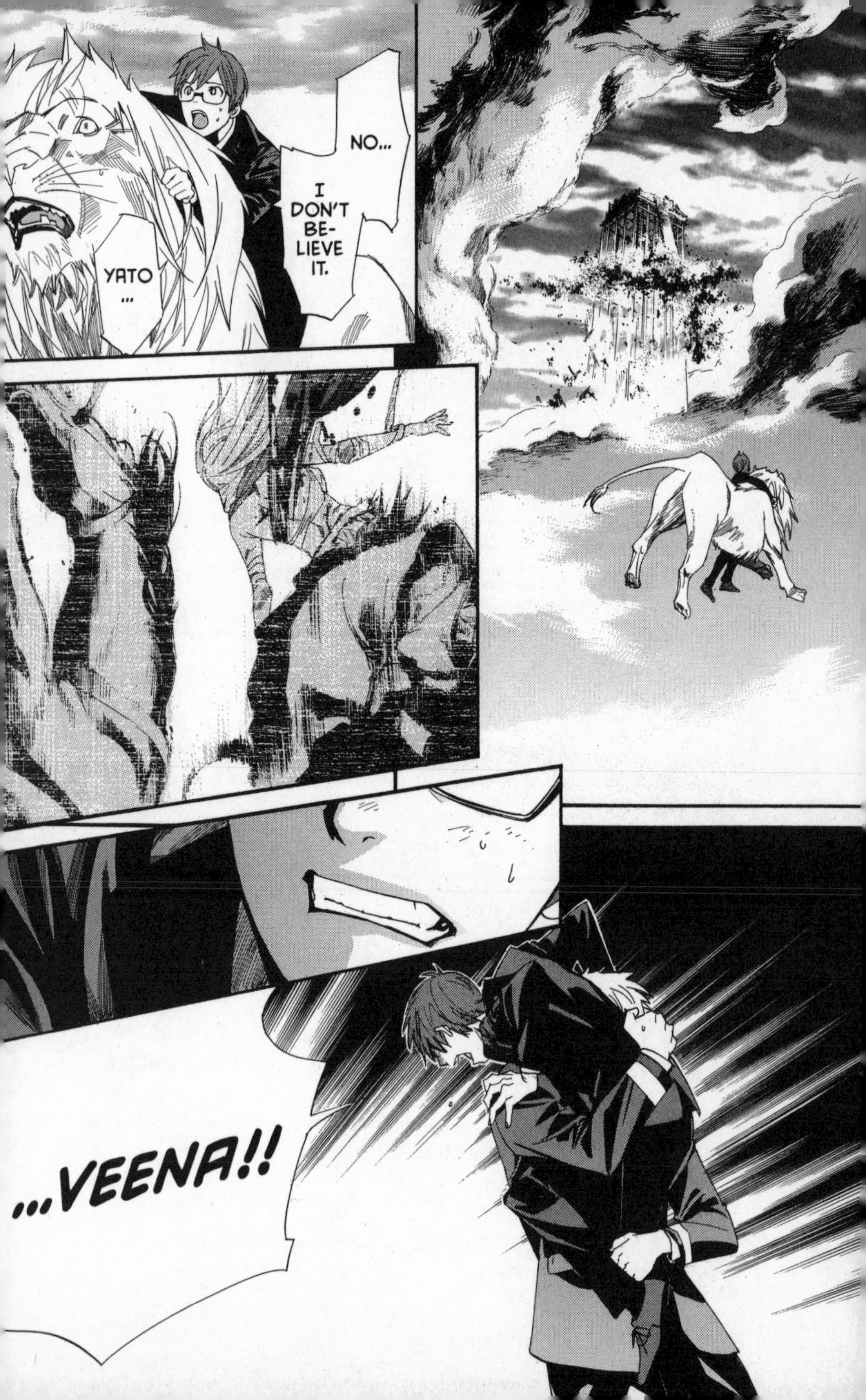
NO...
I DON'T BE-LIEVE IT.
YATO ...
...VEENA!!

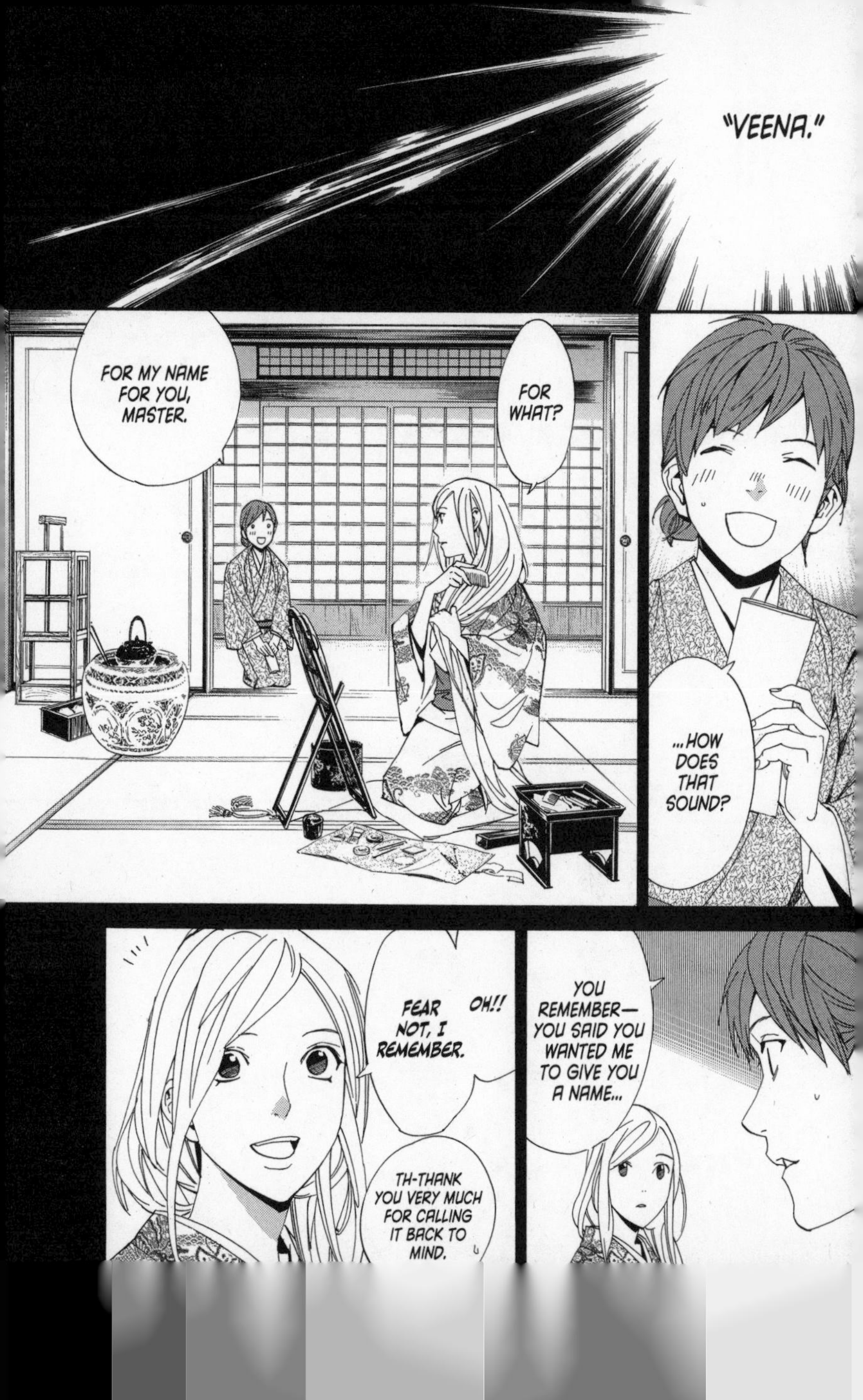
"VEENA."
...HOW DOES THAT SOUND?
FOR WHAT?
FOR MY NAME FOR YOU, MASTER.
YOU REMEMBER—YOU SAID YOU WANTED ME TO GIVE YOU A NAME...
OH!!
FEAR NOT, I REMEMBER.
TH-THANK YOU VERY MUCH FOR CALLING IT BACK TO MIND.

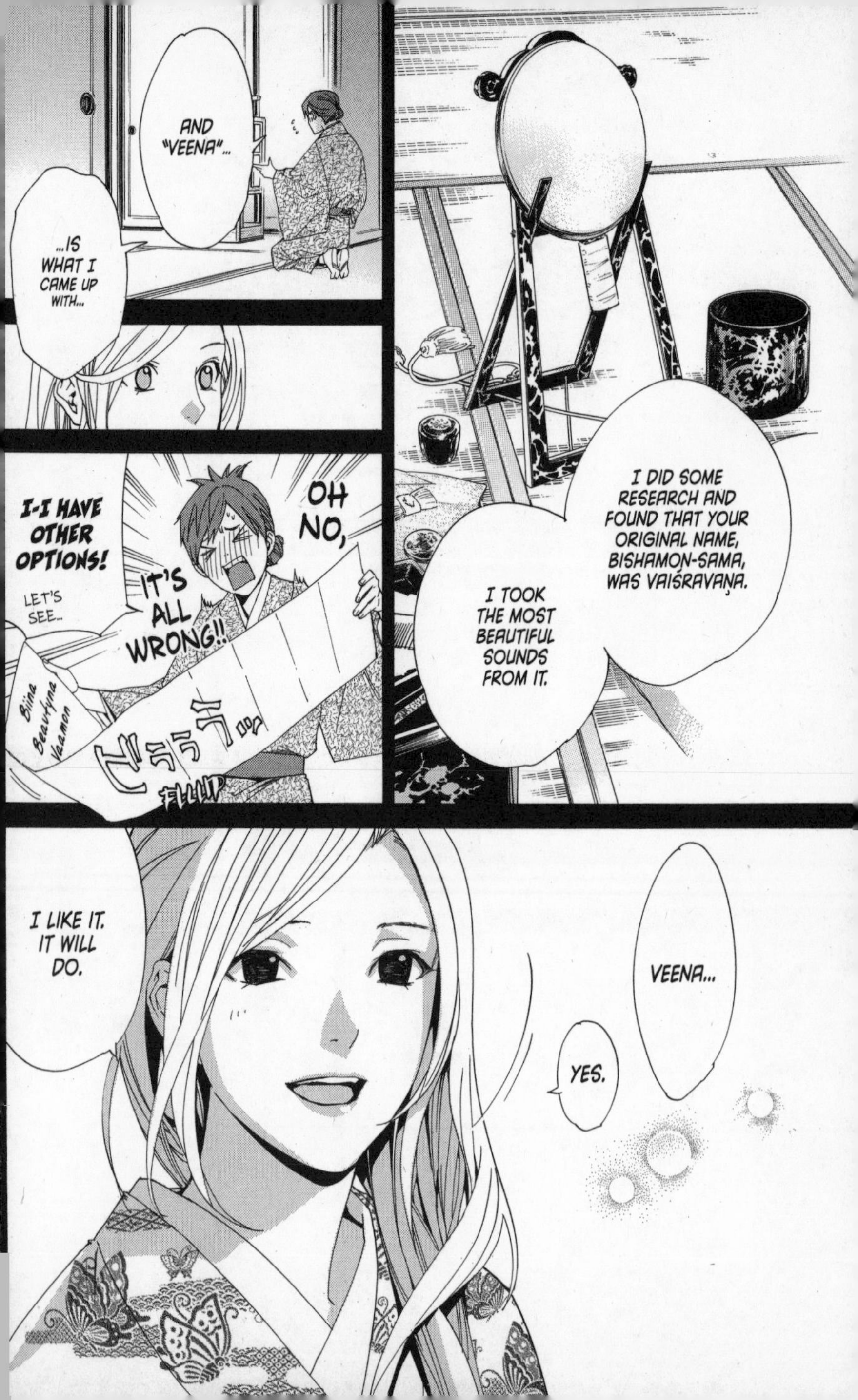
I DID SOME RESEARCH AND FOUND THAT YOUR ORIGINAL NAME, BISHAMON-SAMA, WAS VAIŚRAVAṆA.
I TOOK THE MOST BEAUTIFUL SOUNDS FROM IT.
AND "VEENA"...
...IS WHAT I CAME UP WITH...
OH NO, IT'S ALL WRONG!!
I-I HAVE OTHER OPTIONS!
LET'S SEE...
Biina
Beautyna
Vaamon
ぴらら
FLLLIP
VEENA...
YES.
I LIKE IT. IT WILL DO.

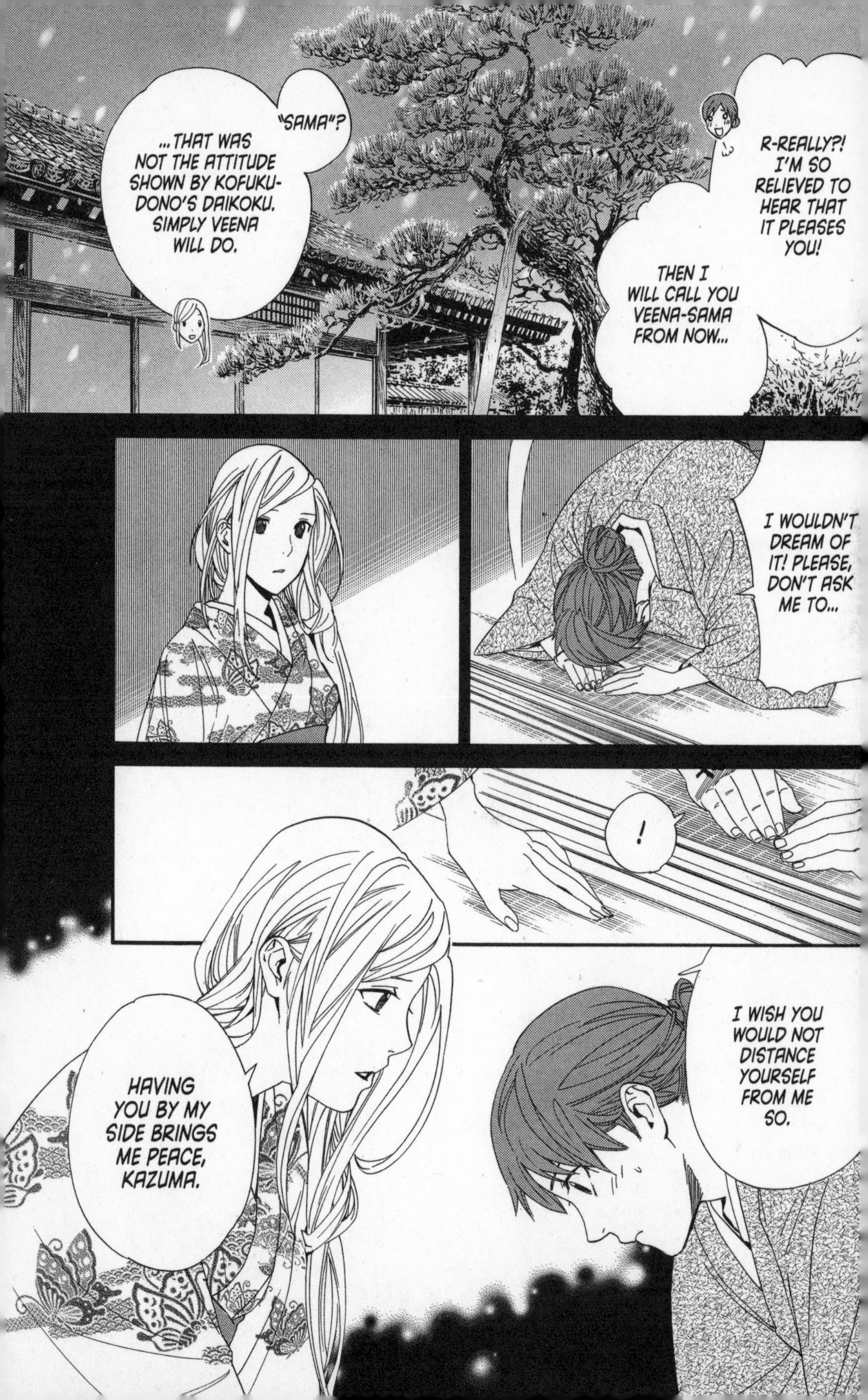
R-REALLY?! I'M SO RELIEVED TO HEAR THAT IT PLEASES YOU!
THEN I WILL CALL YOU VEENA-SAMA FROM NOW...
"SAMA"?
...THAT WAS NOT THE ATTITUDE SHOWN BY KOFUKU-DONO'S DAIKOKU. SIMPLY VEENA WILL DO.
I WOULDN'T DREAM OF IT! PLEASE, DON'T ASK ME TO...
!
I WISH YOU WOULD NOT DISTANCE YOURSELF FROM ME SO.
HAVING YOU BY MY SIDE BRINGS ME PEACE, KAZUMA.

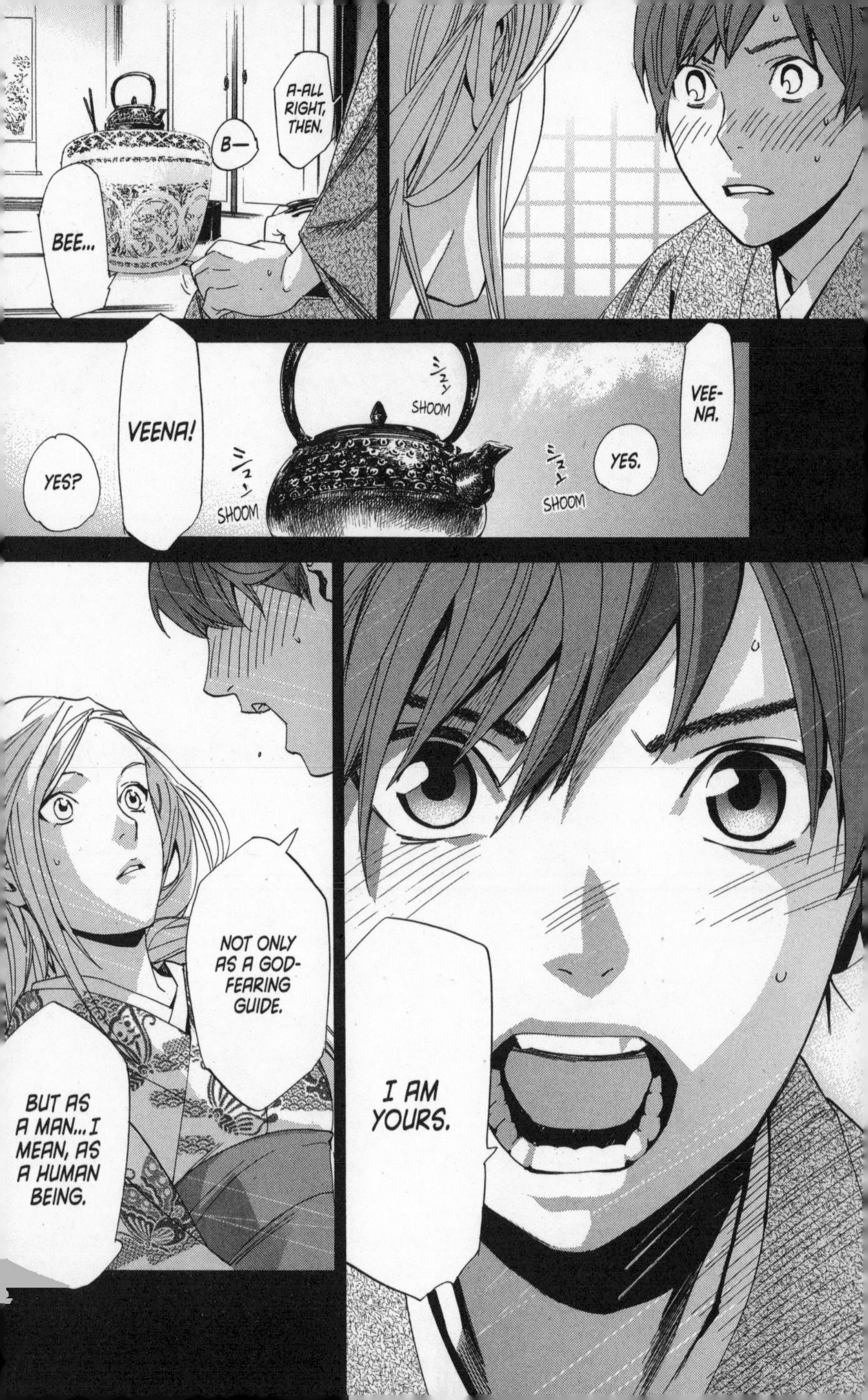
A-ALL RIGHT, THEN.
B—
BEE...
VEE-NA.
YES.
SHOOM
SHOOM
VEENA!
YES?
SHOOM
I AM YOURS.
NOT ONLY AS A GOD-FEARING GUIDE.
BUT AS A MAN... I MEAN, AS A HUMAN BEING.

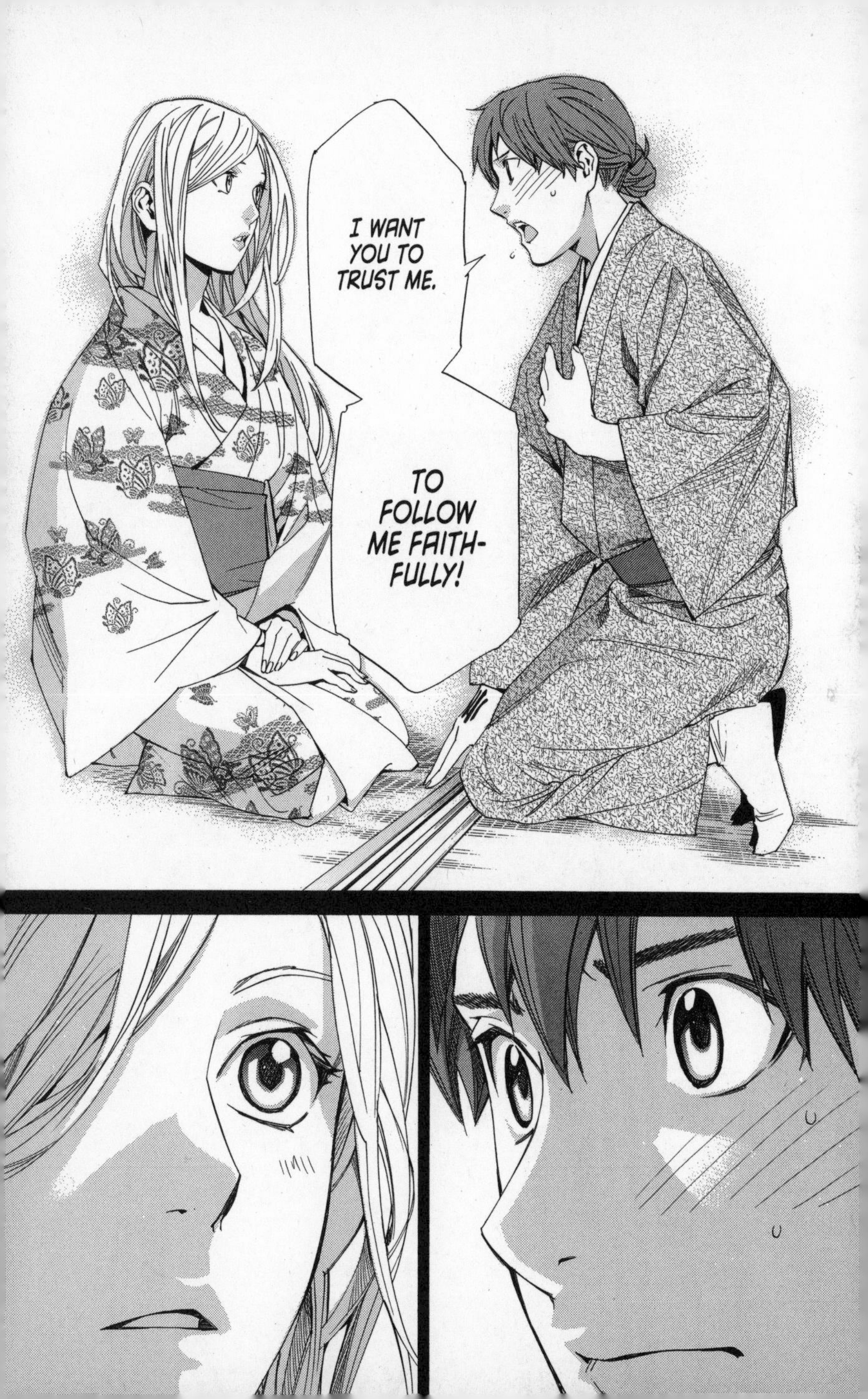
I WANT YOU TO TRUST ME.
TO FOLLOW ME FAITH-FULLY!

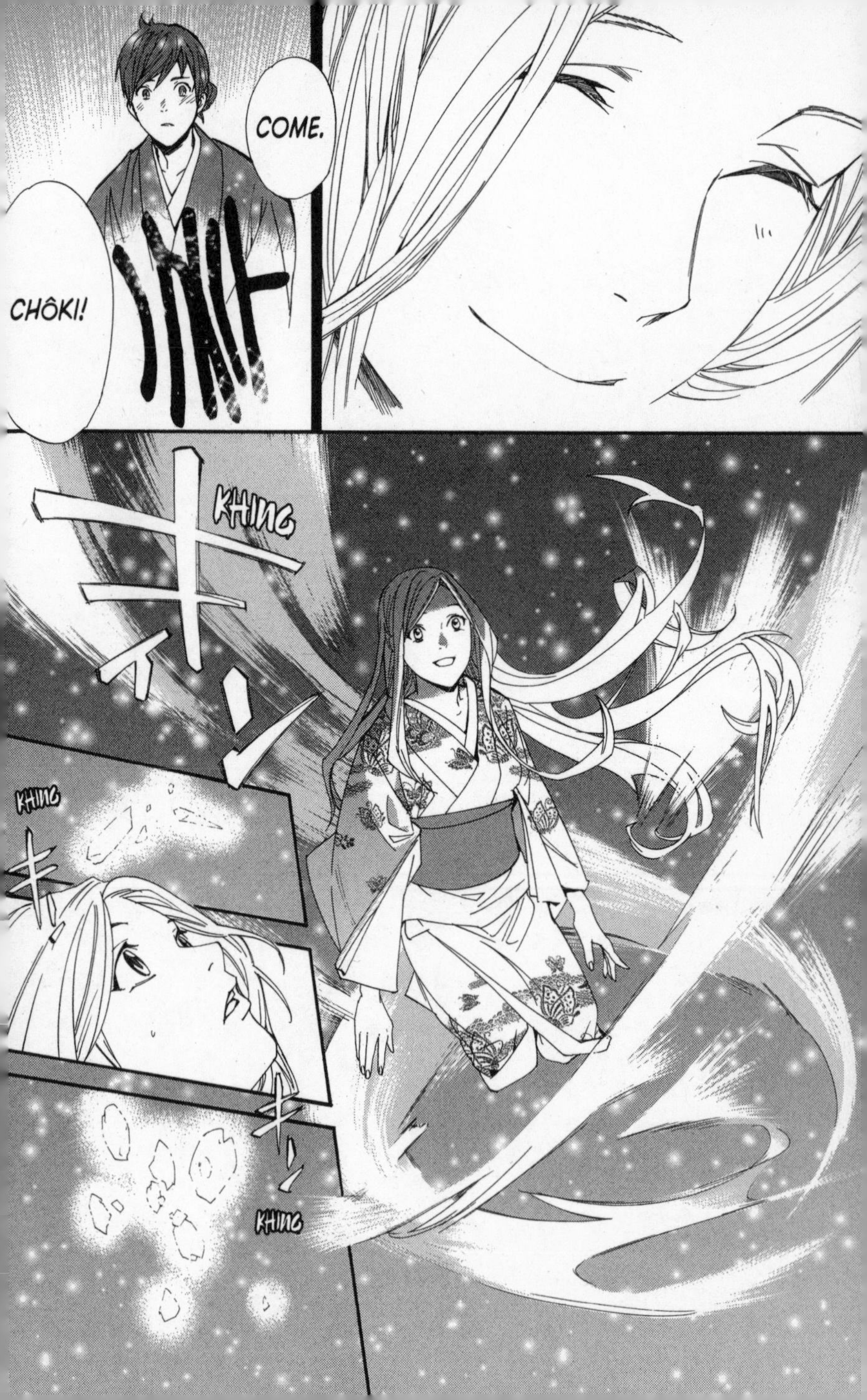
COME.
CHÔKI!
KHING
KHING
KHING

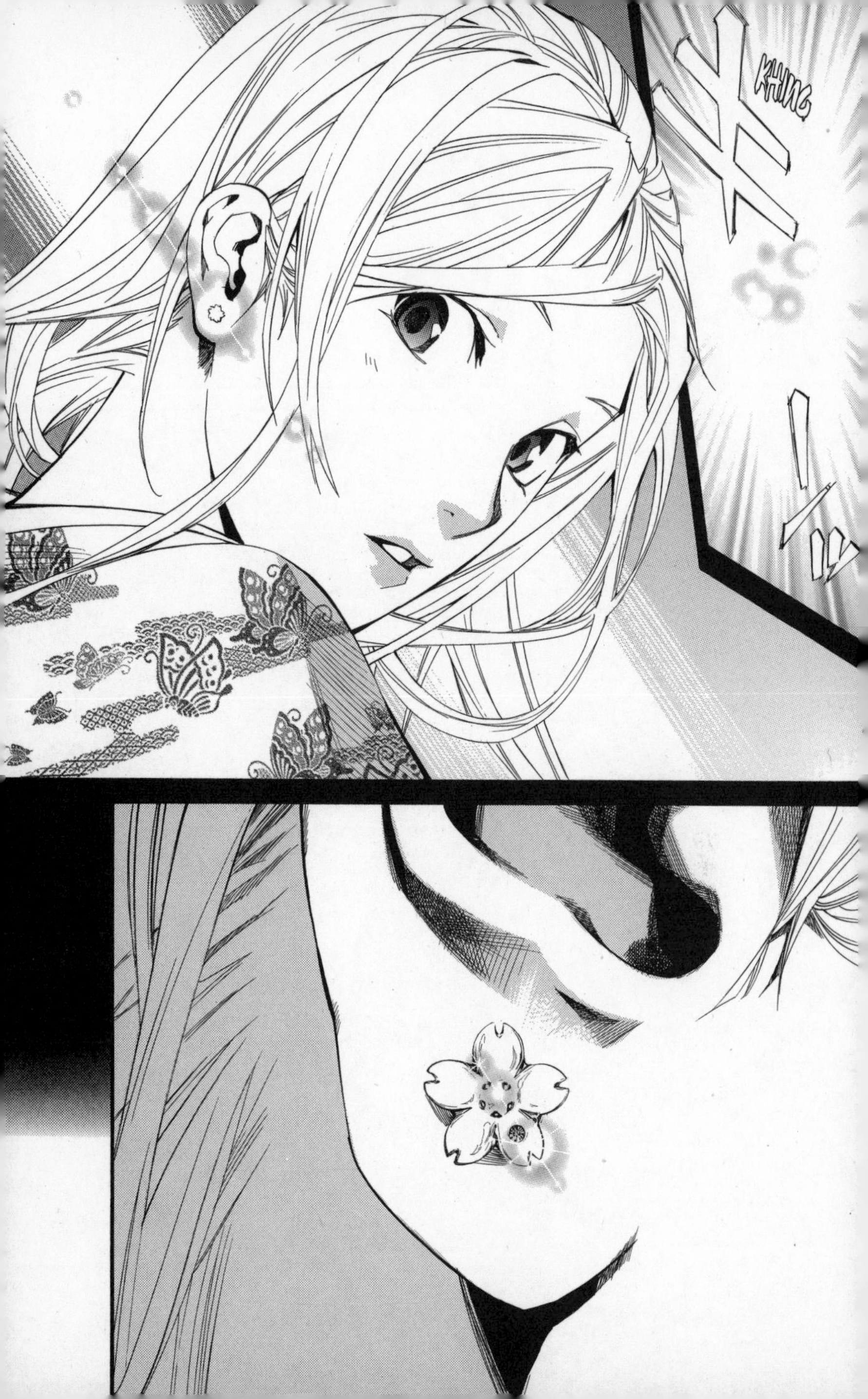
KHING

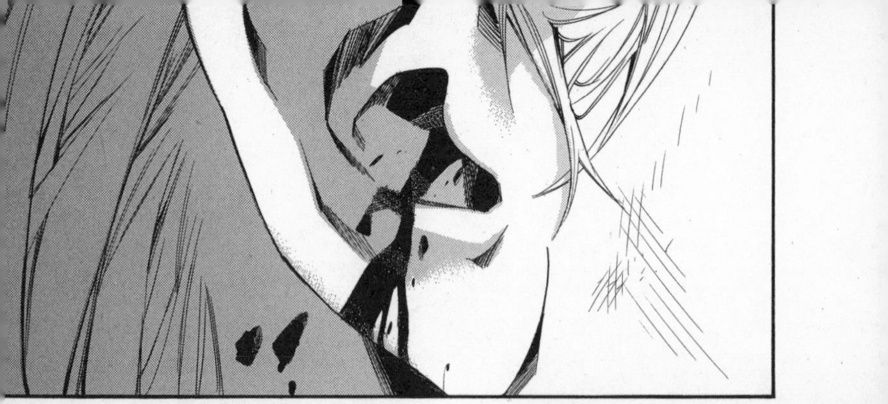

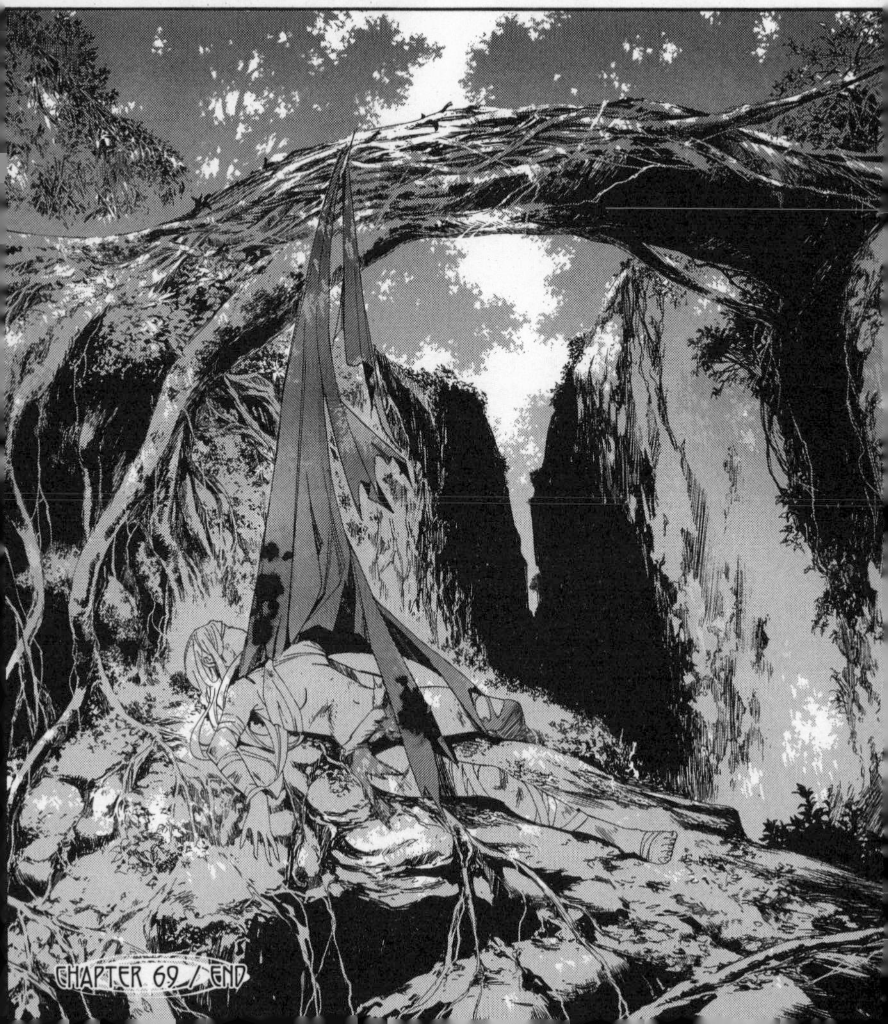
CHAPTER 69 / END

野

是

神

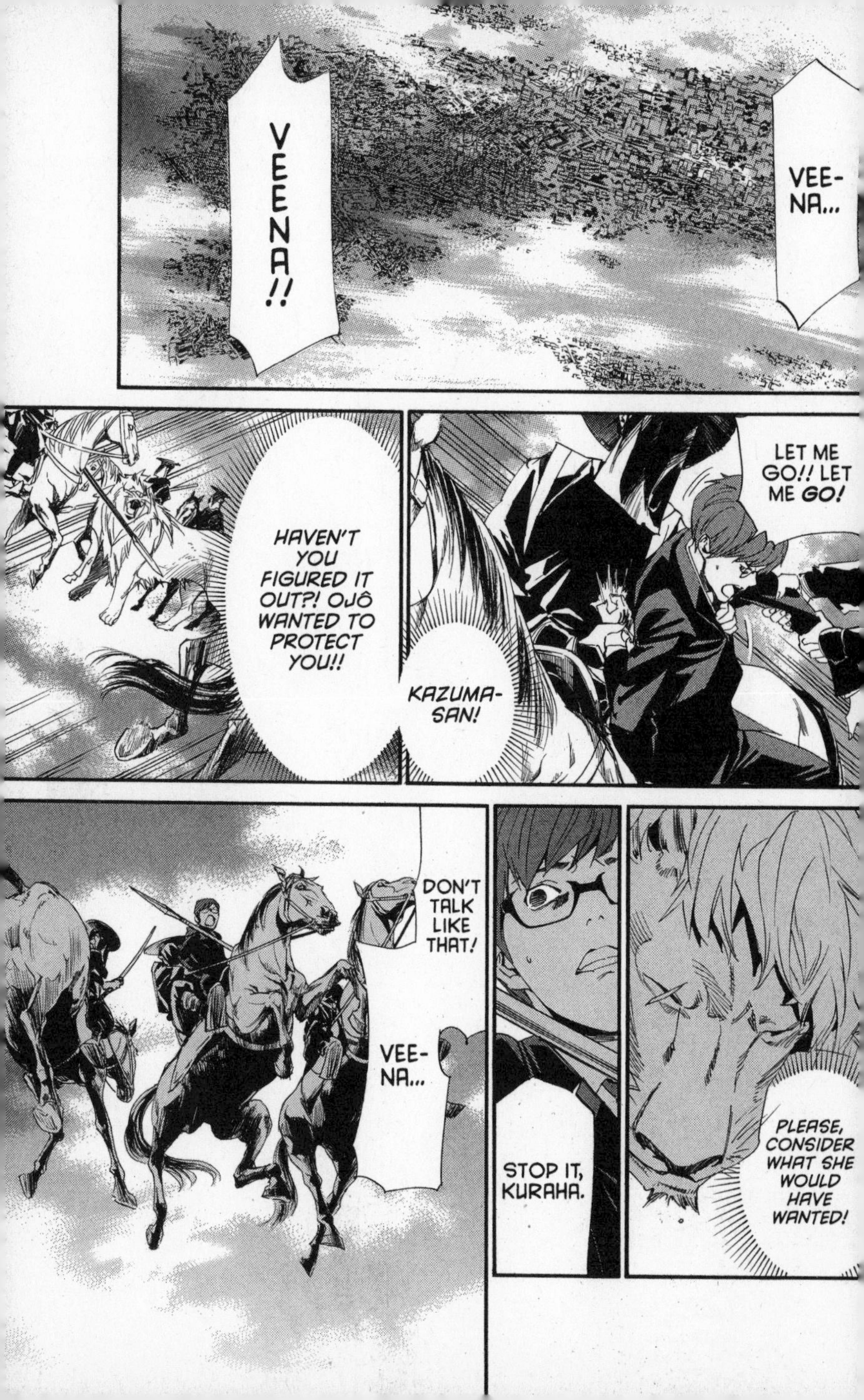
VEE-NA...
VEENA!!
LET ME GO!! LET ME GO!
KAZUMA-SAN!
HAVEN'T YOU FIGURED IT OUT?! OJÔ WANTED TO PROTECT YOU!!
PLEASE, CONSIDER WHAT SHE WOULD HAVE WANTED!
STOP IT, KURAHA.
DON'T TALK LIKE THAT!
VEE-NA...

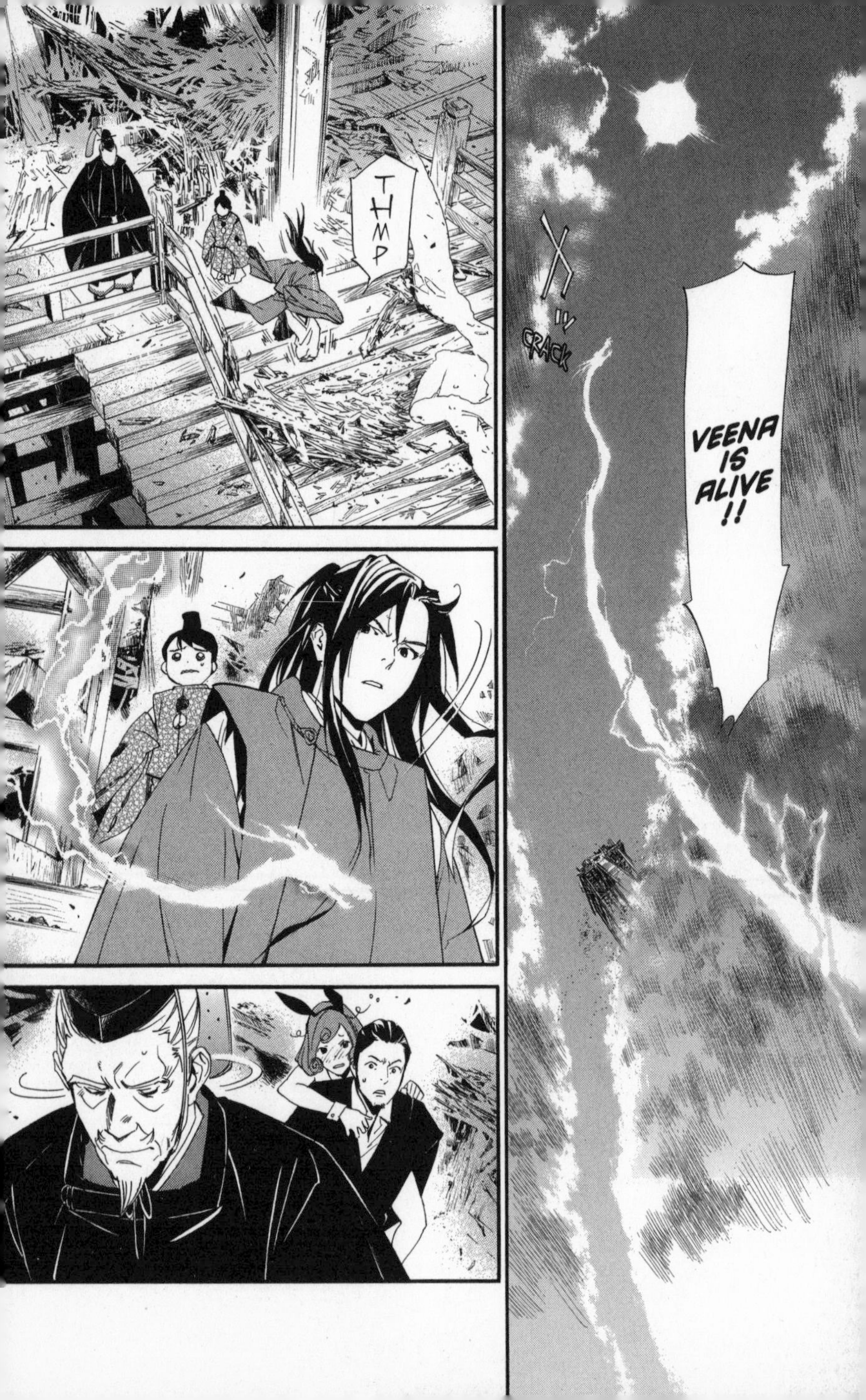
CRACK
VEENA IS ALIVE!!
THMP

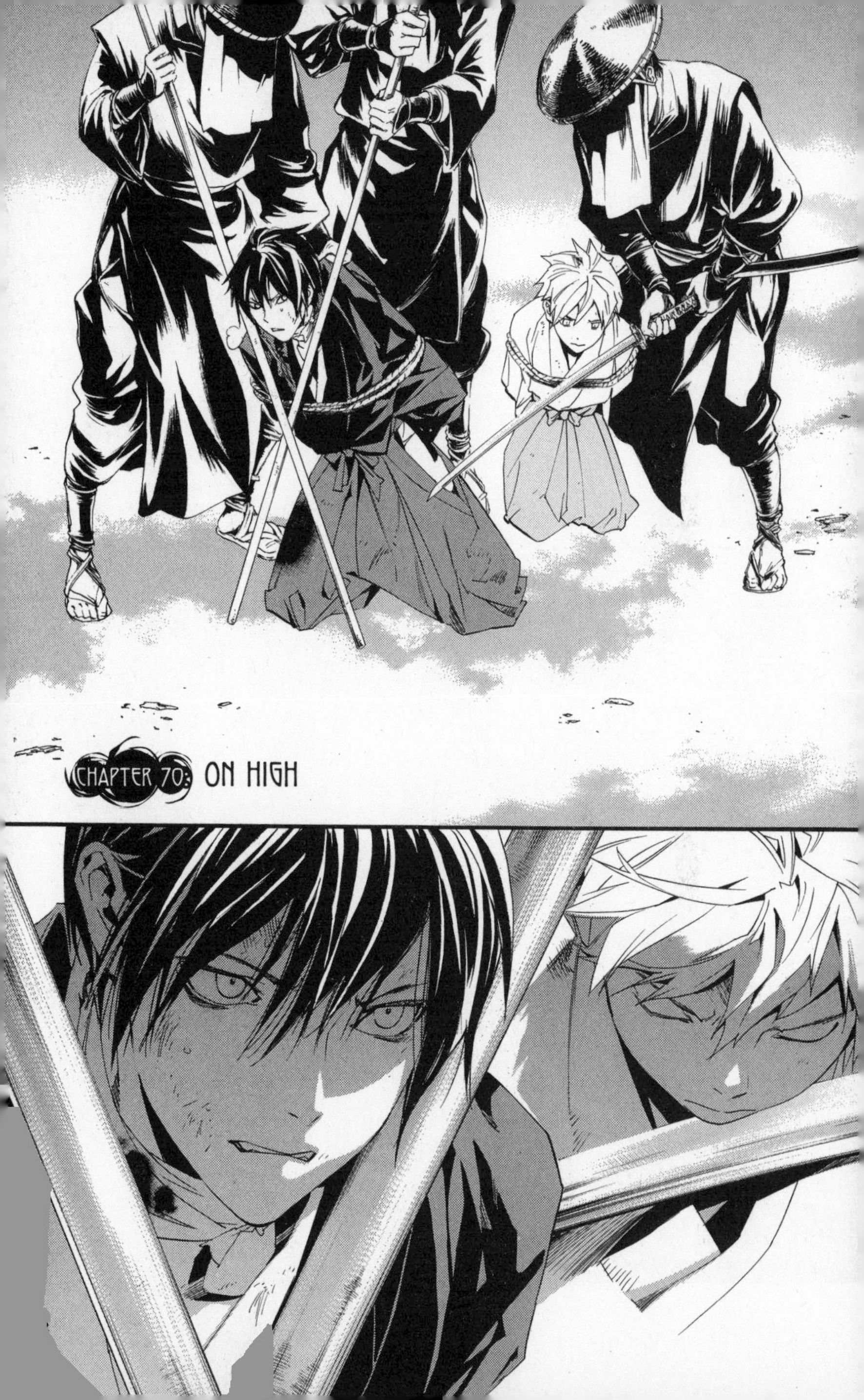
CHAPTER 70: ON HIGH

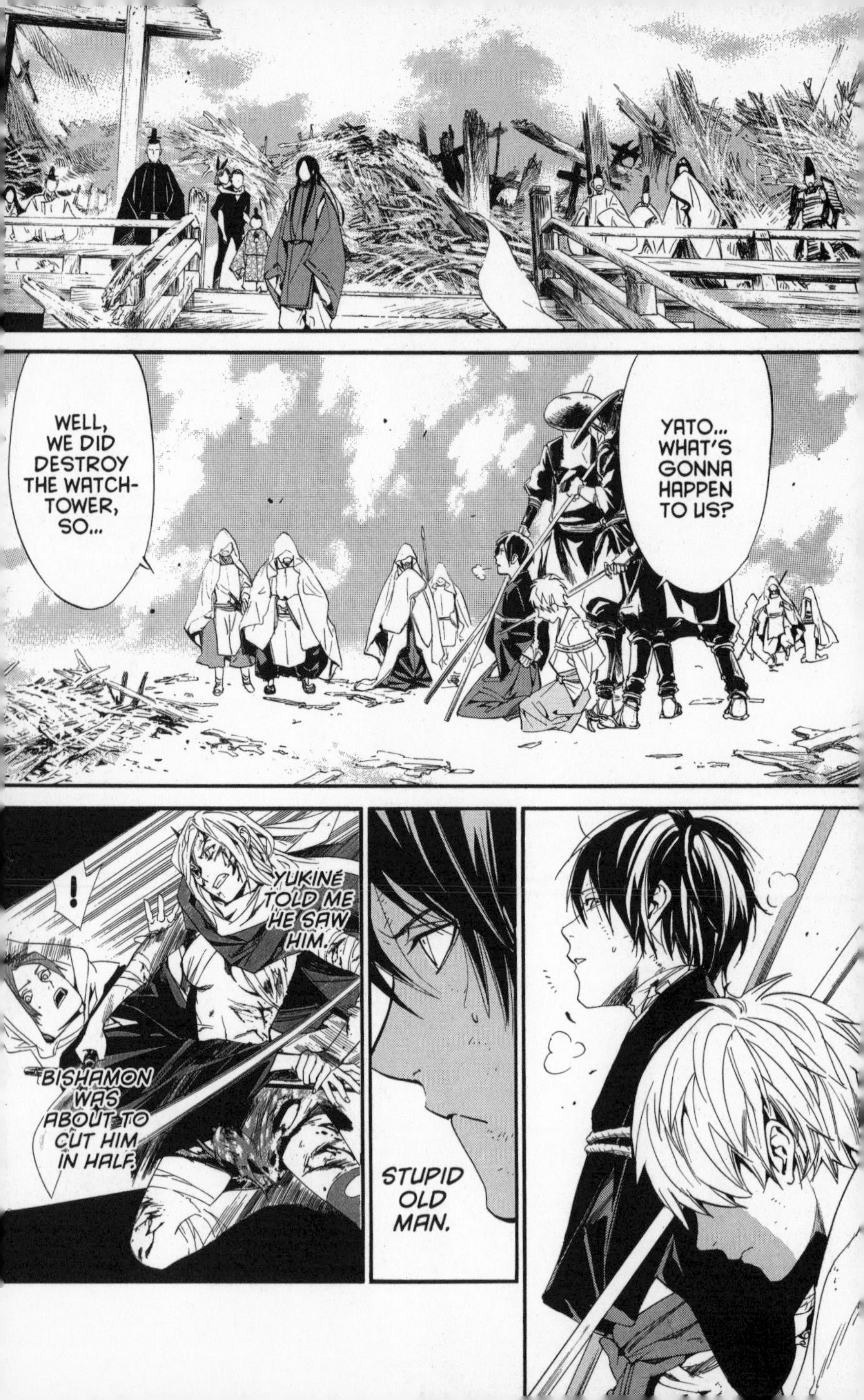
YATO... WHAT'S GONNA HAPPEN TO US?
WELL, WE DID DESTROY THE WATCH-TOWER, SO...
STUPID OLD MAN.
YUKINÉ TOLD ME HE SAW HIM.
!
BISHAMON WAS ABOUT TO CUT HIM IN HALF.

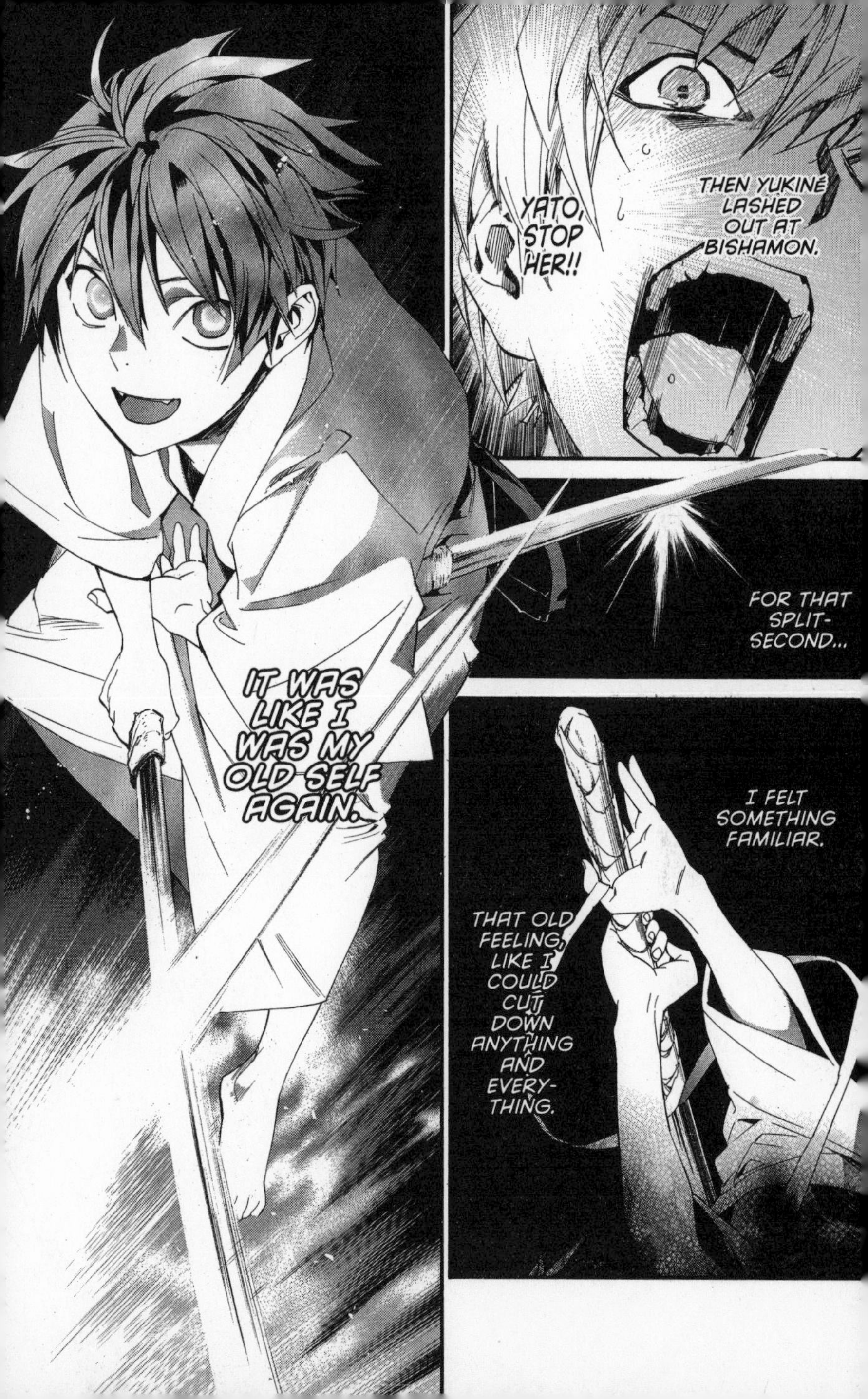
THEN YUKINÉ LASHED OUT AT BISHAMON.
YATO, STOP HER!!
FOR THAT SPLIT-SECOND...
I FELT SOMETHING FAMILIAR.
THAT OLD FEELING, LIKE I COULD CUT DOWN ANYTHING AND EVERY-THING.
IT WAS LIKE I WAS MY OLD SELF AGAIN.

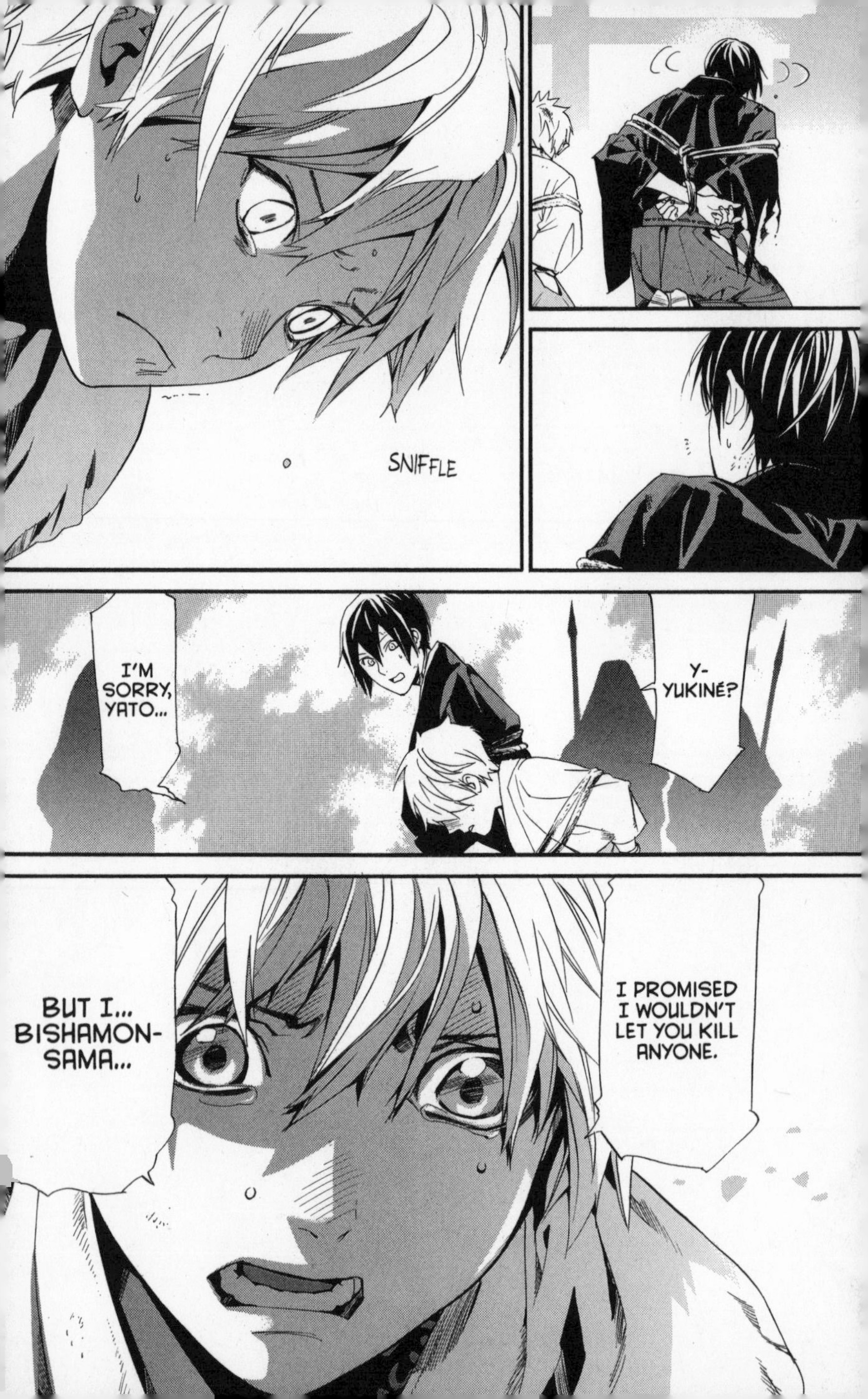
SNIFFLE
Y- YUKINÉ?
I'M SORRY, YATO...
I PROMISED I WOULDN'T LET YOU KILL ANYONE.
BUT I... BISHAMON-SAMA...

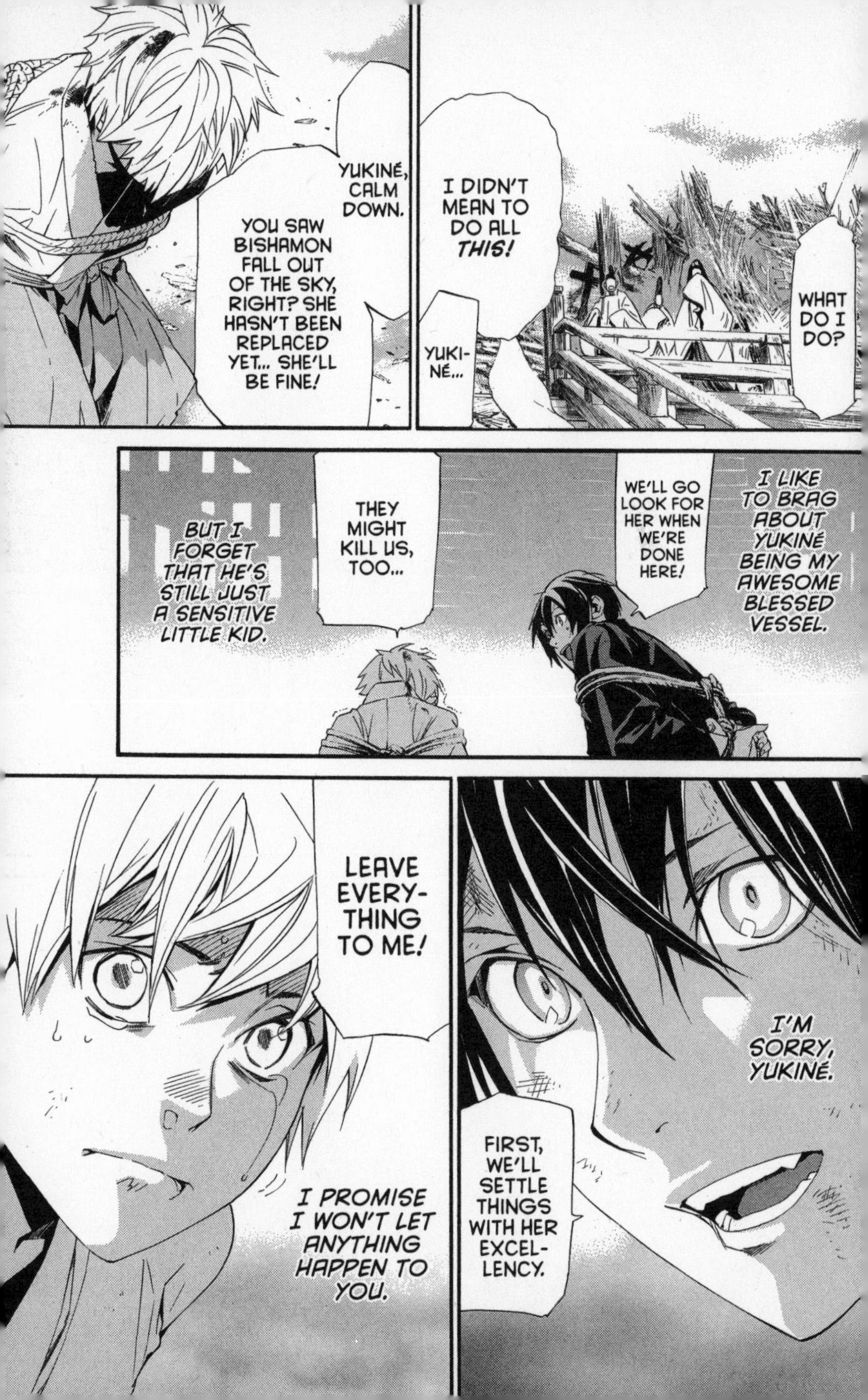
I DIDN'T MEAN TO DO ALL *THIS!*
WHAT DO I DO?
YUKI-NÉ...
YUKINÉ, CALM DOWN.
YOU SAW BISHAMON FALL OUT OF THE SKY, RIGHT? SHE HASN'T BEEN REPLACED YET... SHE'LL BE FINE!
*I LIKE TO BRAG ABOUT YUKINÉ BEING MY AWESOME BLESSED VESSEL.*
WE'LL GO LOOK FOR HER WHEN WE'RE DONE HERE!
THEY MIGHT KILL US, TOO...
*BUT I FORGET THAT HE'S STILL JUST A SENSITIVE LITTLE KID.*
*I'M SORRY, YUKINÉ.*
FIRST, WE'LL SETTLE THINGS WITH HER EXCEL-LENCY.
LEAVE EVERY-THING TO ME!
*I PROMISE I WON'T LET ANYTHING HAPPEN TO YOU.*

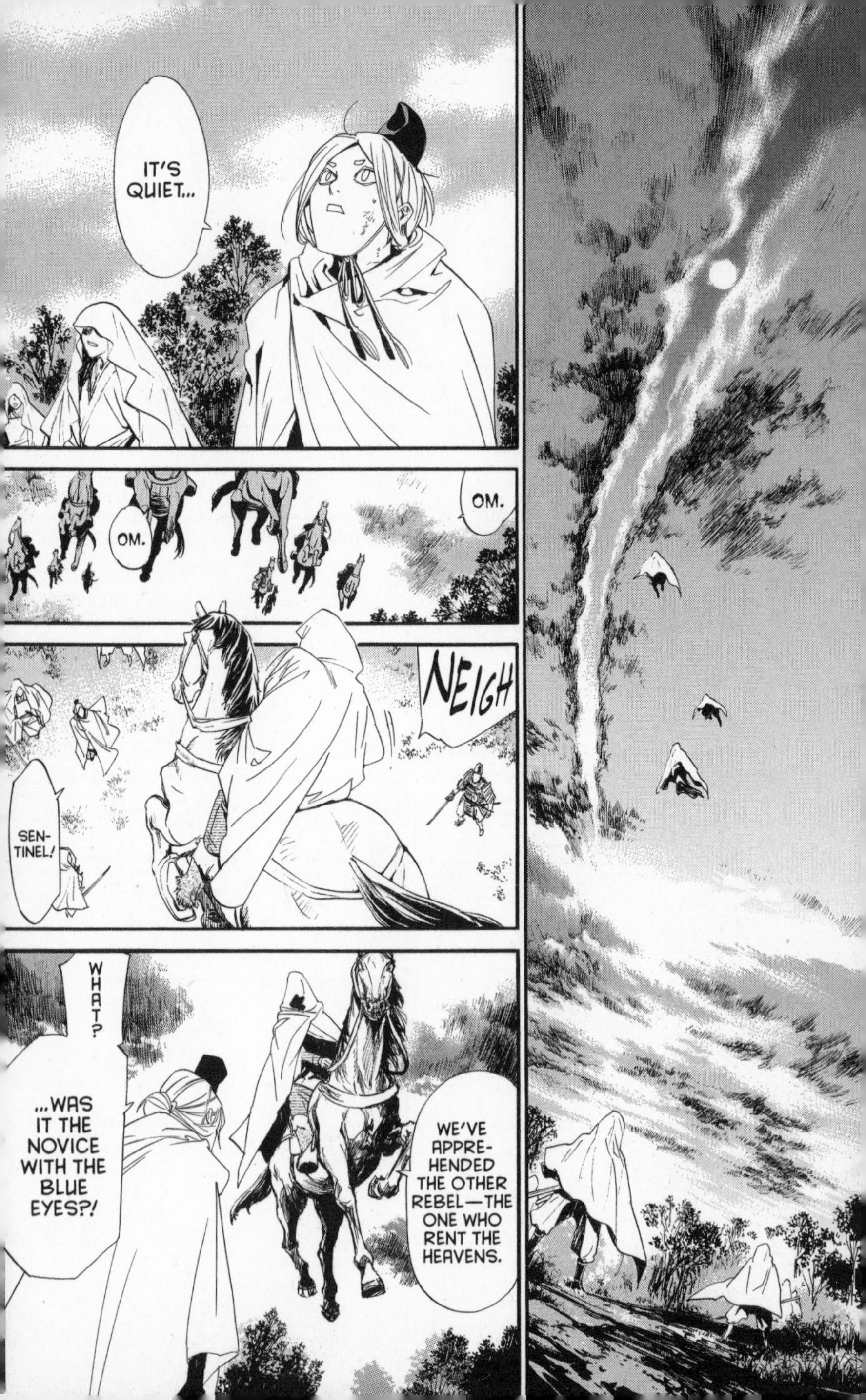
IT'S QUIET...
OM.
OM.
NEIGH
SEN-TINEL!
WE'VE APPRE-HENDED THE OTHER REBEL—THE ONE WHO RENT THE HEAVENS.
WHAT?
...WAS IT THE NOVICE WITH THE BLUE EYES?!

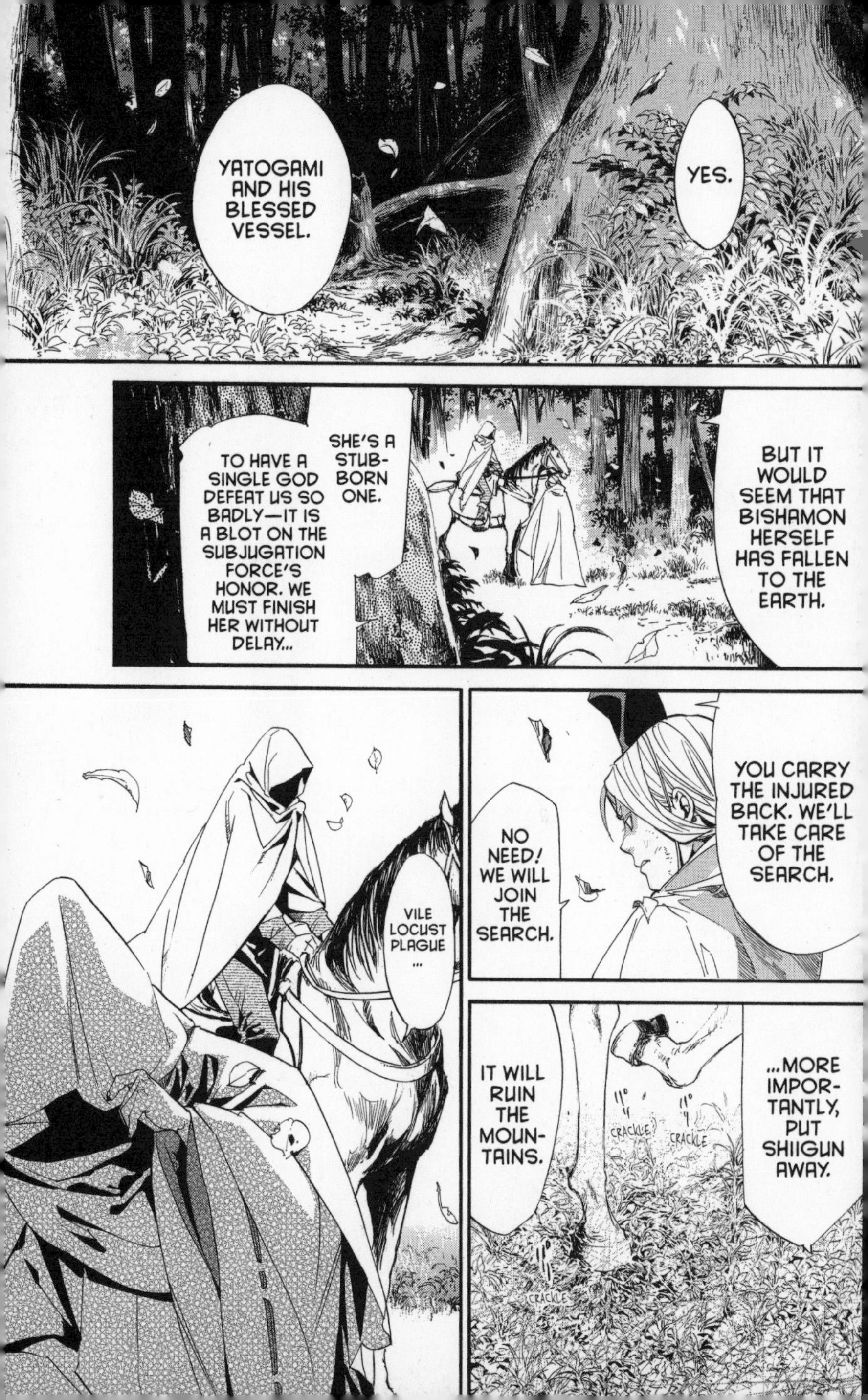
YATOGAMI AND HIS BLESSED VESSEL.
YES.
BUT IT WOULD SEEM THAT BISHAMON HERSELF HAS FALLEN TO THE EARTH.
SHE'S A STUBBORN ONE.
TO HAVE A SINGLE GOD DEFEAT US SO BADLY—IT IS A BLOT ON THE SUBJUGATION FORCE'S HONOR. WE MUST FINISH HER WITHOUT DELAY...
YOU CARRY THE INJURED BACK. WE'LL TAKE CARE OF THE SEARCH.
NO NEED! WE WILL JOIN THE SEARCH.
...MORE IMPORTANTLY, PUT SHIIGUN AWAY.
IT WILL RUIN THE MOUNTAINS.
CRACKLE
CRACKLE
CRACKLE
VILE LOCUST PLAGUE ...

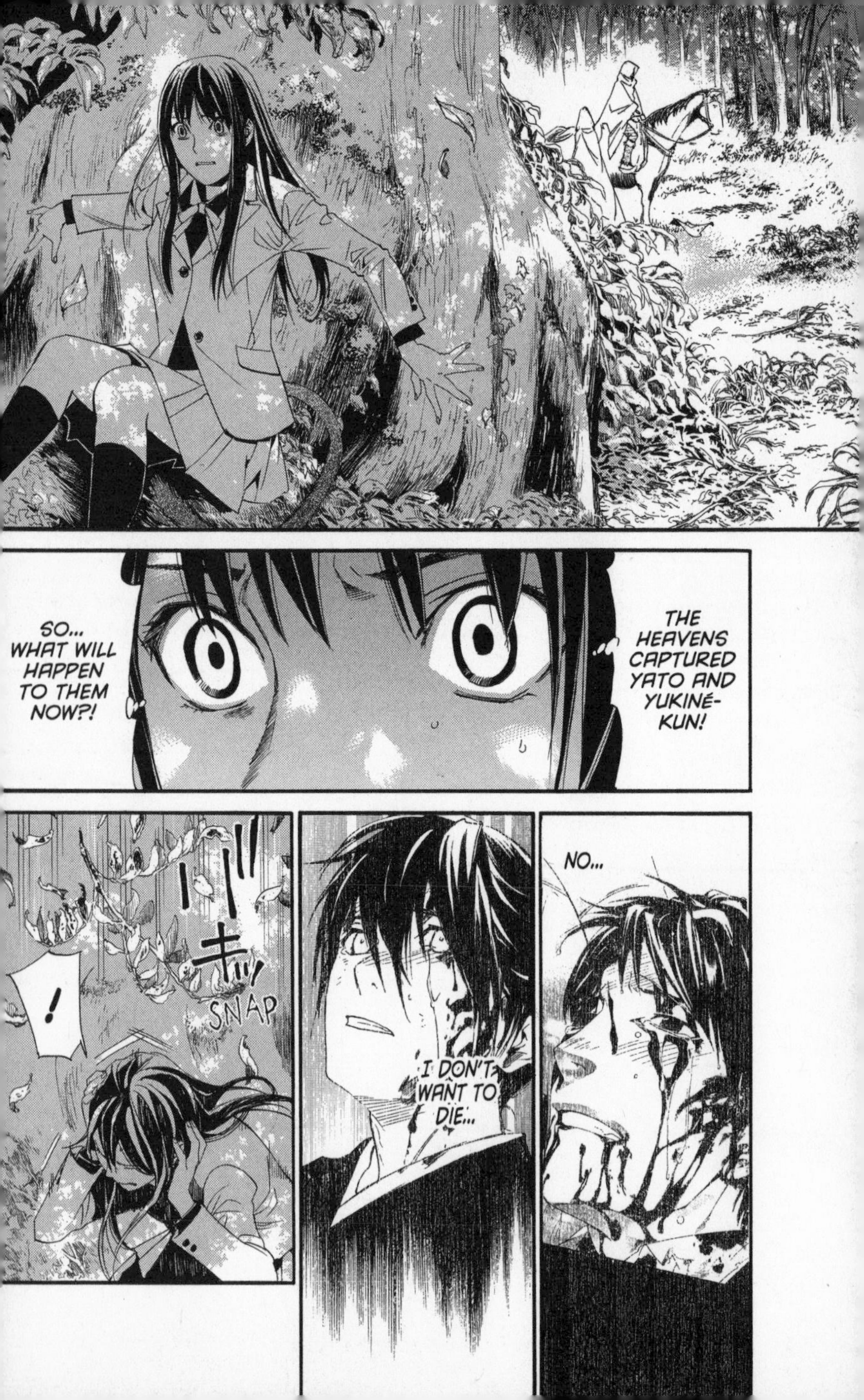
THE HEAVENS CAPTURED YATO AND YUKINÉ-KUN!
SO... WHAT WILL HAPPEN TO THEM NOW?!
NO...
I DON'T WANT TO DIE...
SNAP
!

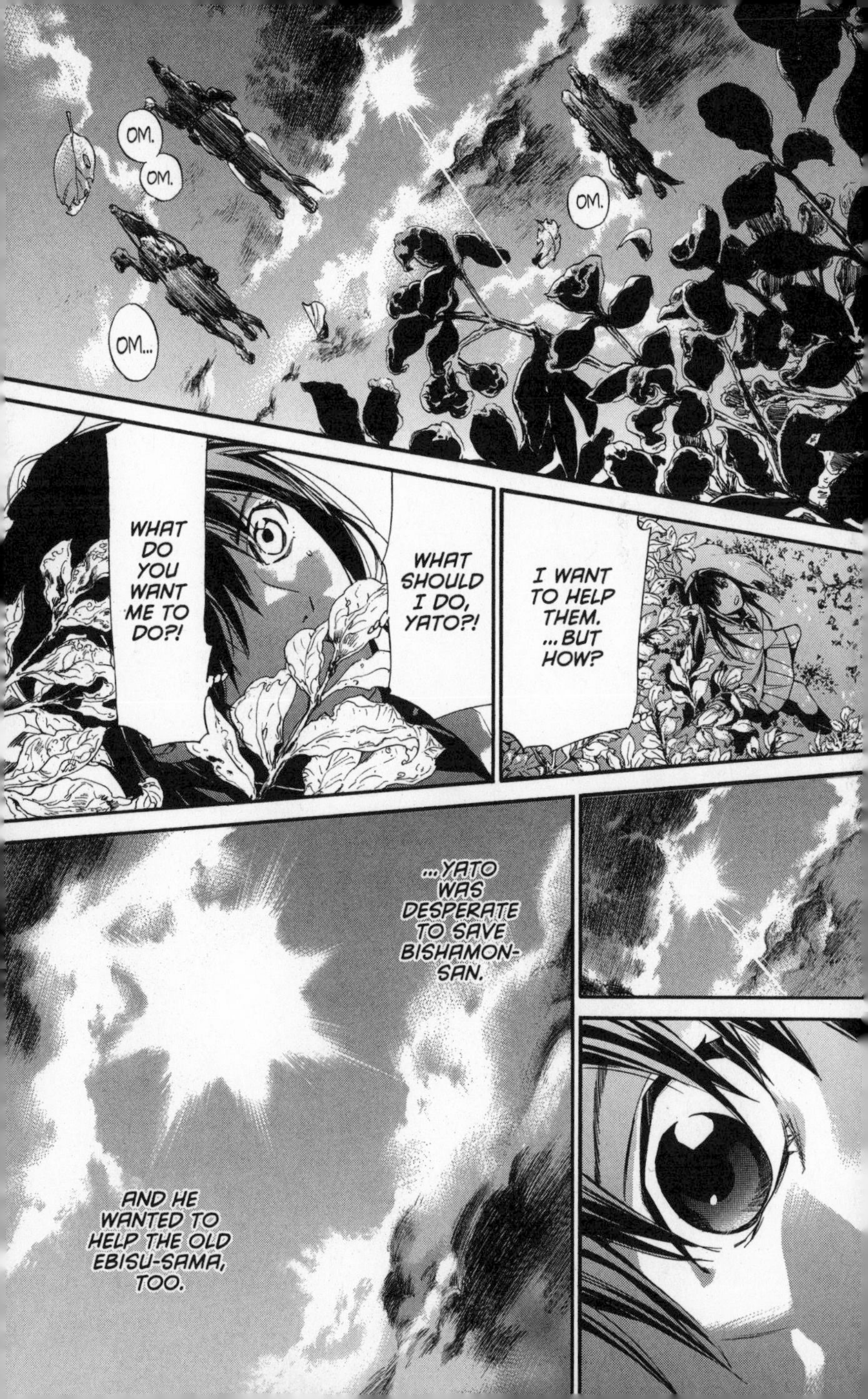
OM.
OM.
OM.
OM...
I WANT TO HELP THEM. ...BUT HOW?
WHAT SHOULD I DO, YATO?!
WHAT DO YOU WANT ME TO DO?!
...YATO WAS DESPERATE TO SAVE BISHAMON-SAN.
AND HE WANTED TO HELP THE OLD EBISU-SAMA, TOO.

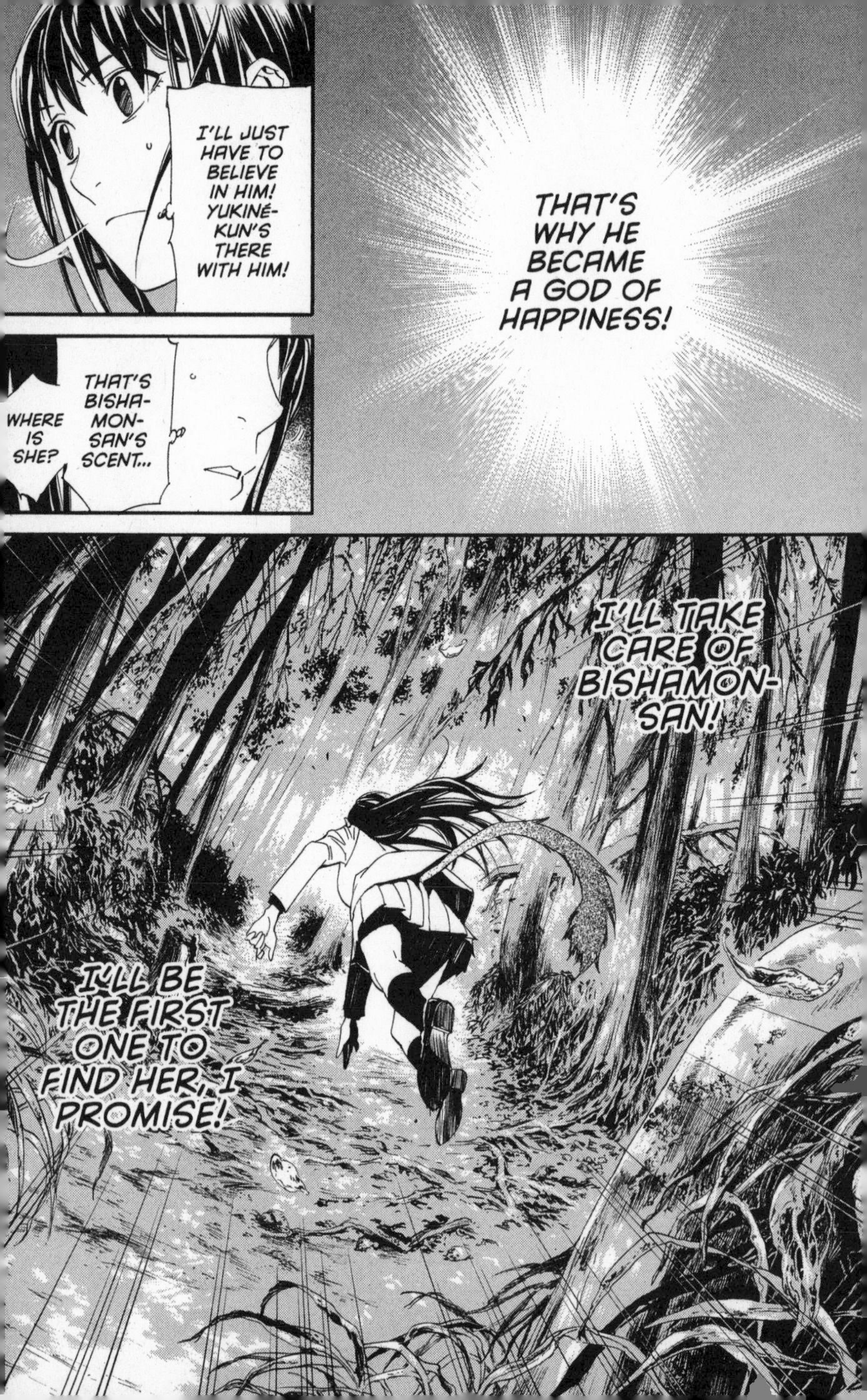
THAT'S WHY HE BECAME A GOD OF HAPPINESS!
I'LL JUST HAVE TO BELIEVE IN HIM! YUKINÉ-KUN'S THERE WITH HIM!
THAT'S BISHAMON-SAN'S SCENT...
WHERE IS SHE?
I'LL TAKE CARE OF BISHAMON-SAN!
I'LL BE THE FIRST ONE TO FIND HER, I PROMISE!

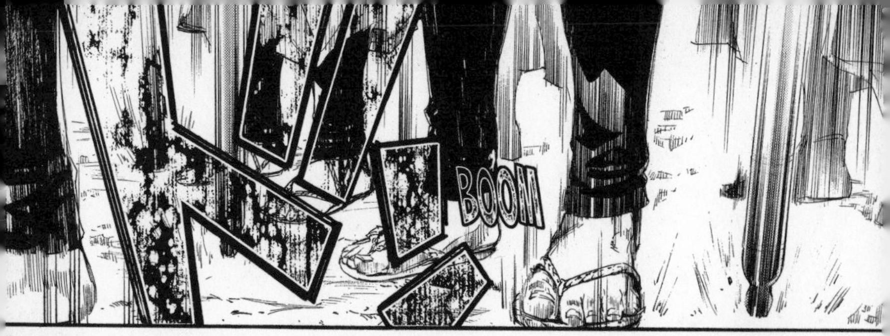
BOOM
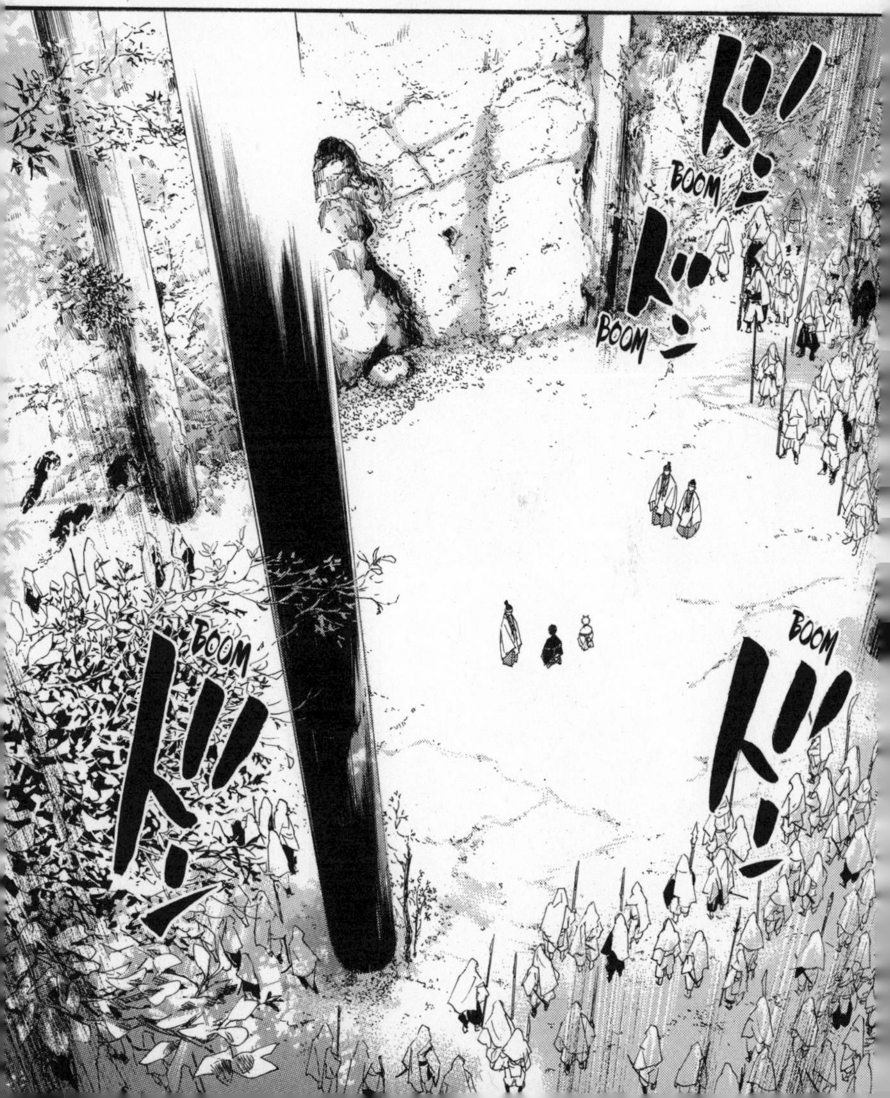
BOOM
BOOM
BOOM
BOOM

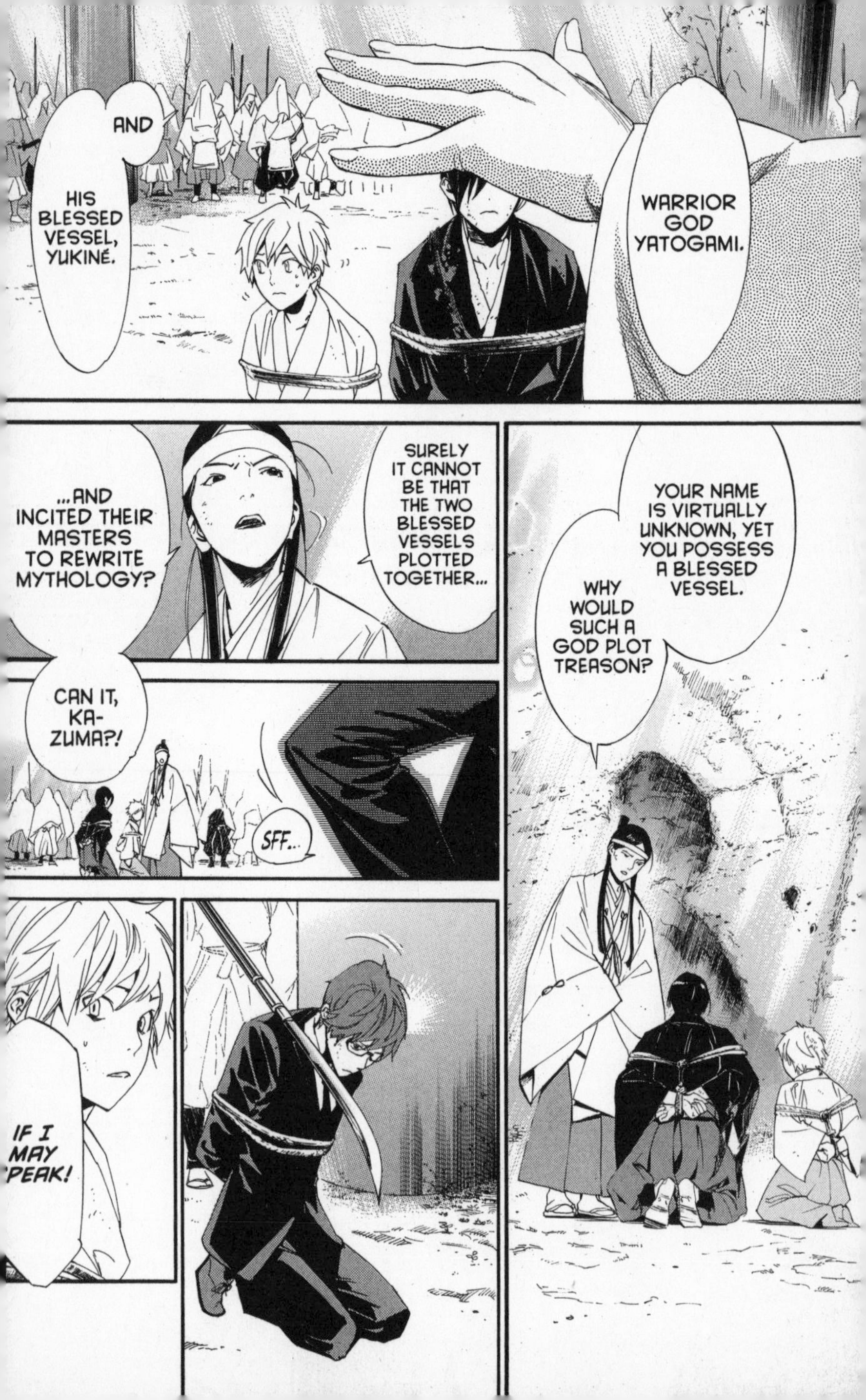
WARRIOR GOD YATOGAMI.
AND
HIS BLESSED VESSEL, YUKINÉ.
YOUR NAME IS VIRTUALLY UNKNOWN, YET YOU POSSESS A BLESSED VESSEL.
WHY WOULD SUCH A GOD PLOT TREASON?
SURELY IT CANNOT BE THAT THE TWO BLESSED VESSELS PLOTTED TOGETHER...
...AND INCITED THEIR MASTERS TO REWRITE MYTHOLOGY?
SFF...
CAN IT, KA-ZUMA?!
IF I MAY PEAK!

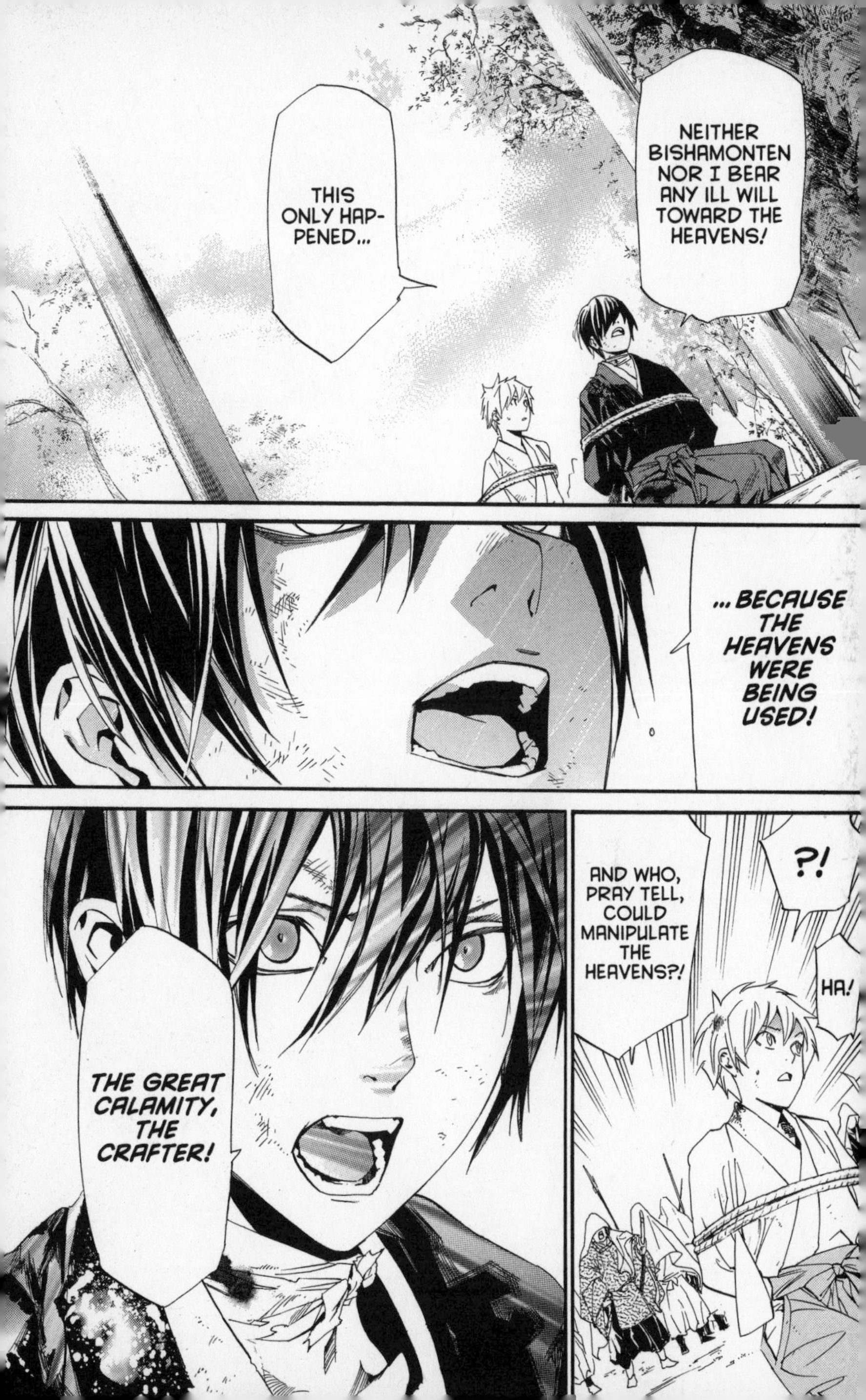
NEITHER BISHAMONTEN NOR I BEAR ANY ILL WILL TOWARD THE HEAVENS!
THIS ONLY HAP-PENED...
...BECAUSE THE HEAVENS WERE BEING USED!
?!
AND WHO, PRAY TELL, COULD MANIPULATE THE HEAVENS?!
HA!
THE GREAT CALAMITY, THE CRAFTER!

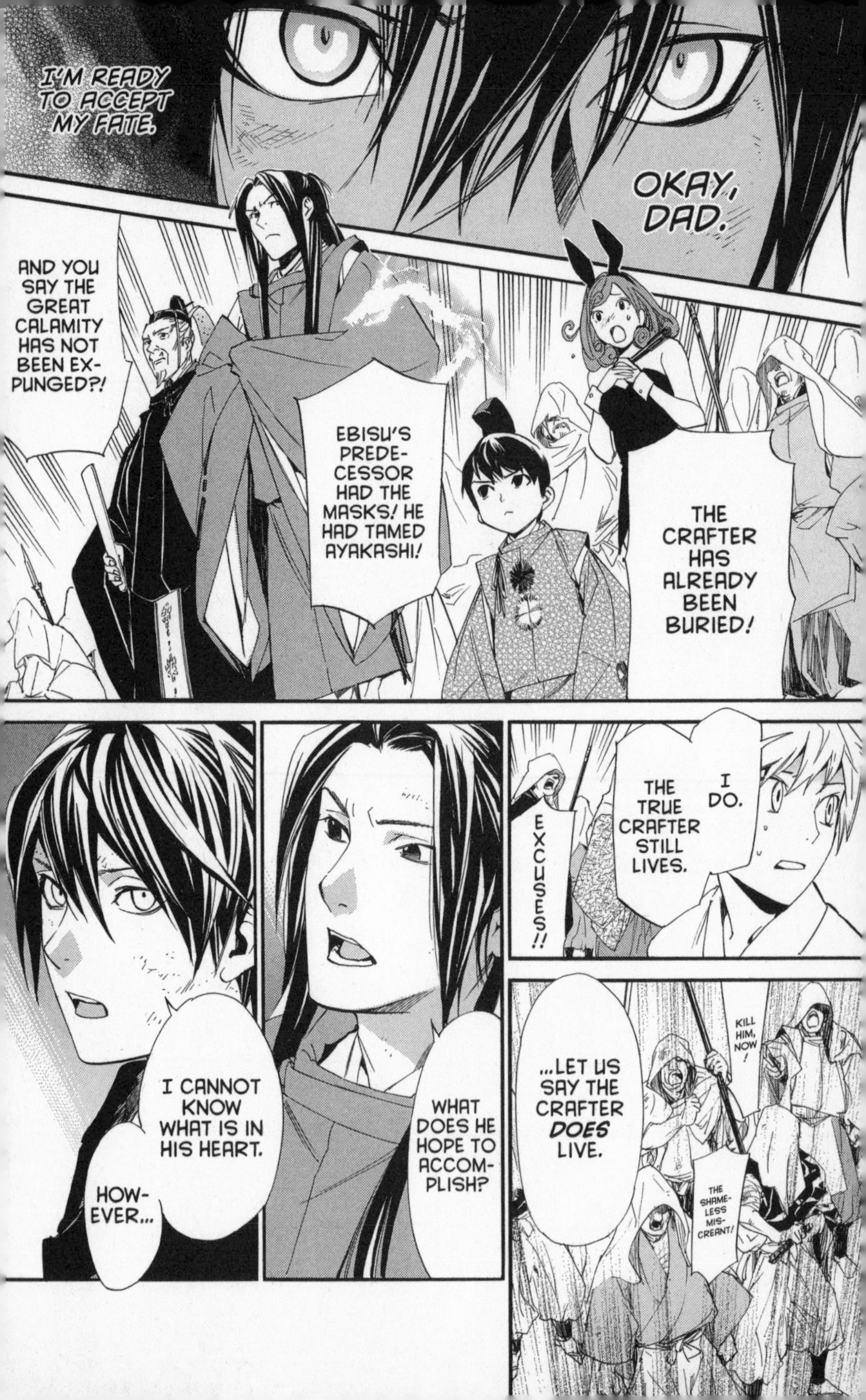
OKAY, DAD.
I'M READY TO ACCEPT MY FATE.
THE CRAFTER HAS ALREADY BEEN BURIED!
EBISU'S PREDECESSOR HAD THE MASKS! HE HAD TAMED AYAKASHI!
AND YOU SAY THE GREAT CALAMITY HAS NOT BEEN EXPUNGED?!
I DO.
THE TRUE CRAFTER STILL LIVES.
EXCUSES!!
...LET US SAY THE CRAFTER *DOES* LIVE.
KILL HIM, NOW!
THE SHAMELESS MISCREANT!
WHAT DOES HE HOPE TO ACCOMPLISH?
I CANNOT KNOW WHAT IS IN HIS HEART.
HOWEVER...

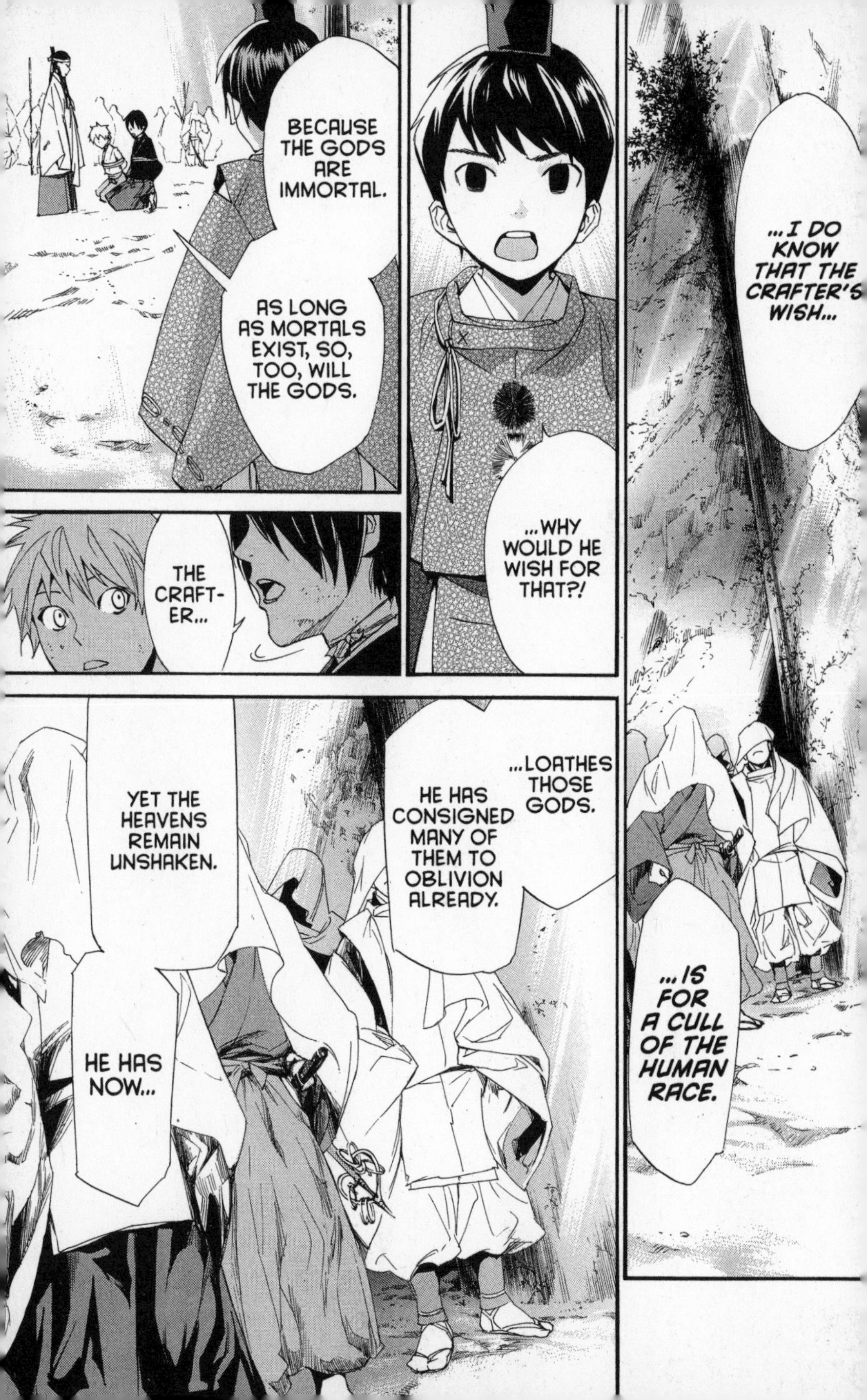
...I DO KNOW THAT THE CRAFTER'S WISH...
...IS FOR A CULL OF THE HUMAN RACE.
...WHY WOULD HE WISH FOR THAT?!
BECAUSE THE GODS ARE IMMORTAL.
AS LONG AS MORTALS EXIST, SO, TOO, WILL THE GODS.
THE CRAFTER...
...LOATHES THOSE GODS.
HE HAS CONSIGNED MANY OF THEM TO OBLIVION ALREADY.
YET THE HEAVENS REMAIN UNSHAKEN.
HE HAS NOW...

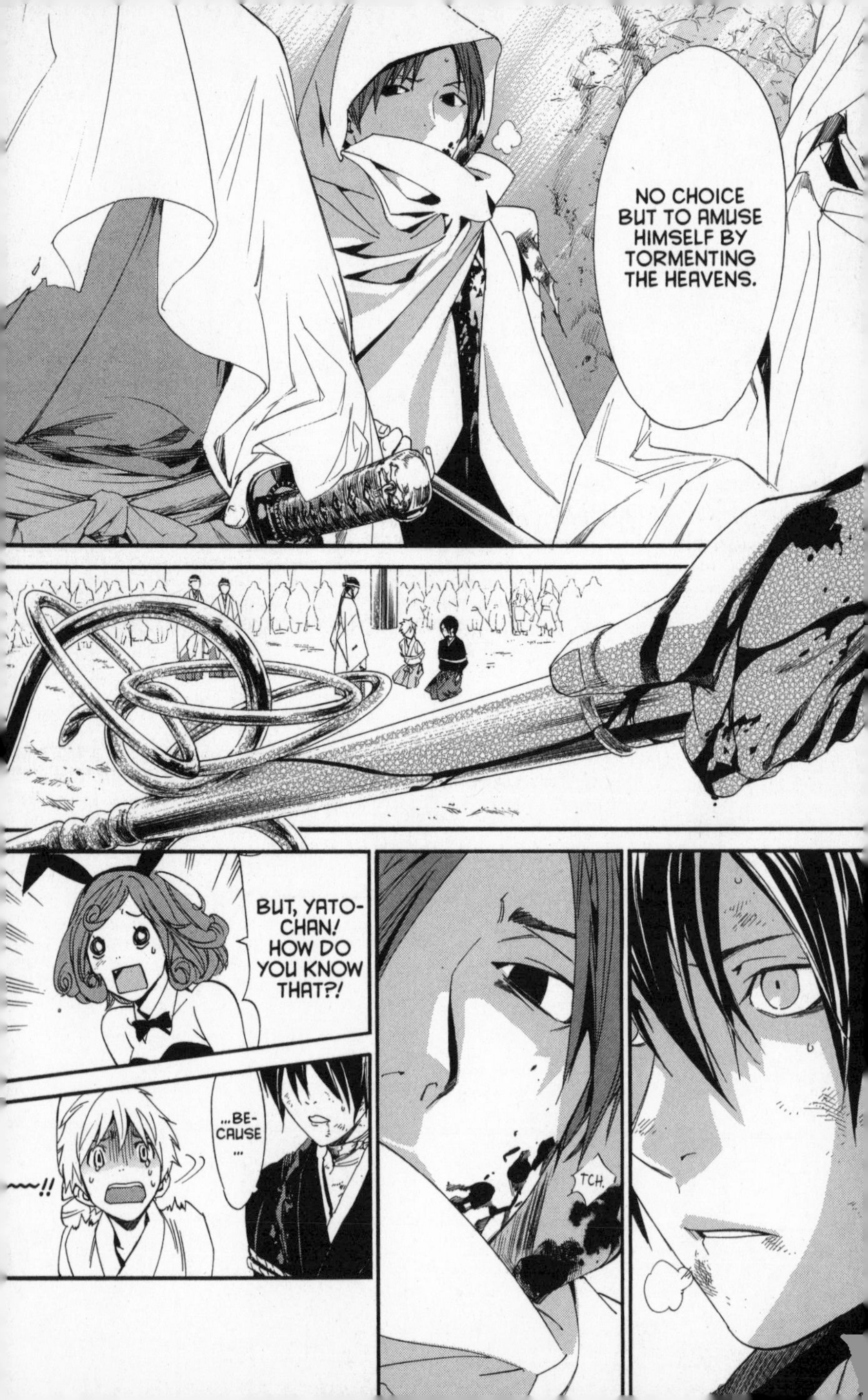
NO CHOICE BUT TO AMUSE HIMSELF BY TORMENTING THE HEAVENS.
TCH.
BUT, YATO-CHAN! HOW DO YOU KNOW THAT?!
...BE-CAUSE ...
~~!!

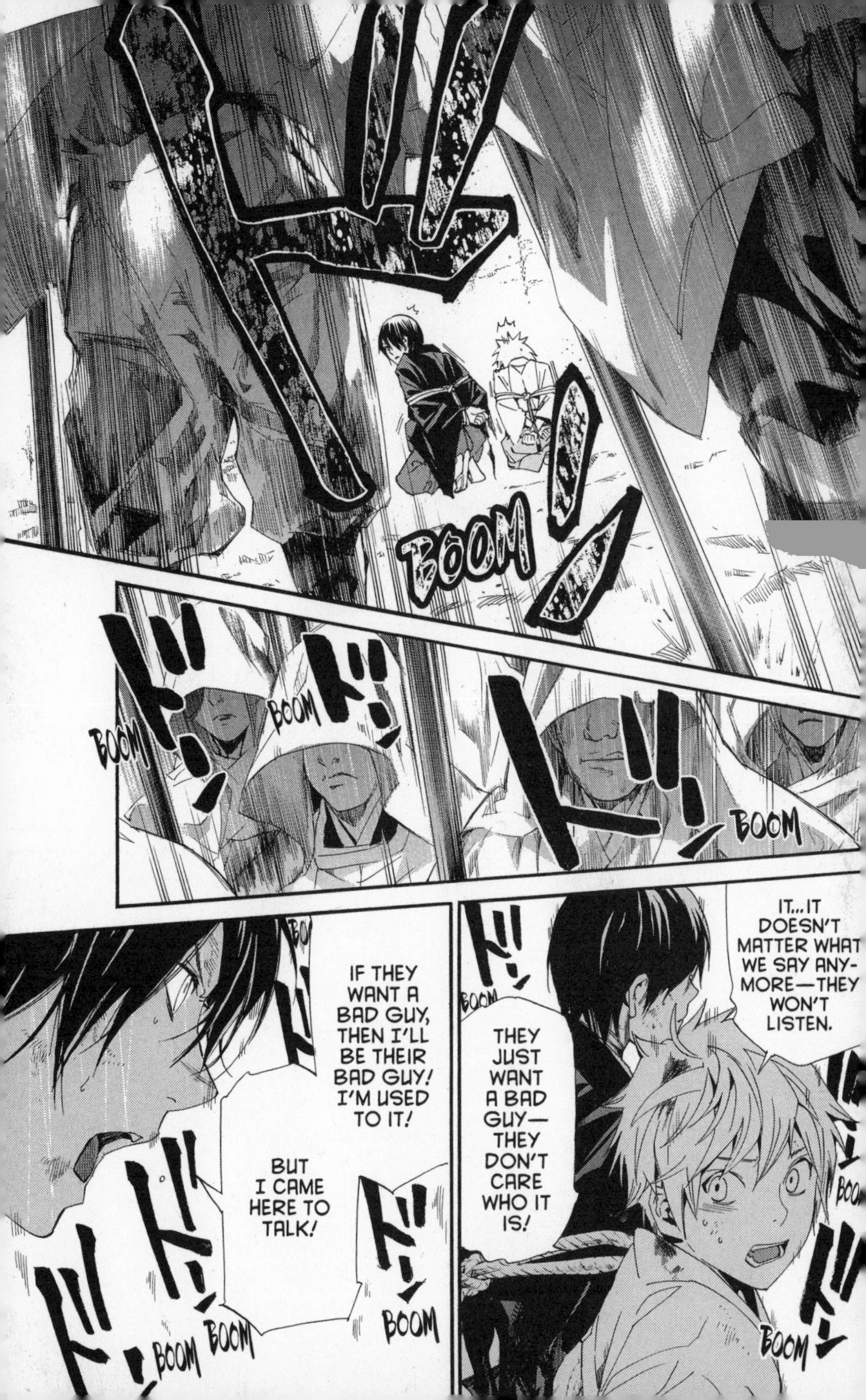
BOOM
BOOM
BOOM
BOOM
BOOM
IT...IT DOESN'T MATTER WHAT WE SAY ANY-MORE—THEY WON'T LISTEN.
THEY JUST WANT A BAD GUY—THEY DON'T CARE WHO IT IS!
BOOM
BOOM
BOOM
IF THEY WANT A BAD GUY, THEN I'LL BE THEIR BAD GUY! I'M USED TO IT!
BUT I CAME HERE TO TALK!
BOOM
BOOM
BOOM

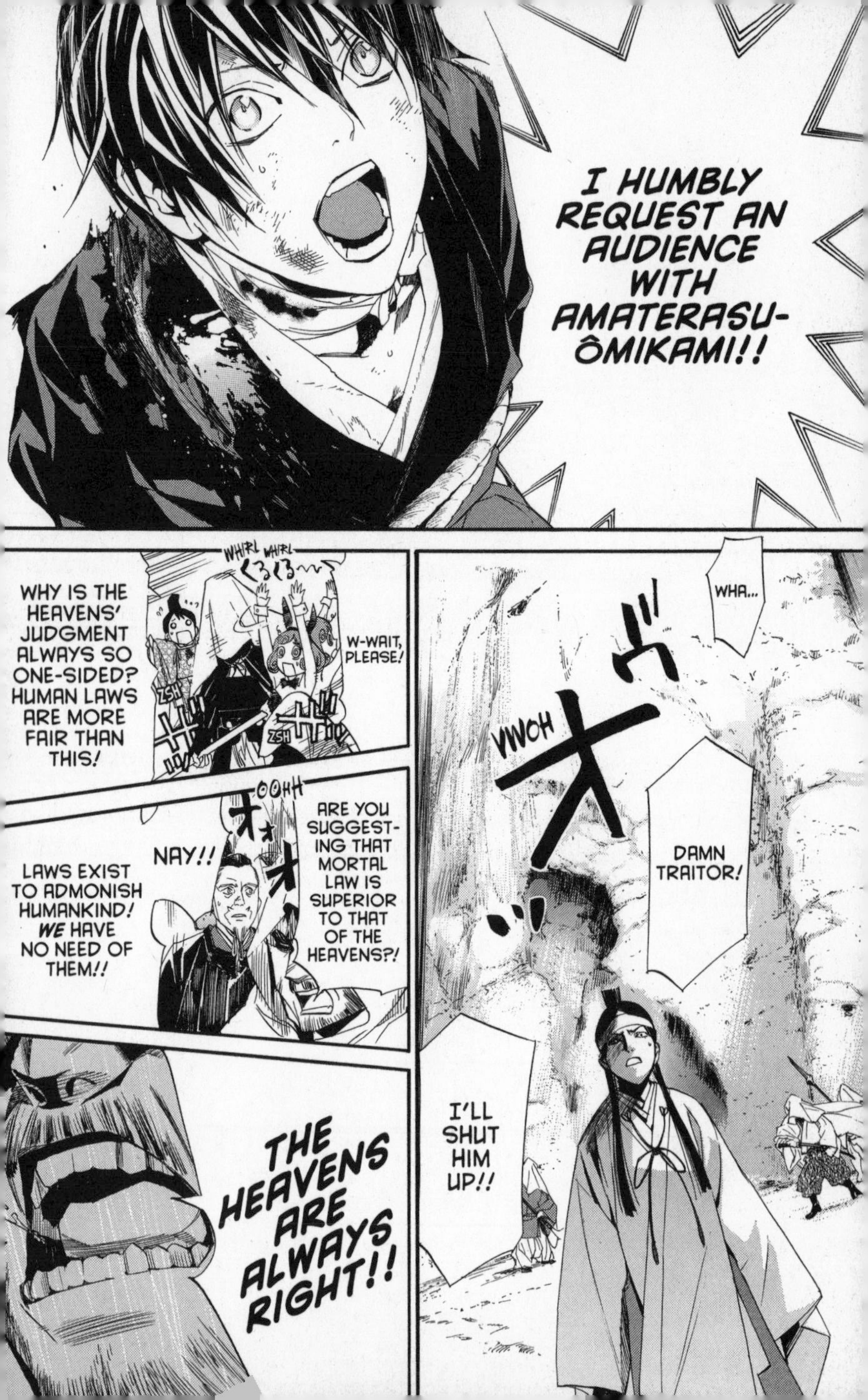
I HUMBLY REQUEST AN AUDIENCE WITH AMATERASU-ÔMIKAMI!!
WHA...
VVVOH
DAMN TRAITOR!
I'LL SHUT HIM UP!!
WHIRL WHIRL
くるくる
W-WAIT, PLEASE!
WHY IS THE HEAVENS' JUDGMENT ALWAYS SO ONE-SIDED? HUMAN LAWS ARE MORE FAIR THAN THIS!
ZSH
ZSH
OOHH
ARE YOU SUGGESTING THAT MORTAL LAW IS SUPERIOR TO THAT OF THE HEAVENS?!
NAY!!
LAWS EXIST TO ADMONISH HUMANKIND! WE HAVE NO NEED OF THEM!!
THE HEAVENS ARE ALWAYS RIGHT!!

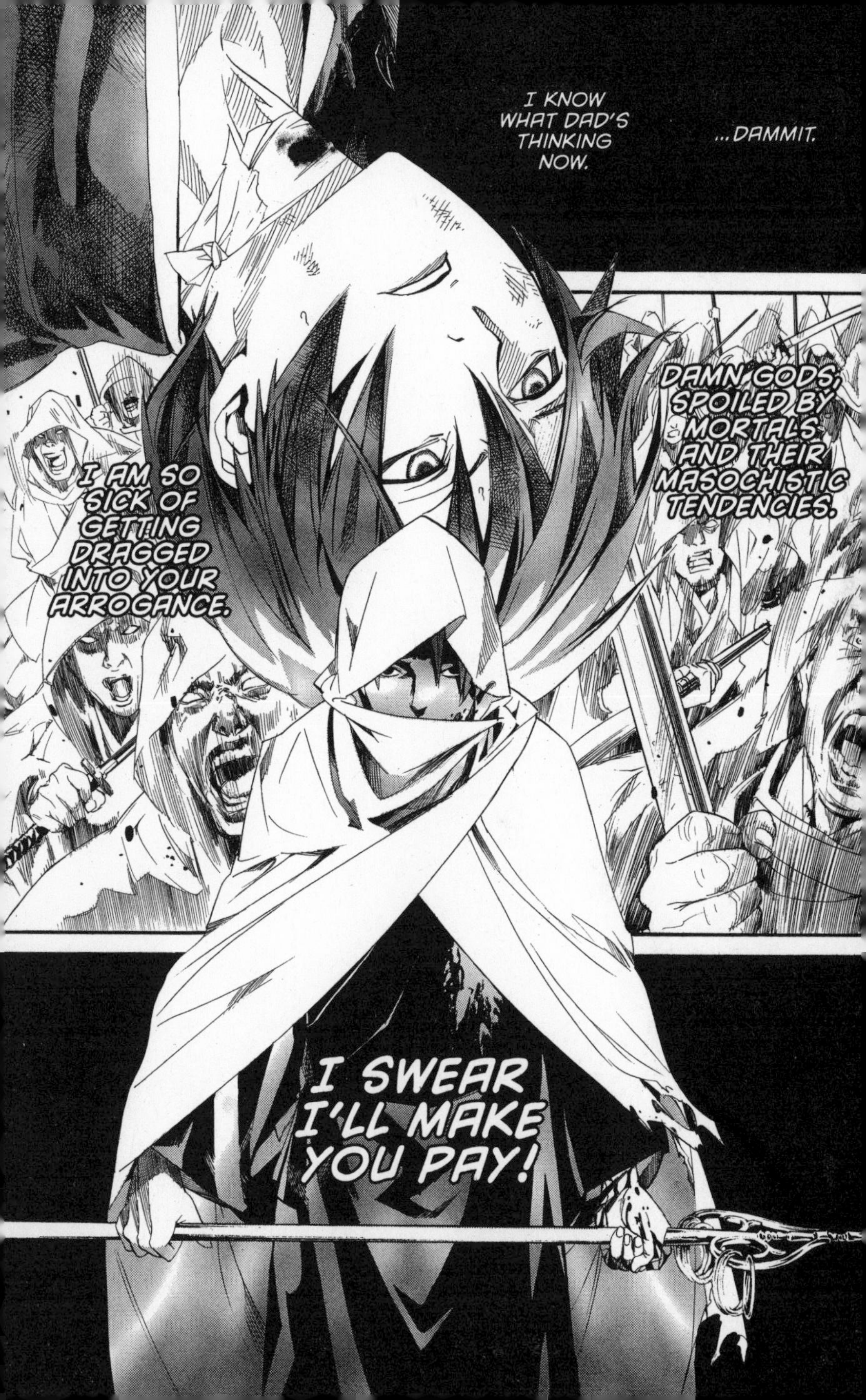
I KNOW WHAT DAD'S THINKING NOW.
...DAMMIT.
DAMN GODS, SPOILED BY MORTALS AND THEIR MASOCHISTIC TENDENCIES.
I AM SO SICK OF GETTING DRAGGED INTO YOUR ARROGANCE.
I SWEAR I'LL MAKE YOU PAY!

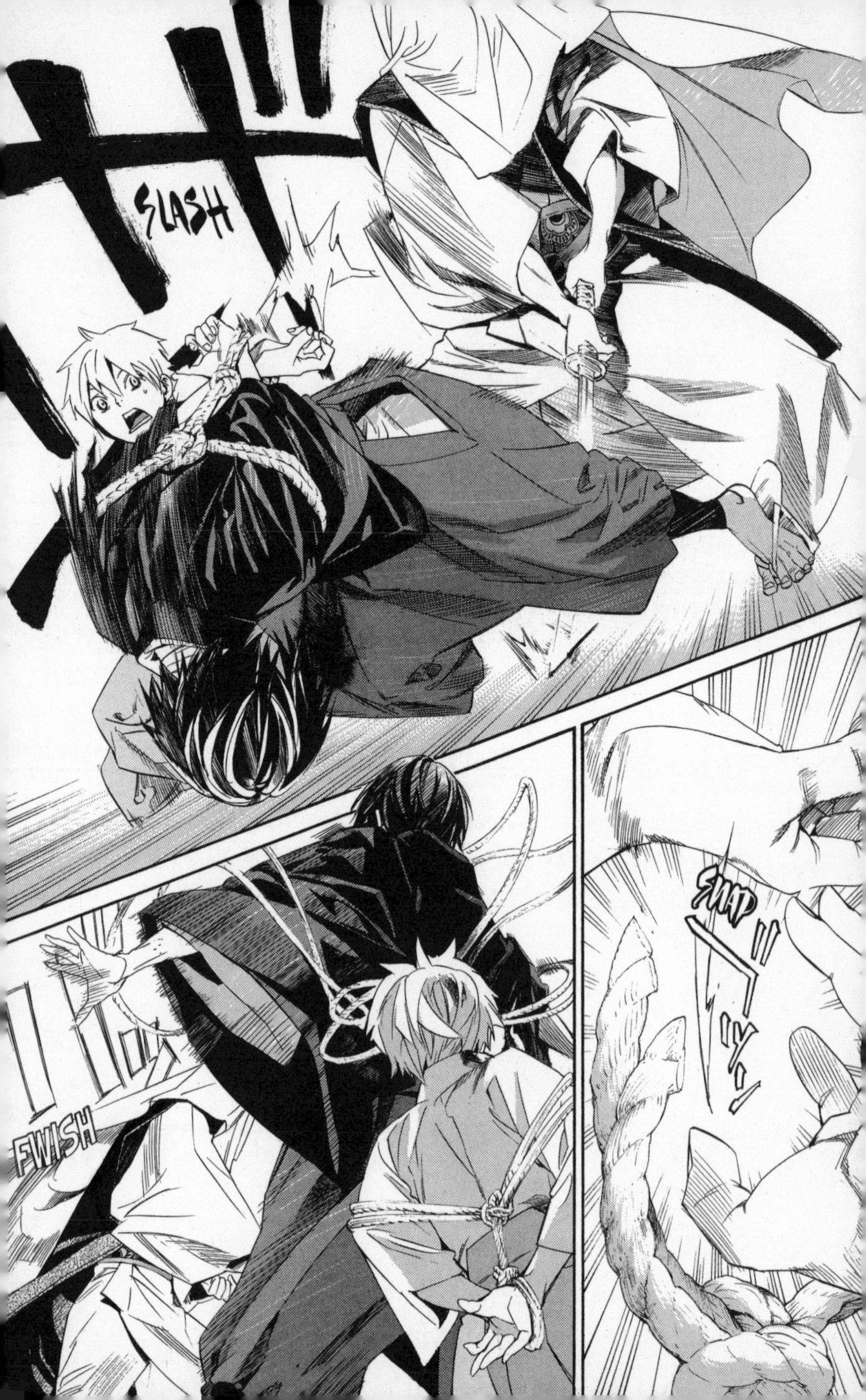
SLASH
SNAP
FWISH

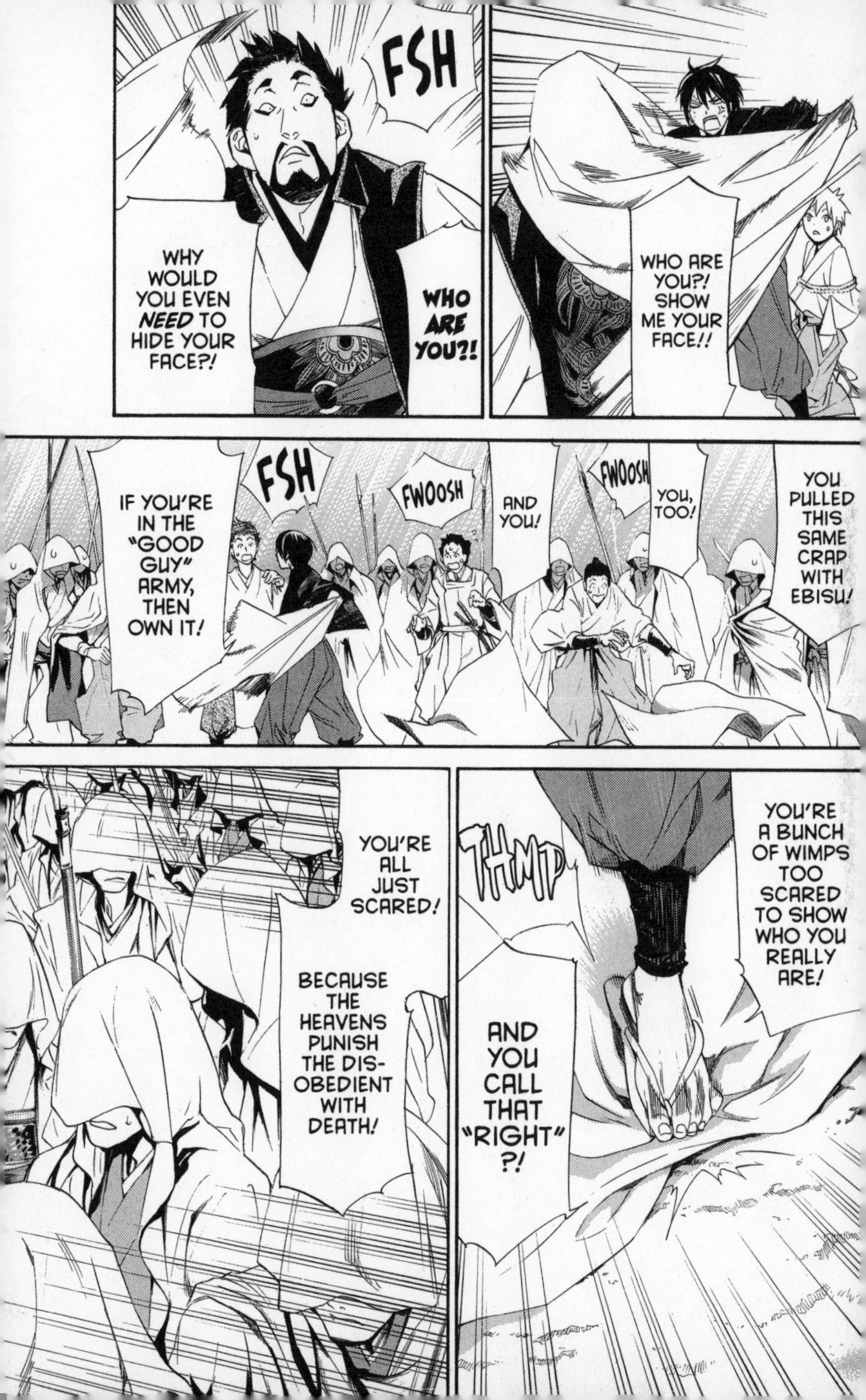
WHO ARE YOU?! SHOW ME YOUR FACE!!
FSH
WHO ARE YOU?!
WHY WOULD YOU EVEN NEED TO HIDE YOUR FACE?!
YOU PULLED THIS SAME CRAP WITH EBISU!
FWOOSH
YOU, TOO!
AND YOU!
FWOOSH
FSH
IF YOU'RE IN THE "GOOD GUY" ARMY, THEN OWN IT!
YOU'RE A BUNCH OF WIMPS TOO SCARED TO SHOW WHO YOU REALLY ARE!
THMP
AND YOU CALL THAT "RIGHT"?!
YOU'RE ALL JUST SCARED!
BECAUSE THE HEAVENS PUNISH THE DIS-OBEDIENT WITH DEATH!

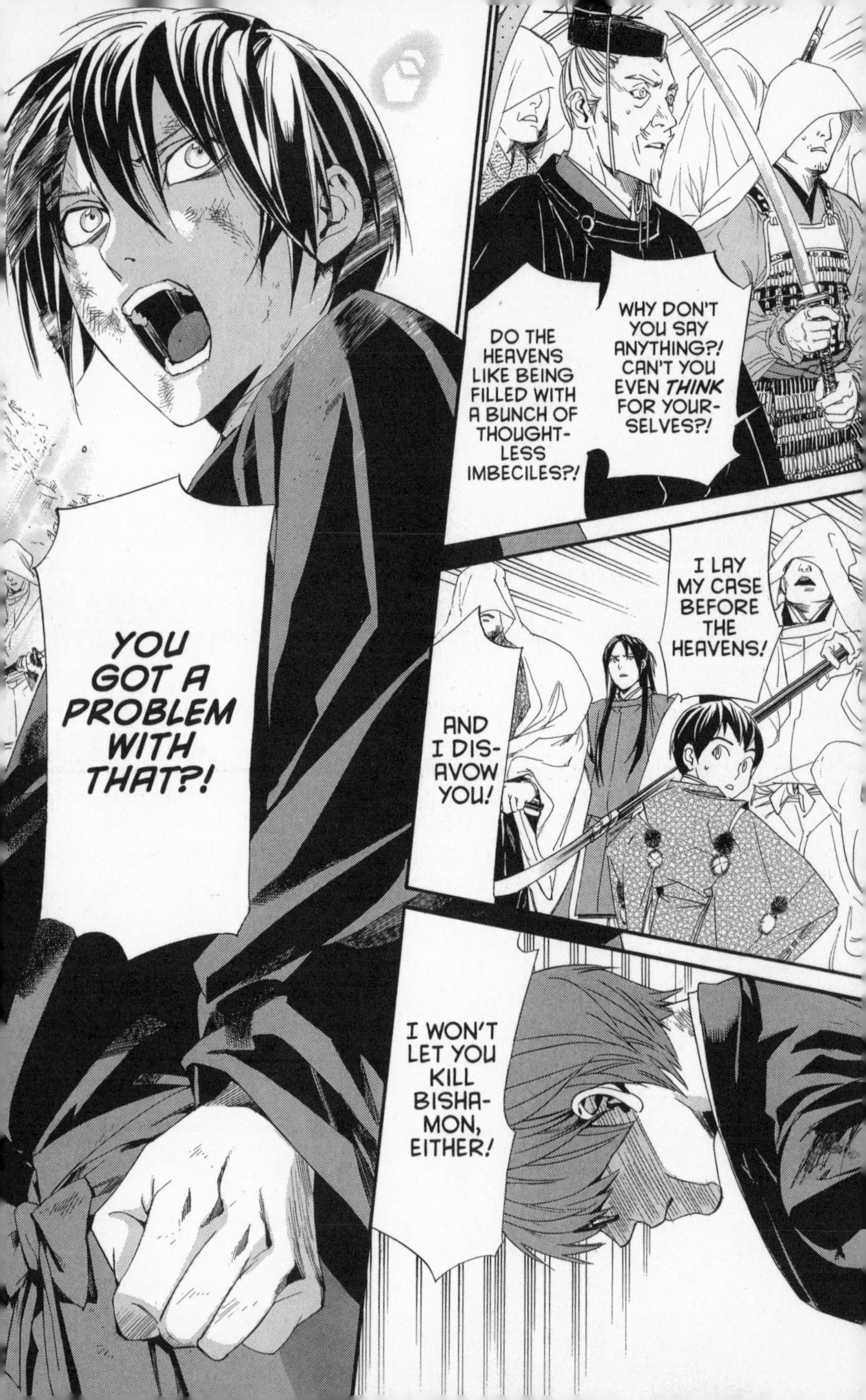
WHY DON'T YOU SAY ANYTHING?! CAN'T YOU EVEN *THINK* FOR YOUR-SELVES?!
DO THE HEAVENS LIKE BEING FILLED WITH A BUNCH OF THOUGHT-LESS IMBECILES?!
I LAY MY CASE BEFORE THE HEAVENS!
AND I DIS-AVOW YOU!
I WON'T LET YOU KILL BISHA-MON, EITHER!
YOU GOT A PROBLEM WITH THAT?!

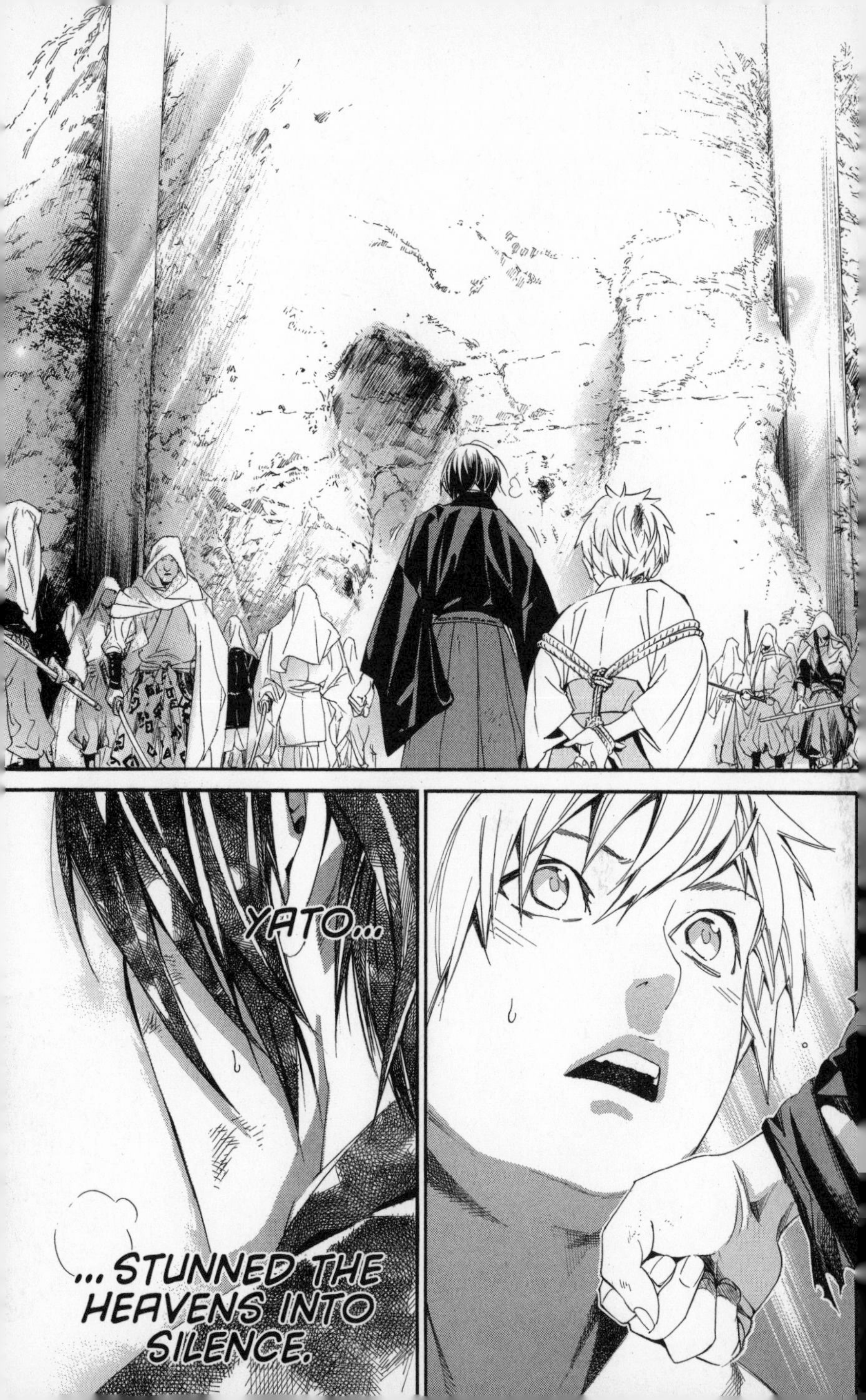
YATO...
...STUNNED THE HEAVENS INTO SILENCE.

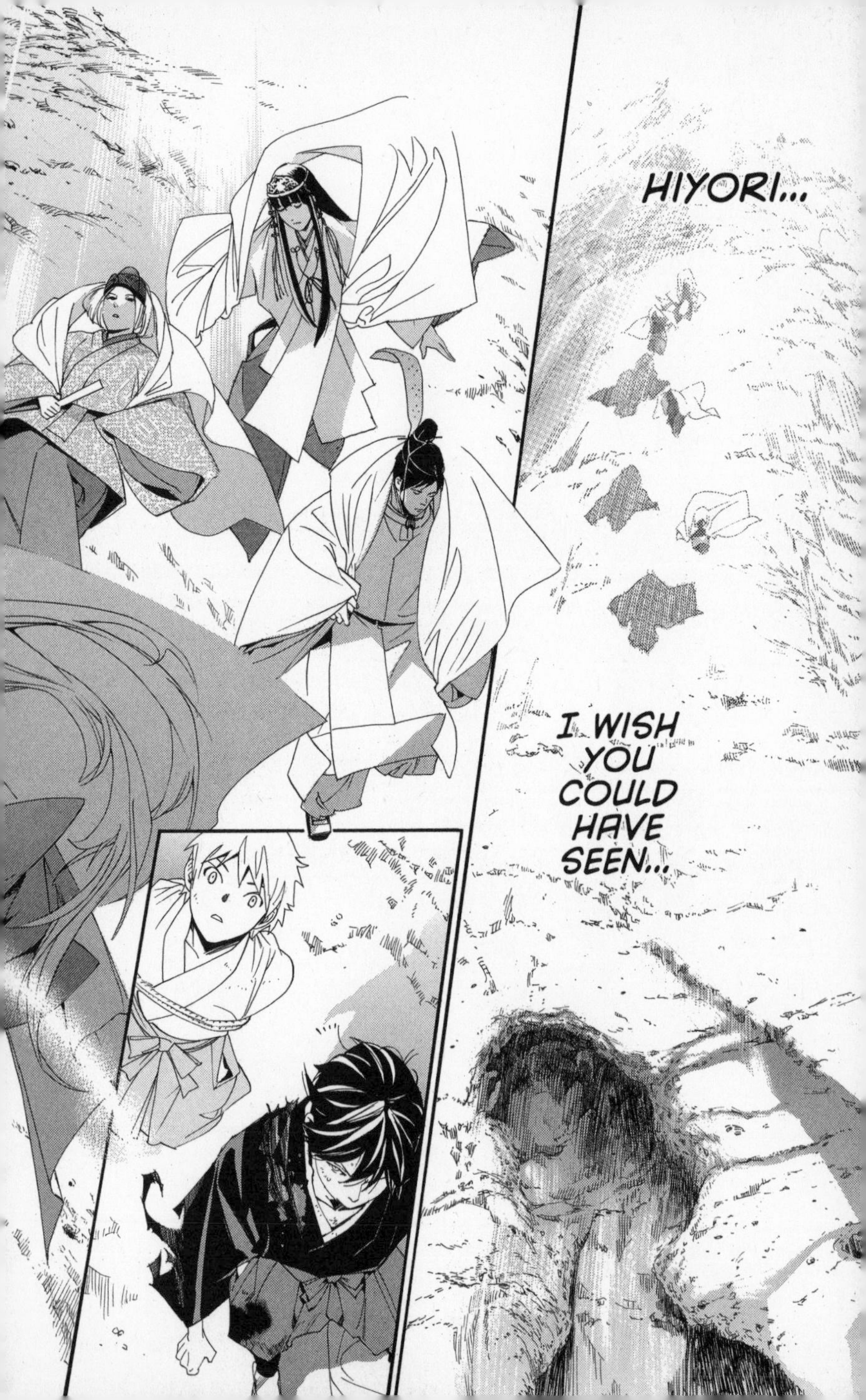
HIYORI...
I WISH YOU COULD HAVE SEEN...

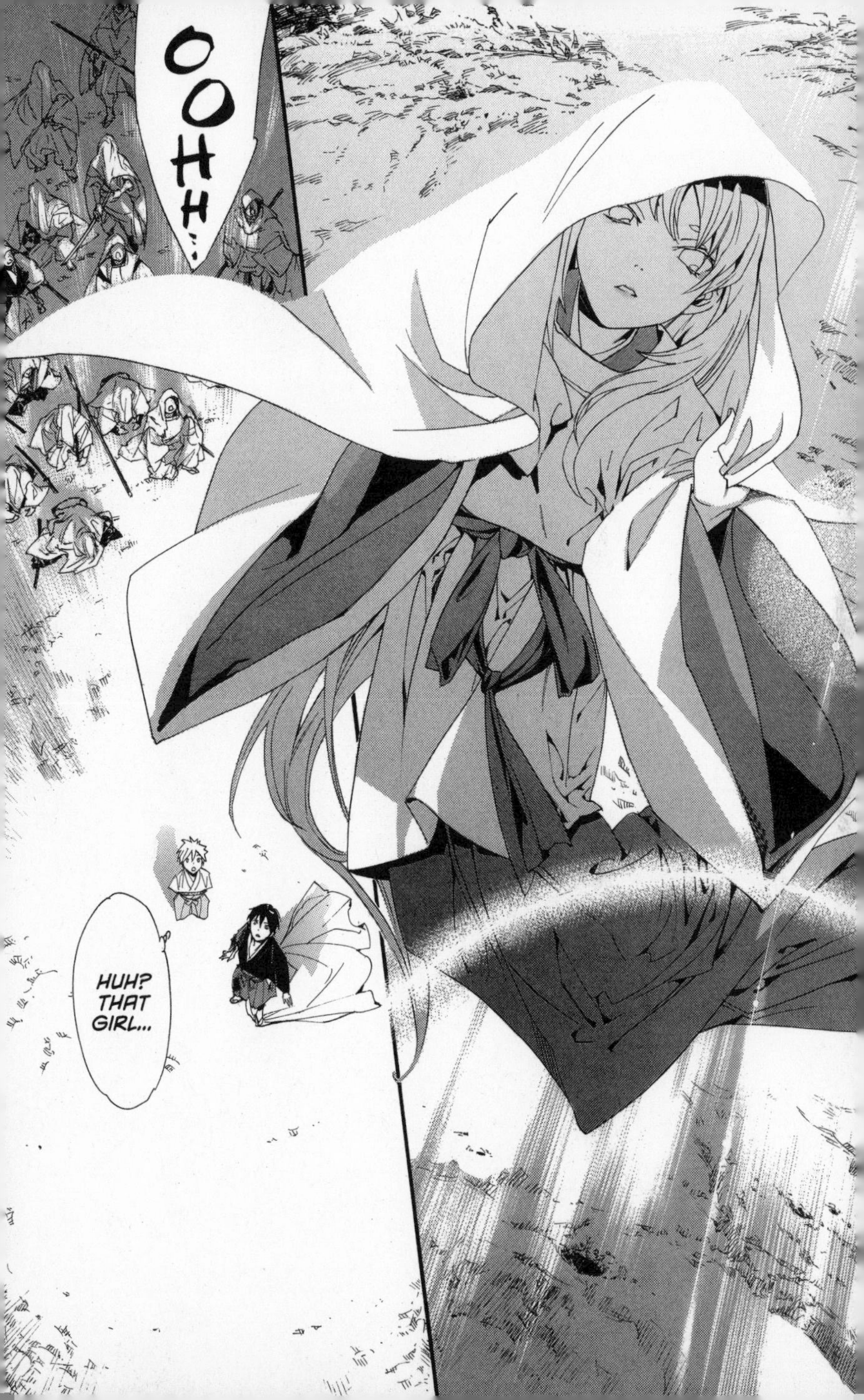
OOHH...
HUH? THAT GIRL...

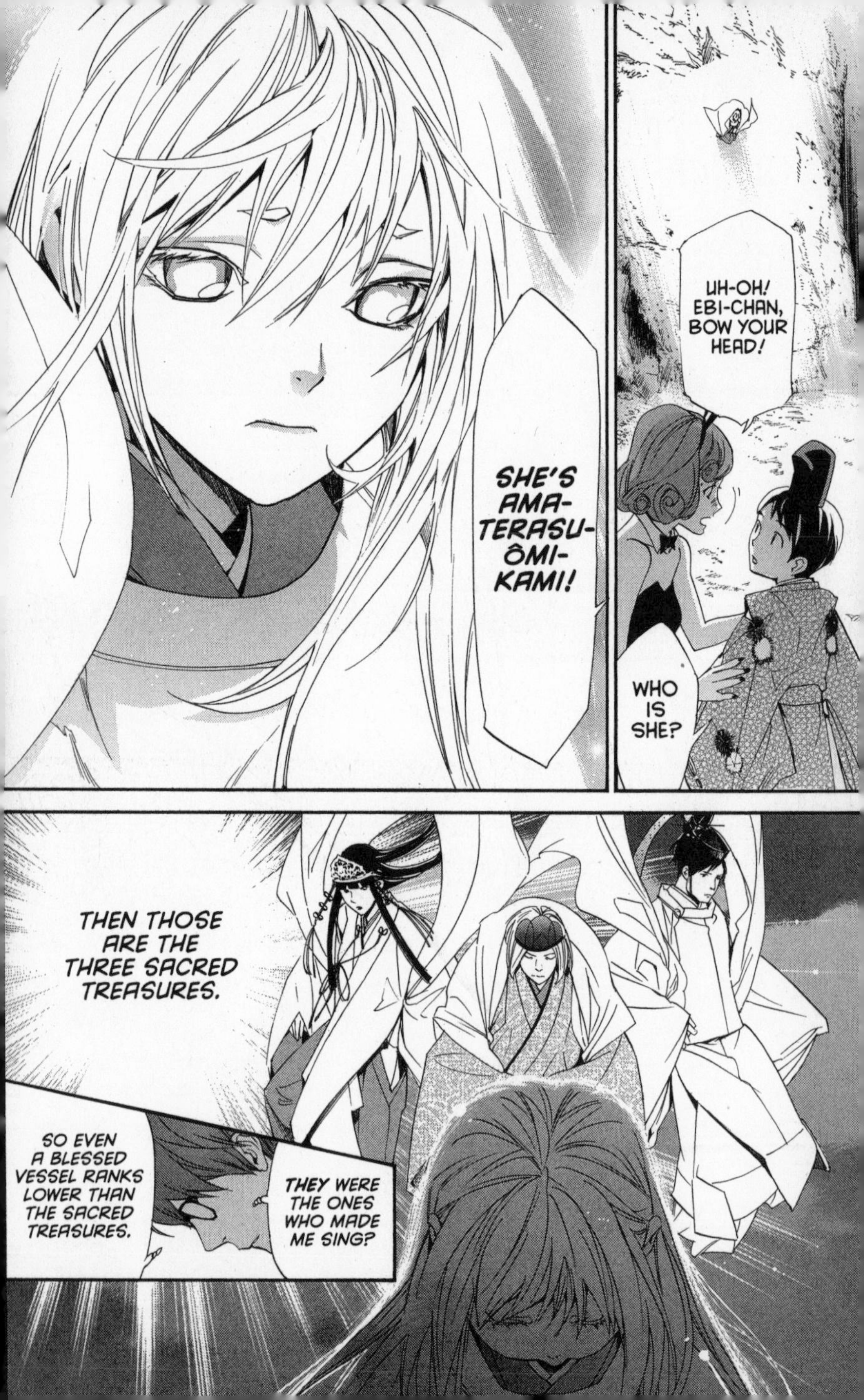
UH-OH! EBI-CHAN, BOW YOUR HEAD!
WHO IS SHE?
SHE'S AMA-TERASU-ÔMI-KAMI!
THEN THOSE ARE THE THREE SACRED TREASURES.
THEY WERE THE ONES WHO MADE ME SING?
SO EVEN A BLESSED VESSEL RANKS LOWER THAN THE SACRED TREASURES.

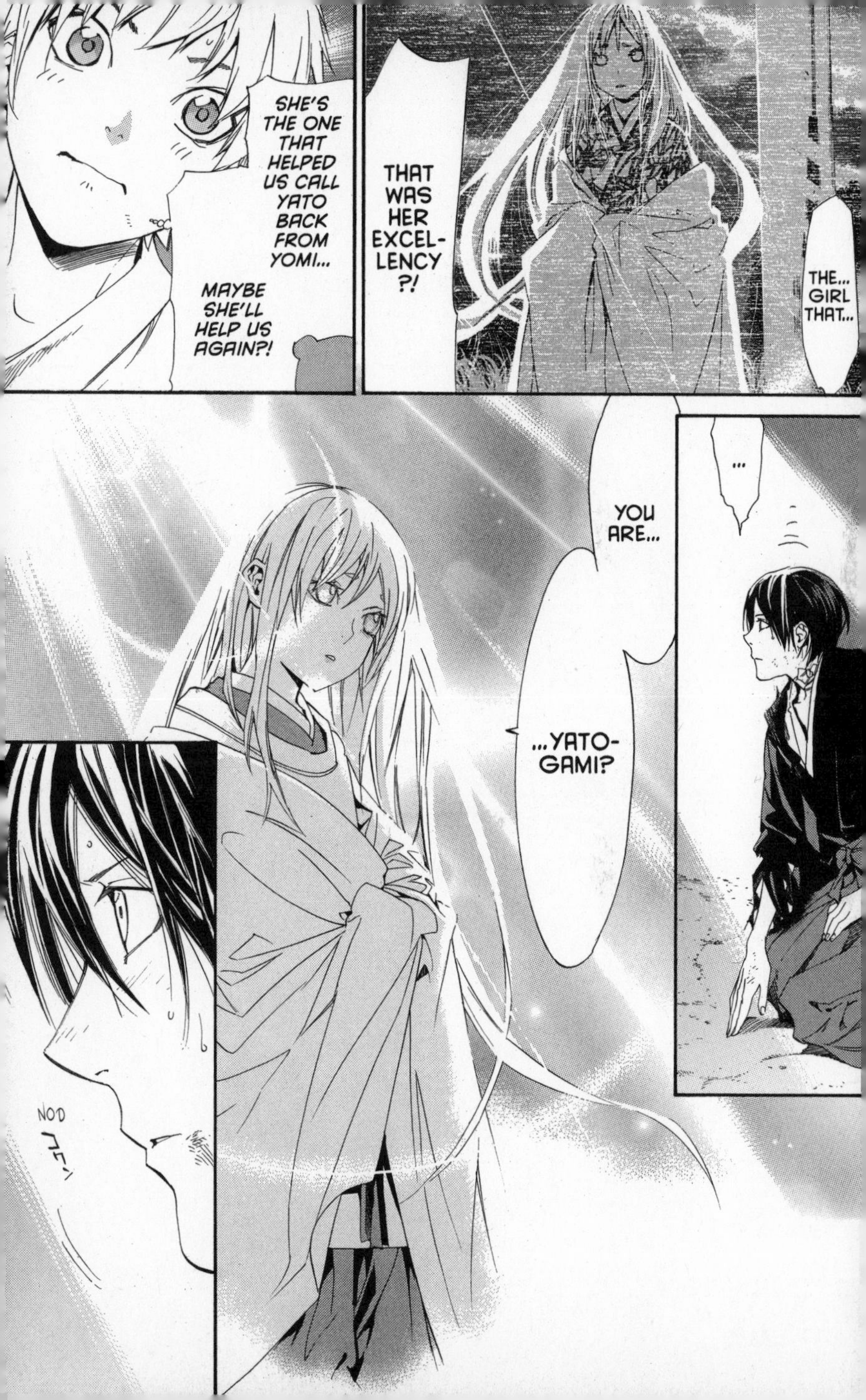
THE... GIRL THAT...
THAT WAS HER EXCELLENCY?!
SHE'S THE ONE THAT HELPED US CALL YATO BACK FROM YOMI...
MAYBE SHE'LL HELP US AGAIN?!
...
YOU ARE...
...YATO-GAMI?
NOD

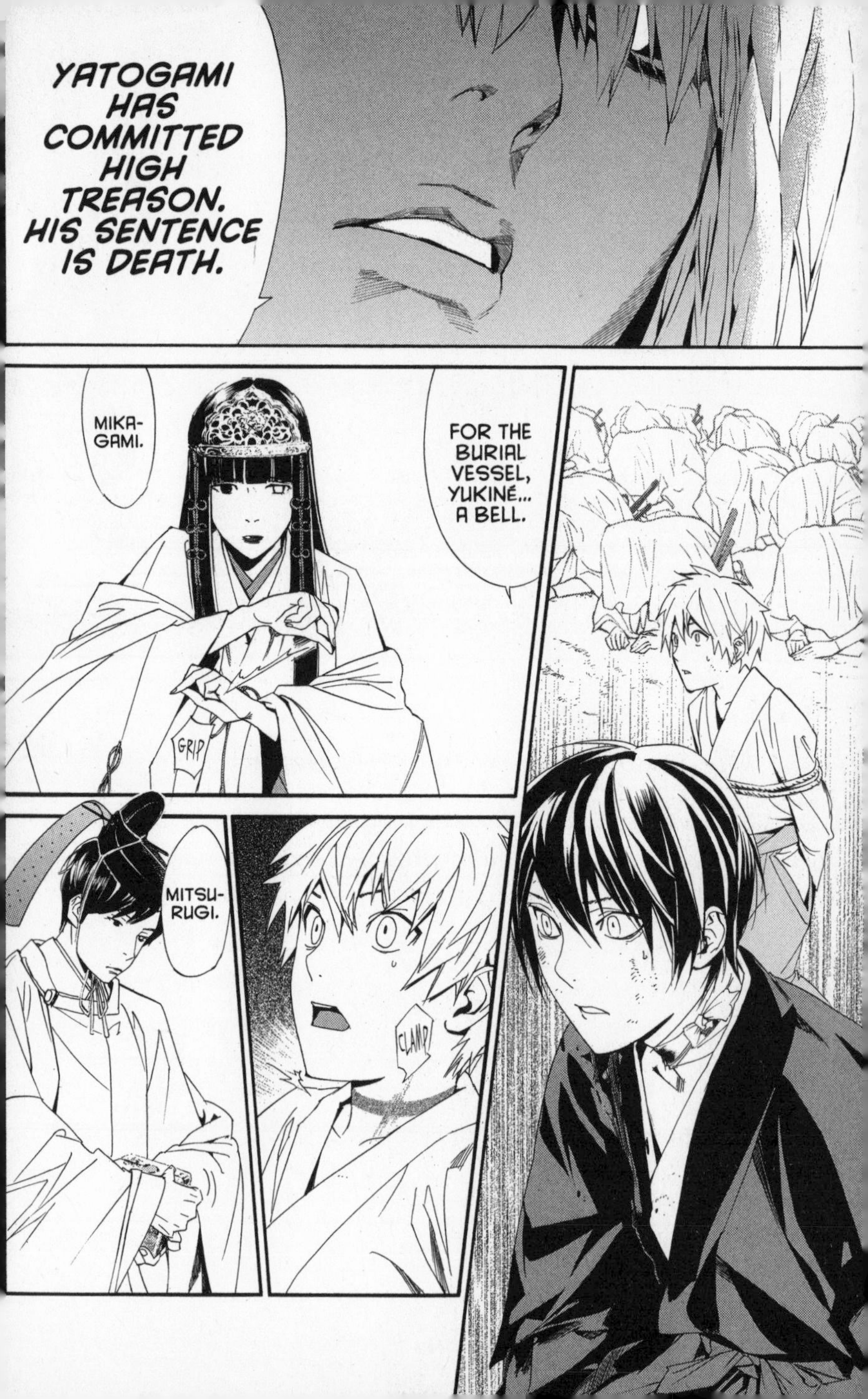
YATOGAMI HAS COMMITTED HIGH TREASON. HIS SENTENCE IS DEATH.
FOR THE BURIAL VESSEL, YUKINÉ... A BELL.
MIKA-GAMI.
GRIP
MITSU-RUGI.
CLAMP

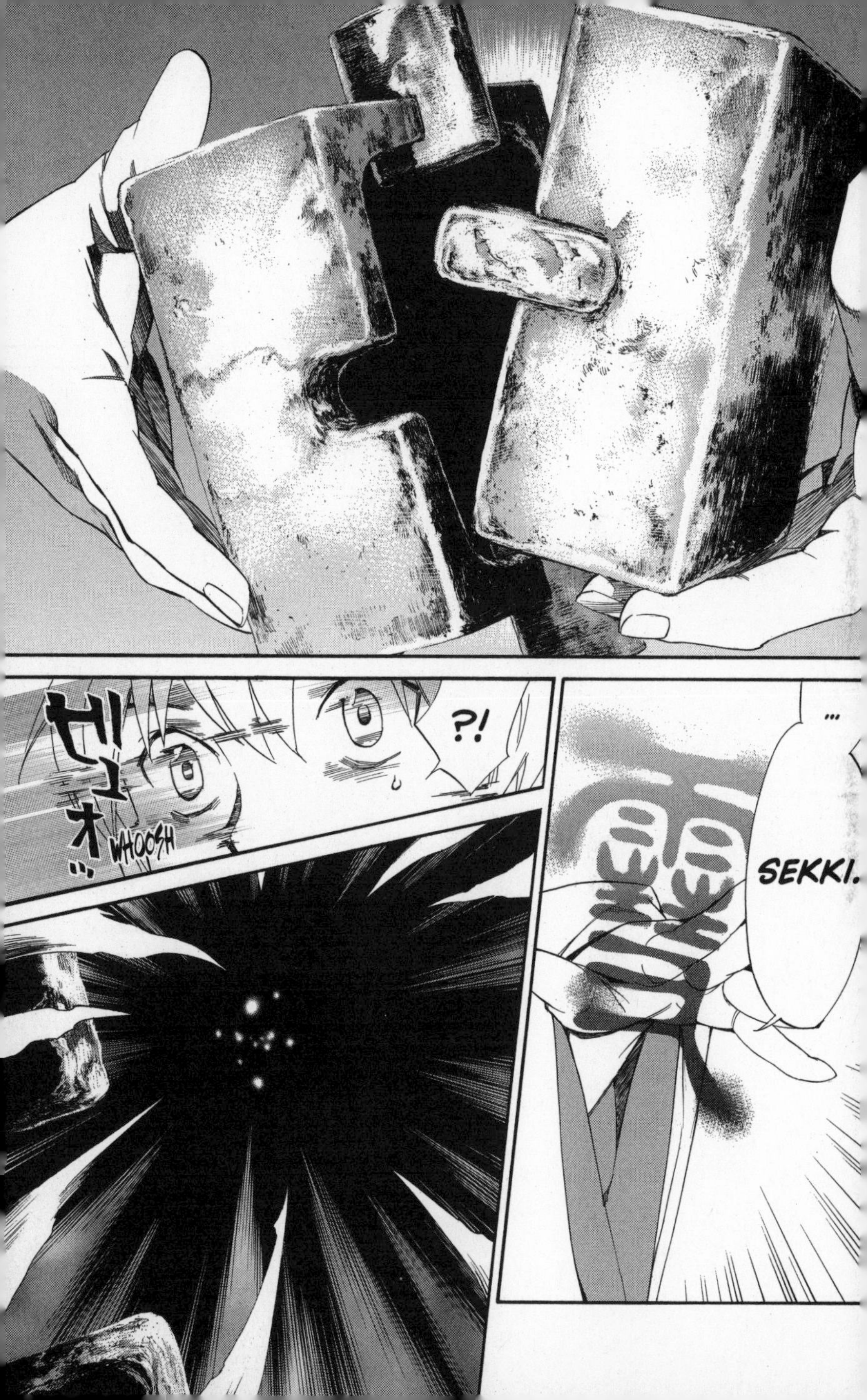
...
SEKKI.
?!
ヒュオッ
WHOOSH

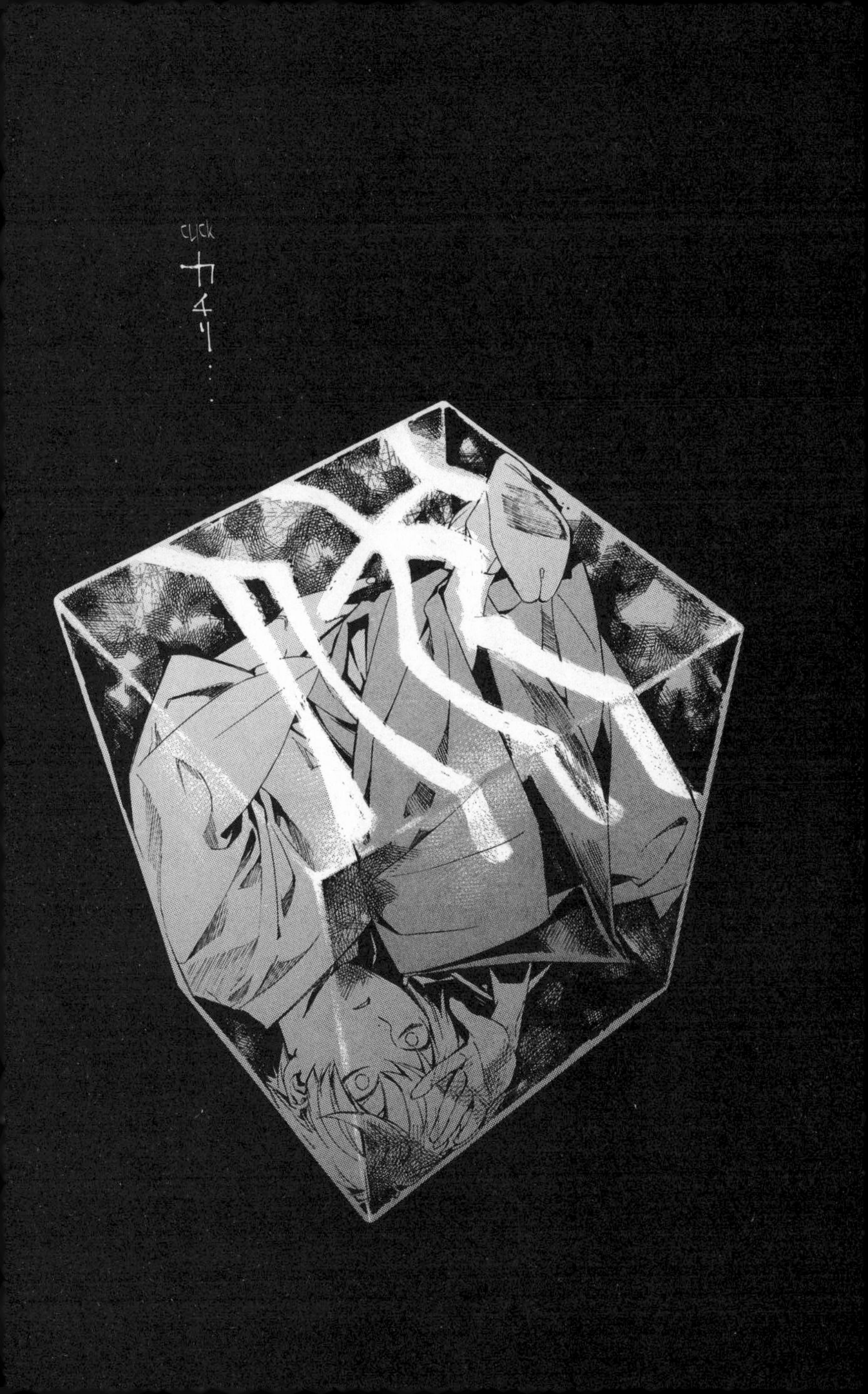
CLICK
カチリ…

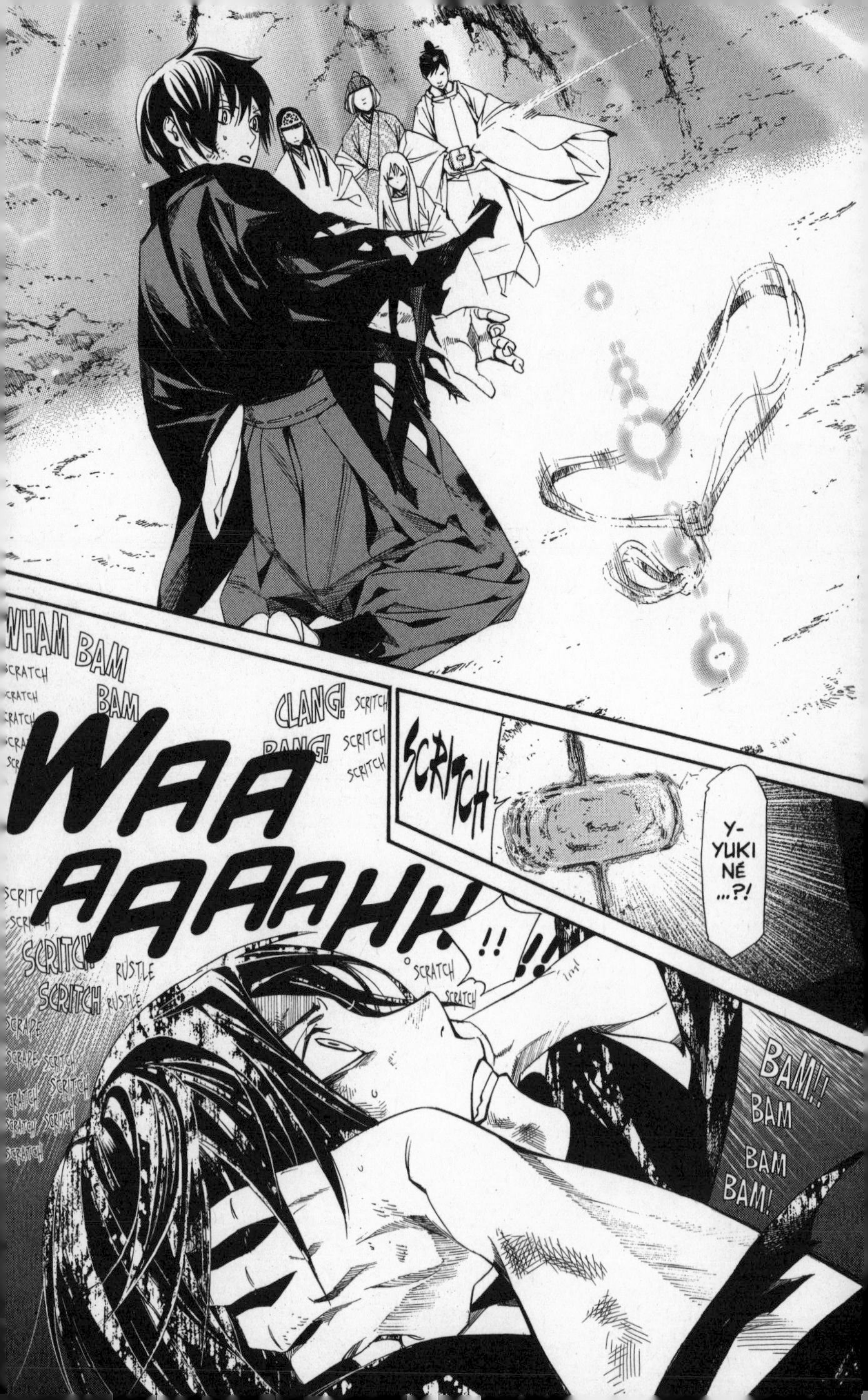

Y-YUKINÉ ...?!
SCRITCH
CLANG!
SCRITCH
BANG!
SCRITCH
SCRITCH
WHAM BAM
SCRATCH
BAM
SCRATCH
SCRATCH
WAAAAAAHK
!!
!!
SCRATCH
SCRATCH
BAM!!
BAM
BAM
BAM!
SCRITCH
SCRITCH
RUSTLE
SCRITCH
RUSTLE
SCRAPE
SCRAPE
SCRITCH
SCRITCH
SCRATCH
SCRATCH
SCRITCH
SCRATCH

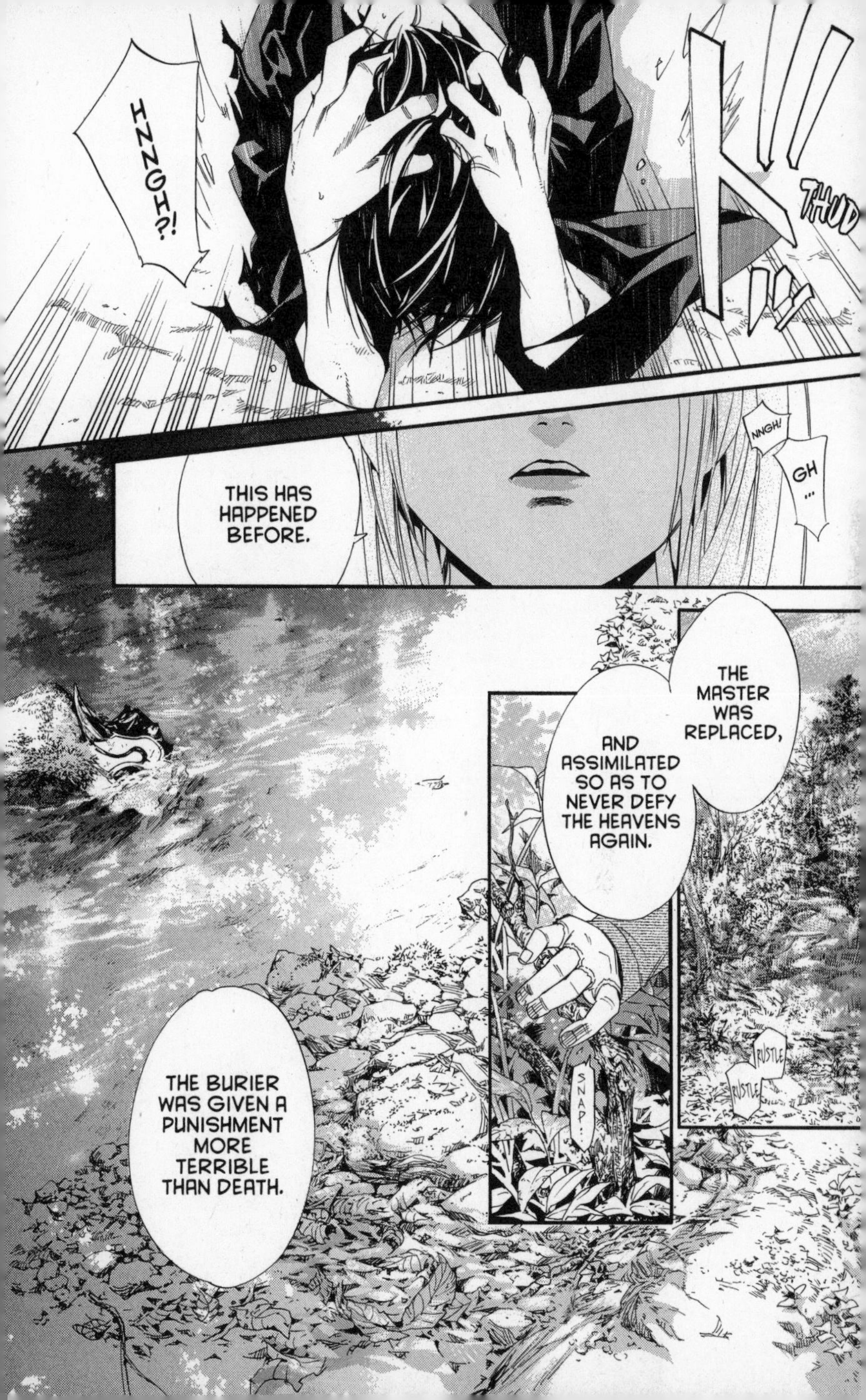
THUD
HNNGH?!
NNGH!
GH ...
THIS HAS HAPPENED BEFORE.
THE MASTER WAS REPLACED,
AND ASSIMILATED SO AS TO NEVER DEFY THE HEAVENS AGAIN.
RUSTLE
RUSTLE
SNAP...
THE BURIER WAS GIVEN A PUNISHMENT MORE TERRIBLE THAN DEATH.

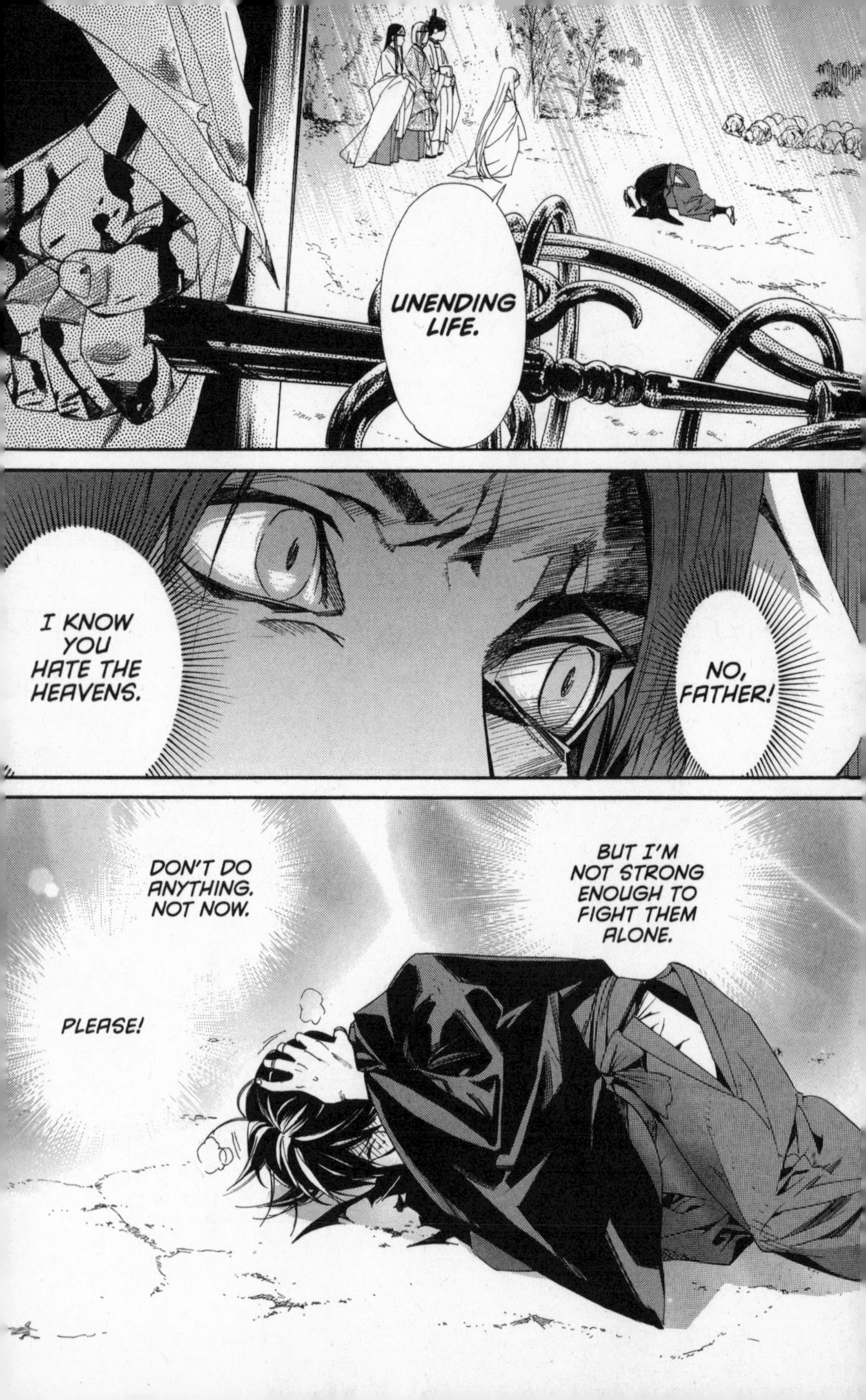
UNENDING LIFE.
NO, FATHER!
I KNOW YOU HATE THE HEAVENS.
BUT I'M NOT STRONG ENOUGH TO FIGHT THEM ALONE.
DON'T DO ANYTHING. NOT NOW.
PLEASE!

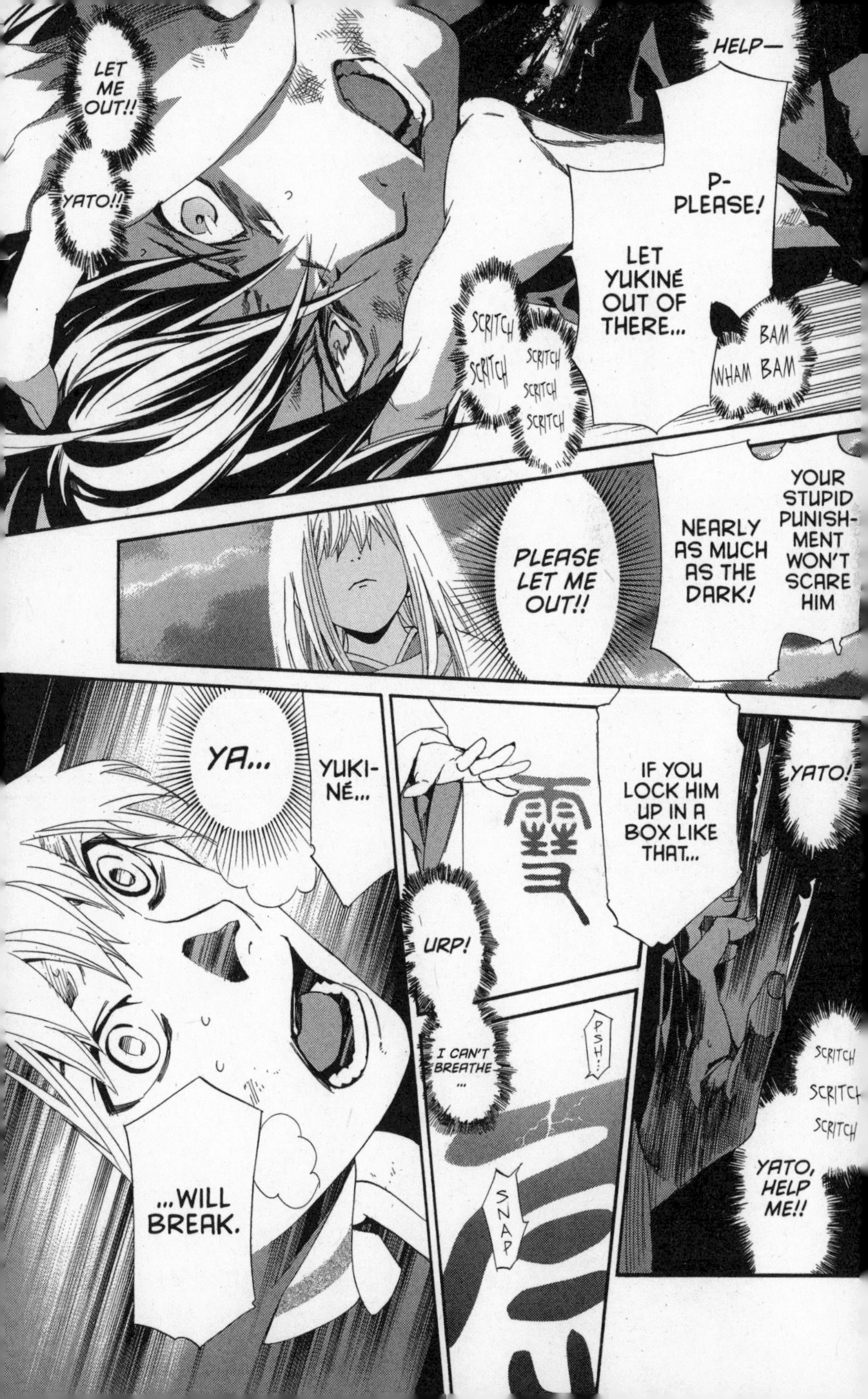
HELP—
P-PLEASE!
LET YUKINÉ OUT OF THERE...
BAM WHAM BAM
SCRITCH SCRITCH SCRITCH SCRITCH SCRITCH
LET ME OUT!!
YATO!!
YOUR STUPID PUNISHMENT WON'T SCARE HIM
NEARLY AS MUCH AS THE DARK!
PLEASE LET ME OUT!!
YATO!
SCRITCH SCRITCH SCRITCH
YATO, HELP ME!!
IF YOU LOCK HIM UP IN A BOX LIKE THAT...
URP!
I CAN'T BREATHE...
PSH..
SNAP
YUKI-NÉ...
YA...
...WILL BREAK.

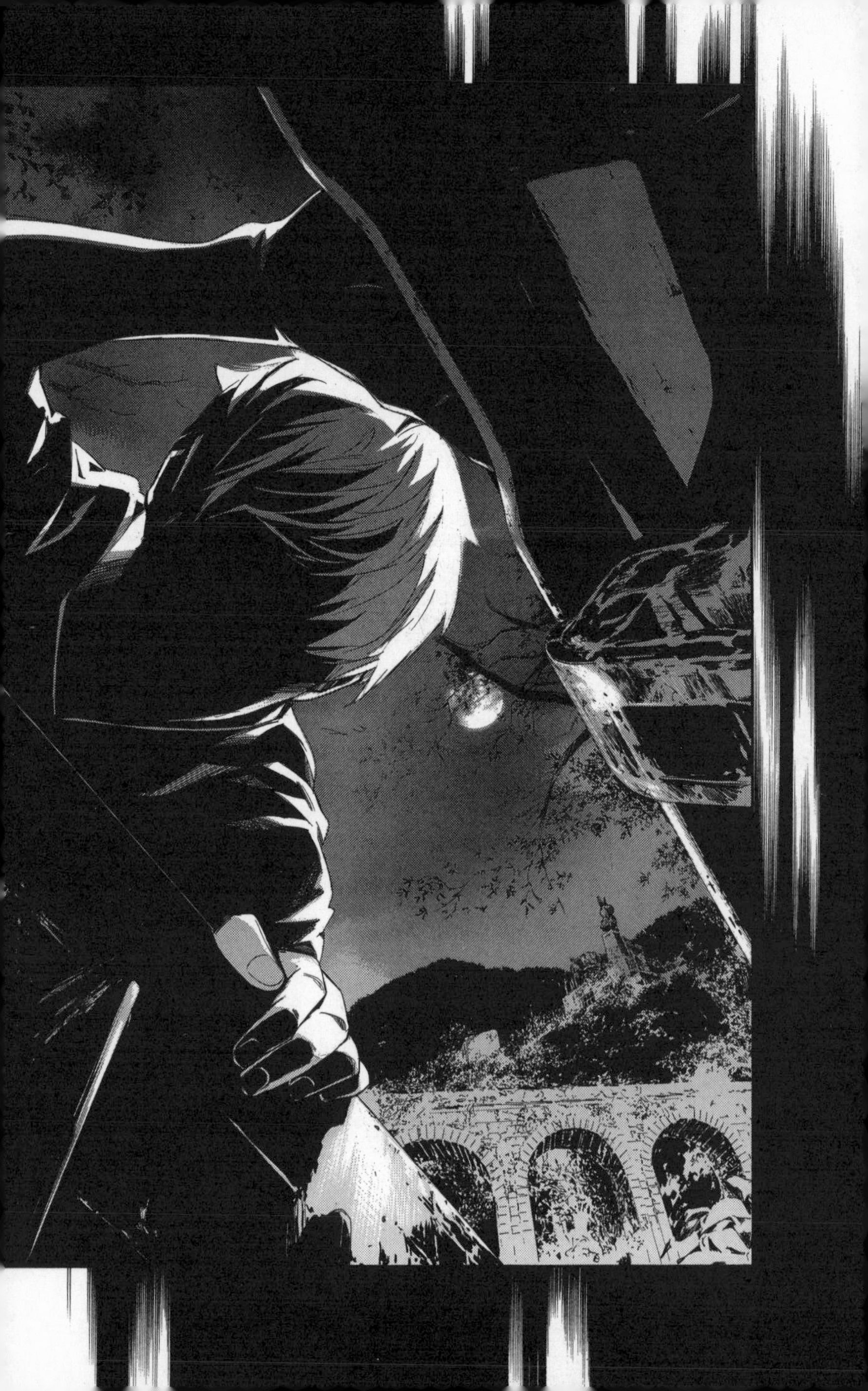

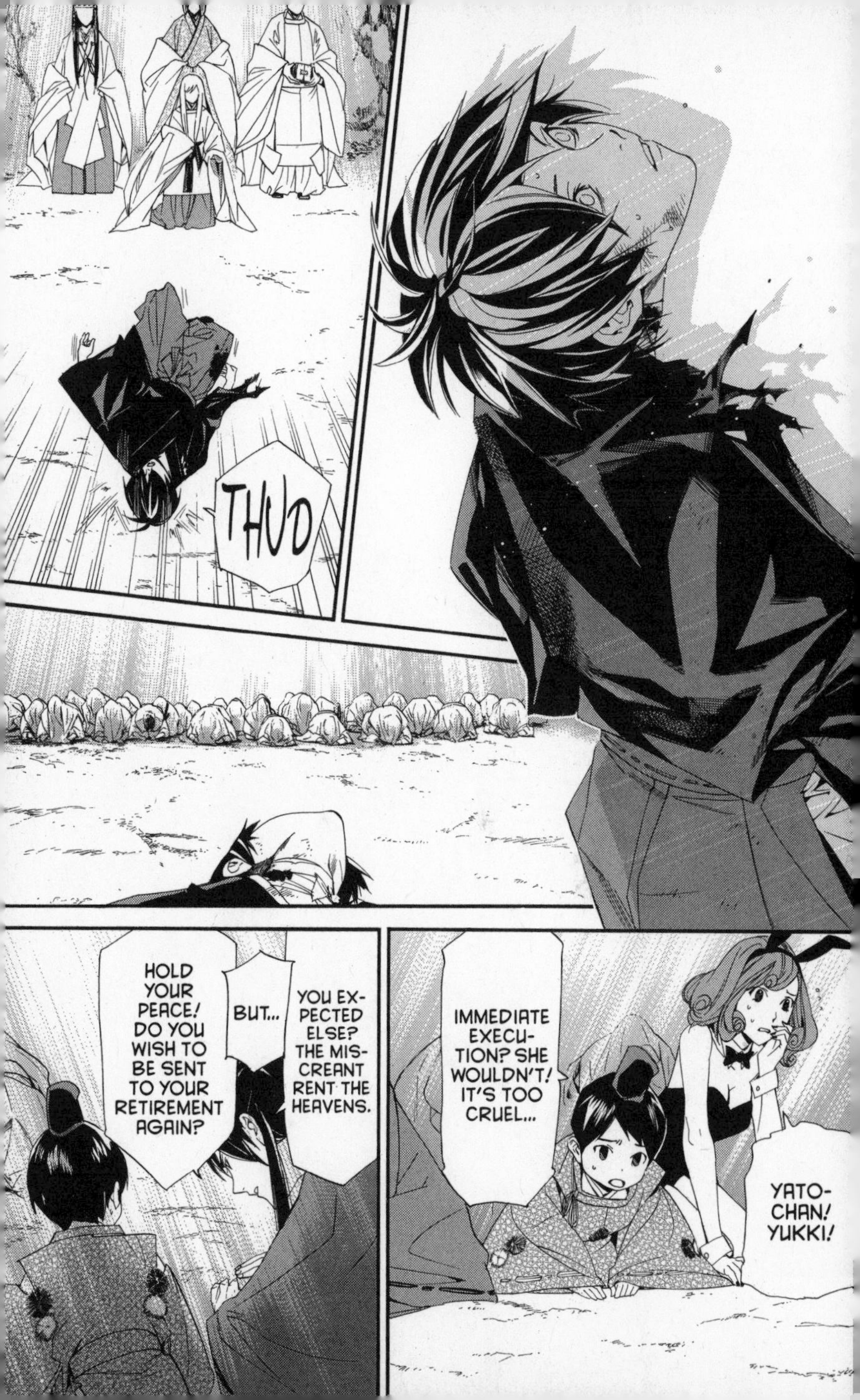
THUD
IMMEDIATE EXECUTION? SHE WOULDN'T! IT'S TOO CRUEL...
YATO-CHAN! YUKKI!
YOU EXPECTED ELSE? THE MISCREANT RENT THE HEAVENS.
BUT...
HOLD YOUR PEACE! DO YOU WISH TO BE SENT TO YOUR RETIREMENT AGAIN?

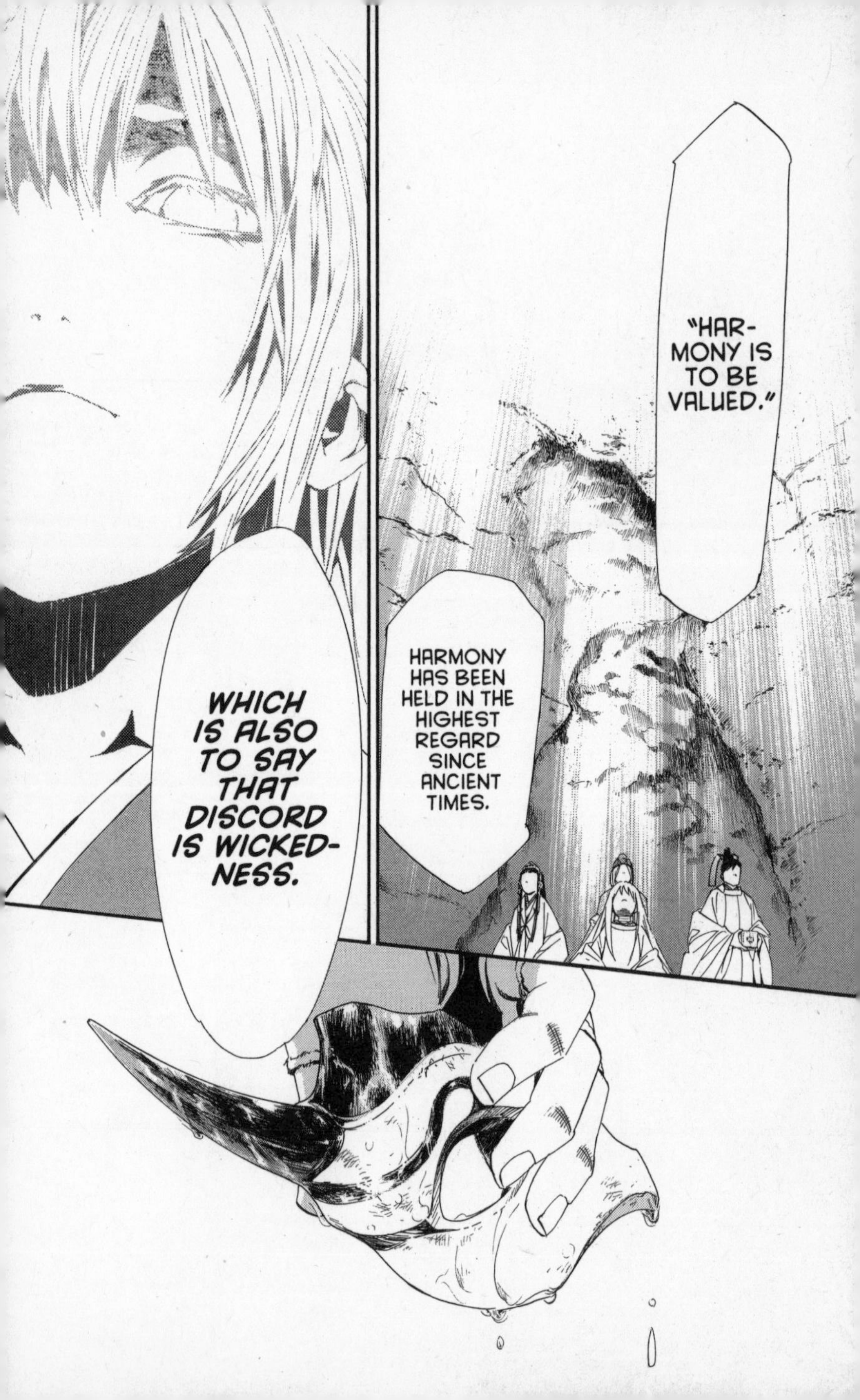
"HARMONY IS TO BE VALUED."
HARMONY HAS BEEN HELD IN THE HIGHEST REGARD SINCE ANCIENT TIMES.
WHICH IS ALSO TO SAY THAT DISCORD IS WICKEDNESS.

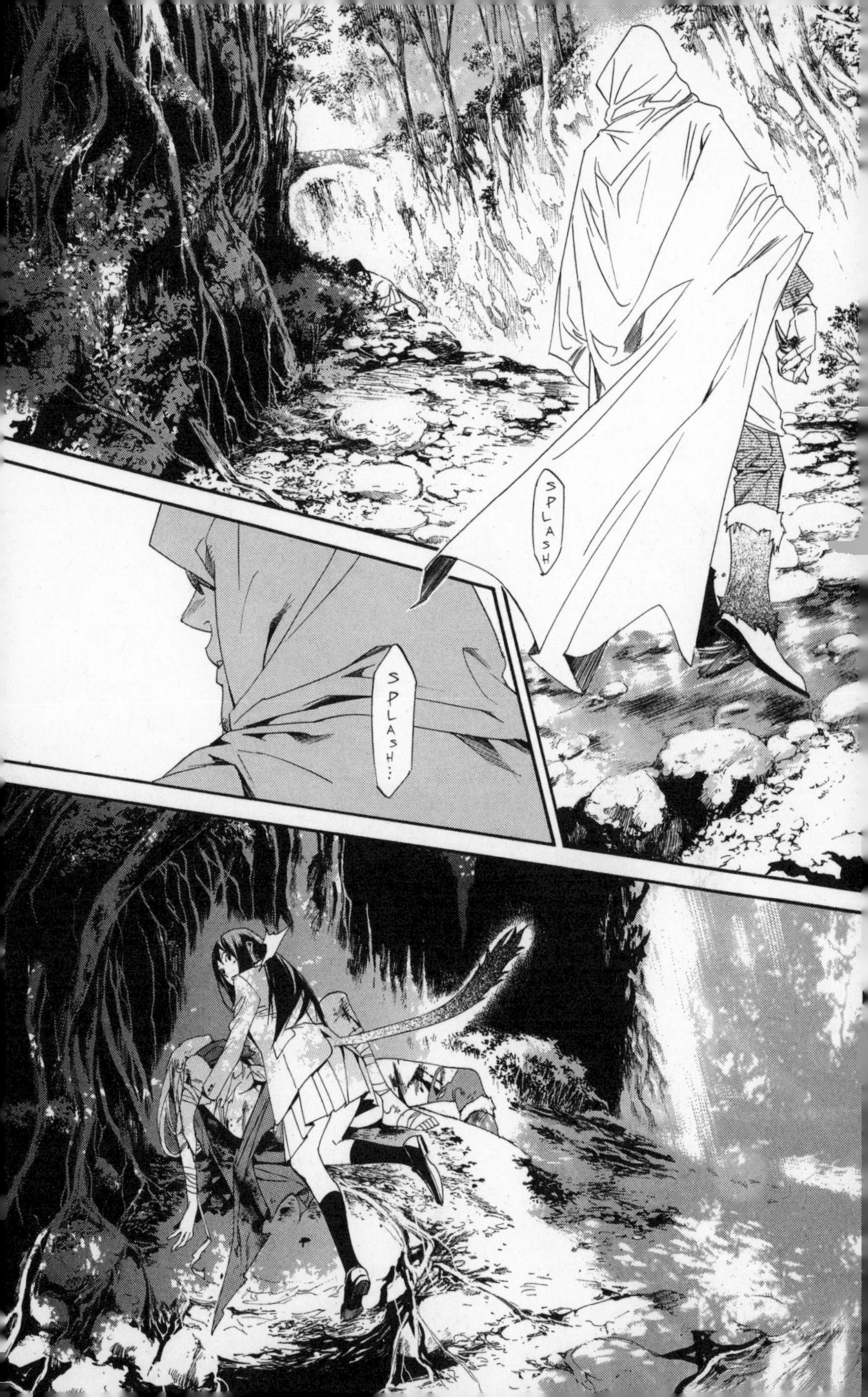
SPLASH
SPLASH...

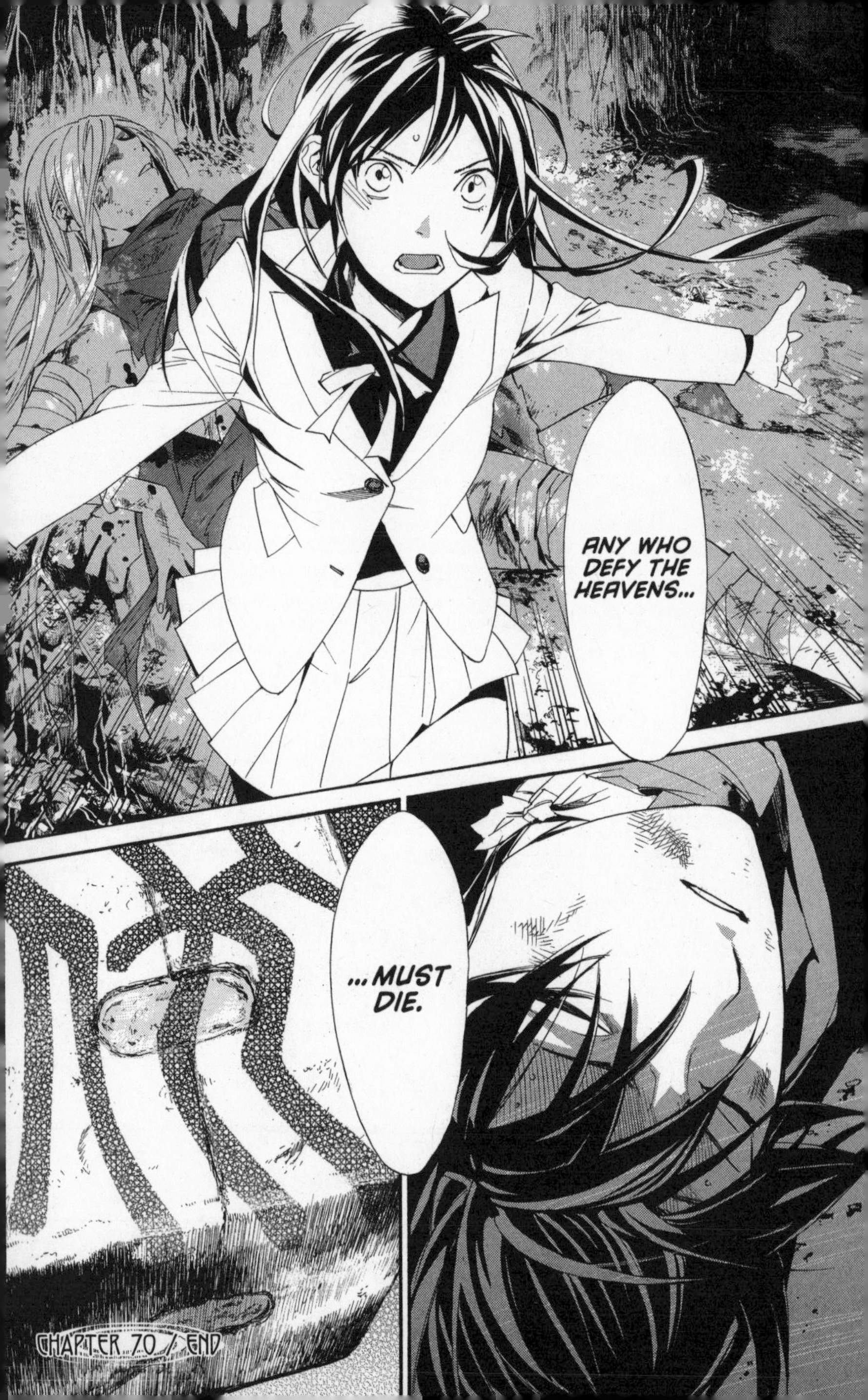
ANY WHO DEFY THE HEAVENS...
...MUST DIE.
CHAPTER 70 / END

野
良
神

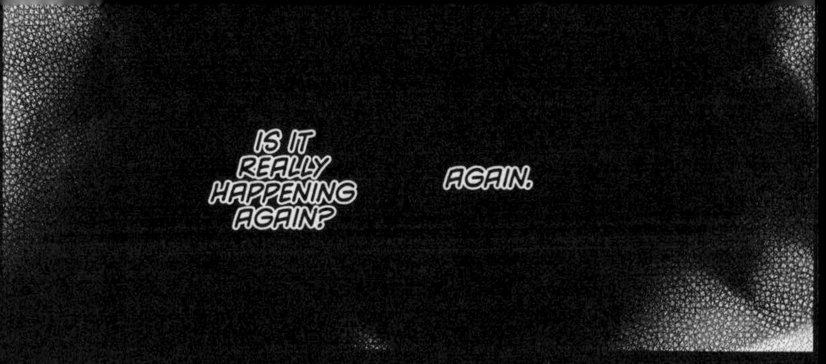
IS IT REALLY HAPPENING AGAIN?
AGAIN.
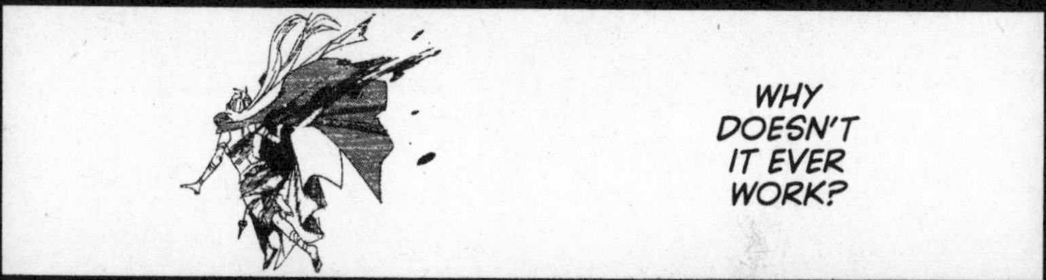
WHY DOESN'T IT EVER WORK?
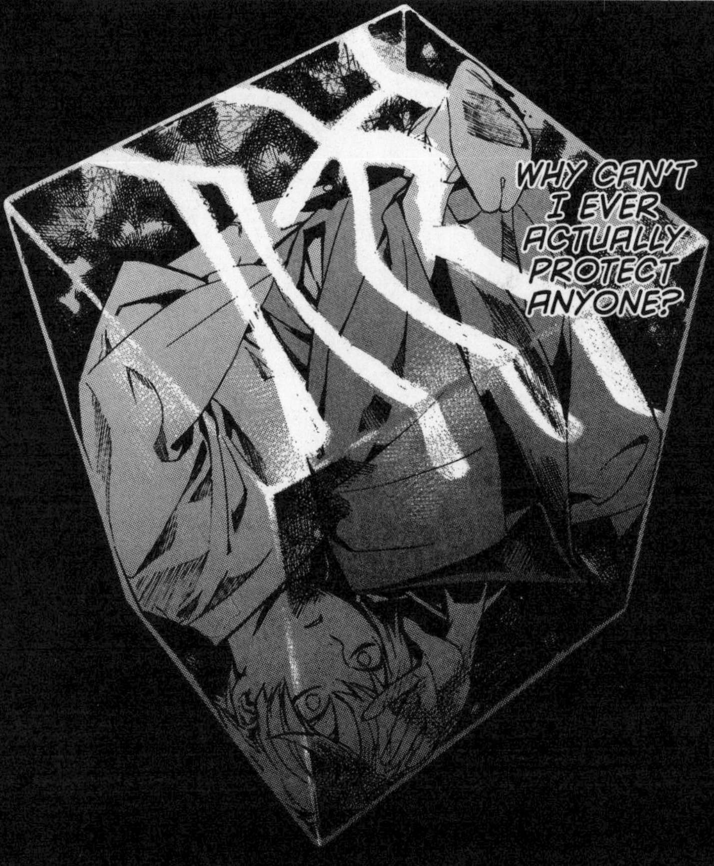
WHY CAN'T I EVER ACTUALLY PROTECT ANYONE?

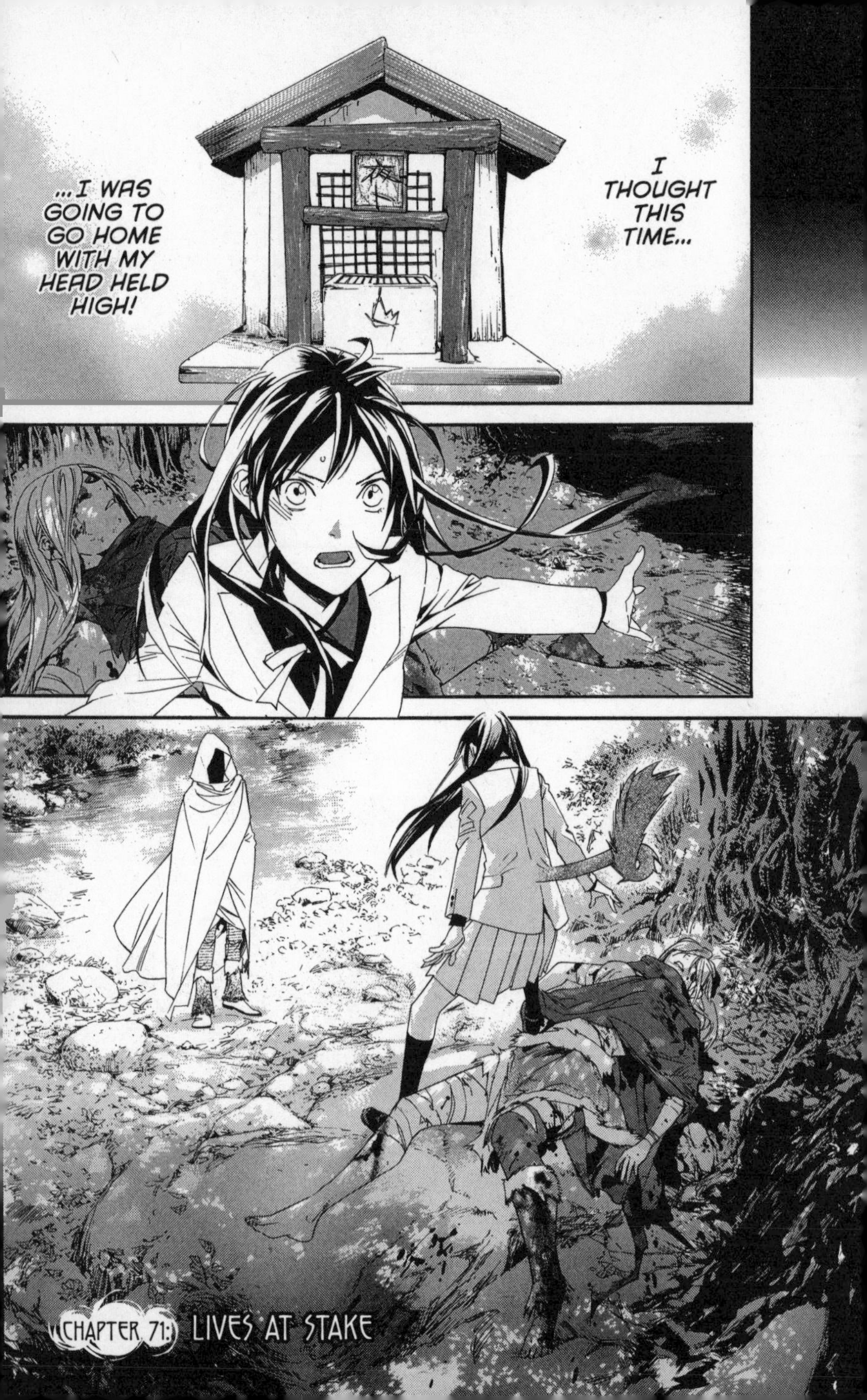
I THOUGHT THIS TIME...
...I WAS GOING TO GO HOME WITH MY HEAD HELD HIGH!
CHAPTER 71: LIVES AT STAKE

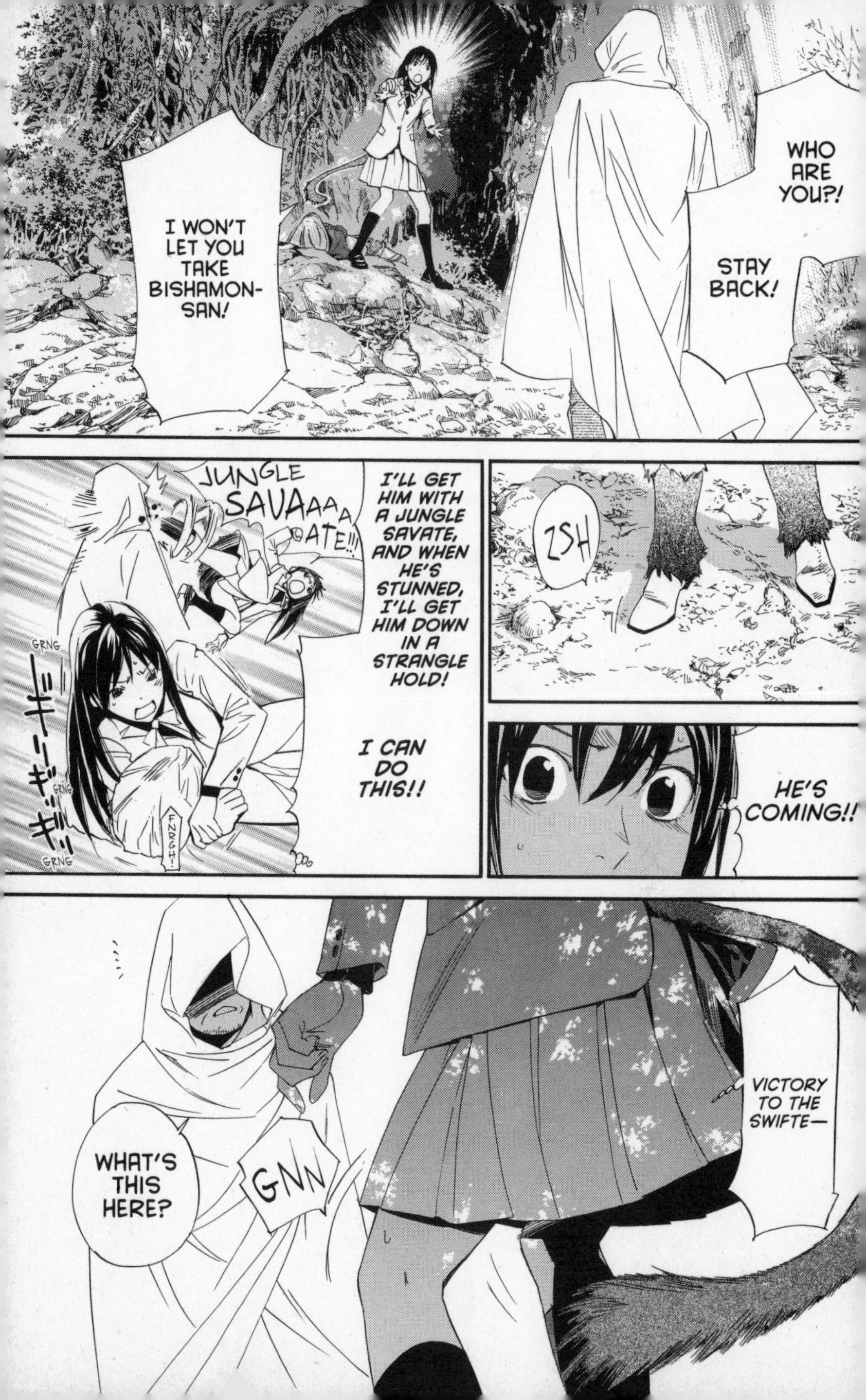
WHO ARE YOU?!
STAY BACK!
I WON'T LET YOU TAKE BISHAMON-SAN!
ZSH
HE'S COMING!!
I'LL GET HIM WITH A JUNGLE SAVATE, AND WHEN HE'S STUNNED, I'LL GET HIM DOWN IN A STRANGLE HOLD!
I CAN DO THIS!!
JUNGLE SAVAAAAATE!!!
GRNG
GRNG
GRNG
FNRGH!
VICTORY TO THE SWIFTE—
GNN
WHAT'S THIS HERE?

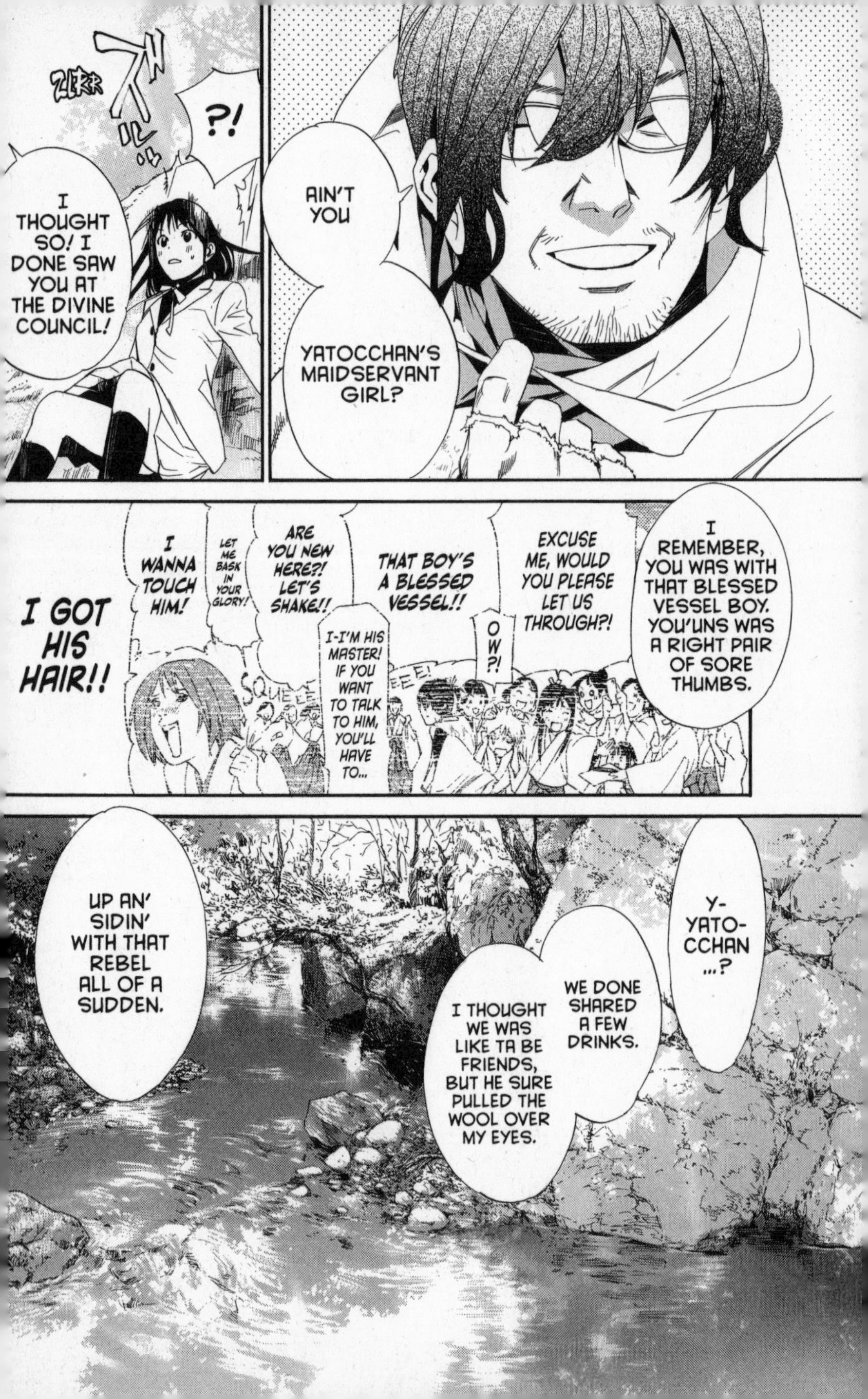
AIN'T YOU
YATOCCHAN'S MAIDSERVANT GIRL?
ZLRRR
?!
I THOUGHT SO! I DONE SAW YOU AT THE DIVINE COUNCIL!
I REMEMBER, YOU WAS WITH THAT BLESSED VESSEL BOY. YOU'UNS WAS A RIGHT PAIR OF SORE THUMBS.
EXCUSE ME, WOULD YOU PLEASE LET US THROUGH?!
OW?!
THAT BOY'S A BLESSED VESSEL!!
I-I'M HIS MASTER! IF YOU WANT TO TALK TO HIM, YOU'LL HAVE TO...
ARE YOU NEW HERE?! LET'S SHAKE!!
LET ME BASK IN YOUR GLORY!
I WANNA TOUCH HIM!
I GOT HIS HAIR!!
Y-YATOCCHAN...?
WE DONE SHARED A FEW DRINKS.
I THOUGHT WE WAS LIKE TA BE FRIENDS, BUT HE SURE PULLED THE WOOL OVER MY EYES.
UP AN' SIDIN' WITH THAT REBEL ALL OF A SUDDEN.

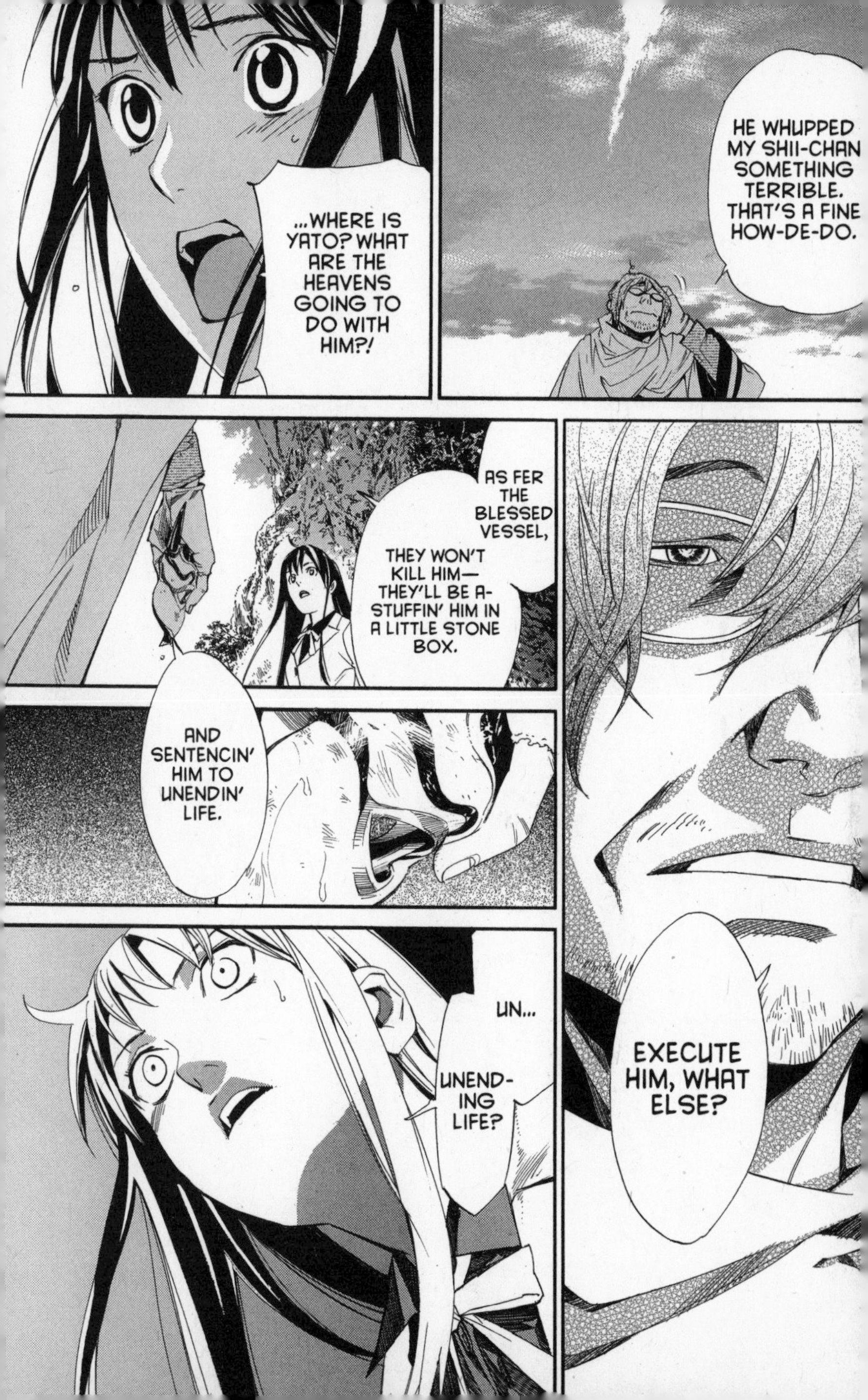
HE WHUPPED MY SHII-CHAN SOMETHING TERRIBLE. THAT'S A FINE HOW-DE-DO.
...WHERE IS YATO? WHAT ARE THE HEAVENS GOING TO DO WITH HIM?!
EXECUTE HIM, WHAT ELSE?
AS FER THE BLESSED VESSEL,
THEY WON'T KILL HIM—THEY'LL BE A-STUFFIN' HIM IN A LITTLE STONE BOX.
AND SENTENCIN' HIM TO UNENDIN' LIFE.
UN...
UNEND-ING LIFE?

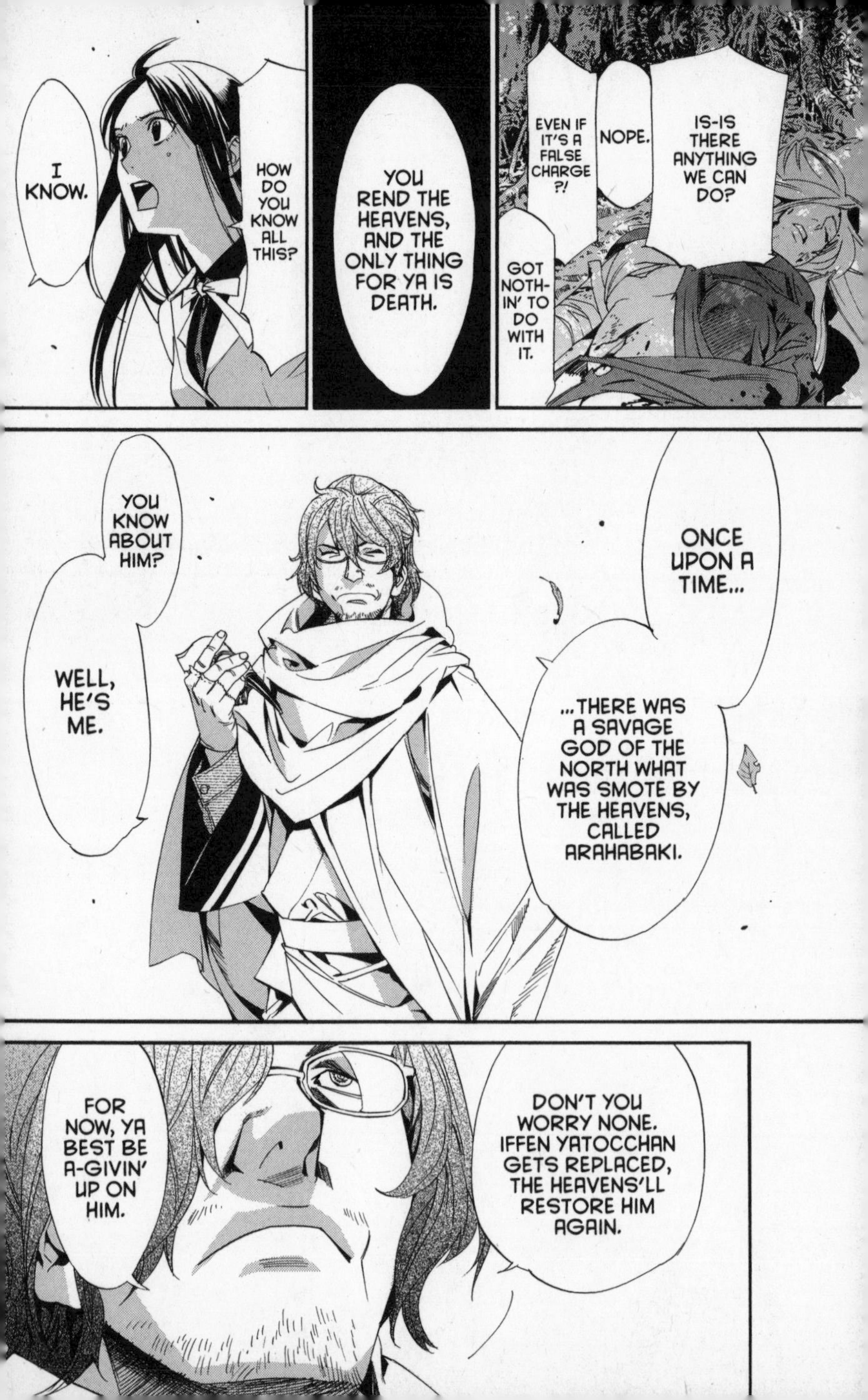
IS-IS THERE ANYTHING WE CAN DO?
NOPE.
EVEN IF IT'S A FALSE CHARGE?!
GOT NOTHIN' TO DO WITH IT.
YOU REND THE HEAVENS, AND THE ONLY THING FOR YA IS DEATH.
HOW DO YOU KNOW ALL THIS?
I KNOW.
ONCE UPON A TIME...
...THERE WAS A SAVAGE GOD OF THE NORTH WHAT WAS SMOTE BY THE HEAVENS, CALLED ARAHABAKI.
YOU KNOW ABOUT HIM?
WELL, HE'S ME.
DON'T YOU WORRY NONE. IFFEN YATOCCHAN GETS REPLACED, THE HEAVENS'LL RESTORE HIM AGAIN.
FOR NOW, YA BEST BE A-GIVIN' UP ON HIM.

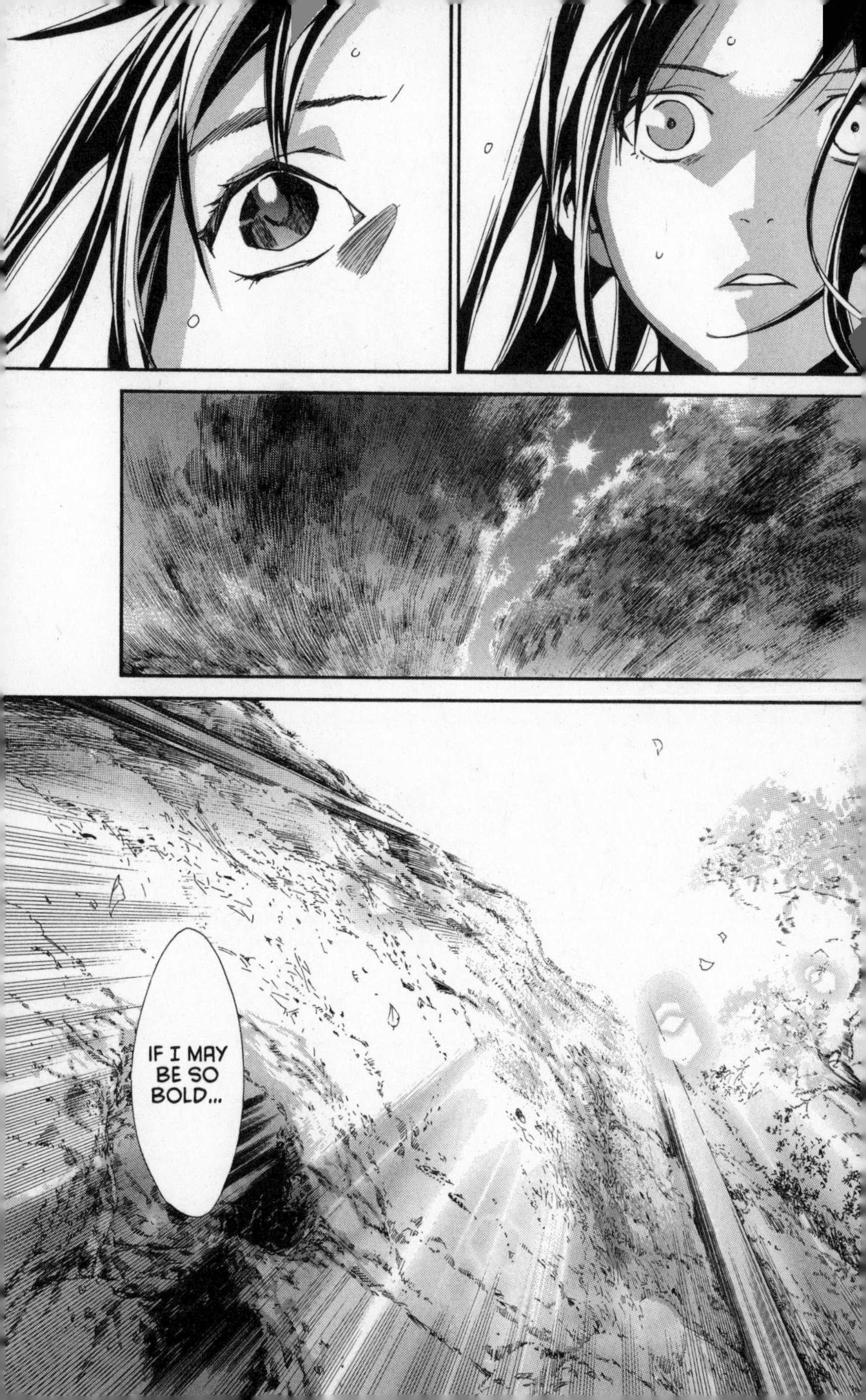
IF I MAY BE SO BOLD...

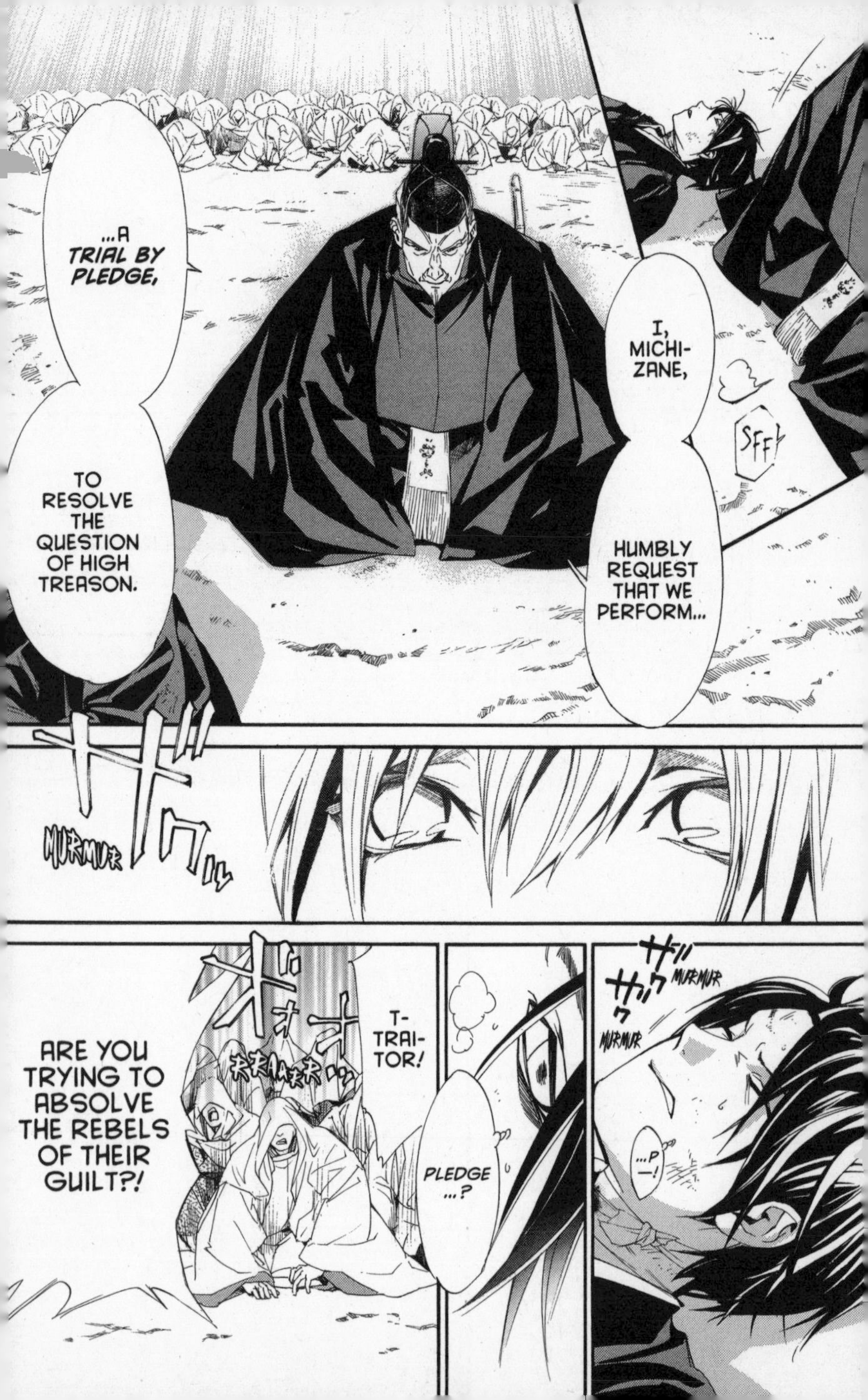
SFF
I, MICHIZANE, HUMBLY REQUEST THAT WE PERFORM...
...A TRIAL BY PLEDGE, TO RESOLVE THE QUESTION OF HIGH TREASON.
MURMUR
MURMUR
MURMUR
...P—!
PLEDGE...?
T-TRAITOR!
ARE YOU TRYING TO ABSOLVE THE REBELS OF THEIR GUILT?!

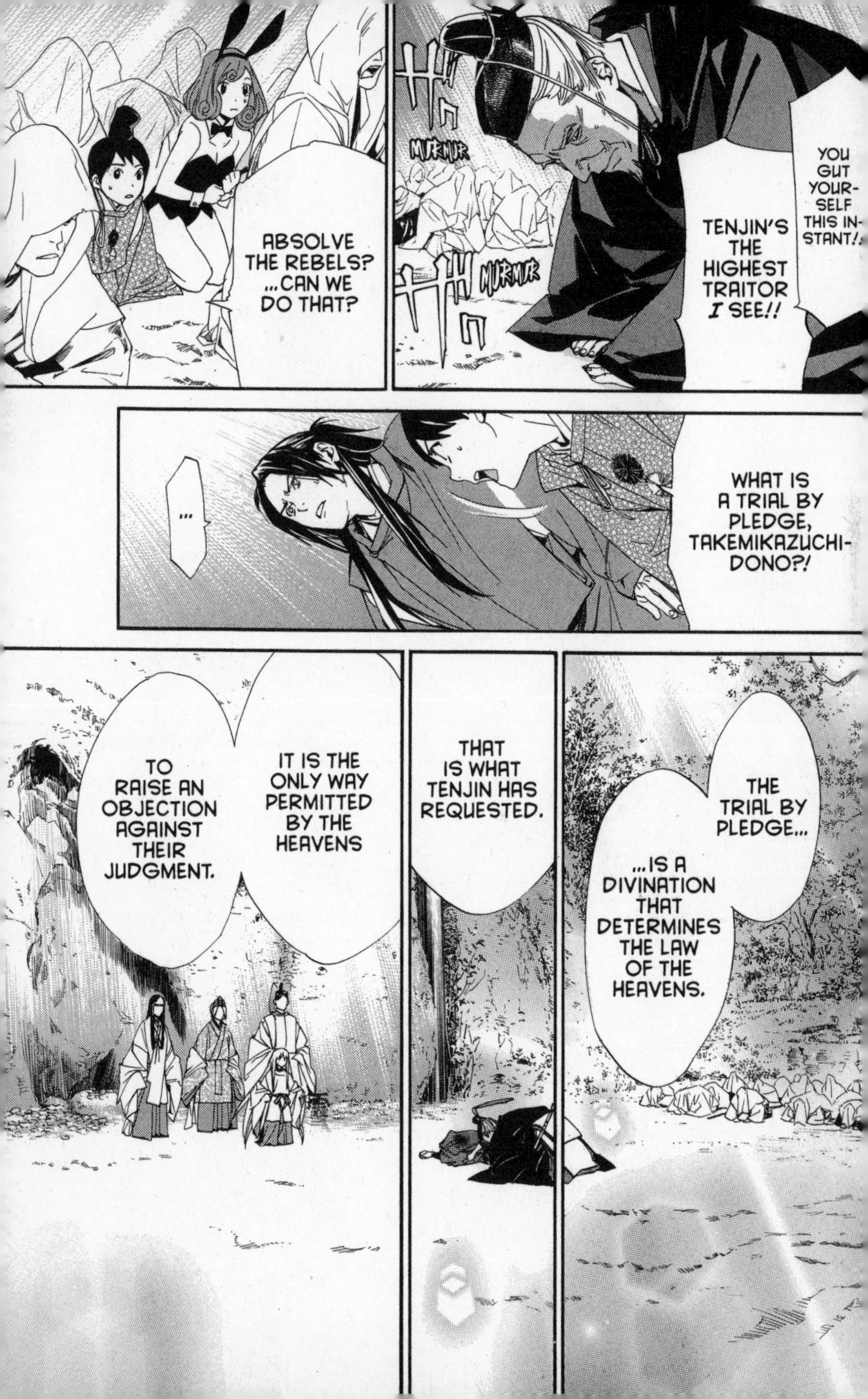
YOU GUT YOURSELF THIS INSTANT!!
TENJIN'S THE HIGHEST TRAITOR I SEE!!
MURMUR
MURMUR
ABSOLVE THE REBELS? ...CAN WE DO THAT?
WHAT IS A TRIAL BY PLEDGE, TAKEMIKAZUCHI-DONO?!
...
THE TRIAL BY PLEDGE...
...IS A DIVINATION THAT DETERMINES THE LAW OF THE HEAVENS.
THAT IS WHAT TENJIN HAS REQUESTED.
IT IS THE ONLY WAY PERMITTED BY THE HEAVENS
TO RAISE AN OBJECTION AGAINST THEIR JUDGMENT.

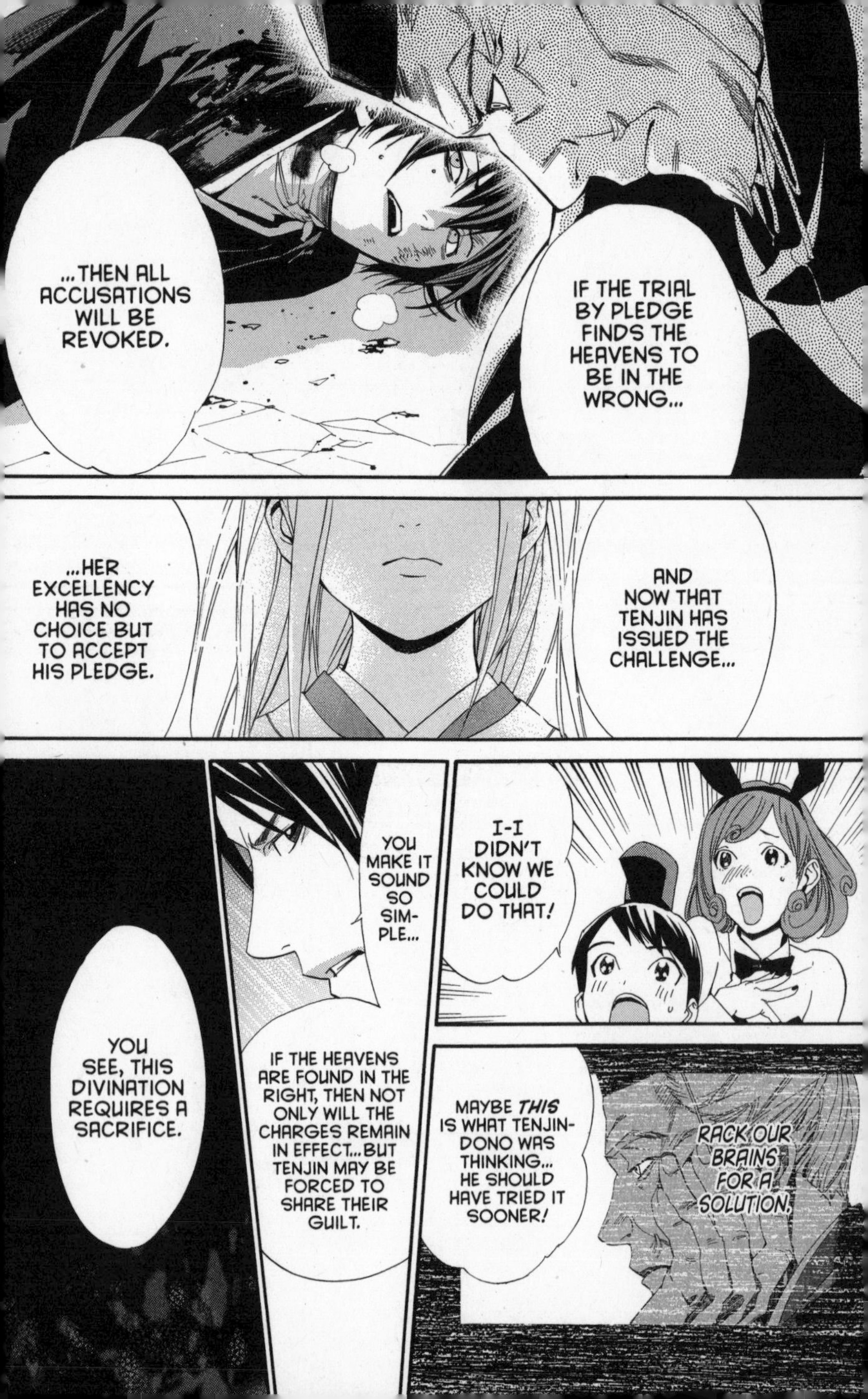
IF THE TRIAL BY PLEDGE FINDS THE HEAVENS TO BE IN THE WRONG...
...THEN ALL ACCUSATIONS WILL BE REVOKED.
AND NOW THAT TENJIN HAS ISSUED THE CHALLENGE...
...HER EXCELLENCY HAS NO CHOICE BUT TO ACCEPT HIS PLEDGE.
I-I DIDN'T KNOW WE COULD DO THAT!
RACK OUR BRAINS FOR A SOLUTION.
MAYBE *THIS* IS WHAT TENJIN-DONO WAS THINKING... HE SHOULD HAVE TRIED IT SOONER!
YOU MAKE IT SOUND SO SIM-PLE...
IF THE HEAVENS ARE FOUND IN THE RIGHT, THEN NOT ONLY WILL THE CHARGES REMAIN IN EFFECT...BUT TENJIN MAY BE FORCED TO SHARE THEIR GUILT.
YOU SEE, THIS DIVINATION REQUIRES A SACRIFICE.

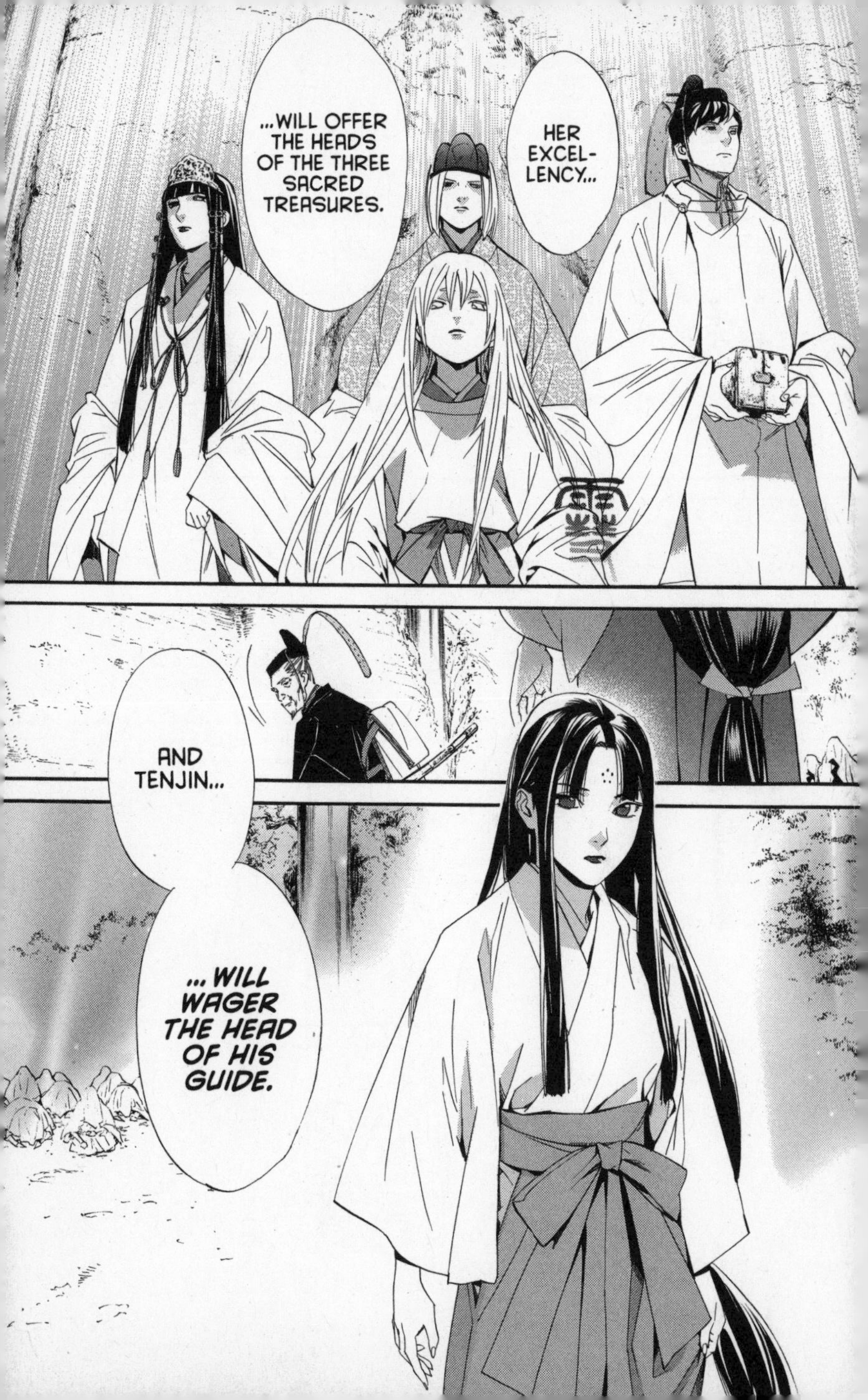
HER EXCELLENCY...
...WILL OFFER THE HEADS OF THE THREE SACRED TREASURES.
AND TENJIN...
...WILL WAGER THE HEAD OF HIS GUIDE.

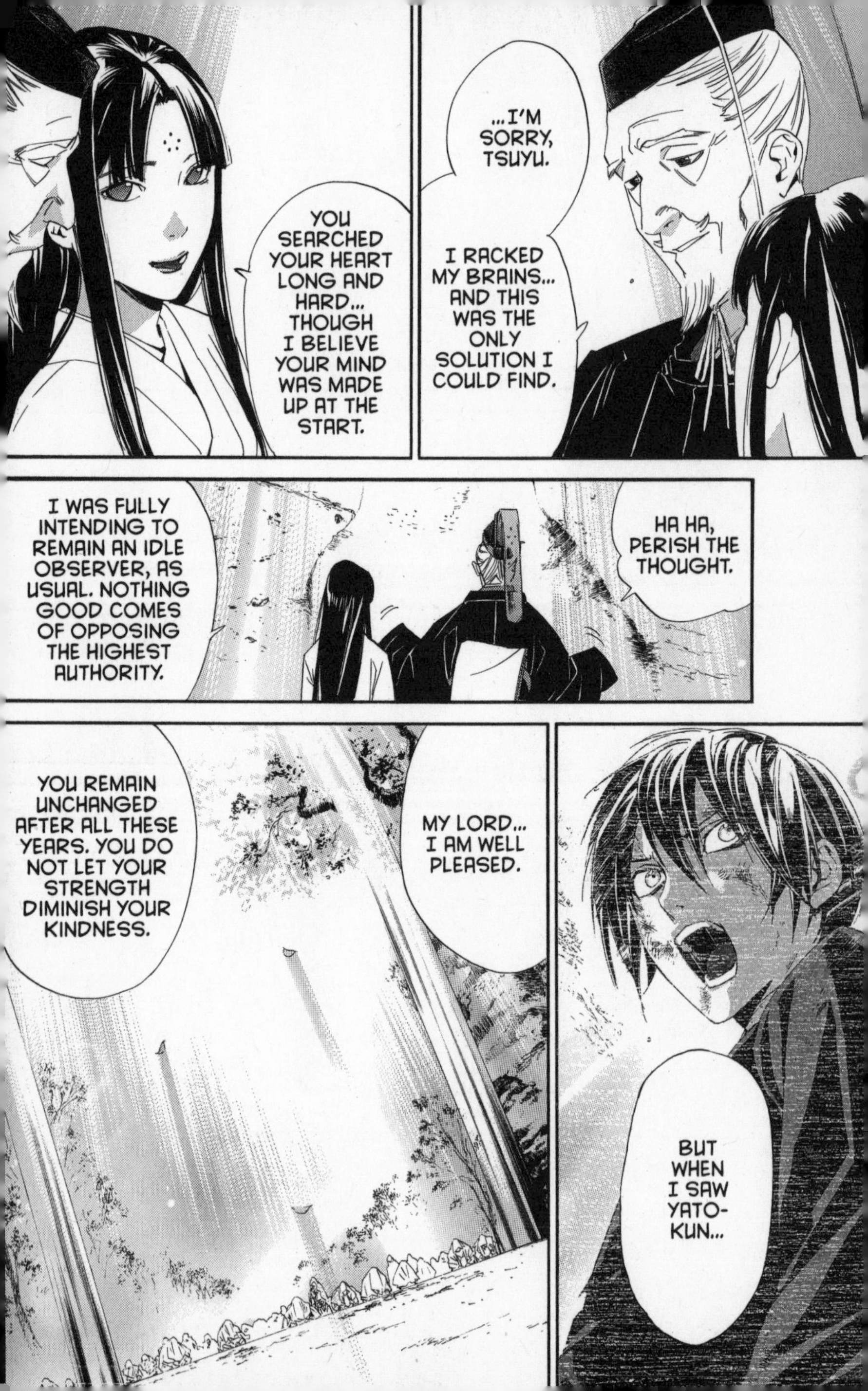
...I'M SORRY, TSUYU.
I RACKED MY BRAINS... AND THIS WAS THE ONLY SOLUTION I COULD FIND.
YOU SEARCHED YOUR HEART LONG AND HARD... THOUGH I BELIEVE YOUR MIND WAS MADE UP AT THE START.
HA HA, PERISH THE THOUGHT.
I WAS FULLY INTENDING TO REMAIN AN IDLE OBSERVER, AS USUAL. NOTHING GOOD COMES OF OPPOSING THE HIGHEST AUTHORITY.
BUT WHEN I SAW YATO-KUN...
MY LORD... I AM WELL PLEASED.
YOU REMAIN UNCHANGED AFTER ALL THESE YEARS. YOU DO NOT LET YOUR STRENGTH DIMINISH YOUR KINDNESS.

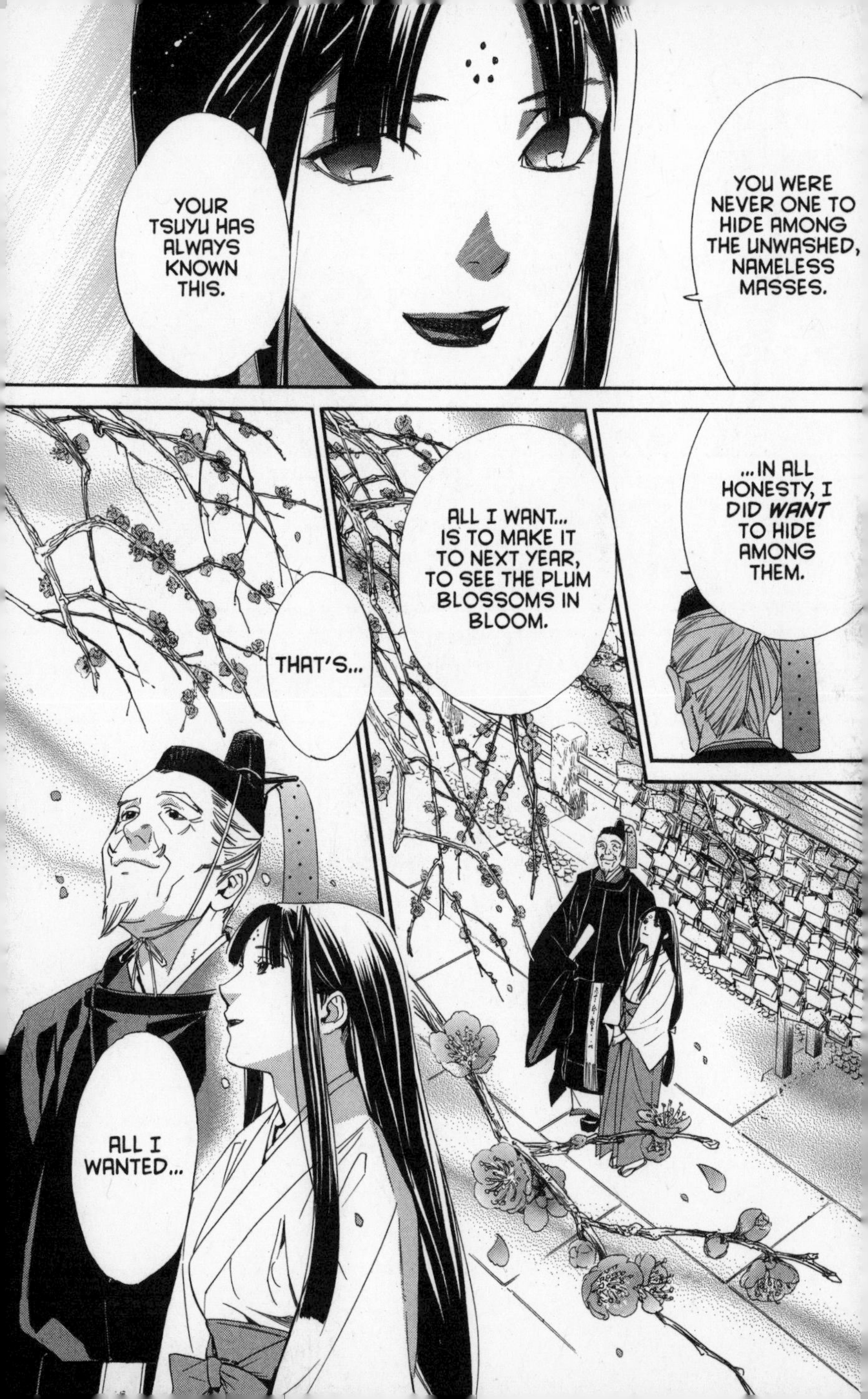
YOU WERE NEVER ONE TO HIDE AMONG THE UNWASHED, NAMELESS MASSES.
YOUR TSUYU HAS ALWAYS KNOWN THIS.
...IN ALL HONESTY, I DID *WANT* TO HIDE AMONG THEM.
ALL I WANT... IS TO MAKE IT TO NEXT YEAR, TO SEE THE PLUM BLOSSOMS IN BLOOM.
THAT'S...
ALL I WANTED...

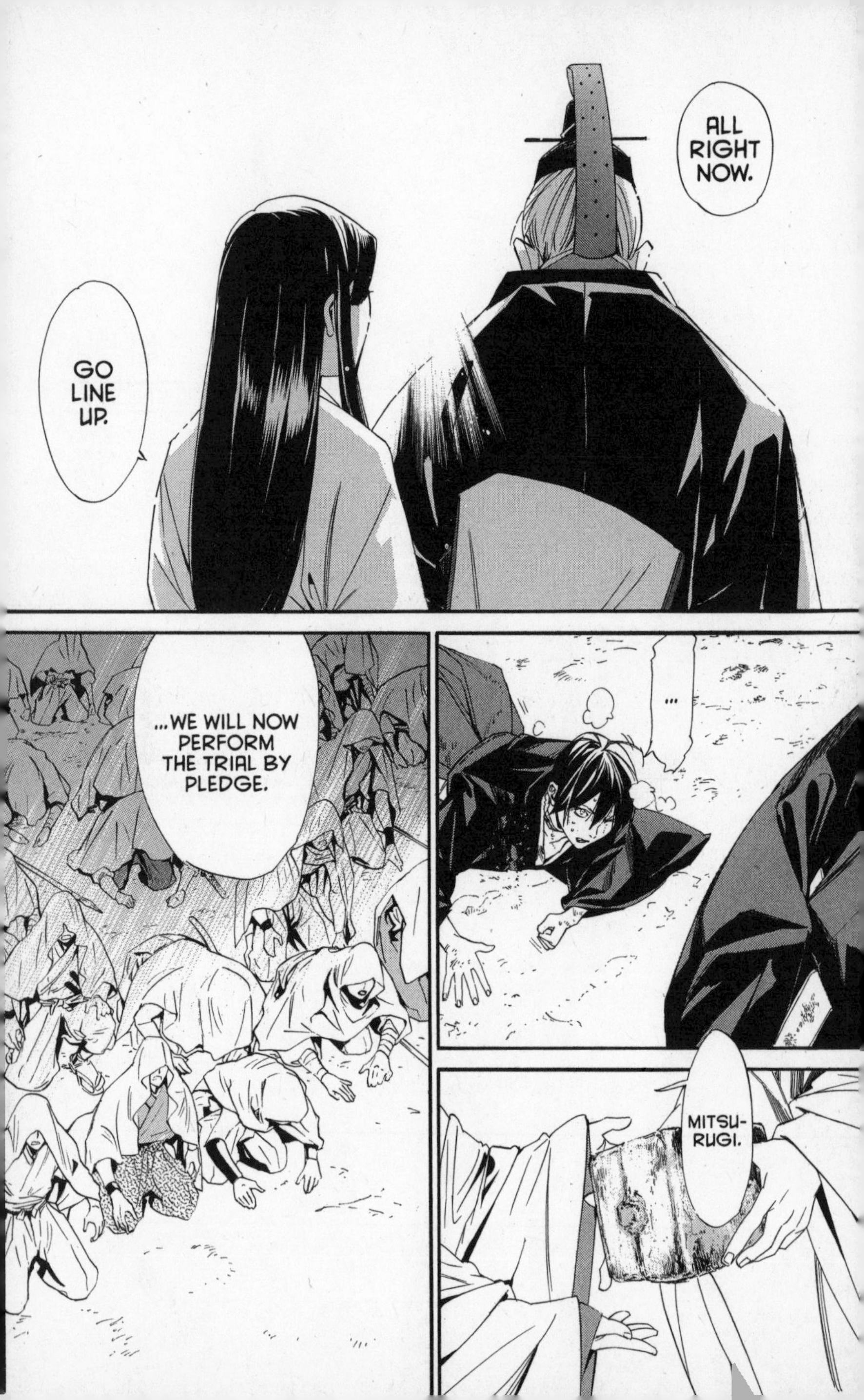
ALL RIGHT NOW.
GO LINE UP.
...
MITSU-RUGI.
...WE WILL NOW PERFORM THE TRIAL BY PLEDGE.

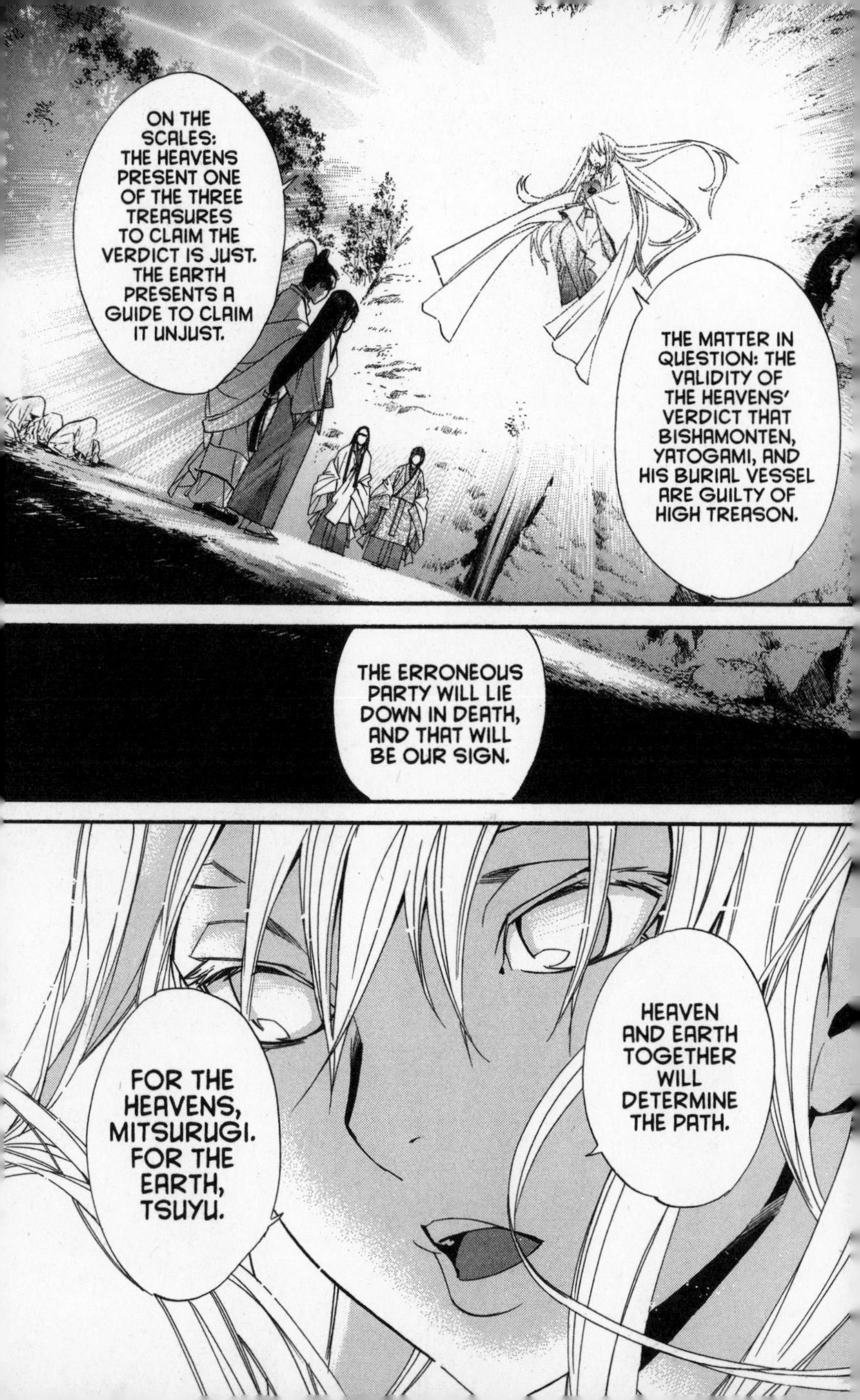
THE MATTER IN QUESTION: THE VALIDITY OF THE HEAVENS' VERDICT THAT BISHAMONTEN, YATOGAMI, AND HIS BURIAL VESSEL ARE GUILTY OF HIGH TREASON.
ON THE SCALES: THE HEAVENS PRESENT ONE OF THE THREE TREASURES TO CLAIM THE VERDICT IS JUST. THE EARTH PRESENTS A GUIDE TO CLAIM IT UNJUST.
THE ERRONEOUS PARTY WILL LIE DOWN IN DEATH, AND THAT WILL BE OUR SIGN.
HEAVEN AND EARTH TOGETHER WILL DETERMINE THE PATH.
FOR THE HEAVENS, MITSURUGI. FOR THE EARTH, TSUYU.

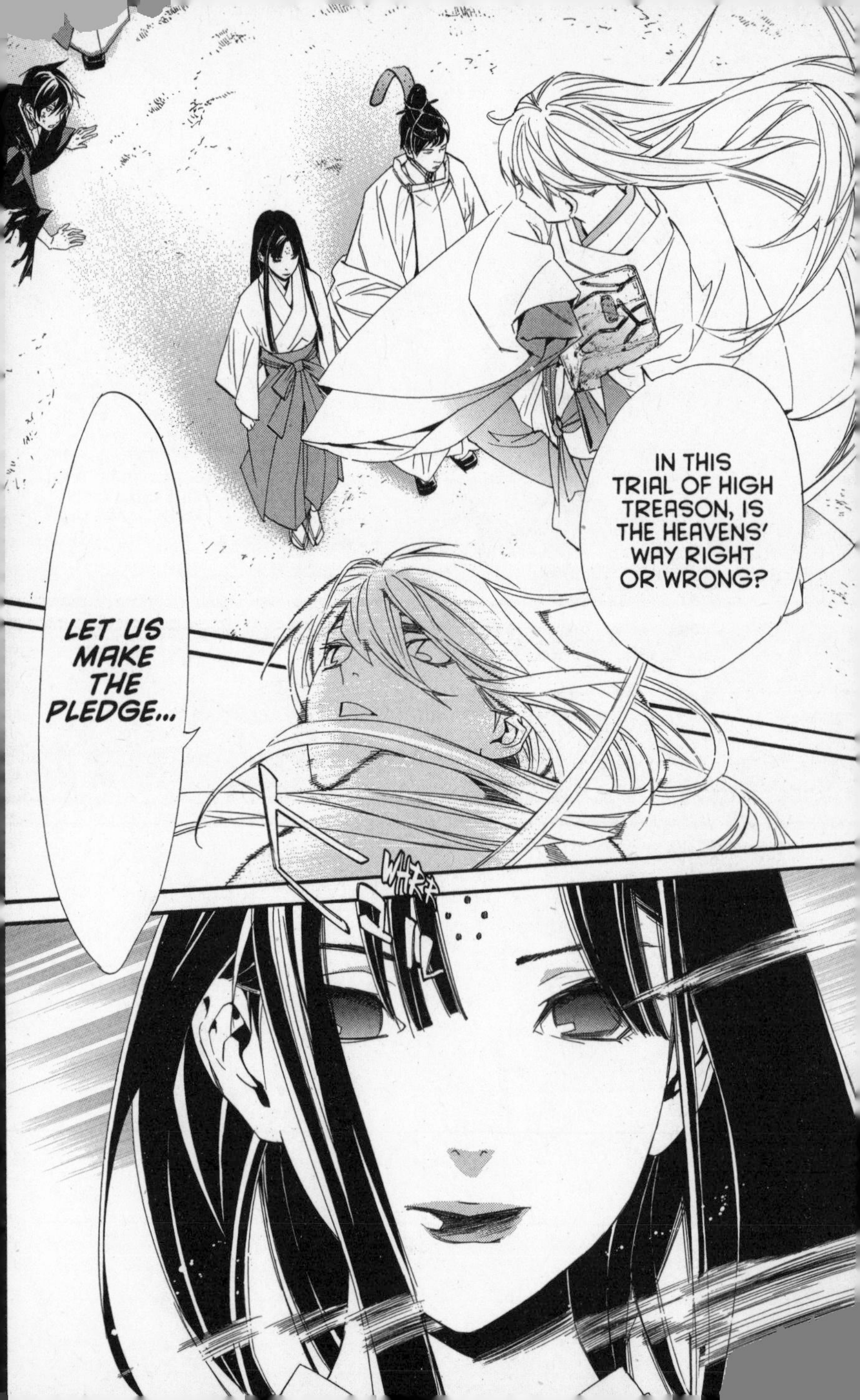
IN THIS TRIAL OF HIGH TREASON, IS THE HEAVENS' WAY RIGHT OR WRONG?
LET US MAKE THE PLEDGE...
WHRR

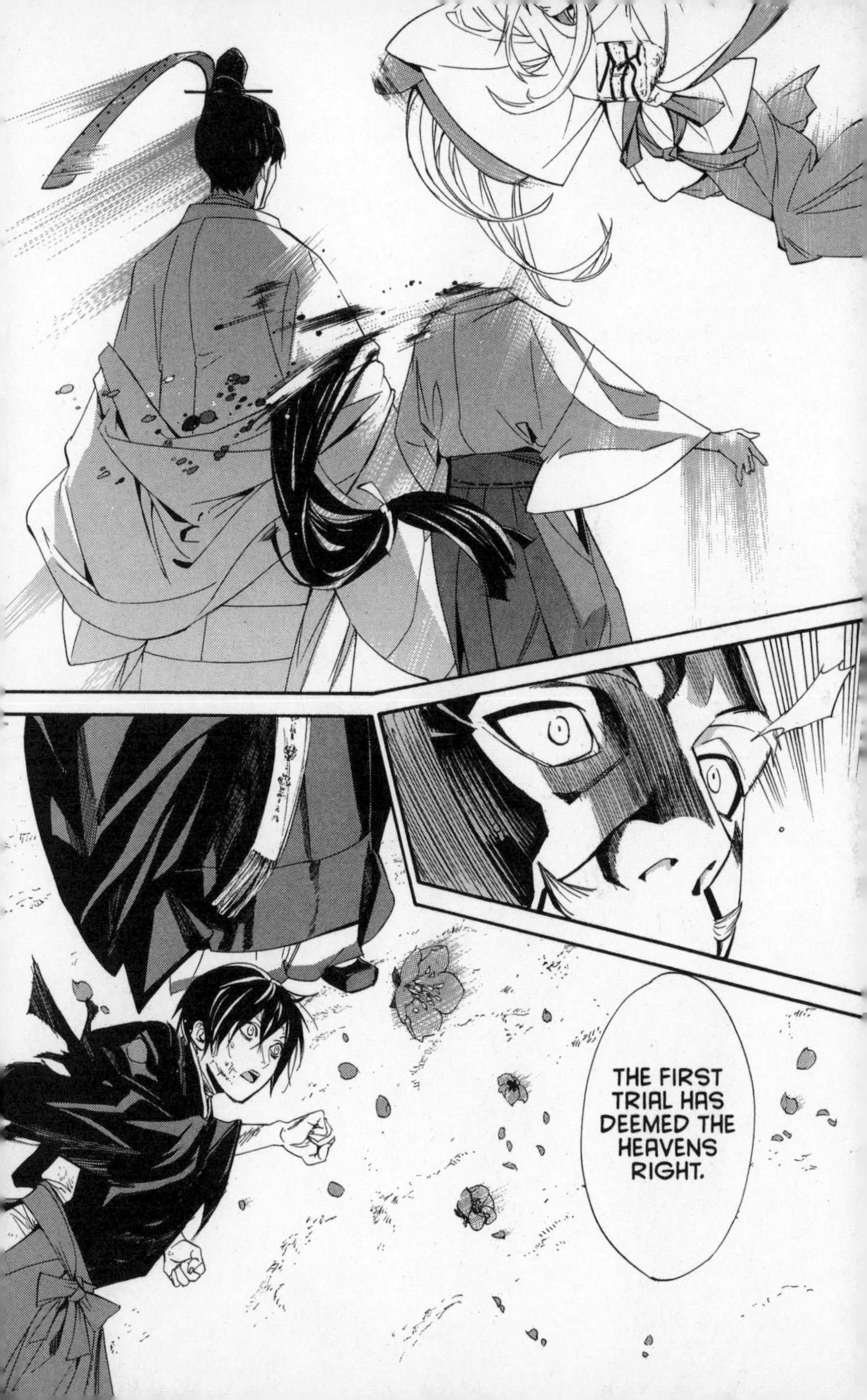
THE FIRST TRIAL HAS DEEMED THE HEAVENS RIGHT.

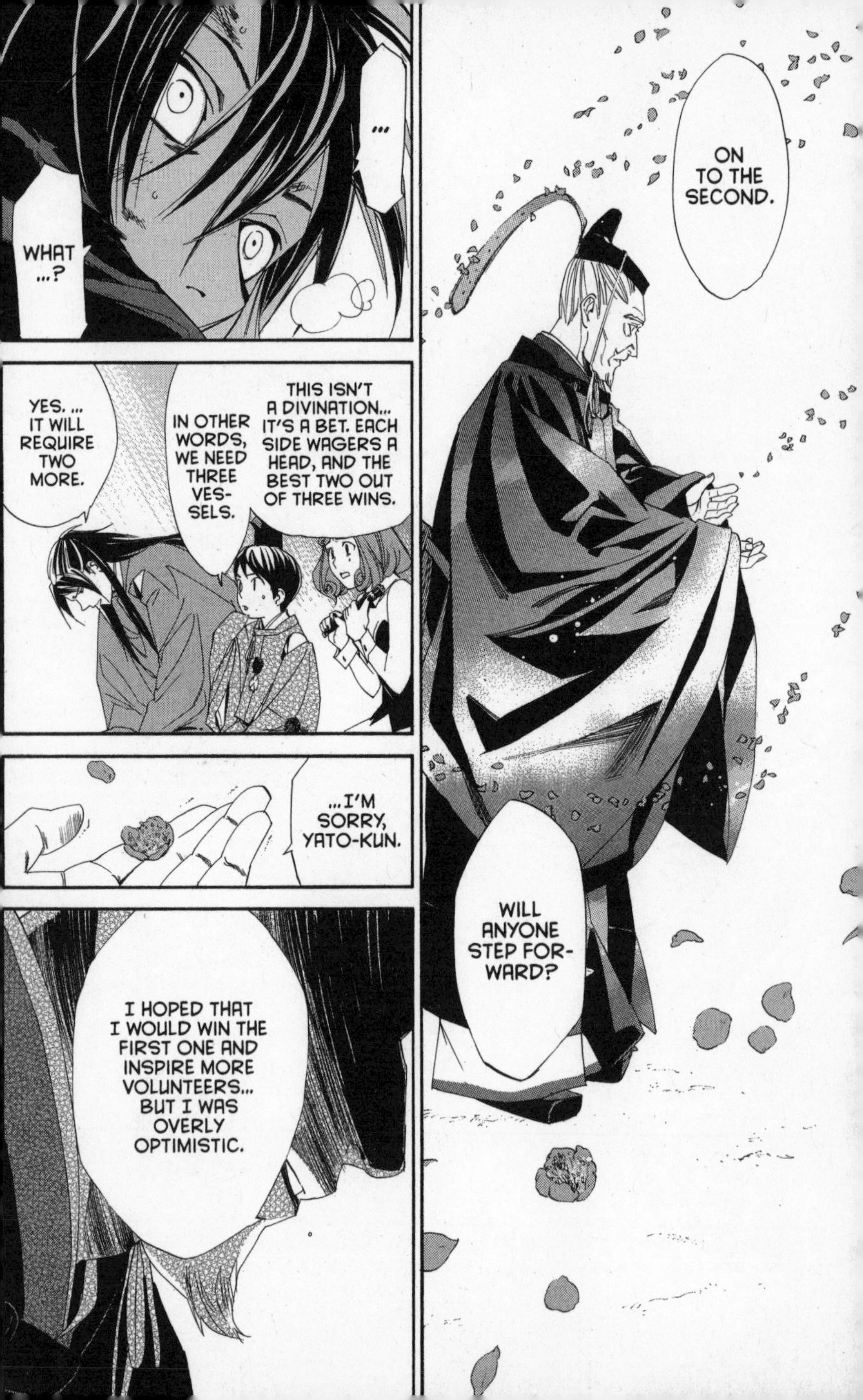

ON TO THE SECOND.
WILL ANYONE STEP FOR-WARD?
...
WHAT ...?
THIS ISN'T A DIVINATION... IT'S A BET. EACH SIDE WAGERS A HEAD, AND THE BEST TWO OUT OF THREE WINS.
IN OTHER WORDS, WE NEED THREE VES-SELS.
YES. ... IT WILL REQUIRE TWO MORE.
...I'M SORRY, YATO-KUN.
I HOPED THAT I WOULD WIN THE FIRST ONE AND INSPIRE MORE VOLUNTEERS... BUT I WAS OVERLY OPTIMISTIC.

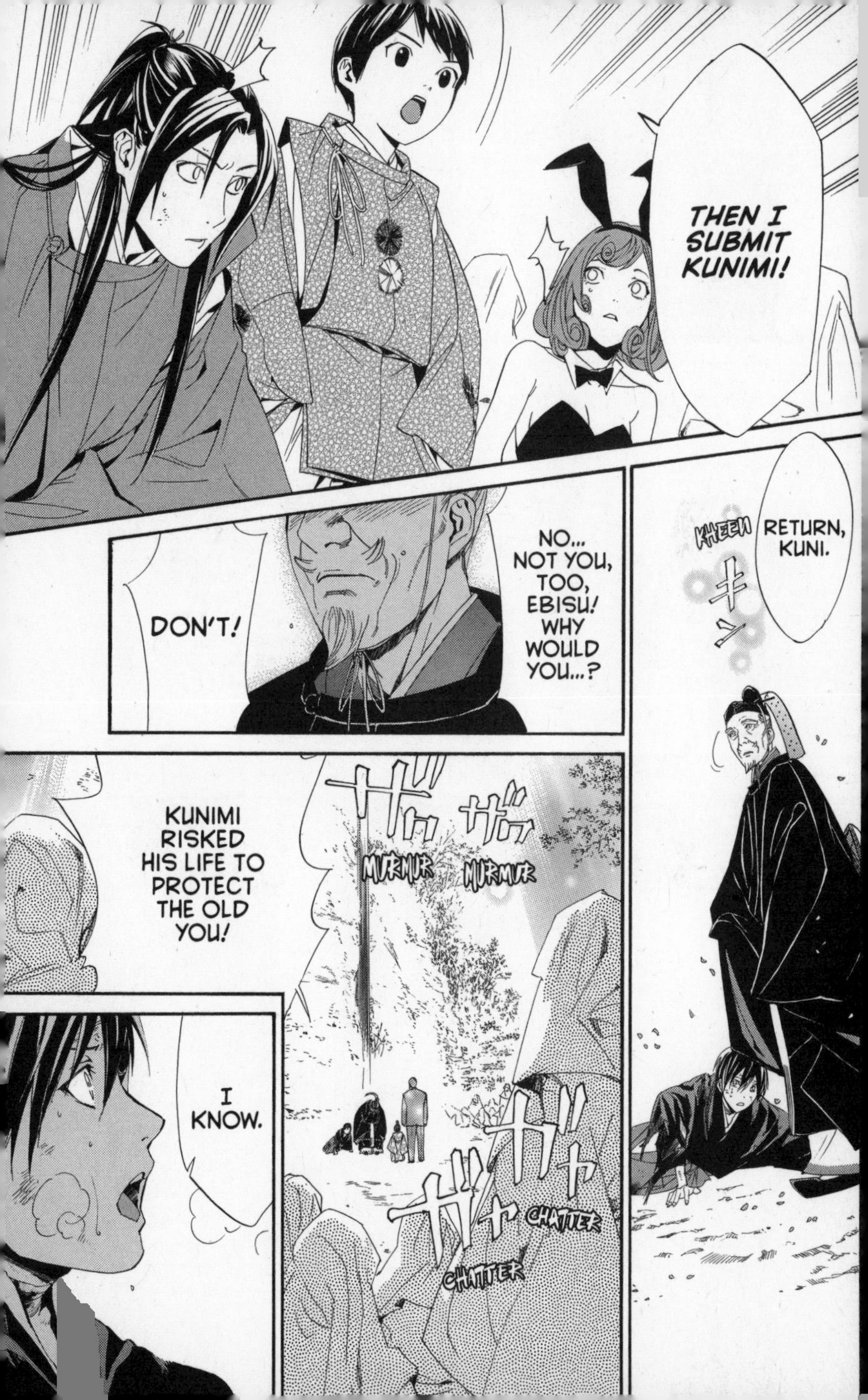
THEN I SUBMIT KUNIMI!
KHEEN
RETURN, KUNI.
NO... NOT YOU, TOO, EBISU! WHY WOULD YOU...?
DON'T!
MURMUR
MURMUR
KUNIMI RISKED HIS LIFE TO PROTECT THE OLD YOU!
CHATTER
CHATTER
I KNOW.

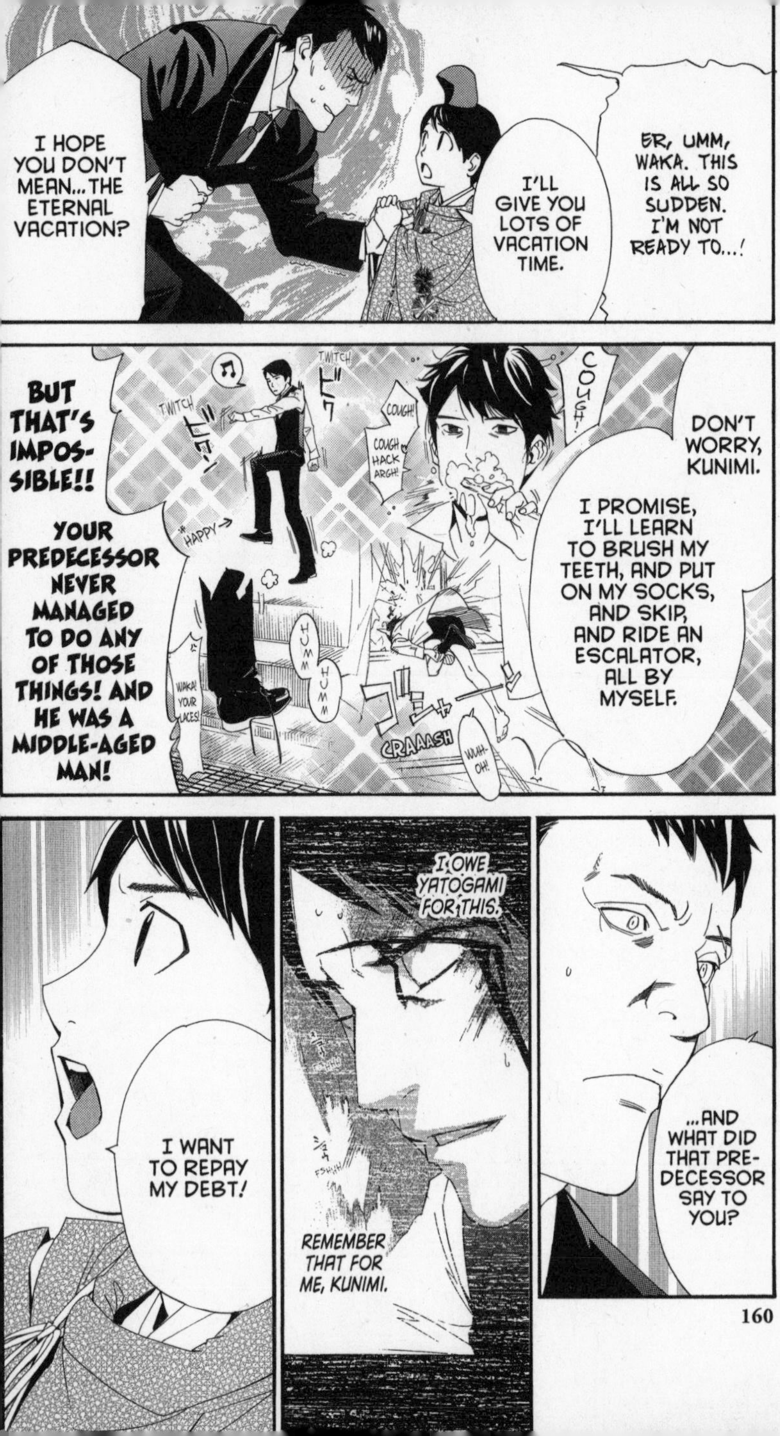
ER, UMM, WAKA. THIS IS ALL SO SUDDEN. I'M NOT READY TO...!
I'LL GIVE YOU LOTS OF VACATION TIME.
I HOPE YOU DON'T MEAN... THE ETERNAL VACATION?
DON'T WORRY, KUNIMI.
COUGH!
I PROMISE, I'LL LEARN TO BRUSH MY TEETH, AND PUT ON MY SOCKS, AND SKIP, AND RIDE AN ESCALATOR, ALL BY MYSELF.
COUGH!
COUGH HACK ARGH!
T.WITCH
T.WITCH
*HAPPY
HUMM
HUMM
WAKA! YOUR LACES!
CRAAASH
WUH-OH!
BUT THAT'S IMPOS-SIBLE!!
YOUR PREDECESSOR NEVER MANAGED TO DO ANY OF THOSE THINGS! AND HE WAS A MIDDLE-AGED MAN!
...AND WHAT DID THAT PRE-DECESSOR SAY TO YOU?
I OWE YATOGAMI FOR THIS.
REMEMBER THAT FOR ME, KUNIMI.
FSHHH
I WANT TO REPAY MY DEBT!

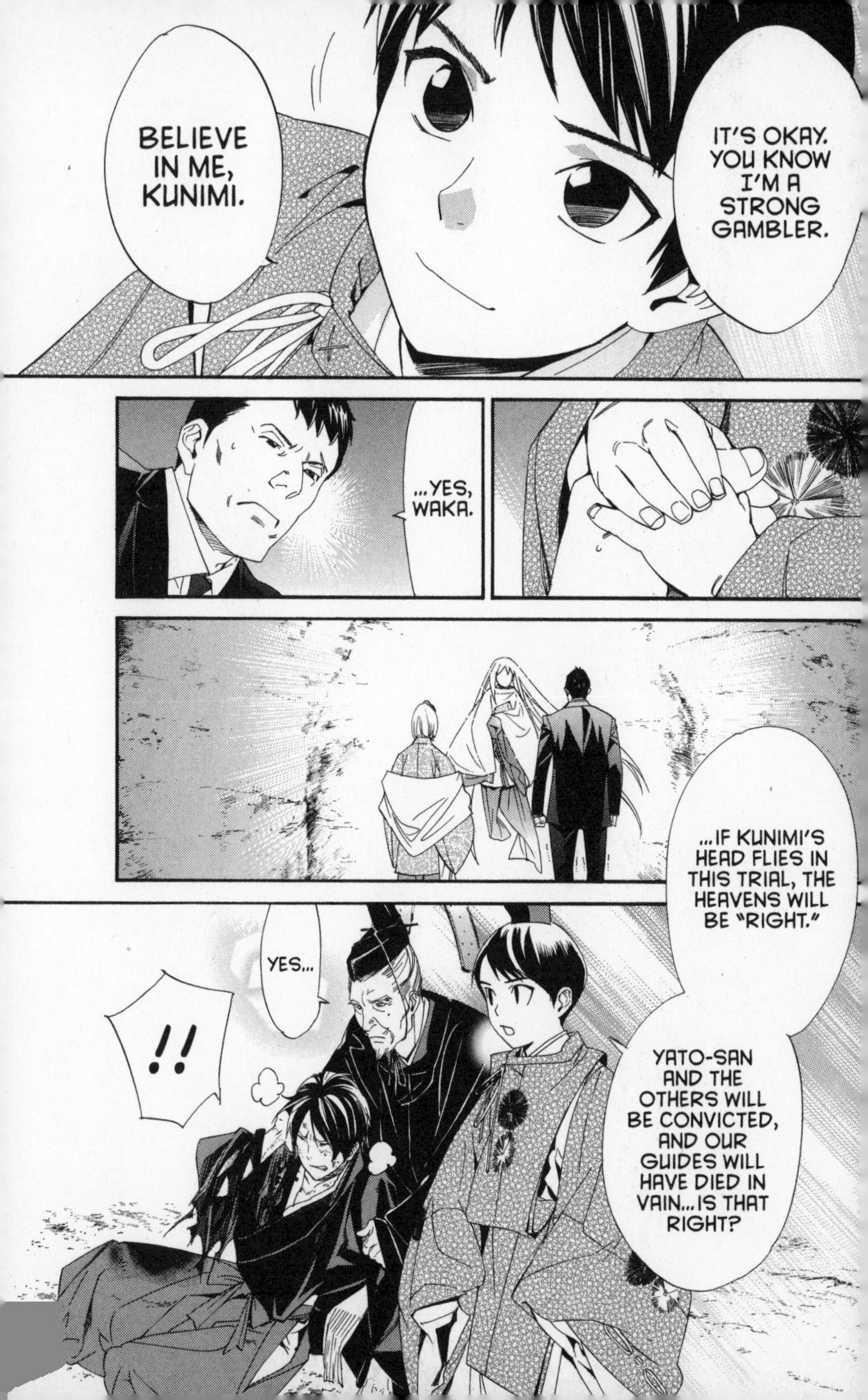

IT'S OKAY. YOU KNOW I'M A STRONG GAMBLER.
BELIEVE IN ME, KUNIMI.
...YES, WAKA.
...IF KUNIMI'S HEAD FLIES IN THIS TRIAL, THE HEAVENS WILL BE "RIGHT."
YATO-SAN AND THE OTHERS WILL BE CONVICTED, AND OUR GUIDES WILL HAVE DIED IN VAIN...IS THAT RIGHT?
YES...
!!

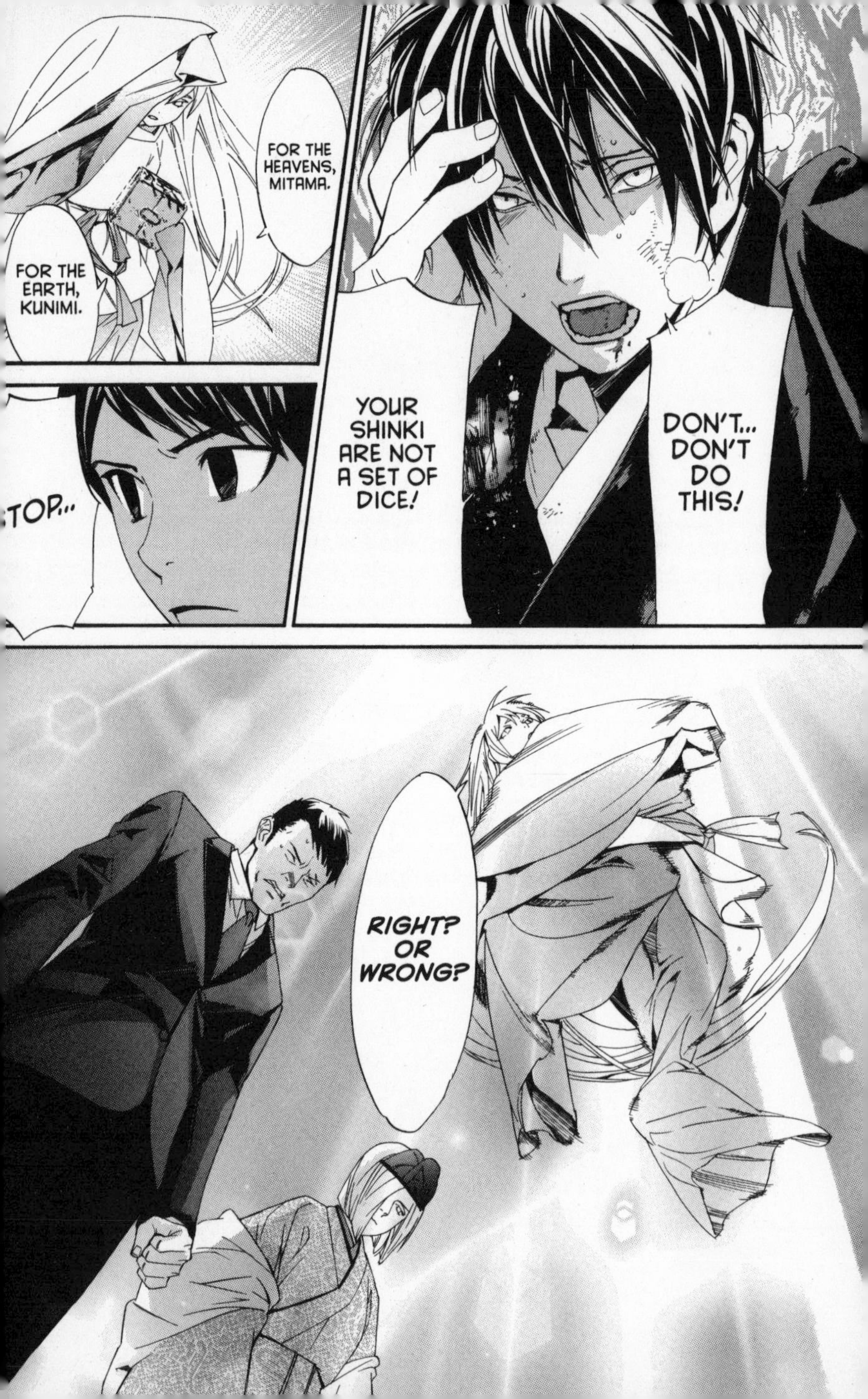
DON'T... DON'T DO THIS!
YOUR SHINKI ARE NOT A SET OF DICE!
FOR THE HEAVENS, MITAMA.
FOR THE EARTH, KUNIMI.
TOP...
RIGHT? OR WRONG?

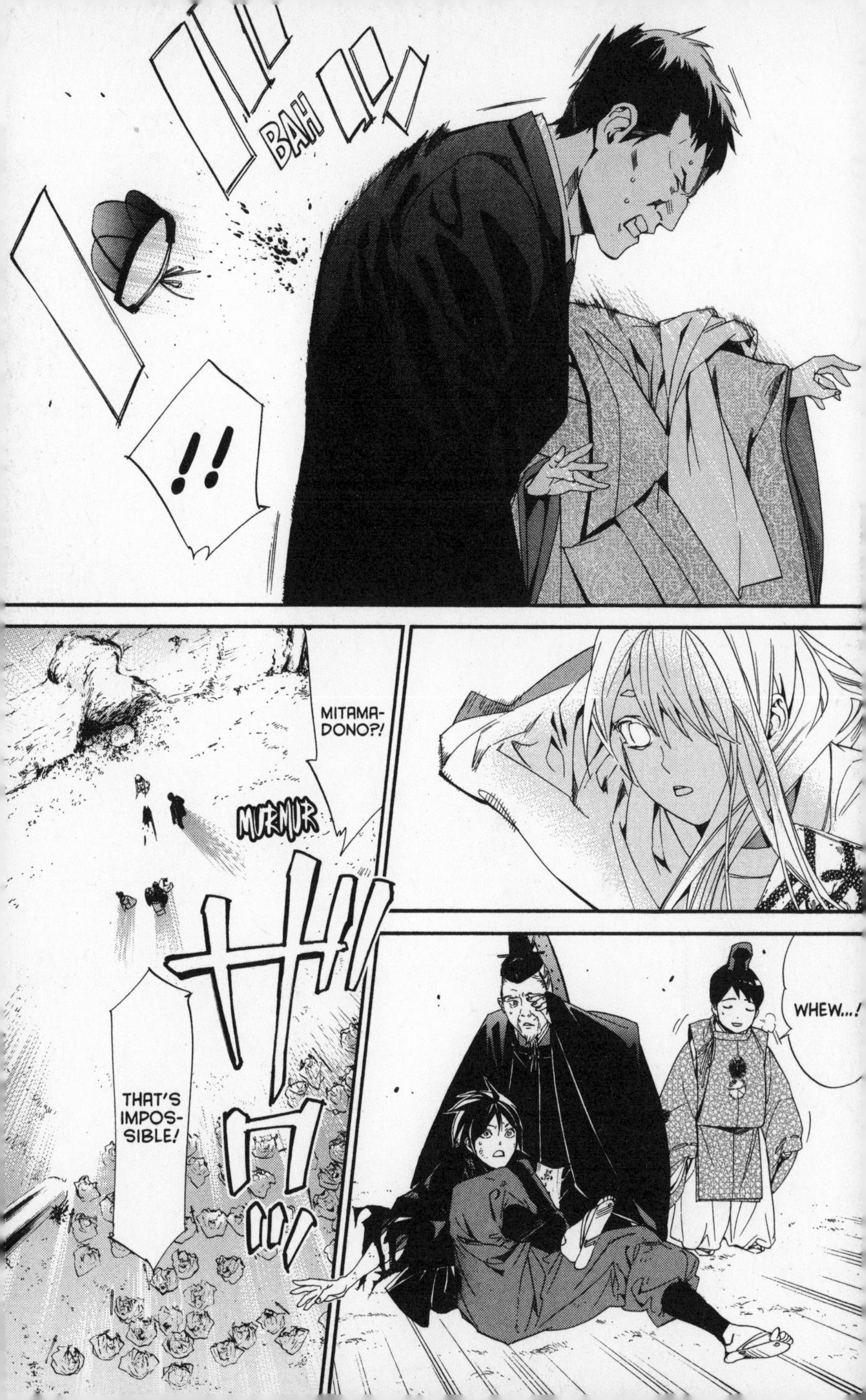
BAH
!!
WHEW...!
MITAMA-DONO?!
MURMUR
THAT'S IMPOSSIBLE!

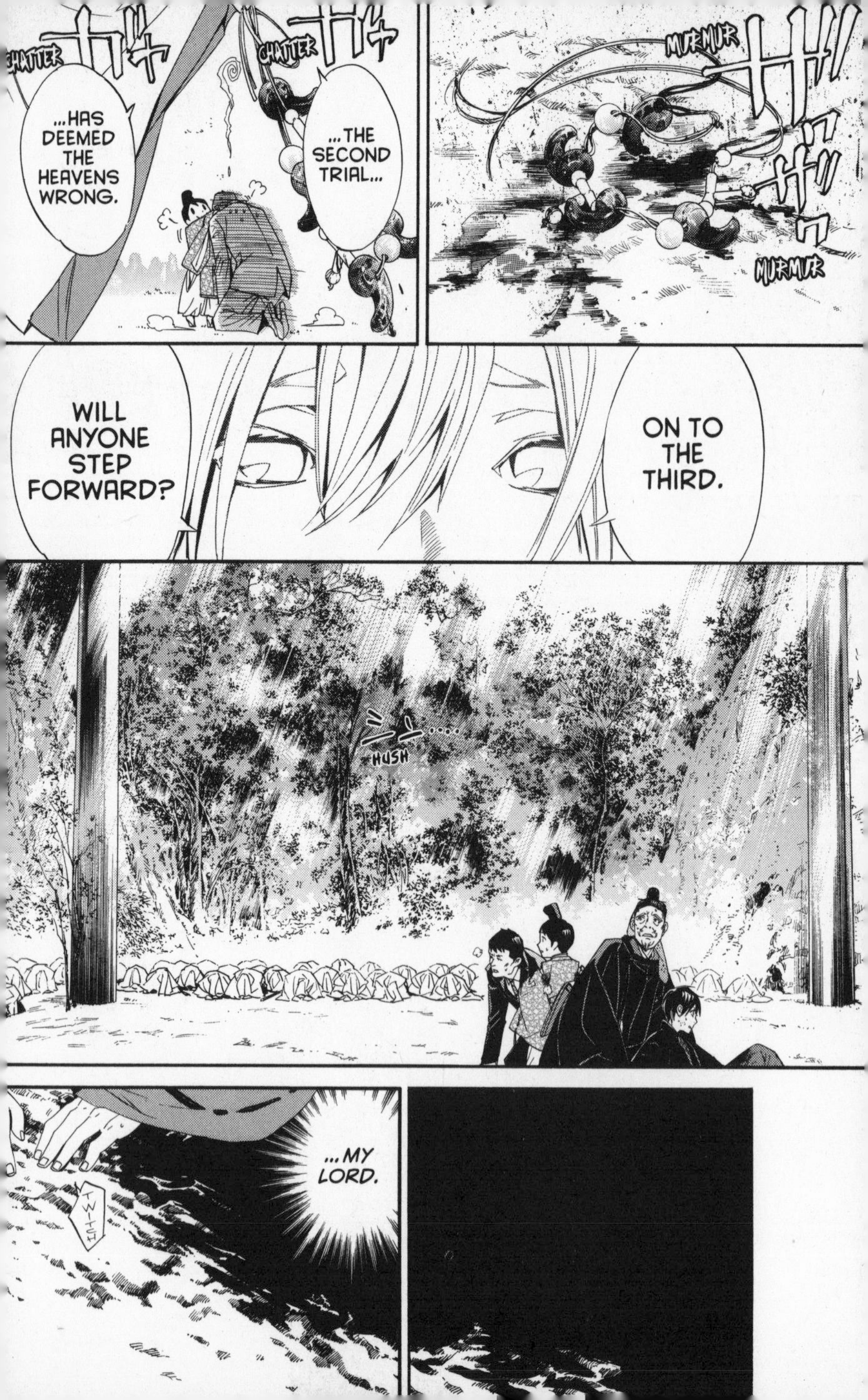
MURMUR
MURMUR
CHATTER
...THE SECOND TRIAL...
CHATTER
...HAS DEEMED THE HEAVENS WRONG.
ON TO THE THIRD.
WILL ANYONE STEP FORWARD?
HUSH
...MY LORD.
TWITCH

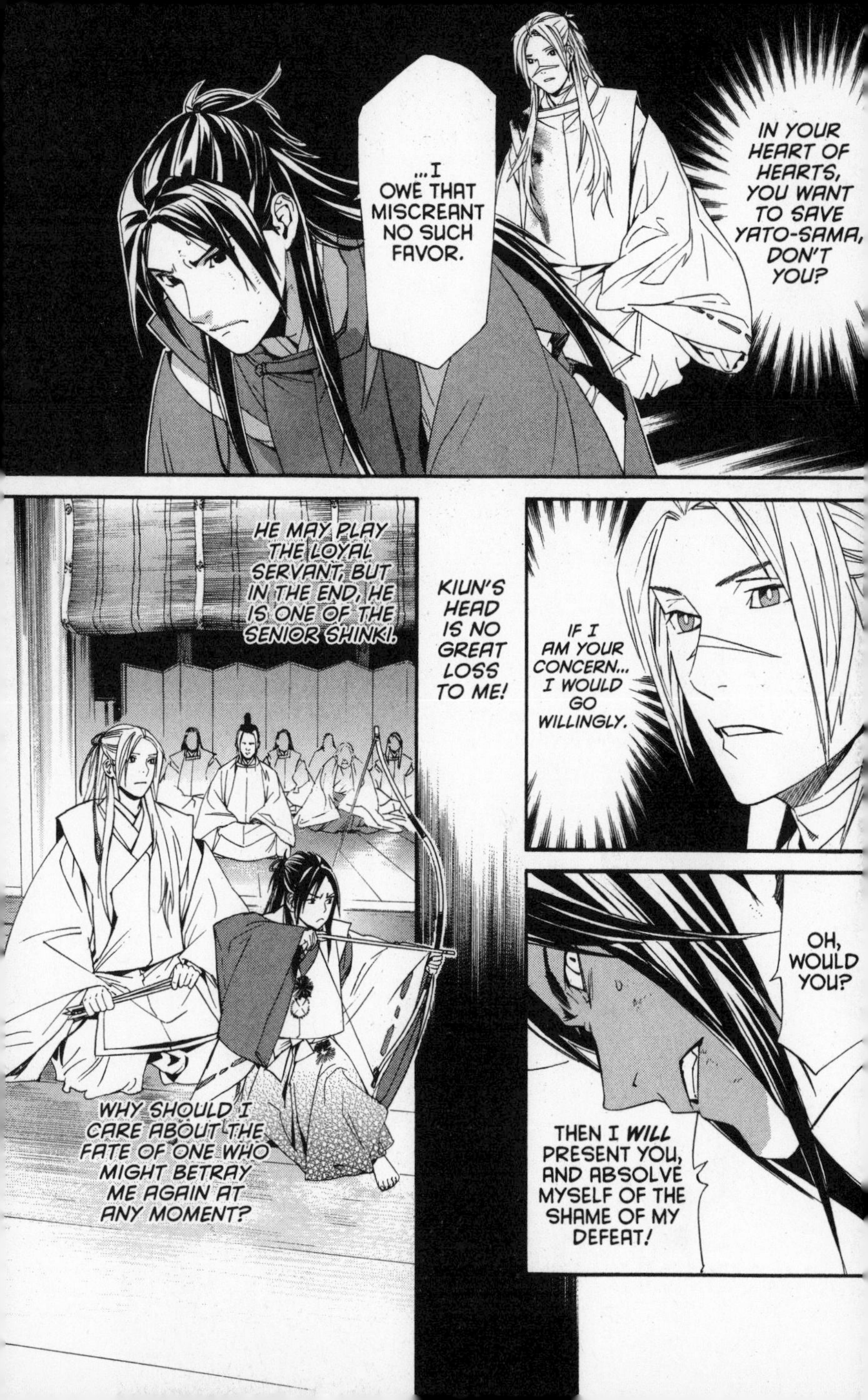
IN YOUR HEART OF HEARTS, YOU WANT TO SAVE YATO-SAMA, DON'T YOU?
...I OWE THAT MISCREANT NO SUCH FAVOR.
KIUN'S HEAD IS NO GREAT LOSS TO ME!
HE MAY PLAY THE LOYAL SERVANT, BUT IN THE END, HE IS ONE OF THE SENIOR SHINKI.
WHY SHOULD I CARE ABOUT THE FATE OF ONE WHO MIGHT BETRAY ME AGAIN AT ANY MOMENT?
IF I AM YOUR CONCERN... I WOULD GO WILLINGLY.
OH, WOULD YOU?
THEN I *WILL* PRESENT YOU, AND ABSOLVE MYSELF OF THE SHAME OF MY DEFEAT!

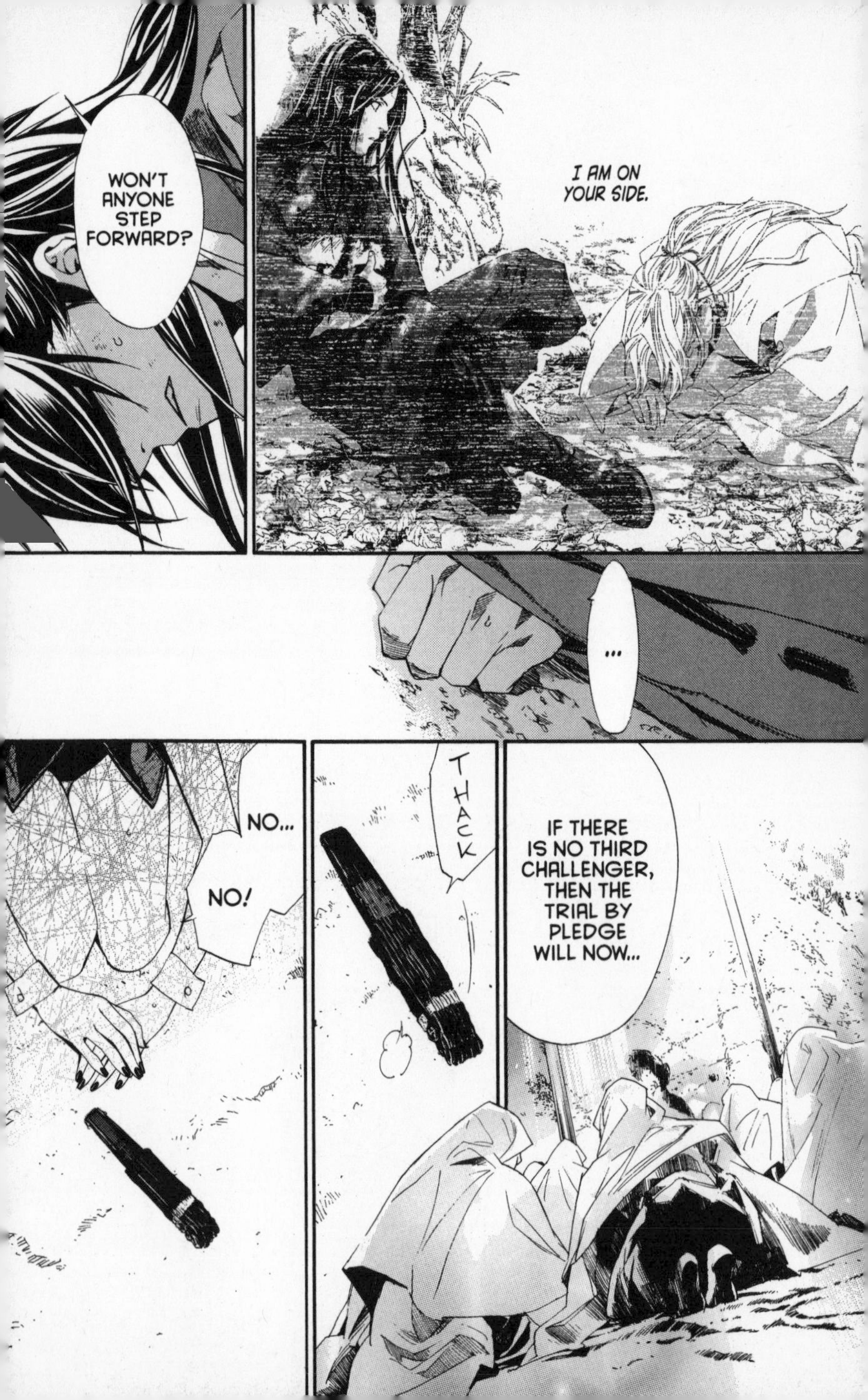
I AM ON YOUR SIDE.
WON'T ANYONE STEP FORWARD?
...
IF THERE IS NO THIRD CHALLENGER, THEN THE TRIAL BY PLEDGE WILL NOW...
THACK
NO...
NO!

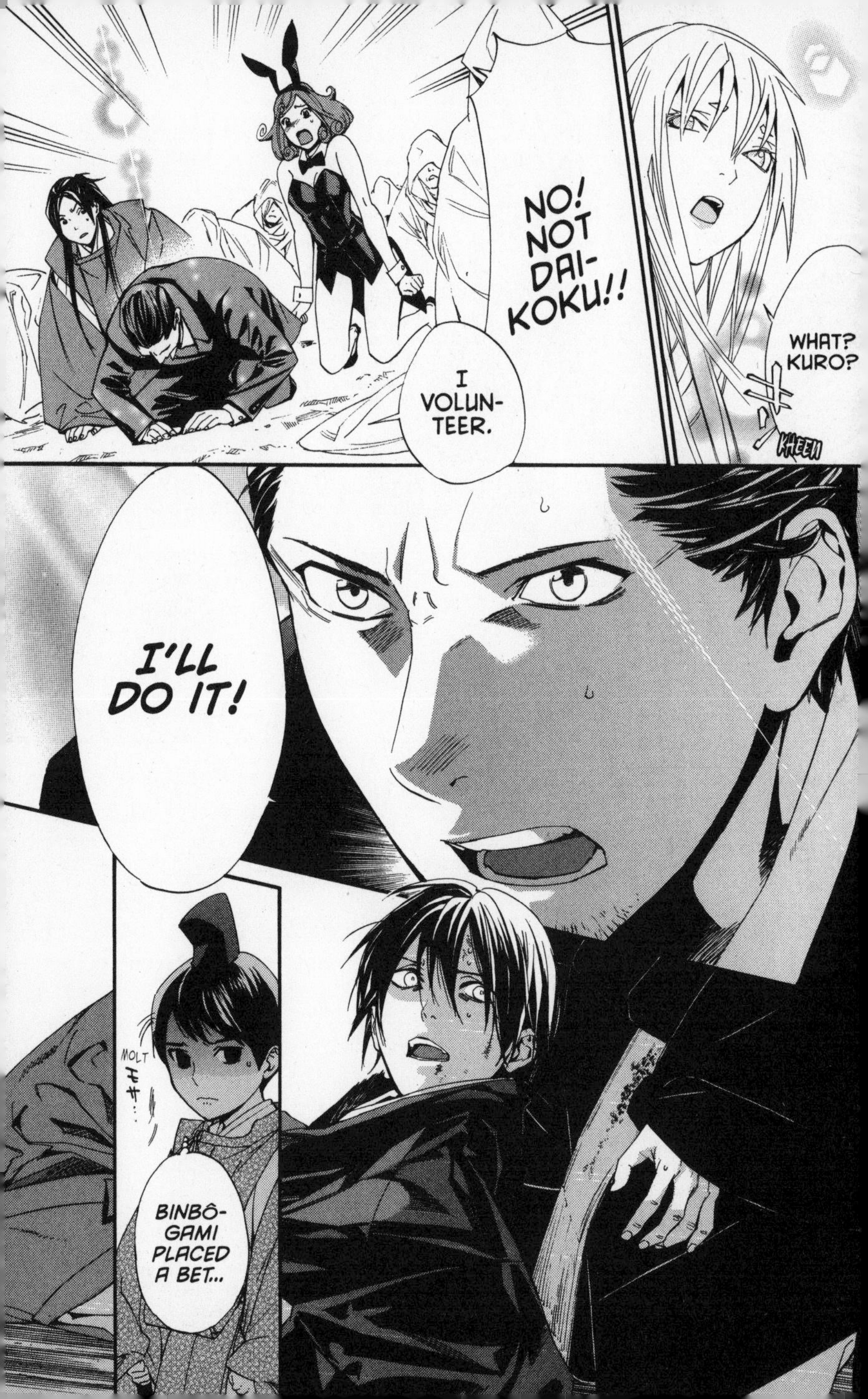
WHAT? KURO?
KHEEN
NO! NOT DAI-KOKU!!
I VOLUN-TEER.
I'LL DO IT!
MOLT
BINBÔ-GAMI PLACED A BET...

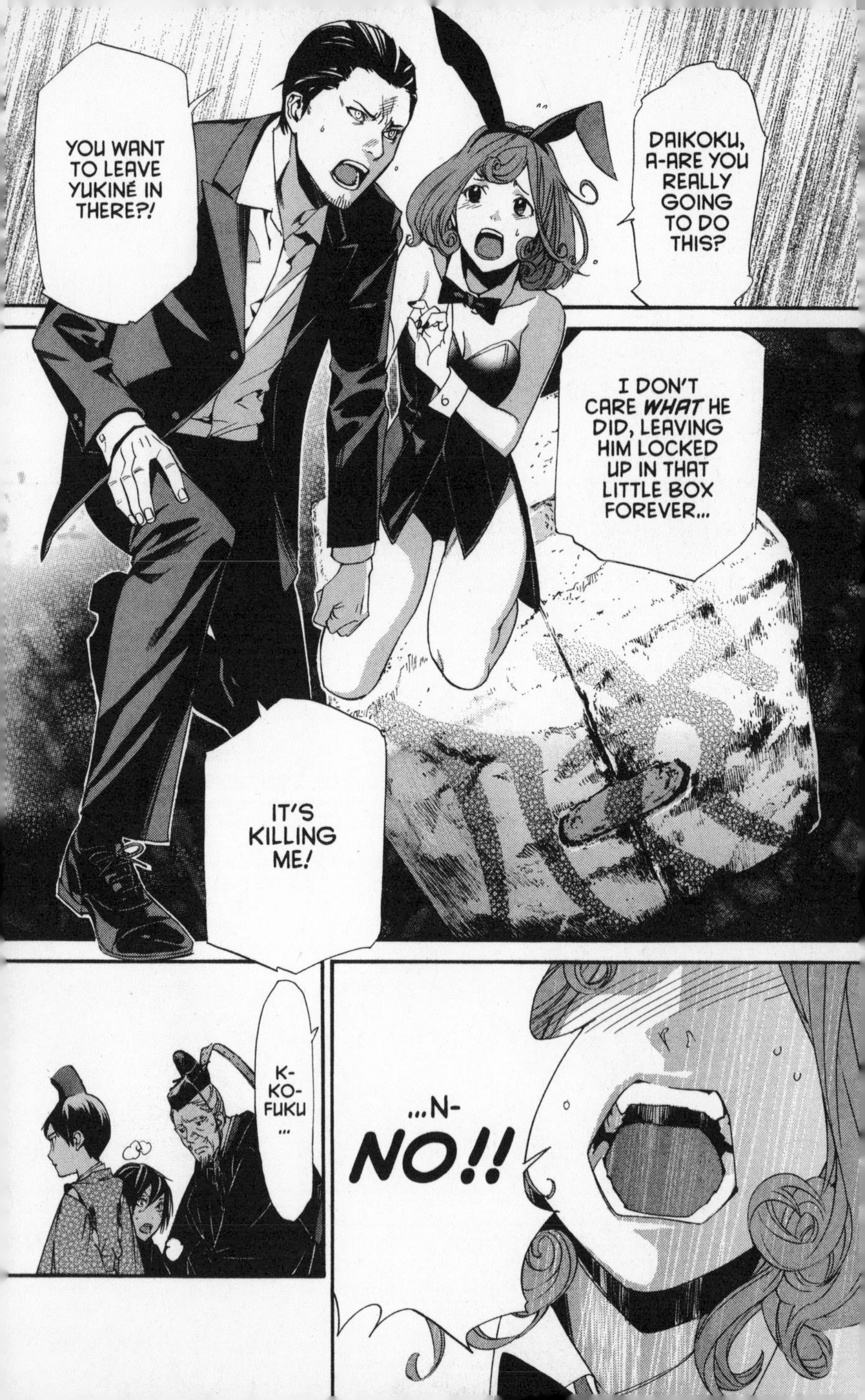
DAIKOKU, A-ARE YOU REALLY GOING TO DO THIS?
YOU WANT TO LEAVE YUKINÉ IN THERE?!
I DON'T CARE *WHAT* HE DID, LEAVING HIM LOCKED UP IN THAT LITTLE BOX FOREVER...
IT'S KILLING ME!
...N- NO!!
K-KO-FUKU ...

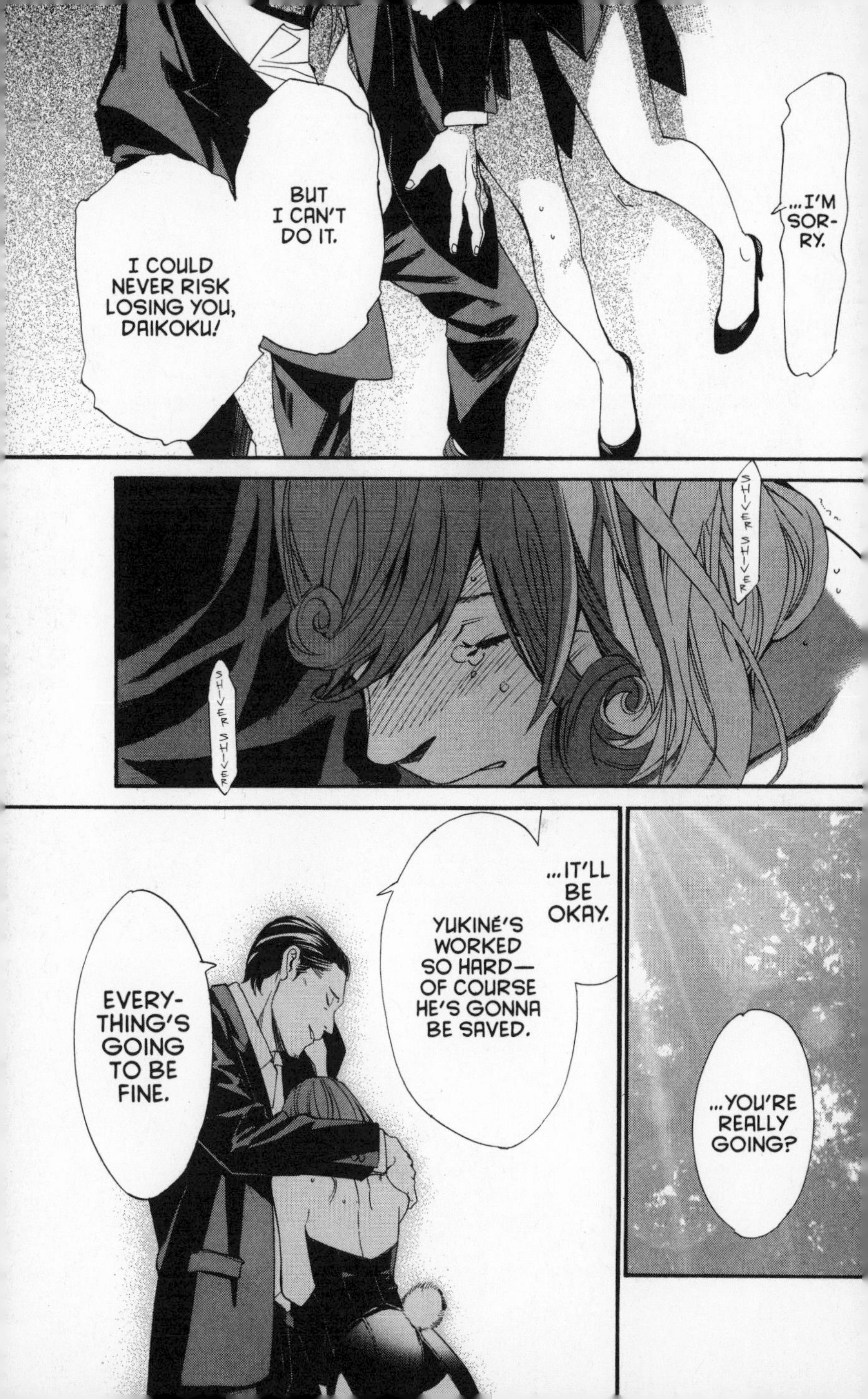
...I'M SOR-RY.
BUT I CAN'T DO IT.
I COULD NEVER RISK LOSING YOU, DAIKOKU!
SHIVER SHIVER
SHIVER SHIVER
...YOU'RE REALLY GOING?
...IT'LL BE OKAY.
YUKINÉ'S WORKED SO HARD— OF COURSE HE'S GONNA BE SAVED.
EVERY-THING'S GOING TO BE FINE.

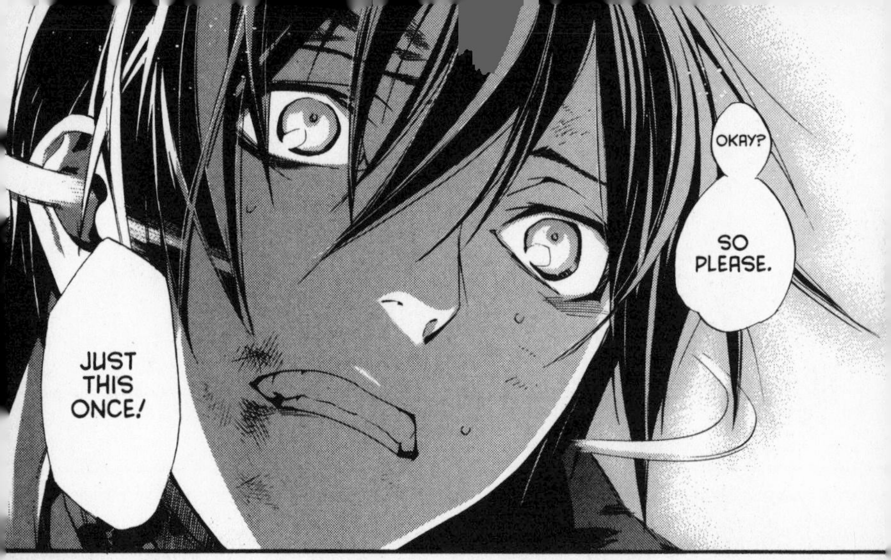
OKAY?
SO PLEASE.
JUST THIS ONCE!
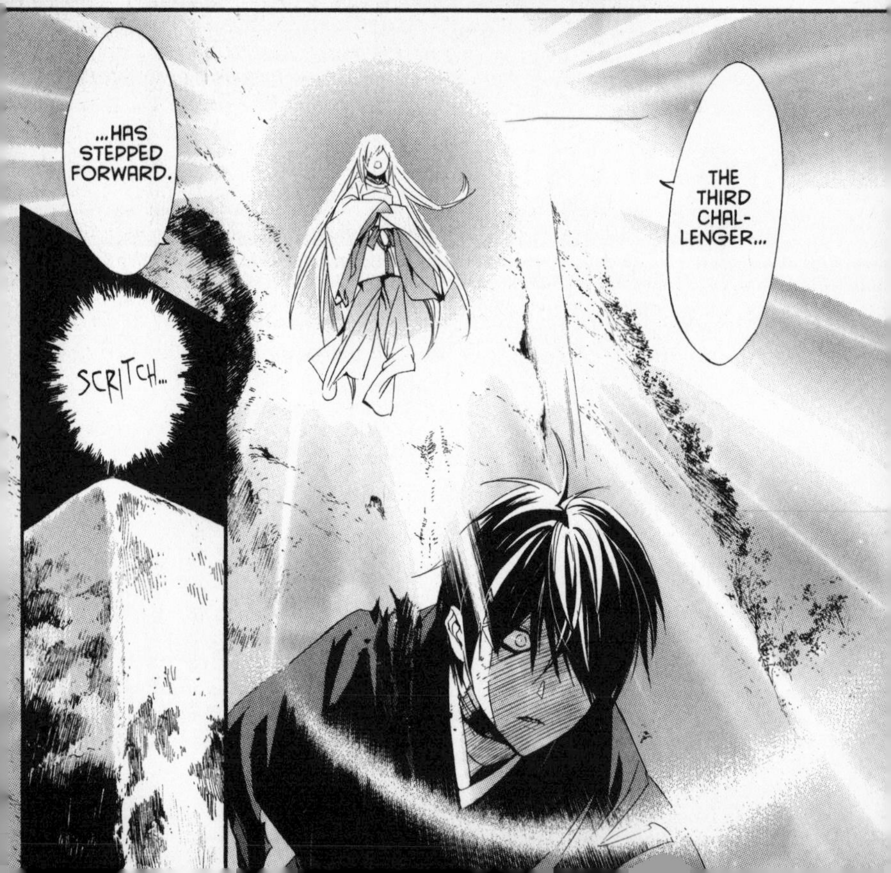
THE THIRD CHAL-LENGER...
...HAS STEPPED FORWARD.
SCRITCH...

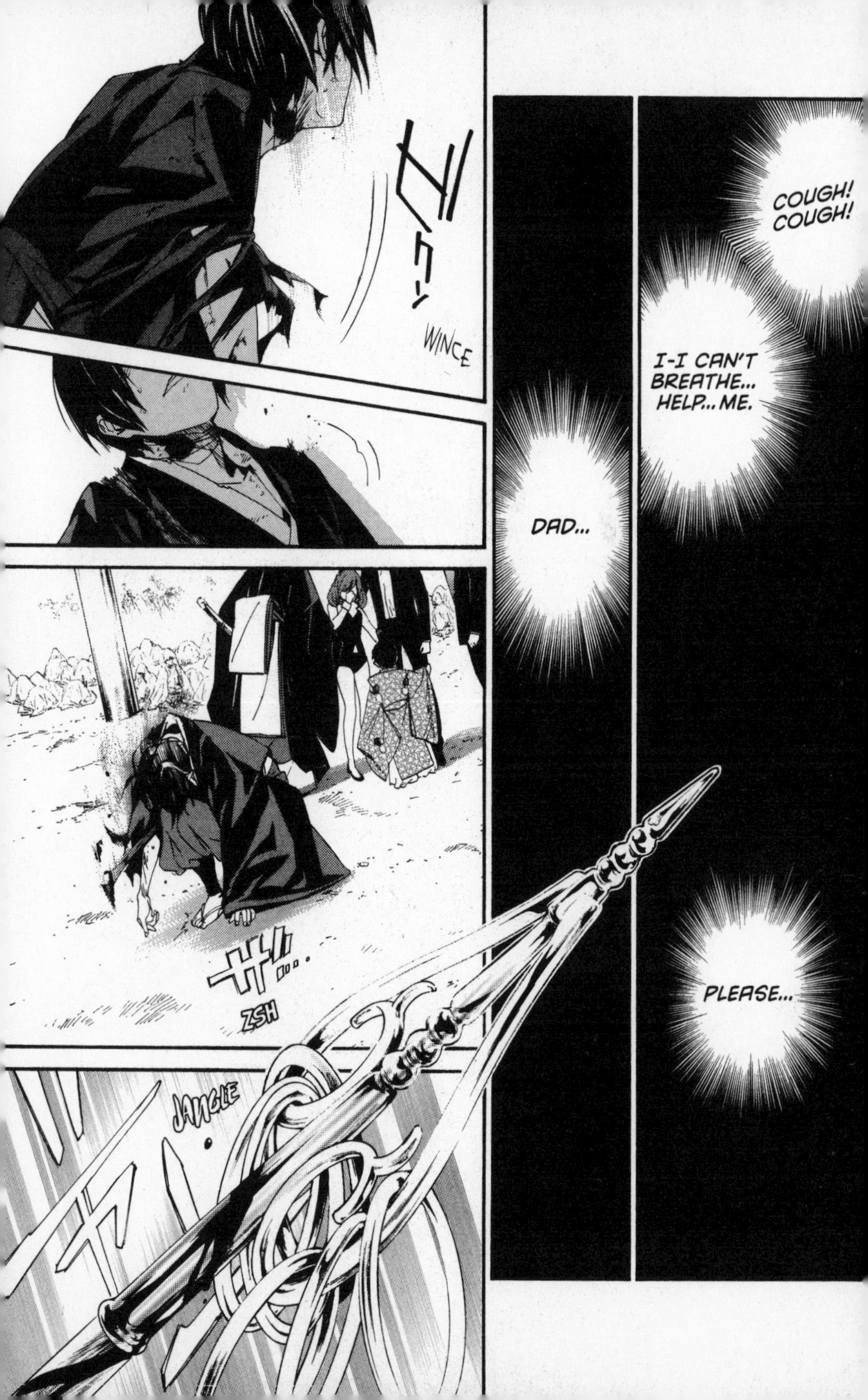
COUGH! COUGH!
I-I CAN'T BREATHE... HELP... ME.
PLEASE...
DAD...
WINCE
ZSH
JANGLE

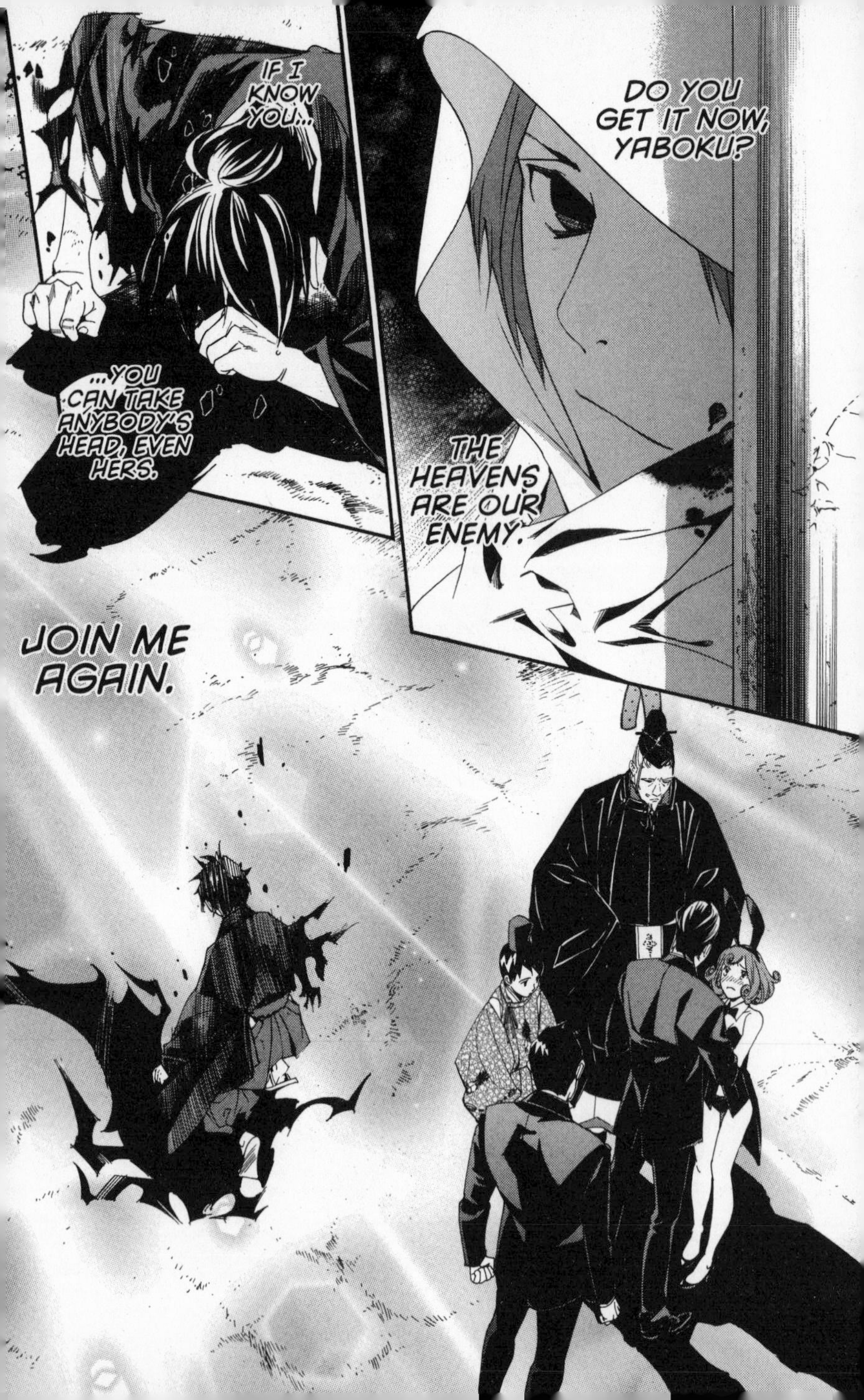
DO YOU GET IT NOW, YABOKU?
THE HEAVENS ARE OUR ENEMY.
IF I KNOW YOU...
...YOU CAN TAKE ANYBODY'S HEAD, EVEN HERS.
JOIN ME AGAIN.

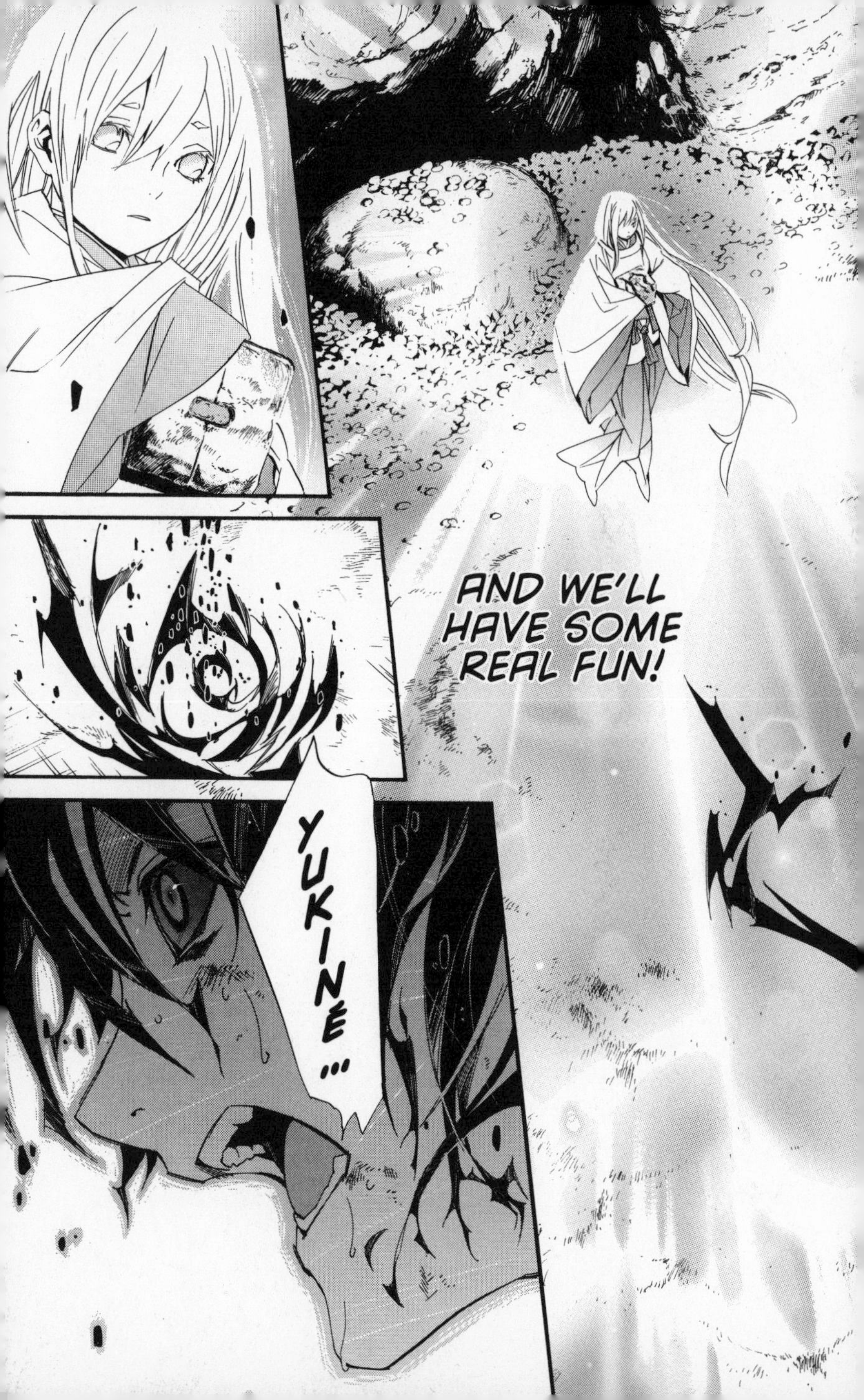
AND WE'LL HAVE SOME REAL FUN!
YUKINE...

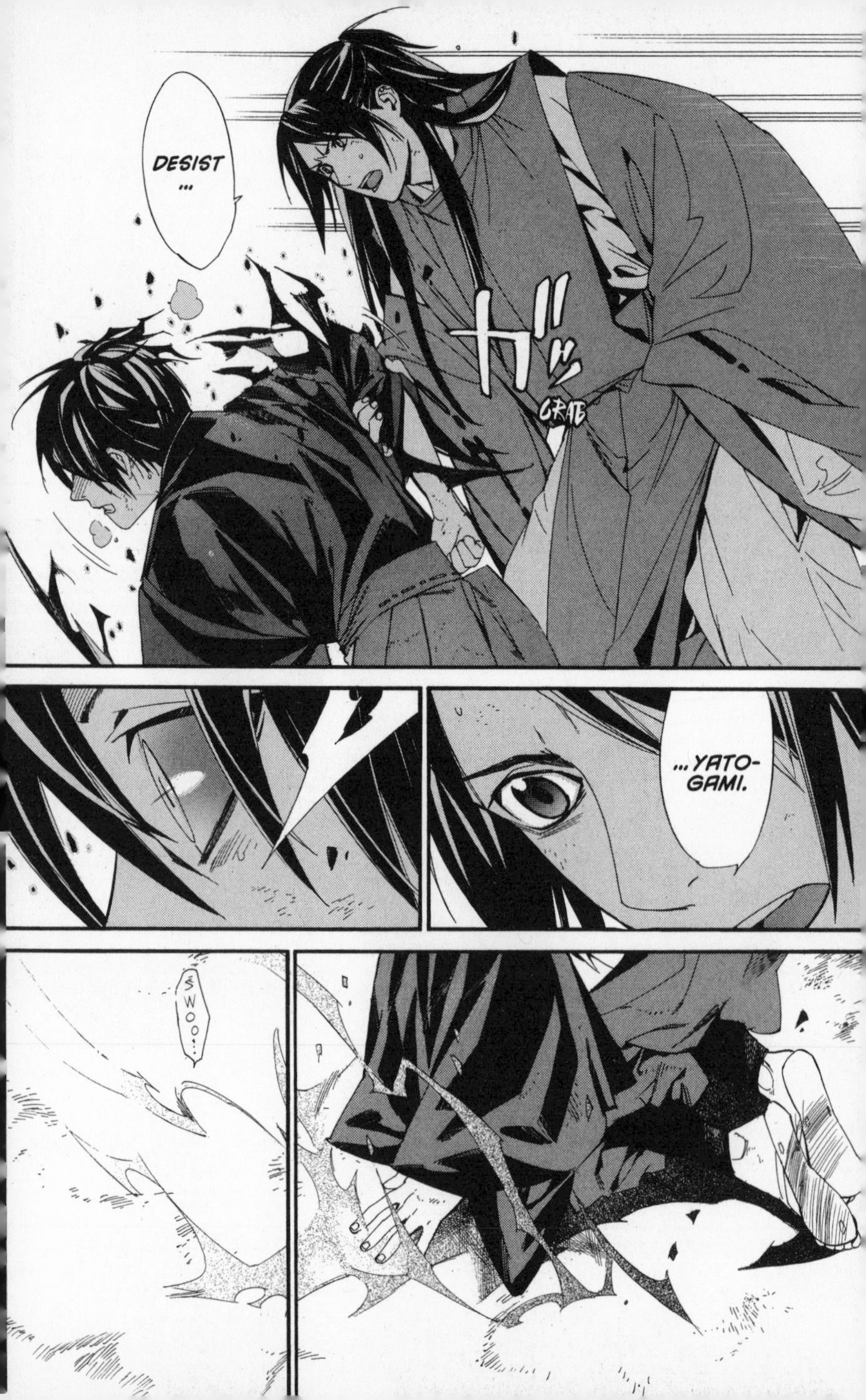
DESIST ...
ガッ
GRAB
...YATO-GAMI.
SWOO...

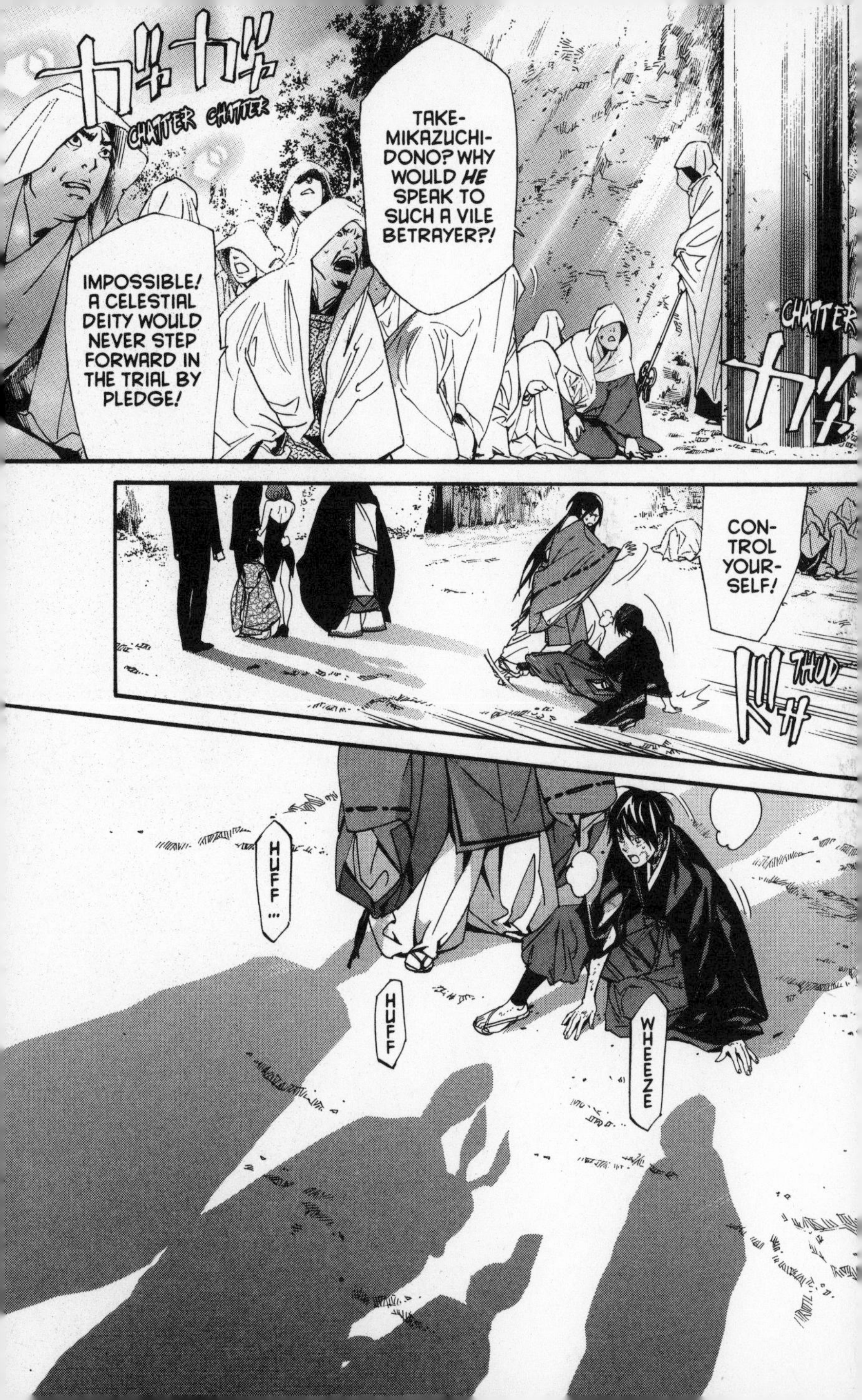
CHATTER
TAKE-MIKAZUCHI-DONO? WHY WOULD HE SPEAK TO SUCH A VILE BETRAYER?!
IMPOSSIBLE! A CELESTIAL DEITY WOULD NEVER STEP FORWARD IN THE TRIAL BY PLEDGE!
CHATTER CHATTER
CONTROL YOURSELF!
THUD
WHEEZE
HUFF
HUFF...

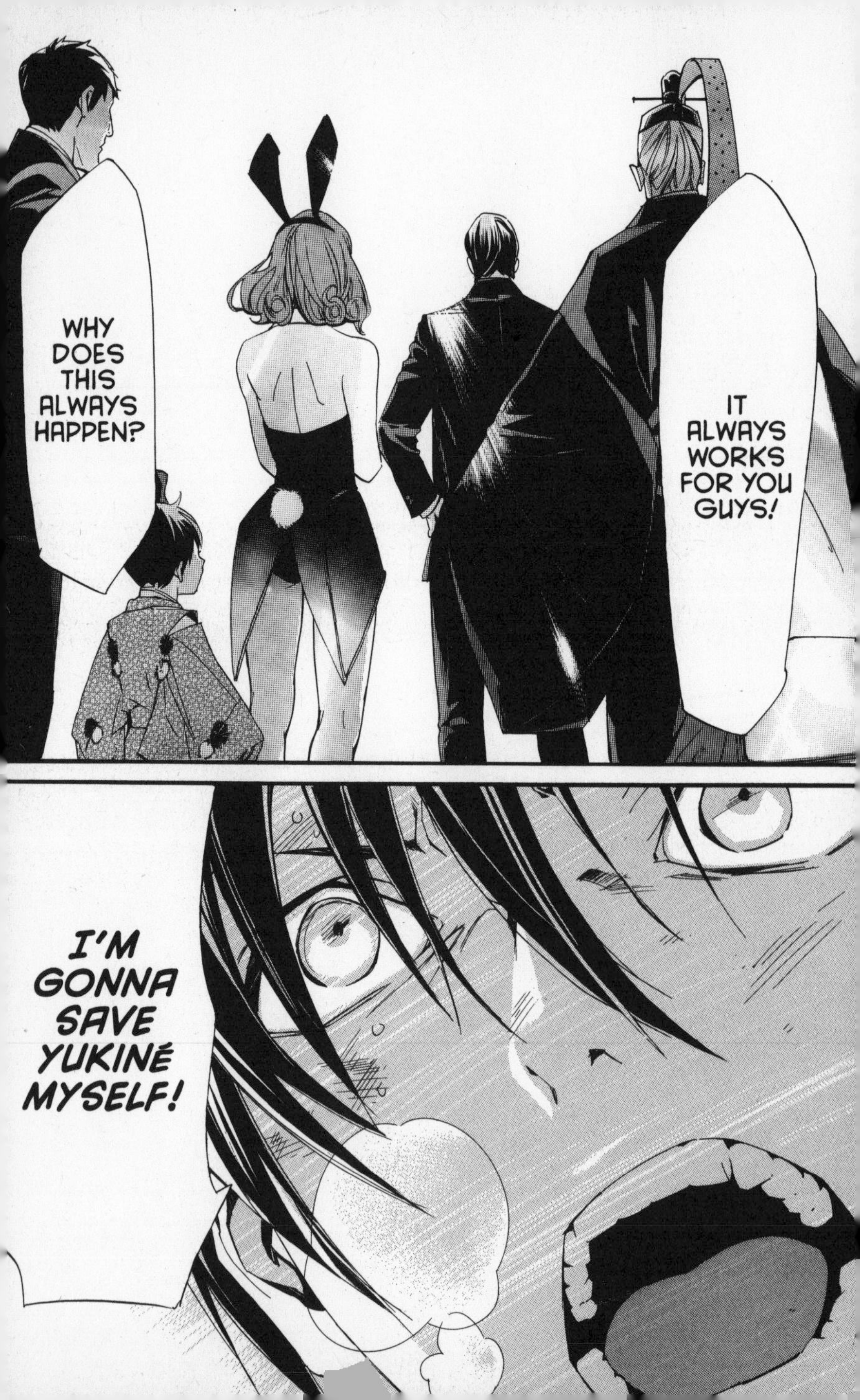
WHY DOES THIS ALWAYS HAPPEN?
IT ALWAYS WORKS FOR YOU GUYS!
I'M GONNA SAVE YUKINÉ MYSELF!

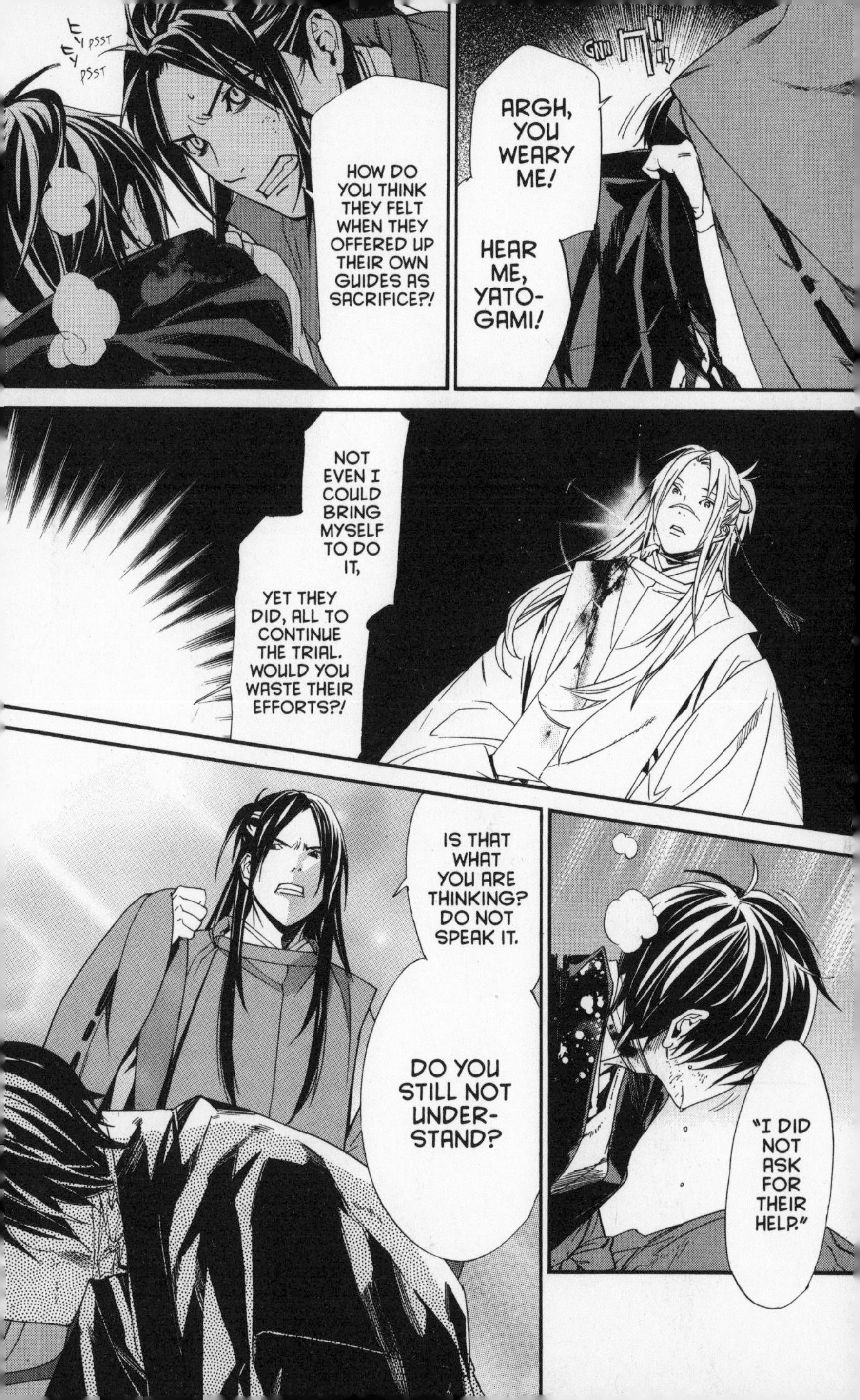
GNN
ARGH, YOU WEARY ME!
HEAR ME, YATO-GAMI!
PSSST PSSST
HOW DO YOU THINK THEY FELT WHEN THEY OFFERED UP THEIR OWN GUIDES AS SACRIFICE?!
NOT EVEN I COULD BRING MYSELF TO DO IT,
YET THEY DID, ALL TO CONTINUE THE TRIAL. WOULD YOU WASTE THEIR EFFORTS?!
"I DID NOT ASK FOR THEIR HELP."
IS THAT WHAT YOU ARE THINKING? DO NOT SPEAK IT.
DO YOU STILL NOT UNDER-STAND?

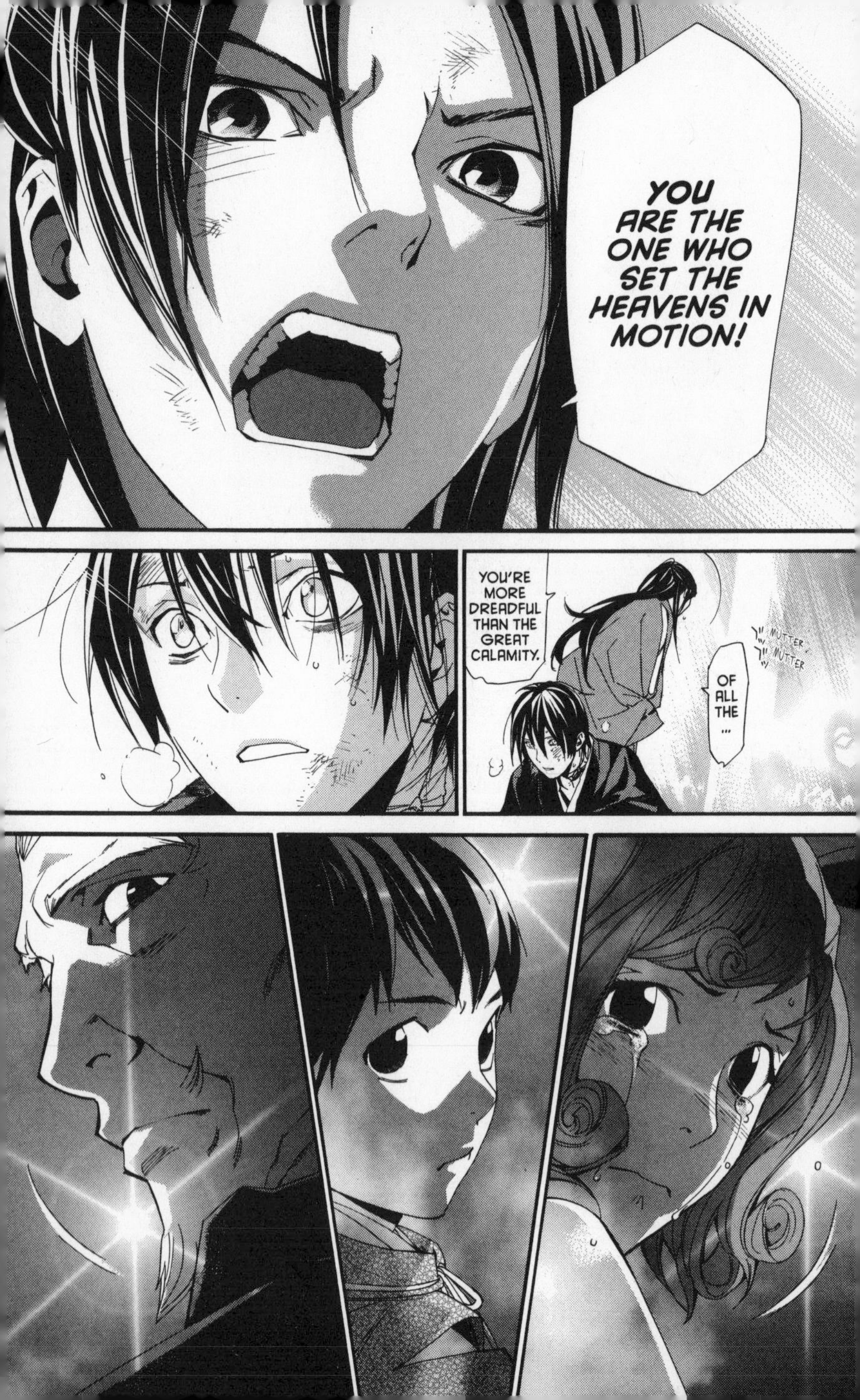
YOU ARE THE ONE WHO SET THE HEAVENS IN MOTION!
OF ALL THE ...
MUTTER MUTTER
YOU'RE MORE DREADFUL THAN THE GREAT CALAMITY.

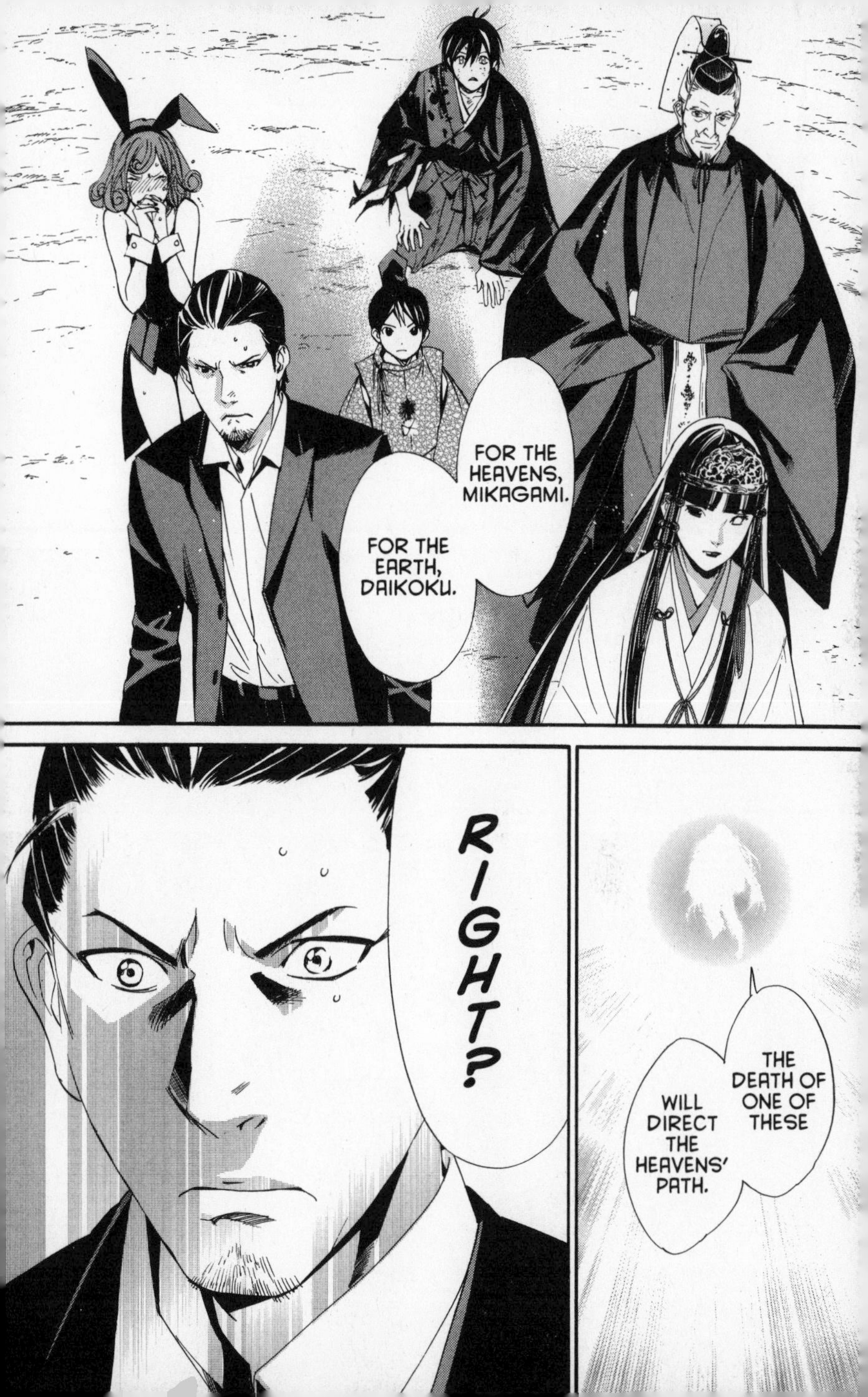
FOR THE HEAVENS, MIKAGAMI.
FOR THE EARTH, DAIKOKU.
THE DEATH OF ONE OF THESE
WILL DIRECT THE HEAVENS' PATH.
RIGHT?

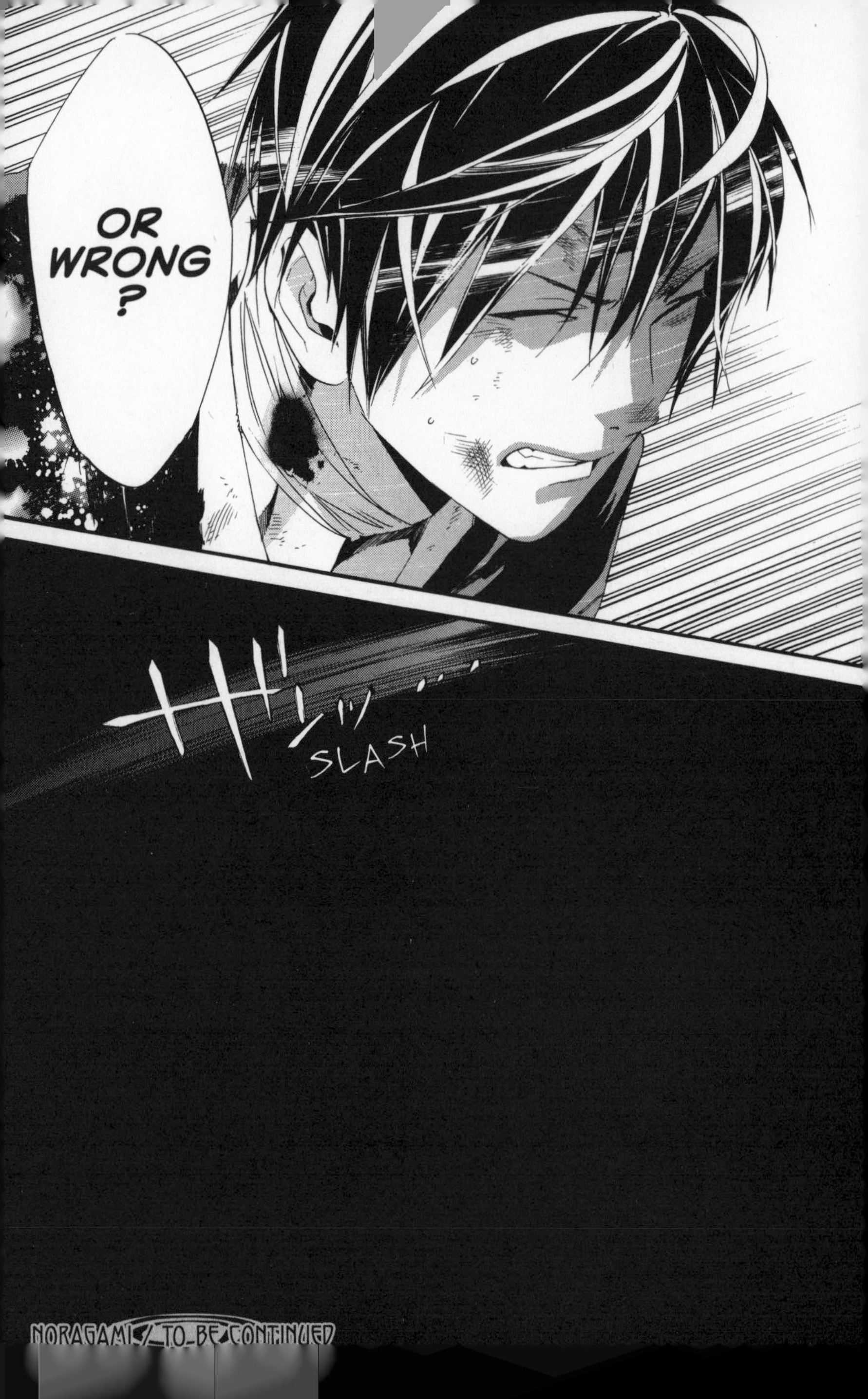
OR WRONG?
ザシュッ
SLASH
NORAGAMI / TO BE CONTINUED

野

良

神

# ATROCIOUS MANGA

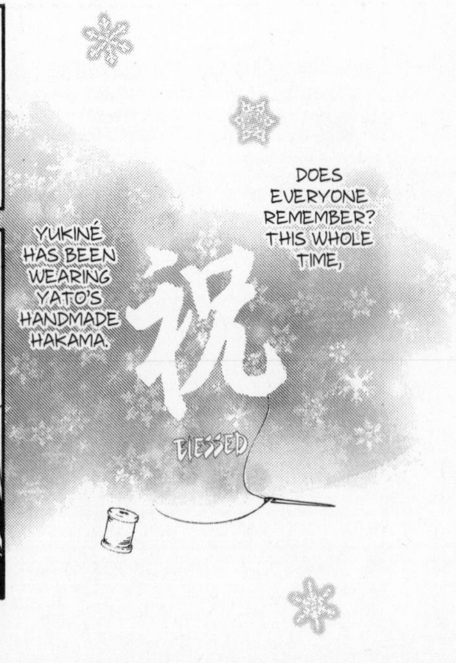
DOES EVERYONE REMEMBER? THIS WHOLE TIME,
YUKINÉ HAS BEEN WEARING YATO'S HANDMADE HAKAMA.
BLESSED

YOU SOUND LIKE A DESPERATE HOODLUM

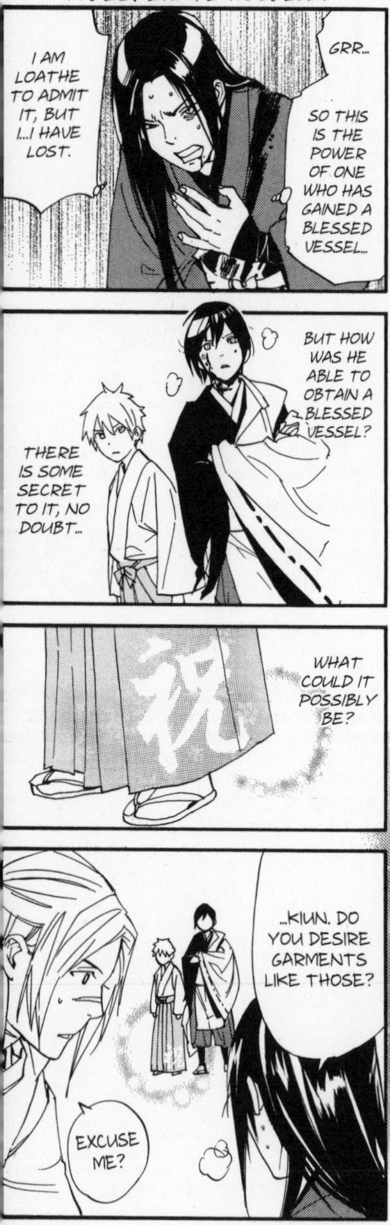
GRR...
SO THIS IS THE POWER OF ONE WHO HAS GAINED A BLESSED VESSEL...
I AM LOATHE TO ADMIT IT, BUT I...I HAVE LOST.
BUT HOW WAS HE ABLE TO OBTAIN A BLESSED VESSEL?
THERE IS SOME SECRET TO IT, NO DOUBT...
WHAT COULD IT POSSIBLY BE?
...KIUN. DO YOU DESIRE GARMENTS LIKE THOSE?
EXCUSE ME?

FAMILY

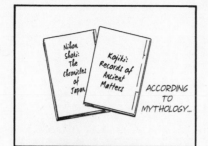

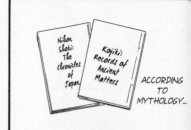

Nihon Shoki: The chronicles of Japan
Kojiki: Records of Ancient Matters
ACCORDING TO MYTHOLOGY...
CHILD OF IZANAGI & IZANAMI
...EBISU AND AMATERASU-ÔMIKAMI...
...HAVE THE SAME FATHER.
CHILD OF IZANAGI
ONII-CHAN!
TAME ANOTHER AYAKASHI, AND I'LL KILL YOU!
ぱぁぁ BEEE
ぁあ EEAM
Nihon Shoki: The chronicles of Japan
Kojiki: Records of Ancient Matters
ACCORDING TO MYTHOLOGY...
...TAKE-MIKAZUCHI...
...WAS BORN FROM THE BLOOD OF KAGUTSUCHI AFTER IZANAGI KILLED HIM.
Dad
FATHER?
WH-WHAT SHALL I CALL YOU?
KAGU-TSUCHI WILL BE FINE.
INCIDENTALLY, EBI IS KAGU'S BIG BROTHER.
EH HEH HEH! I'M A BIG BROTHER!

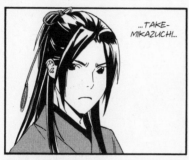

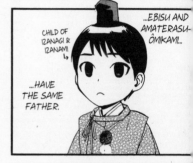

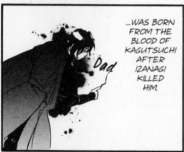

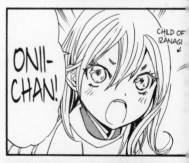

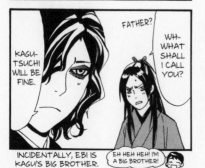

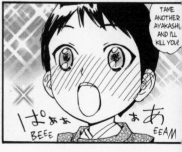

## TOBACCO HATER

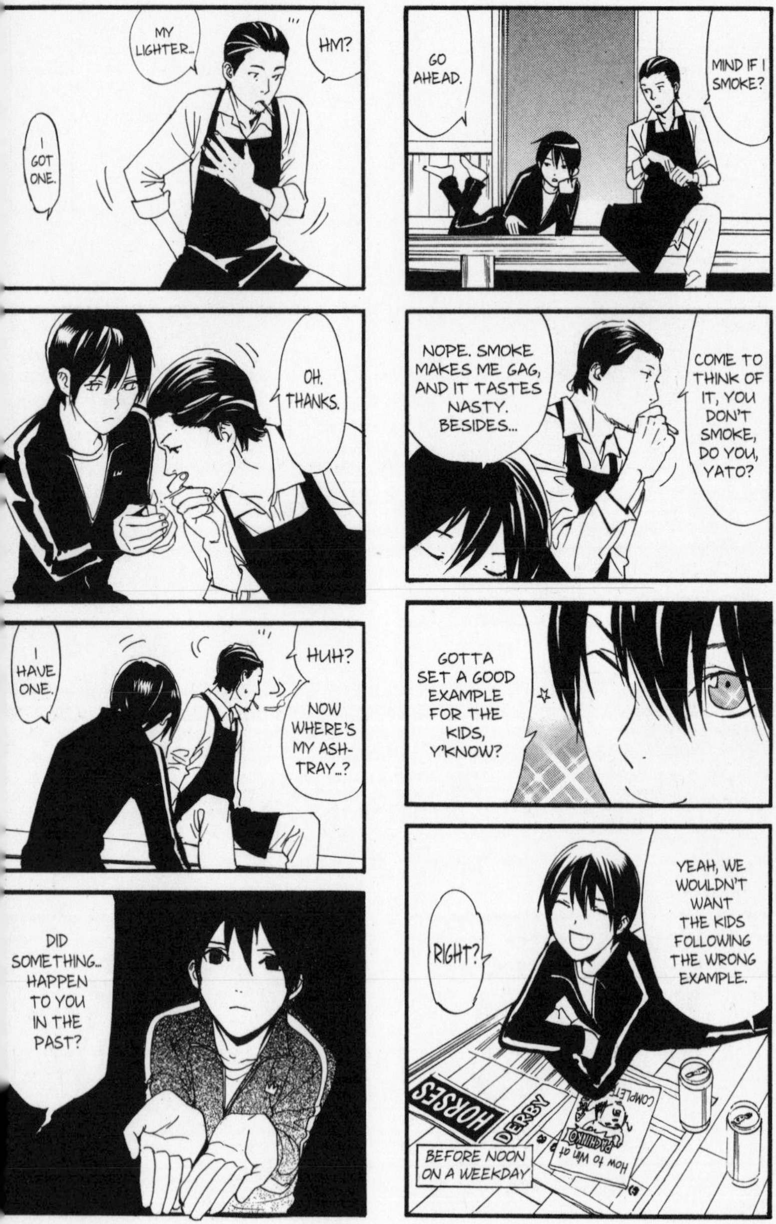
MIND IF I SMOKE?
GO AHEAD.
COME TO THINK OF IT, YOU DON'T SMOKE, DO YOU, YATO?
NOPE. SMOKE MAKES ME GAG, AND IT TASTES NASTY. BESIDES...
GOTTA SET A GOOD EXAMPLE FOR THE KIDS, Y'KNOW?
YEAH, WE WOULDN'T WANT THE KIDS FOLLOWING THE WRONG EXAMPLE.
RIGHT?
HORSES
DERBY
How to Win at PACHINKO
BEFORE NOON ON A WEEKDAY
HM?
MY LIGHTER...
I GOT ONE.
OH. THANKS.
HUH?
NOW WHERE'S MY ASH-TRAY...?
I HAVE ONE.
DID SOMETHING... HAPPEN TO YOU IN THE PAST?

LEVELS OF CONSCIOUSNESS

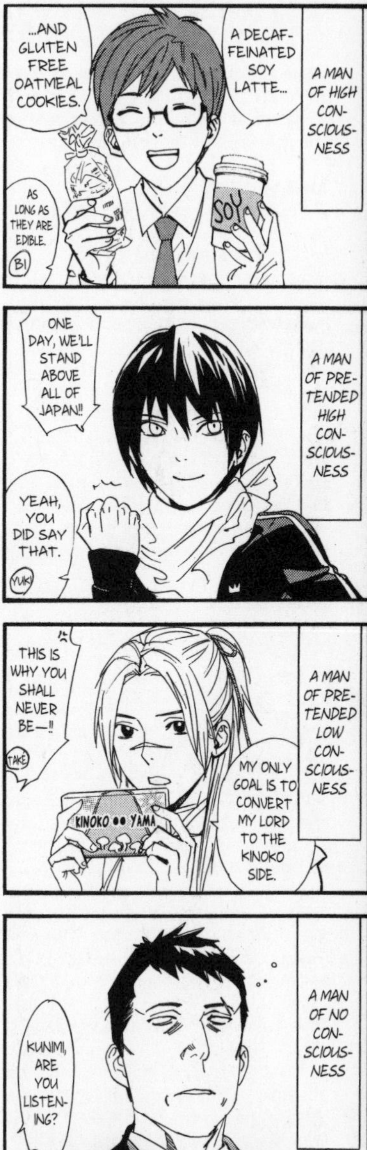
A MAN OF HIGH CONSCIOUSNESS
A DECAFFEINATED SOY LATTE...
...AND GLUTEN FREE OATMEAL COOKIES.
SOY
AS LONG AS THEY ARE EDIBLE.
BI
A MAN OF PRETENDED HIGH CONSCIOUSNESS
ONE DAY, WE'LL STAND ABOVE ALL OF JAPAN!!
YEAH, YOU DID SAY THAT.
YUKI
A MAN OF PRETENDED LOW CONSCIOUSNESS
THIS IS WHY YOU SHALL NEVER BE—!!
TAKE
MY ONLY GOAL IS TO CONVERT MY LORD TO THE KINOKO SIDE.
KINOKO oo YAMA
A MAN OF NO CONSCIOUSNESS
KUNIMI, ARE YOU LISTENING?
E

MOSTLY LAPOTA CONSCIOUS

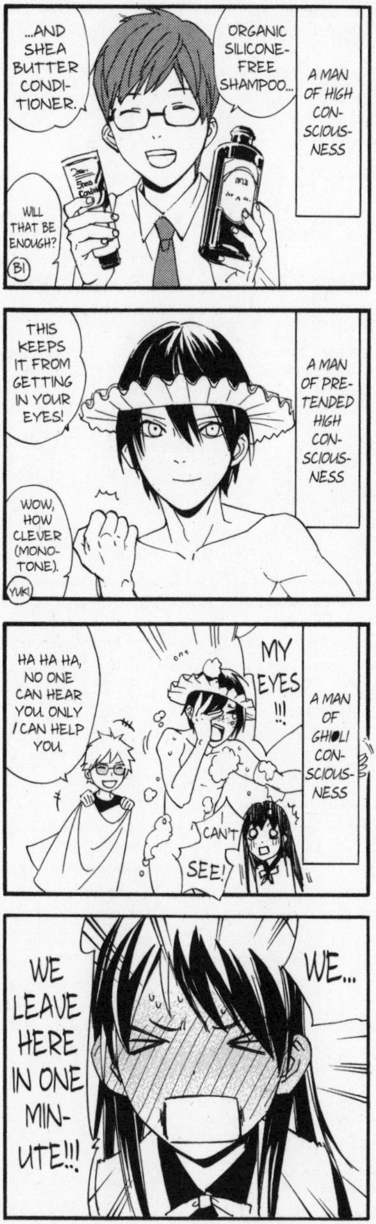
A MAN OF HIGH CONSCIOUSNESS
ORGANIC SILICONE-FREE SHAMPOO...
...AND SHEA BUTTER CONDITIONER.
WILL THAT BE ENOUGH?
BI
A MAN OF PRETENDED HIGH CONSCIOUSNESS
THIS KEEPS IT FROM GETTING IN YOUR EYES!
WOW, HOW CLEVER (MONOTONE).
YUKI
A MAN OF GHIOLI CONSCIOUSNESS
MY EYES!!!
HA HA HA, NO ONE CAN HEAR YOU. ONLY I CAN HELP YOU.
I CAN'T SEE!
WE...
WE LEAVE HERE IN ONE MINUTE!!!

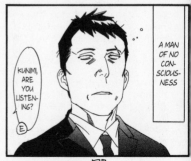

THANK YOU TO EVERYONE WHO READ THIS FAR!

# TRANSLATION NOTES

Japanese is a tricky language for most Westerners, and translation is often more art than science. For your edification and reading pleasure, here are notes on some of the places where we could have gone in a different direction in our translation of the work, or where a Japanese cultural reference is used.

### Sumo, page 6

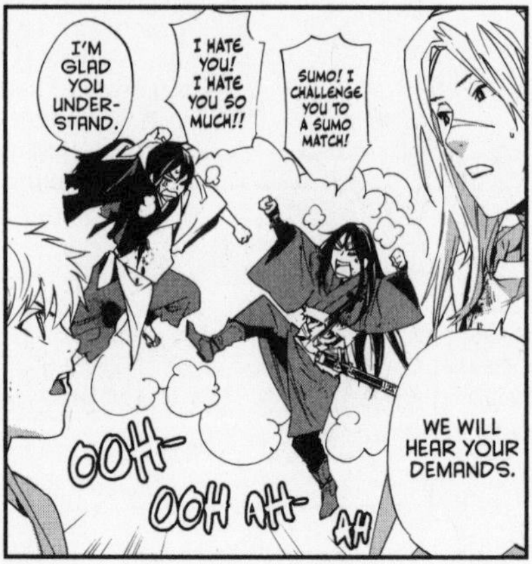
SUMO! I CHALLENGE YOU TO A SUMO MATCH!
I HATE YOU! I HATE YOU SO MUCH!!
I'M GLAD YOU UNDER-STAND.
WE WILL HEAR YOUR DEMANDS.
OOH-
OOH AH-
AH

Many readers may already have a passing knowledge of Japan's national sport, in which two wrestlers fight to force each other out of a ring. These matches have been associated with Shinto rituals, and have even been used to predict the outcome of the coming harvest. According to myth, the very first sumo match was fought between Takemikazuchi and the son of Ôkuninushi. Based on Takemikazuchi's confidence, the reader can safely assume that he was the winner, and is now considered to be the inventor of sumo.

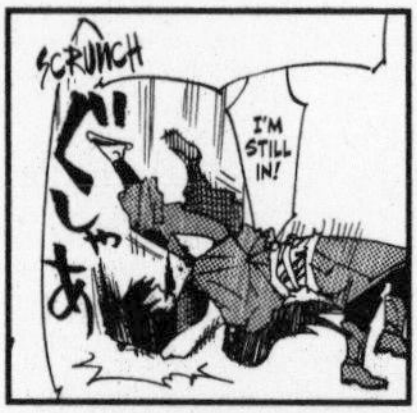
SCRUNCH
ぐしゃあ
I'M STILL IN!

### Ready, go, page 7

Technically, the translators should have left this and "I'm still in" in Japanese, because in international sumo, these calls remain untranslated. "Ready, go" comes from *hakkeyoi*, which is what the *gyôji* (referee) says when a match is stalled—he taps each of them on the back and says *hakkeyoi* to let them know that it's time to get back into action. In this case, there is no *gyôji*, so Takemikazuchi and Yato are making their own calls. Yato, upon being thrown by his opponent, calls *nokotta* (still in), to indicate that he hasn't been pushed out of the ring yet, and therefore has not been defeated. Normally, a *gyôji* would call this to let a *rikishi* (wrestler) know that he hasn't been beaten yet, and to encourage him to keep fighting. Of course, the rules of sumo state that a *rikishi* has lost if any part of his body other than the soles of his feet touches the ground, so Yato's claim that he is "still in," while his feet are in the air and his head is on the ground, is patently false.

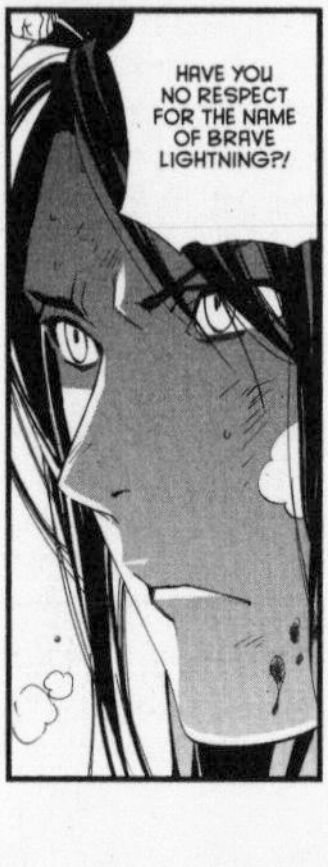
HAVE YOU NO RESPECT FOR THE NAME OF BRAVE LIGHTNING?!

### The name of Brave Lightning, page 11

In case any readers have been curious as to the meaning of Takemikazuchi's name, Sekiun has kindly provided the answer. Rather than stating the god's name, Sekiun refers to the god he serves as *Takeki Ikazuchi. Takeki* is the adjective form of *také*, which means "brave," and *ikazuchi* means "lightning." The name becomes Takemikazuchi by combining *ikazuchi* with prefix *mi*, which elevates the word in a show of respect. It may be interesting to note that Sekiun did not feel the need to use that prefix here.

### Shinki, page 52
As noted all the way back in Volume 1, shinki refers to the tools of the gods, personified in this manga by souls who have passed. Though this chapter is simply called "shinki," it refers to not only the people involved, but their true nature as instruments or vessels of the divine.

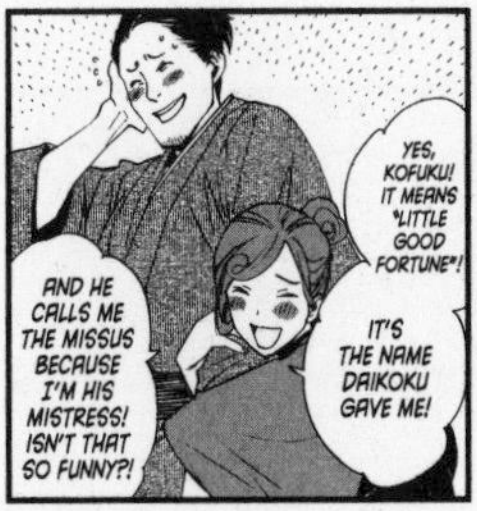
YES, KOFUKU! IT MEANS "LITTLE GOOD FORTUNE"!
IT'S THE NAME DAIKOKU GAVE ME!
AND HE CALLS ME THE MISSUS BECAUSE I'M HIS MISTRESS! ISN'T THAT SO FUNNY?!

### Kofuku means..., page 53
While Kofuku is no doubt very excited about the meaning of her name, telling Bishamon actually serves another purpose (in addition to sharing her joy). As the reader knows by now, the Japanese writing system uses *kanji*, where one sound can be written using a variety of different characters. So by telling Bishamon what her name means, she is also explaining how to write or "spell" it.

### Kazuma's envious face, page 55

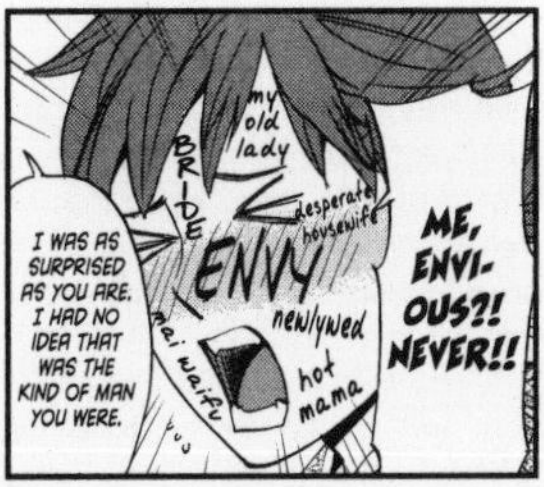
ME, ENVI-OUS?! NEVER!!
my old lady
BRIDE
desperate housewife
ENVY
newlywed
hot mama
mai waifu
I WAS AS SURPRISED AS YOU ARE. I HAD NO IDEA THAT WAS THE KIND OF MAN YOU WERE.

Apparently Kazuma is so envious of Daikoku's relationship with Kofuku that he looked into the future and found slang terms for wives. The translators confess to adapting some of them for more immediate comprehension. "Desperate housewife" is a translation of *danchi-zuma*, literally "apartment wife," a term made popular by the x-rated video of the same name, which was subsequently made into a whole series. "My old lady" comes from *ané-san nyôbô*, which means "older-sister wife." Here it is important to remember that in Japanese, women are addressed as "sister" whether or not there is a blood relation to the speaker. In this case, it refers to a wife who is slightly older than her husband. "*Mai waifu*" is the Japanese pronunciation of the English phrase "my wife." Generally it seems to be used by anime fans to refer to the character to whom they wish they were married, but as the term didn't come into popular use until centuries after this event, Kazuma could hardly be expected to know that.

### Om, page 66
Readers may be familiar with the word "Om" as a mantra that is used during meditation. The mantra is described as being the sound of the universe, and it has spiritual meaning in various Eastern religions. The *om* spoken here, however, has quite the opposite meaning (although it may not be a coincidence that it has the same sound). This *om* is spoken with the *kanji* character meaning "grudge" or "hate," specifically in reference to grievances over having been wronged. In other words, it would seem that Shiigun, or the god who commands them, has been wronged in the past, and is still seeking justice.

### On High, page 99
The title of this chapter is a single *kanji* character, one with a myriad of possible pronunciations, none of which having been specified by the author. Perhaps the most common reading would be *ue*, meaning "up" or "above," and this symbol can refer to just about anything that is above anything else—the higher floor of a building, a realm that exists above the earth, someone who is of a higher social standing, etc. In other words, this chapter refers to all kinds of superiority (which comes from a Latin word meaning "above" or "higher"), including Amaterasu's

superiority, her shinki's superiority, and the gods' superiority in general. One other way to read this *kanji* is *kami*, which is the origin of other words referring to things above a person, such as the hair on top of a person's head, or a god above human beings. Perhaps most importantly, *kami*, or rather, the more polite *okami*, is a form of address used when speaking to the highest authority in the land, or in this case, the skies. The translators chose to call the chapter "On High" in English, because that phrase can put people in mind of the heavens.

### The Three Sacred Treasures, page 124

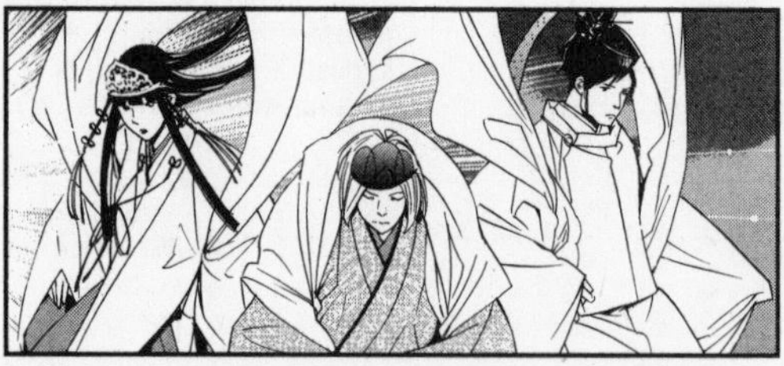

Also known as the Imperial Regalia of Japan, these are the three most well-known shinki in Japan. They consist of a sword, a mirror, and a jewel, and although there are variations, the *Kojiki* ("Records of Ancient Matters") explains their origins thus: Upon being insulted by her brother Susa-no-o, Amaterasu hid in a cave, plunging the world into darkness. Thinking this situation less than ideal, the gods devised a plan to lure her out. They hung jewels and a mirror on a tree, then held a party. When she heard all the merrymaking, she opened the door of her cave to see how a world in darkness could possibly be having so much fun. The gods told her they had another sun god, and showed her her own reflection in the mirror. This startled her long enough for them to grab her and drag her out into the open. As for the sword, it was presented to Amaterasu by Susa-no-o, who found it in the tail of the slain Yamata-no-Orochi (see volume 15, "Gods at the Divine Council").
In the human world, it is said that Amaterasu gave them to her grandson Ninigi when he went down from heaven to tame the islands, and he gave them to his descendant, Jimmu, the first emperor of Japan, as a symbol of his divinity and right to rule. They are now presented to each new emperor when he takes the throne.

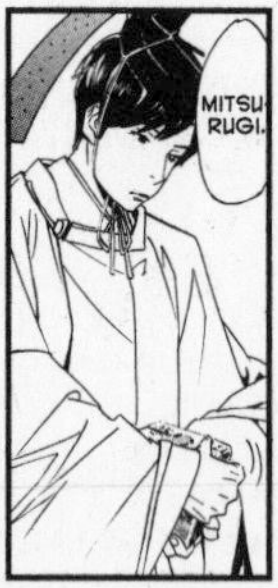
MITSU-RUGI.

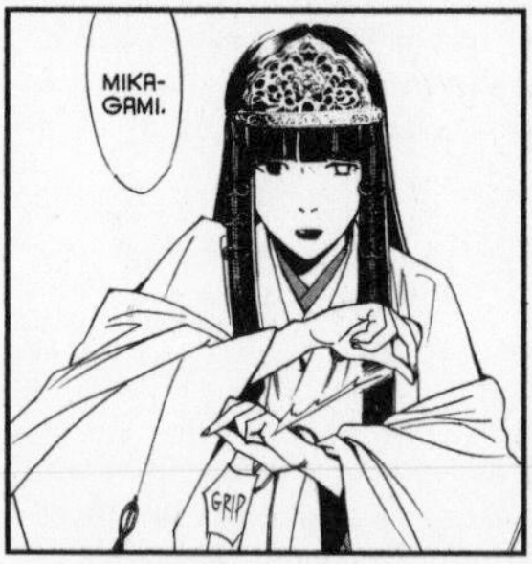
MIKA-GAMI.
GRIP

### Mikagami and Mitsurugi, page 126

The Japanese reader will likely know immediately that these names are honorific terms for "mirror" and "sword," respectively, but it is worth noting is that, while most shinki have names represented in the Chinese *kanji* characters, the names of these Sacred Treasures are written in *hiragana*—characters exclusive to Japan. This may be to represent that Amaterasu herself is exclusive to Japan, as opposed to imported gods (like Bishamon) or syncretic gods (gods whose identities have been fused with those of gods of other lands) like Ôkuninushi. Or it may simply be because *kanji* characters were not used in Japan when Amaterasu first employed these shinki. Of course, *hiragana* was based off of *kanji*, so in that case, the names of the Sacred Treasures would be most properly represented by an entirely different, and by now illegible, writing system, or may have been purely oral.

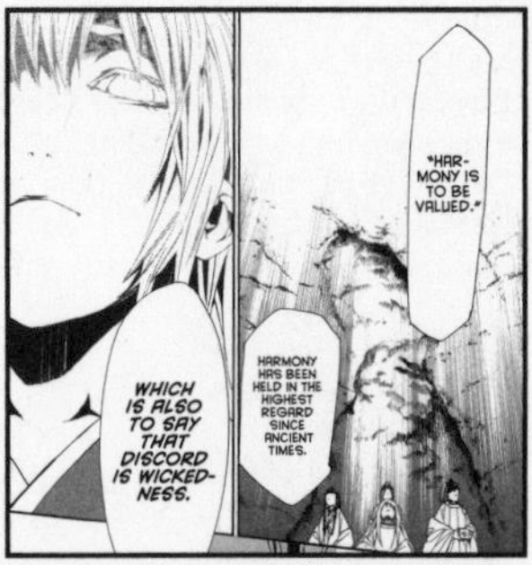
*HARMONY IS TO BE VALUED.*
HARMONY HAS BEEN HELD IN THE HIGHEST REGARD SINCE ANCIENT TIMES.
WHICH IS ALSO TO SAY THAT DISCORD IS WICKEDNESS.

**Harmony is to be valued, page 136**
This is the first article of the Seventeen-Article Constitution written by the semi-legendary Prince Shôtoku back in the seventh century. This constitution was a guideline for the proper behavior of government officials, based heavily on Buddhist and Confucian ideals. The fact that "harmony is to be valued" is the very first guideline listed indicates just how valuable it is.

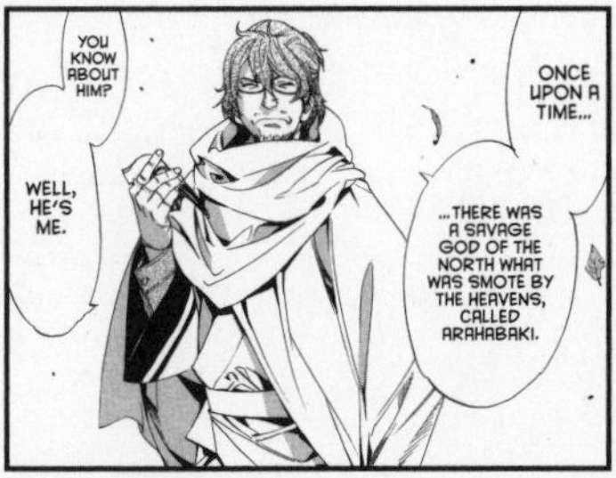
ONCE UPON A TIME...
...THERE WAS A SAVAGE GOD OF THE NORTH WHAT WAS SMOTE BY THE HEAVENS, CALLED ARAHABAKI.
YOU KNOW ABOUT HIM?
WELL, HE'S ME.

**Arahabaki and Shiigun, page 146**
Arahabaki is perhaps the most well-known god of the peoples indigenous to northern Japan, making him the number one opponent to Amaterasu's reign. Before she took over, the people worshiped him as a *sae no kami*, sentinel god, who protected them from war and other disasters. His shinki, Shiigun, is named after the chinquapin tree, or *shii*, and may be a reference to an old poem from the *Man'yôshû* poetry collection. The short poem was written by a man in exile, and translates roughly to, "At home, I would serve my rice in a bowl, but on my journey, I use the *shii* leaves as my vessel."

**Trial by pledge, page 148**
The trial by pledge, or *ukei*, is a form of divination that has been used in Shinto for many centuries, which could also be seen as a form of gambling. Basically how it works is, when there is a question that has two answers (yes or no, red or blue, are the Heavens right or wrong, etc.), an act is performed and the answer is determined based on the outcome, much like flipping a coin. In one famous instance, Amaterasu wanted to know if her brother Susa-no-o meant her ill will or not, so each of them offered up items from which were born children. Susa-no-o had determined, as the rules of this trial by pledge, that the gender of the children would prove his guilt or innocence. Because five male children, and only three female children, were born, he declared himself innocent. The English word "pledge" is significant, because it indicates a promise made (the literal translation of *ukei*) as well as an item offered as proof of sincerity in making that promise.

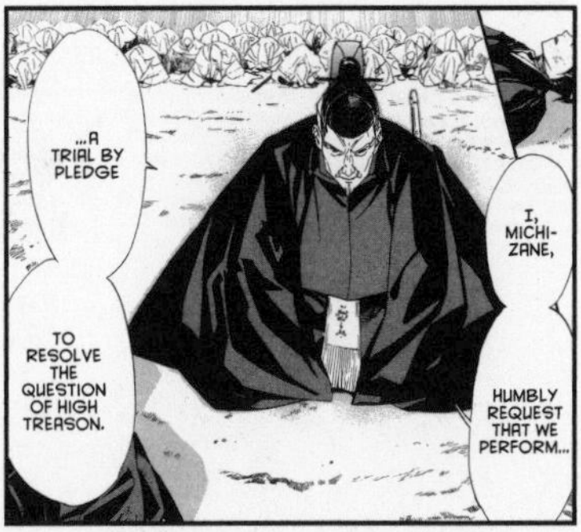
I, MICHIZANE,
HUMBLY REQUEST THAT WE PERFORM...
...A TRIAL BY PLEDGE
TO RESOLVE THE QUESTION OF HIGH TREASON.

**Gut yourself, page 149**
When crowds get worked up, they tend to shout unfriendly things at each other. In this case, one of the gods present has suggested to Tenjin that he slit his belly, referring to the *seppuku* ritual suicide used to restore honor to disgraced

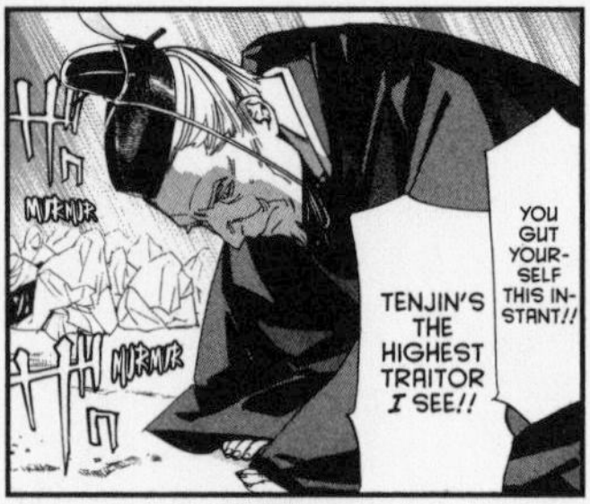
YOU GUT YOURSELF THIS INSTANT!!
TENJIN'S THE HIGHEST TRAITOR I SEE!!
MURMUR
MURMUR

samurai. While this might merely be an extreme way of suggesting that he take responsibility for his actions (sometimes people will say such things as, "If I'm wrong, I'll cut my belly," to show the willingness to answer for their deeds), more likely it is meant to say that Tenjin's suggestion is so offensive that the only possible way to restore his honor is through ritual suicide.

## Consciousness, page 185

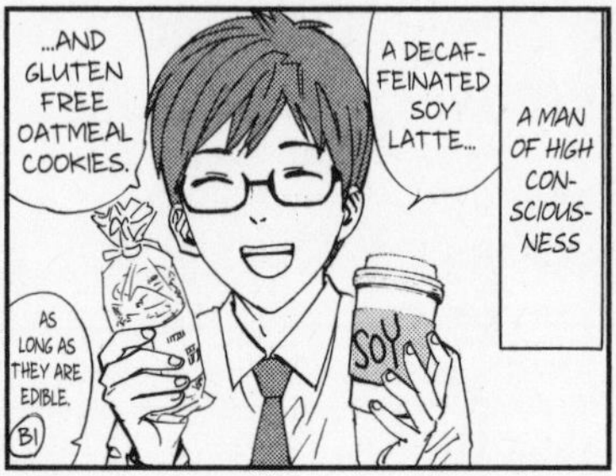
A MAN OF HIGH CONSCIOUSNESS
A DECAFFEINATED SOY LATTE...
...AND GLUTEN FREE OATMEAL COOKIES.
AS LONG AS THEY ARE EDIBLE.
SOY

When referring to people who are very conscious about health, the environment, etc., there are two groups: the *ishiki takai*, or "high consciousness," group, and the *ishiki takai kei* or "high-consciousness style," group. The former refers to people who are actually concerned about all of these things, while the latter is more concerned about making sure the rest of the world knows that they are concerned about these things. In contrast, a *ishiki hikui kei*, or "low-consciousness style," person is someone who wants people to think that they don't care.

## My eyes, page 185

As the reader may have guessed, Yato and pals are quoting the famous Studio Ghibli film, *Laputa: Castle in the Sky*. Because this is the English version of *Noragami*, the translators used the latest official English version of the script. However, when translating a movie from one language into another, there tends to be a heavy amount of adaptation. There may be any number of reasons for this to happen, not the least of which being that the words in each line have to match the way the characters' mouths move as closely as possible. That being the case, the most recent edition of *Castle in the Sky* has dialogue that is different enough from the original Japanese that the translators felt the readers might be interested in reading a closer translation and will provide it here. (Yato and Yukiné's lines were both from Colonel Muska, and Hiyori's line is from Dola.)

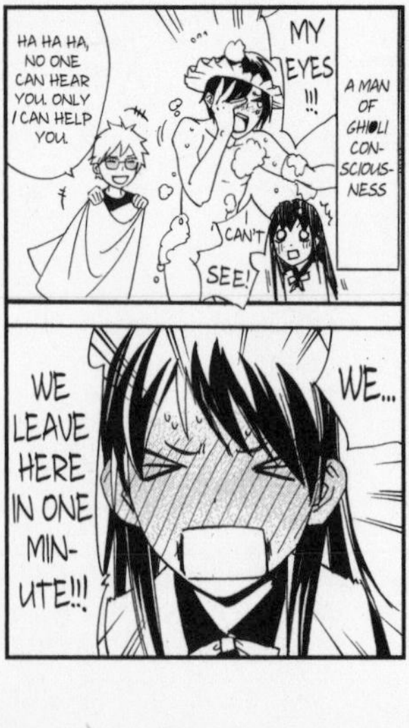
A MAN OF GHIBLI CONSCIOUSNESS
MY EYES!!!
HA HA HA, NO ONE CAN HEAR YOU. ONLY I CAN HELP YOU.
I CAN'T SEE!
WE...
WE LEAVE HERE IN ONE MINUTE!!!

Yato: My eyes!!! My eeeeyyyes!
Yukiné: Ha, ha, ha, ha. Where do you think you're going, hm?
Hiyori: B-Be ready in 40 seconds!!!

野 N O R A 良 G A M I 神

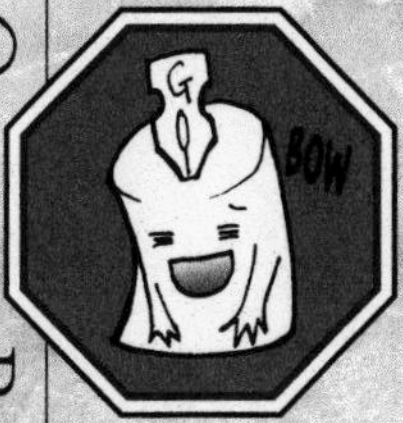
BOW

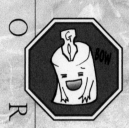

With this cover, I tried switching to high-quality watercolor paper.
It really brings out the intensity of the colors, but it might be a little harder to scrub out pigments like I could on cheap paper.

Adachitoka

A Kodansha Comics Trade Paperback Original.

*Noragami: Stray God* volume 18 copyright © 2017 Adachitoka
English translation copyright © 2017 Adachitoka

Published in the United States by Kodansha Comics, an imprint of Kodansha USA Publishing, LLC, New York.

Publication rights for this English edition arranged through Kodansha Ltd., Tokyo.

First published in Japan in 2017 by Kodansha Ltd., Tokyo.

ISBN 978-1-63236-345-9

Printed in the United States of America.

www.kodanshacomics.com

9 8 7 6 5 4 3 2 1

Translation: Alethea Nibley & Athena Nibley
Lettering: Lys Blakeslee
Editing: Lauren Scanlan
Kodansha Comics edition cover design: Phil Balsman